NINA SIMONE

NiNA SiMONE

THE BIOGRAPHY

DAVID BRUN-LAMBERT

First published in Great Britain
2009 by Aurum Press Ltd
7 Greenland Street, London NW1 0ND
www.aurumpress.co.uk

Copyright © Éditions Flammarion, 2005, translated from the original
French: *Nina Simone: une vie* by David Brun-Lambert

Published by arrangement with Éditions Flammarion, France

A catalogue record for this book is available from the British Library.

ISBN 978 1 84513 430 3

1 3 5 7 9 10 8 6 4 2
2010 2012 2013 2011 2009

Translation by Paul Morris & Isabelle Villancher
Printed by MPG Books Ltd, Bodmin, Cornwall

CONTENTS

PROLOGUE

NINA SIMONE died on 21 April 2003 in Carry-le-Rouet, a village in the south of France not far from Marseille. Her death didn't cause much of a stir in the media – European or American. It was said merely that a bad-tempered but successful diva from the world of jazz had passed away. That was about it.

Just about everyone seems to have a story about Nina Simone, Toni Morrison's 'every woman'. The flamboyant artist, the tireless warrior, the submissive then forsaken woman, the diffident lover addicted to men, the loose cannon, the breathless fighter, the absolute diva, the visionary creator, the dramatist, the voice of doom. Not to mention the first black classical concert player, who was such a success despite all the tricks that fate played on her. Finally, the little girl with her back against the wall.

Nina Simone's life spanned half a century of music and major social upheavals. She was a fellow-traveller of many of the great black figures of America (Martin Luther King, Stokely Carmichael, Malcolm X...), the equal in status and destiny of some of the great divas of the century (Maria Callas, Billie Holiday...) and the author of a repertoire peerless in American music.

This black girl, born in 1933 to a poor religious family in North Carolina, boasted incomparable talents – at two and a half years of age she was playing hymns by ear on the family pedal organ, at four she was accompanying her preacher mother on the Tryon church organ, and at six she began her classical training with a white teacher. At twenty, determined to become the first African-American classical concert performer in a still overtly segregationist country, she was rejected by the white jury from a music school. We could say that Eunice Waymon – for that was her name – died on that day, along with her dreams. But her anger never did – it persisted, swelled, grew, until another creature entirely came into being, belligerent, charismatic, resolute, gifted: Nina Simone. An artist with a mission.

Born by chance in an Atlantic City dive, in a few years Nina Simone would become an American singing star. From interpreter to songwriter to flag-carrier of a revolution – the civil rights movement.

In her struggles, at times Nina Simone abandoned everything or had it taken away: her family, her career, her influence, even her art. Her odyssey was a long wandering stalked by the illness that lurked in her brain and threatened to destroy her, from the beaches of Barbados to the Liberian coast, from the banks of Lake Geneva to the streets of Paris, from the drizzle of Holland to sun-baked Aix-en-Provence. Finally, the swansong to her pain, the loneliness of a villa in Carry-le-Rouet.

The story of Nina Simone is one of inconsolable solitude, of an artist wracked and torn by destructive forces. Under life's blows and her depression, she became her own worst enemy, a woman singing of lost love and revolution who would find neither the man of her dreams nor peace.

But before looking at the life of this diva, we should go back to the little talented girl Eunice Kathleen Waymon, the descendant of slaves, who grew up in a town in North Carolina. A young girl wise and talented beyond her years, who showed promise as a concert performer and carried with her the hopes of a community. This was her drama, the first wound, the precursor and shaper of all her future battles, her thirst for success and her emotional problems. A wound whose scars would reopen at regular intervals when her illness or disillusionment drowned out her desire for harmony and happiness.

The child prodigy and the messenger. The little girl spurned by the classical art of the white community and the diva proud of her blackness determined to take on the establishment. This is the story of a little girl, Eunice, who, like a chrysalis, sheltered the soul of one of the great tragic players of the century: Nina Simone.

1

THE FIRST NOTES
OF THE MELODY

She does not know her beauty
She thinks her brown body has no glory
If she could dance naked under palm trees
And see her image in the river she would know
Yes. she would know
But there are no palm trees in the street
No palm trees in the street
And dishwater gives back no images

NINA SIMONE, 'IMAGES'

PLUNGE into the story of Nina Simone and you always come back to a small anonymous town in North Carolina. Tryon, lost in the agricultural heartland of the east of the state, is a few miles from the Mason–Dixon line, that invisible frontier separating America into two different poles: the north and south. Two rival economic systems, but ones that both practised strict racial segregation.

North Carolina is a region rich in tobacco plantations, the vast majority of its inhabitants being highly religious and conservative rural folk. Here, meagre ivy-choked trees stretch as far as the eye can see in a sombre green landscape against which modest homes can be made out. Tryon is not a tourist destination. From New York it is two full days' travel by train then a bus before you reach its dreary streets. As soon as you reach your destination, you are struck by a sense of torpor. There is nothing of interest in the town – it's just like any other city in the Midwest. Its stores serve bad hamburgers, and shop windows display dresses long since out of fashion. A poor place, built on the ashes of Indian encampments burnt down to build a railway line to the neighbouring town of Landrum. Once the work had finished, some went further west. Others didn't have the energy or means, so stayed there. Little by little the town grew, and in 1891 it was christened Tryon, after the peak that overlooks it.

This is where Nina Simone was born, where little Eunice Waymon's spark took life. The same spark that would accompany her from the first revivals she attended as a child to the New York stages where she was allowed to fulfil her destiny.

But before Nina's tormented destiny was to be fulfilled, there was a child: Eunice Kathleen Waymon.

On 21 February 1933, the sixth child of deacon John Divine Waymon and his wife, the Reverend Mary Kate Waymon, came into the world.

Mary Kate's origins can be traced back to an Indian from South Carolina and a black slave, a mixed-race marriage common at the time between enslaved minorities. The couple gave birth to a mixed-race child, the great-grandmother of Eunice Waymon. In turn, this mixed-race girl married a slave and it appears they had a son. Their child, Eunice's grandfather, was born into slavery. He died young and never knew his granddaughter. This man, a mixture of African and Indian blood, married a mixed-race slave – African and Irish – who was the result of what was then an unnatural union. Looking back, it is hard not to think of one of the verses in Nina Simone's song 'Four Women': 'My skin is yellow, my hair is long, between two worlds I do belong. My father was rich and white. He forced my mother late one night.'

In 1902 this mixed-race couple had a daughter: Mary Kathleen, an olive-skinned mixture of African, Irish and Indian blood, and who would become Mary Kathleen Waymon.

Mary Kate's family included no less than fifteen Methodist Baptist preachers. She was raised in this religion and would in turn embrace a 'career' as a reverend, but before this she married John Divine Waymon in 1922, in Inman, South Carolina.

Nothing is known of her husband's origins, except that he was also the son of a slave. John Divine Waymon was uneducated but everyone saw him as an intelligent, hard-working and upstanding boy. He knew how to get himself liked and respected, the type of man with a natural gift for life. In Tryon he was nicknamed 'Whistler', as he could whistle two tunes at a time, and his children would long remember nights spent listening to him whistle old tunes on the street corner.

John Divine spent his youth touring as a professional singer and dancer, performing in the music halls around Pendleton, but he gave this up when he married Mary Kate. The couple set up home in South Carolina, where John Divine was a dry-cleaner, qualified barber and finally preacher.

The Waymons' first child, John Irvine, was born in 1923. Then came Lucille, at the beginning of the following year, and the next year Carrol and Harold. But at just six weeks old Harold caught spinal meningitis. He survived, but would be left paralysed down one side, leaving him 'tough', according to Nina. '[Y]ou could almost call him mean,' she would later write. 'Maybe that was because he never forgave the world for the injustice it had inflicted on him.'[1]

A respected figure in an ecclesiastical society to which she was completely devoted, Mary Kate Waymon was ordained as a reverend after the birth of the twins. She was a loving mother, but in her own way. Chaste, pious, lacking warmth with her children, she left it to her husband to show affection, which she did through the church.

At the end of the 1920s, life was comfortable for the Waymons. John Divine's temperament was a counterweight to the stiffness of his wife. Here was an ambitious, positive man – for him anything was possible. Tired of working as an employee in a dry-cleaning store with a salary he felt too low, he set himself to improving his lot by creating a small road haulage company with a friend. But he soon learned that Tryon, North Carolina was in need of a hairdresser and barber. He put his plans off until another day, took the job and set up home with his family in a big house in Tryon with a slide, a swing and a basketball hoop in the yard, and a tennis court next to the house. It was here, on 7 March 1929, just two weeks after their arrival, that their fifth child, Dorothy Waymon, was born.

The family soon integrated into life in Tryon. Here, the climate was perfect year-round, and once spring was under way the town turned into a resort hosting rich white tourists escaping the scorching heat of Florida and enjoying the attractions of moonshine whisky.

In Tryon, like everywhere else in North Carolina, segregation was strictly enforced, although not as zealously as elsewhere. White and black communities lived in peace – there were no lynchings in Tryon, no racial violence of any sort, the two communities even cohabiting to the extent that there was no clear demarcation between black and white neighbourhoods.

Religious life reflected this entente – one Sunday the congregation of black churches (Methodist, Baptist, Episcopalian, Pentecostalists) would go to a white church to worship, the next week the white congregation would go to a black church. Thus, black and white pastors interacted almost daily. Of course, anywhere people came into intimate contact was still segregated (bars, hotels, etc.), but basically, and without conflict, 'blacks and whites took part in all sorts of activities together long before desegregation'.[2]

Business was good for John Divine in Tryon, and the family wanted for nothing. He worked both as a barber in a town-centre shop reserved for black customers, and as a dry-cleaner in a store for whites only. In a few months he became a respected figure among the tradesmen of the town. A hard worker and born thrifty, he knew how to make himself liked by his customers. In just one year he was able to buy a truck with his partner, and in the evenings and at weekends he transported the cargo he picked up from the four corners of the state.

For her part, Mary Kate joined the church council. The Waymons' was a religious household in which the fear of God was instilled, and she wanted her family to be an exemplary Christian household: no alcohol, no swearing, hard-working, pulling their weight. At the heart of her concerns was the respectability of her family within the community. A model and submissive wife, as tradition dictated, Mary Kate bowed to the authority of her husband. It was a harmonious marriage – there was no violence or crisis in their home, and they all grew up following the doctrine of 'a moderate bliss, a moderated bliss'.[3]

The 24th and then the 29th of October 1929. Like millions of American homes, the life of the Waymons suddenly took a turn for the worse. The stock market crash tipped the middle classes into poverty, and the poor into destitution. In just a few days consumption plummeted, social problems rose to the surface and much of the population was suddenly at risk of famine.

Tryon was not spared. The old resort saw its tourists fade away. Businesses closed one after the other, and by winter 1931 it was no more than a ghost town. For the Waymons, the consequences of the recession were disastrous. John Divine found himself unemployed, unable to cover the household costs, his savings being eaten away by raging inflation. He was forced to sell his truck to feed his family, which only survived thanks to their vegetable patch and the conserves made by Mary Kate.

Christmas of 1931 saw the family without the funds to heat their home. John Divine accepted whatever work was going, at the lowest pay. Mary Kate became a cleaning lady for some of the few middle-class families in the area who could still afford such a luxury, then took on work sewing the uniforms of soldiers for $2 a week at a relief centre set up by the government, work they would usually give to the guys at the penitentiary.

The family somehow managed to stay afloat, and then John Divine learnt that as part of the National Relief Agency, a government welfare scheme, the federal government was hiring drivers charged with delivering food to the most needy. He got himself hired and won the right to the extra rations awarded to drivers. Other than this, the Waymons scratched a living as best they could – they wheeled and dealed and swapped the meagre harvest from their vegetable patch (tomatoes, green beans, chard) for sugar or flour.

In the autumn of 1932, Mary Kate announced to her husband that she was pregnant again, news unlikely to have been welcome to anyone. And for Mary Kate there was no chance of taking time off work

– the expectant mother had to work right up to the week before giving birth.

Eunice Kathleen Waymon was born at 6 a.m. on the morning of 21 February 1933 in Tryon, and on her birth certificate her dad put his profession as 'barber' although he hadn't been that for two years, and her mum as 'housewife' although she was the only one with regular work. Poor they may have been, but they still had their pride.

The misery of the depression started to ease shortly after summer 1933. Finally tourists trickled back to Tryon, a lakeside camp opened up and John Divine was taken on as a cook.

Eunice's childhood memories were happy ones. Thanks to the family vegetable patch she never went hungry, and the family plot became a real little farm, where they raised the hogs they slaughtered in winter, chickens and a cow.

Some of Nina's first memories were of her mother's voice. With her high, trilling voice she would sing songs like 'I'll Fly Away', 'If You Pray Right' or 'Heaven Belongs to Me', which became the soundtrack to little Eunice's life, songs she would rediscover a few years later at Bible readings with her mother, and that sealed the loving relationship between the mother and her sixth child.

For the Waymons music was everywhere. It was a means of communication and an integral part of their life. After dinner John Divine would pick up his guitar or harmonica, invite his wife to accompany him on the organ, and the whole family would take turns on the instruments, every evening revisiting the same hymns, the same gospels.

In 1935, work became scarce again and the Waymons could no longer afford the rent on their house, and although their plot of land had guaranteed their survival, with heavy hearts they moved to a smaller house outside Tryon – more of a shack with few amenities, and at night they had to go out of the house and climb the outside staircase to bed.

Soon John Divine fell seriously ill and had to quit his job at the lake camp. The family's fate was in her hands, so Mary Kate took on all the work she could get.

Better times are ahead, they used to say, but the family had been in the new house for less than a year when the stove caught fire and the house burnt down. True to their nature, the first thing to be saved was the organ.

As a temporary measure the family moved to a house above an Episcopal school centre while they looked for somewhere else, but just a few days later John Divine was rushed to hospital with a blockage in his intestine. He was operated on within the hour. He would survive but had to spend several months convalescing.

With his wife working all day long and his kids at school, Dad and little Eunice, then four, spent their days together for almost a year. Eunice's childhood was over.

Ten times a day the ugly wound left by the operation on her father's stomach had to be washed, and she was the one who had to prepare his concoction of milk and raw eggs beaten up with a little sugar and vanilla, and help him to drink it. There were good days too – listening to his stories, her sides splitting with laughter, learning popular tunes and humming them with him. He had an answer to all of her questions and they became intimates, hugging and sharing their own special moments. She became Daddy's favourite: 'For the rest of my childhood I relied on him more than anyone else in the world, and he never let me down.'[4]

It soon became clear that they couldn't stay in the Episcopal centre – it was too noisy and busy, and John Divine couldn't get the peace and quiet he needed. In any event, it had been made clear to the Waymons that they couldn't stay there indefinitely, but with Mary Kate the sole breadwinner, the family were now too poor to afford a house in Tryon, and there was no question of going back to South Carolina to stay with one of their families – too complicated, but above all too expensive. They had to move far from town where rent was more affordable, and found a tiny house in the village of Lynn, some thirteen miles from Tryon. It was an isolated and 'primitive' spot as Nina recalls, mainly inhabited by unemployed black families. Even the most rudimentary notions of hygiene seemed to have passed the place by, and the new arrivals were the first to build their own bathroom. Nearly the entire family of their closest neighbours, the Knoxes, were crippled by rickets, and at just five, Eunice developed a fear of deformity, a fear which she would soon focus on Harold, her paralysed brother. One day she declared to her father, 'You have to get rid of Harold because we're a black family and he's gonna hold us down and we have to move fast.'[5] The child was just beginning to make sense of her family's social position: the need to survive in a hostile environment.

For Mary Kate, religion pushed doubts to one side, helped her ignore them while seeking to vanquish them. Religion was at the heart of her life, and to some extent even came before her family. Soon her job as a reverend meant that she dedicated herself entirely to it. 'As far as church was concerned Momma was a fanatic,' wrote Nina. She 'became a minister, which meant she had to travel all around preaching and leading services. By the time I was four the church had come to dominate her life.'[6] And as a result, her children's lives. Because being the child of a preacher in such a close-knit black community as Tryon meant there was a duty of excellence, a constant responsibility to live up to her family's position in the community. Nina had to be beyond reproach, a model child – humble, impeccably polite and totally submissive to the teachings of the church. She had to do everything with distinction yet remain modest at all times, whether in sport or her studies. And once her gift became apparent, excellence was not enough – people expected miracles.

Still only small, Eunice had an ear for music. 'My mother told me that when I was a baby, I only had to see an image, hear a radio advert of two or three notes of music, and I was off singing. It was in me, she told me. Music was in me.'[7] Her mother told her that she would raise herself on her arms and look around whenever she heard music playing.

The ladies at church had been amazed to see this baby in her crib tapping to the rhythm of the hymns. Everyone agreed that it must surely be a divine manifestation, in the Lord's own house! The village buzzed with the rumours of the miracles that took place at the Waymon home. It was said that aged two and a half, the first time that Eunice touched the keyboard of the organ she played the hymn 'God Be with You Till We Meet Again'. 'It's a spiritual in the key of *fa* which my mother used to play. At just two and a half years of age I had learnt it by heart, and my parents literally fell to their knees to see me sat before the pedal organ playing something that clearly nobody had ever taught me. "It's a gift from God," they cried. Few are lucky enough to have such a gift – Callas, Rubinstein, Horowitz, me and a few others.'[8]

Eunice was also compared to Mozart, and we think of his sister Nannerl, who at eleven was playing 'on the harpsichord or the piano the most difficult sonatas and concertos of the great masters, with the greatest of clarity, incredible ease and the best of taste'.[9] The extraordinary experience of the four-year-old Eunice opening Sunday services with her music was interpreted by the community as a divine manifestation. It should be remembered that this was a community in which Christian rituals evoked ancient spirits and magic. Had the grace of God filled this child? Had a spirit possessed her body? These religious rituals were the fruit of 'intangible expressions of African culture',[10] and the child had immersed herself in it well before discovering classical music. When she played on Sundays, 'the walls of the church trembled'.[11] The faithful came from far and wide (some more than fifty miles there and back) to hear the young prodigy. Eunice immersed herself in Bach at six years of age, and was an expert player at twelve. How could miracles not be expected of such a child?

In Tryon, Eunice was nicknamed 'the little prodigy'. At the same time an attraction, an object of curiosity, a sign of God's will and a hope for the black community of the town, was this child not evidence that God had heard their prayers over all these generations?

Even so, Mary Kate warned her against getting above her station. For her this gift was indeed a divine manifestation, and no reason for pride. On the contrary, it was a reason for humility and the recognition of God's will.

At five years of age, Eunice became the regular pianist at the Tryon Methodist church. This is where she learnt her sense of rhythm, her instinctive understanding of certain mystical rhythms she would use later in life. Most of all she loved the music in the Holiness church, which hosted revivals, neo-Pentecostalist ceremonies in which the faithful reaffirmed their faith in God, falling into trances and speaking in tongues. During these ceremonies she became familiar with other, more powerful, spiritual energies that believers used and strengthened until reaching a trance state. She became aware of the power of rhythm, the hypnotic power of music, the effect it had such as the look of joy on the faces of the faithful, or their gyrations. Eunice Waymon attended these services from childhood, before the age of six. 'Over the years those lessons slipped into my blood and became part of me.'[12] Everything came together here: music, religion, mystical teaching, and the community. But it had already existed within her, as if dormant, a seed waiting to be grown. It was a faith, an avalanche of feelings that submerged her, a familiar emotion which could almost have come from her distant ancestors.

She embraced this feeling that manifested itself in her body as if it had always been part of her.

When still a little girl, Eunice used to listen to her mother telling stories of her people during sermons at the Tryon Baptist church. Facing an audience of puritans, students, devout matriarchs, carpenters, peasants, old women and young, Reverend Mary Kate Waymon would evoke the marshlands of the south, the resistance to white oppression through faith in God and the church as the first spiritual experience of her people in this land.

As her sixth birthday drew near, Eunice Waymon's life was divided between church, music, her stamp collection and prayer. She would listen to Mary Kate's sermons, guessing that her mother spoke of the gift within her. Egged on by her mother and her community, Eunice subjected herself to a strict schedule. On Sundays she went to church at nine in the morning, played at eleven then accompanied the choir, and once more at six in the evening. She would play on Wednesday night at the prayer meeting and Friday night at choir rehearsals. And whenever she could, she would go to Holiness church revivals. The rest of the time the child would practise on the family organ.

She would observe this schedule until she turned twelve. She was forbidden to play anything but hymns in public, but on the sly, and with her father's help, she would learn lighter songs, popular melodies or jaunty old tunes.

In 1938 the Waymons relocated to Tryon and little Eunice enrolled in the school for black children. Five hundred pupils, five schoolmistresses and one headmaster. She proved to be a serious, committed and above all humble student, despite her 'prodigy' reputation with the other kids. A little role model in every respect, true to her position as pastor's daughter.

And all the more so as Mary Kate became a prominent religious figure in the Tryon area. She was appointed a Methodist minister and would travel all over the district every week to preach, henceforth dedicating all her time to the Church. This was a path that – unconsciously perhaps, in the guise of devoting herself to a noble purpose – allowed her gradually to detach herself from the family and children whom her sense of propriety wouldn't let her cherish. Eunice would bear her distant mother's emotional and physical withdrawal like an open wound, spending her life trying to fill this void, and repeating the cycle with her own and only daughter. Before her sixth birthday, the seed of her future failures as a mother had been planted.

The responsibilities of the household then fell on Lucille, the elder of the Waymon daughters.

Lucille, a radiant fifteen-year-old, was a self-confident teenager with poise and character. She became Eunice's first surrogate mother and her best friend. Lucille – as housewife, cook, childminder, housekeeper and sister – was subjected to a hellish schedule from adolescence: she was the first to rise in the morning to light the stove, make breakfast and take the little ones to school. Then she would make lunch and dinner, clean, serve the food, clear the table, wash the dishes, do the laundry, tidy up, do the ironing, never once complaining. When the younger girls came in from school, she would help them wash, comb and braid their hair, listen to them chatting about boys and answer their questions, teaching them the basics of womanhood. She would watch over her brothers, sometimes even having to call the police when a fight broke out, looking after her father who was growing ever weaker. In the evenings she would wash the dishes, then finally sleep and start all over again the next day.

Lucille played an essential part in Eunice's childhood. She was her one source of female affection, the only person to lend a caring ear to the child's doubts, her sorrows or little girl's troubles. But a decisive meeting was about to take place that would open up a brand new world to Eunice, one little known to her community, that Mary Kate had only glimpsed while working for the middle-class Millers. The world of whites.

Mrs Miller was a nice lady who would come and hear Eunice play at church every Sunday and would tell Mary Kate what a terrible shame it would be for a child of such talent not to take classical piano lessons. But the Waymons couldn't afford that kind of thing, though it pained Mary Kate to admit it. Mrs Miller offered to pay for Eunice's classes for one year, after which, she said, if she made good progress, they would no doubt find some sort of solution. She mentioned Eunice to a local piano teacher: Muriel Massinovitch.

Muriel was a charming and dainty woman of around fifty who wore her silver hair in a bun and spoke with a refined English accent. She asked to hear the young prodigy play, and a few days later saw a shy black girl appear on her doorstep, clutching her school bag close to her chest, not daring to meet her eyes.

With Muriel Massinovitch, Eunice would discover a kind of refinement she didn't know existed, the peace and quiet of a wealthy home where everything was delicate, sophisticated, filled with beauty and *joie de vivre*. She took in the paintings that covered the walls of the house, most of them works of 'Miz Mazzy's' husband, who was an artist of Russian descent and rumoured to be famous. 'The first time I went to Mrs Massinovitch's house I almost fainted – it was so beautiful.'[13] The child was led into a brightly lit room that opened onto a garden. At the end of this room proudly stood a baby grand piano. The child, awestruck, had never played on such an instrument. Mazzy asked her to play what she fancied. When Eunice finished playing, she called up

Mrs Miller: 'She is filled with music, her tonality is flawless; she has a smooth touch and her fingering is remarkable! I would be delighted to give her lessons.'

The Waymons saw no reason to object. That a white person would teach Eunice an art – a white art – didn't bother anyone. Mary Kate concealed her pride at seeing her daughter in the hands of a middle-class lady, whereas John Divine was downright gleeful at the thought.

Up until her twelfth year, when she started high school, Eunice Waymon would make the journey to the house in the woods every Saturday morning. She walked those two miles like a ritual and would always stop halfway to go to Owen's, a drugstore close to the railway, and buy a cheese sandwich which she'd eat outside, standing up. It wasn't allowed for a black person, even a child, to sit down in the restaurant or even to use the bathroom. Did Eunice question those rules, whose consequences she would soon come to understand?

During her lessons with Mazzy, Eunice learnt classical music's equivalent of algebra: solfeggio. She learned to decipher musical scores, to read and write music, understand the rhythms and sing a tune; the role of the right hand, which played themes and melodies, and the left, usually focused on rhythm and harmonies. The child learned all that with ease, so her teacher allowed herself to skip a few stages in her tuition. She taught her easy pieces, introduced her to a few composers, woke her up to Mozart and had her learn a few of his early works. Then she introduced her to Liszt, Czerny and, most importantly, to Bach. She immersed the child in his two-part inventions, his fugues and contrapuntal writing. She made her study the preludes, then later *The Art of Fugue*, the toccatas...

Through Bach, Eunice rediscovered emotions that she'd already felt in church, and that reached beyond music alone. Nothing in the nuances she deciphered could explain how she felt; it was as though a higher force flowed from the harmonies she played, like some kind of presence, a gateway to a sacred dimension. 'Once I understood Bach's music I never wanted to be anything other than a concert pianist,' she wrote in her memoirs; 'Bach made me dedicate my life to music'.[14]

Now eight years old, Eunice Waymon, the great-granddaughter of slaves, the youngest of this Christian African-American family, was discovering through a white person the path she would devote her life to: classical piano. Bach's mathematics gave her an insight into the white psyche, subtly opening up a cultural gap between her and her people. This was a clash between two universes: Bach's rigour and the vertigo of gospel, purity and mysticism, discipline and the secular.

Years later, in an interview she gave to the BBC, Nina Simone said: 'I admire Bach more than any other composer in the world. In terms of technique, he was pure; there's not a single arbitrary note with him. And it wasn't just his technique that was perfect, he was emotionally perfect too, but the most amazing thing was his actual detachment from his own music. He's the hardest composer of all to play. This man's principles were simple, you had to get them into your own head and listen to them; he'd just take a melody and surround it with another five or six voices. But to play this melody well, you have to alter the emotional mood every time a new voice came in, which needs tremendous discipline. He's a master, you need a great deal of discipline to play Bach well. If you don't play Bach well, it sounds all jumbled, but played correctly, those same notes you keep on repeating take on great significance. And that's what's hard. If you play a piece just for yourself, and you let yourself get carried away by your feelings, to the point of disregarding technique, you're in trouble. But if at the same time you manage to distance yourself from your feelings and put yourself in the audience's shoes and hear what they're hearing, there's nothing like it. That's what Bach means to me. I believe that Bach could play Bach with just about any score, without necessarily being guided by any experience.'

Between the ages of six and ten, Eunice Waymon practised the piano three hours a day. Then she gradually increased this to four, then to six hours. From age ten to eleven she would play six or seven hours a day. On top of this schedule came her school work, playing at church on Sundays, prayer evenings, revivals...

Those years were also an introduction to pain: she learned to lean forward a little, always a bit off balance, so that each note came from her lower back and made its way to her fingertips, hurting her her hands and back.

But what the girl was discovering in return for her efforts, this pain and sacrifice, was priceless. Her progress in classical piano was one thing, but Mazzy herself had taken on a vital role in her life, filling the void Mary Kate had left when she decided to devote herself full-time to her ministry. With her teacher, Eunice discovered affection, the tenderness of kisses. Mazzy actually came to be her 'white momma',[15] the more so as the little girl noticed Mary Kate moving further away from her, keeping her distance even when the two of them were alone together. But how could she begin to tell her how this distance hurt her? How she missed her mother? Communication between them seemed to have broken down.

Yet Mary Kate had great things in mind for her daughter – perhaps she thought her motherly love could wait. Would she, who immersed herself body and soul in her religion, become, like Leopold Mozart, the kind of parent who can only find fulfilment through her child and 'to a certain extent at [his or her] expense'?[16] As with Amadeus and Leopold, soon the only link remaining between the two women was the dream they shared, reaching a higher ground through music.

After consulting Eunice's parents, Miz Mazzy set up the Eunice Waymon Fund to collect donations that would allow her pupil to continue her musical education in an institute the year she was due to start college. She wrote to the local paper to place an ad calling for donations. The parishes of Tryon joined in her quest for funds, and eventually the local council organized a fund-raiser .

This was a lot of pressure to put on a child. 'I had no choice,' she would say. Eunice would become what her mother and Mazzy had decided for her. After such a mobilization on her behalf, how could she fail to believe she was somehow different, a prodigy as some would whisper? Despite what her mother kept telling her, she knew she wasn't like the other kids. Hadn't her destiny just been taken over by a fund that was mainly the doing of whites? Could any other black child in Tryon claim the same? Gradually, Eunice began to act like those who 'instinctively feel that they belong to the chosen ones'.[17]

It was agreed that the young pianist would play regular recitals at a venue in Tryon, so that fund contributors could follow her progress and congratulate themselves on their donations. Eunice was told of her mother's and teacher's plans. As well as giving her piano lessons, Mazzy taught her how to take the stage, how to hold her head, the dignity required at every step, every movement.

At barely ten, Eunice was already being forced into success. She would one day say that from that moment on her childhood became a kind of sacrifice. The weight not only of her community's hopes, but also those of a town where blacks and whites united around her destiny, rested on her frail shoulders.

Her talents must have been truly outstanding for the more affluent class of a small provincial town in segregationist 40s America to contemplate the thought of a black child becoming a concert pianist. Indeed, on paper, anyone from Tryon would have told you: 'Black children don't get to be concert pianists.'

The little girl shielded from violence would grow up to discover the fate of blacks in America and become acquainted with Jim Crow, 'the most elaborate and formal expression of sovereign white opinion upon the subject'[18] of racism. Eunice would cross that invisible line and learn the meaning of a word – racism – around which the society she lived in was, in part, built. Beyond that boundary, she would have to give up her innocence.

Budding breasts were soon followed by her first period. In just a year she had suddenly grown all at once. Despite her status in Tryon, Eunice had become a black woman and was subjected to the same laws, the same bans as the members of her community. She started to question things like why she couldn't sit down at Owen's Pharmacy or use the bathroom at gas stations, this distance imposed between the two communities. She was told it had always been that way. The way men looked at her had changed too; they no longer saw a child, but rather something else, something threatening. Prey, or perhaps an enemy. Even Mrs Miller's attitude towards her was now different. Before, when Eunice went to her house to help her mother do the cleaning, she would play with David, Mrs Miller's youngest son, but lately she noticed they were being kept apart from each other.

Eunice heard that one of her father's friends had left town in a hurry after an affair with a white woman. No one around her talked about it. She noticed that the Tryon barber, a very light-skinned black man who could pass for white, was treated as one of their own by the white men whose hair he cut. But outside his working hours he lived in the black neighbourhood and was considered black. Later she was told that a lynching had taken place in a nearby county. She didn't know the word, and asked her father about it. He didn't answer.

1941. The United States had just gone to war following the attack on Pearl Harbor. President Roosevelt, then in his third term, granted blacks the right to work in the arms industry. It was rumoured that in the North, in Detroit, blacks could hope to be paid a dollar a day working in the Ford or Chrysler factories, these having halted their car production to build tanks and B-52s. The city became 'the arsenal of democracy'.

Spring 1943. The Waymon family was all set to marry off Lucille, and John Divine had just found a job as foreman in Landrum, five miles from Tryon. Business was picking up. The Waymons relocated again and moved into a big house with a veranda, a garden and, for the first time, running water.

Eunice had just celebrated her tenth birthday when she was invited to give a recital at the Tryon town hall with all the high officials in attendance: the mayor, doctors, businessmen, the local police chief and representatives of the community.

For Miz Mazzy, who had organized the event with the white ladies of her support fund, this was all about a demonstration of strength: on the one hand, showing all the benefactors the progress her pupil had made, and on the other, that the girl (a black girl at that!) was indeed on the road to a career as a concert pianist. The first step in her ascension would dazzle them. It was impossible to ignore the stakes of such a challenge. Eunice had spent weeks rehearsing, practising for six hours every day, which left her exhausted, her back aching relentlessly, her hands screaming in pain. On the eve of the recital, sleep eluded her, melodies swam around her head. In the morning she began to feel nauseous even before breakfast. Despite her mother's insistence, she barely ate a thing. Eunice was overcome with an alien emotion, some kind of fear, stage fright, a terrible apprehension that threatened to engulf her.

That day was filled with pride. Dressed in their finest clothes, the Waymons rode to the town hall in their old Ford, none of them speaking a word. They parked at a short distance and walked towards the forecourt, John Divine savouring the polite nods of good society.

Clad in a white muslin dress Lucille had made for her, Eunice stepped into the town hall for the first time, discovering the shrine of Tryon's white power, surprised to find it so modestly decorated. A baby grand piano awaited her in the reception room on the first floor. Joining her, Miz Mazzy took her hand, introduced her to the mayor, the local notables, their wives. The girl curtsied, avoiding her benefactors' amused glances, and strode towards the instrument.

On her teacher's signal, as her beaming parents took their seats in the first row, Eunice sat down. She noticed how her father held Mary Kate's hand, a gesture she'd only seldom seen him allow himself with her mother. Not that John Divine was a timid man, but Mary Kate seemed to flounder at the slightest display of affection.

The recital was about to start, her audience awaited. Eunice had carefully laid out her scores: she would start with the toccatas then carry on with *The Art of Fugue*. She could feel all the eyes on her, as she realized how familiar this actually was. After all, hadn't she been preparing for this moment for the last four years? She'd just managed to clear her thoughts when suddenly she sensed movement in the audience. A couple of whites were asking her parents to give up their seats. She saw her father's pained expression, read the resignation on Mary Kate's face. The girl stood up from her piano stool and protested, declaring that she wouldn't play unless her parents remained in their seats. She heard a lady from Tryon choke with laughter, saw the men's nervous smiles. Then silence. Eunice met her father's gaze; he seemed to be telling her: 'Do you realize what you're doing?' Her mother remained completely silent, her eyes riveted to the floor, as though dying with shame. In the room, stupor gave way to scoffing. Some said: 'Charming girl, but what a nerve!' Visibly annoyed, the white couple took their seats further back, leaving the Waymons theirs. This first performance would leave a different taste in her mouth. 'All of a sudden it seemed a different world, and nothing was easy any more,'[19] she would write later.

This was the first time Eunice came up against everyday racism, and her first rejection of the violence it entailed. Paradoxically, the first applause the young musician ever gleaned came from white hands.

In the summer of 1944, Detroit witnessed violent race riots, events soon forgotten by the US media in favour of the landing of Allied troops in Normandy. Thousands of black GIs had gone to battle in the Old World, convinced that by thus serving their country they would be rewarded with honour and recognition. They'd been led to think that white people were a united and invincible race, and now African-American soldiers came to Europe and saw whites fighting whites. Back in their home country, they told their people what they had witnessed. Those reports roused passionate discussions within the community. If whites could kill each other like that, their race was to be pitied; it was digging its own grave.

The Waymon boys had pretty much escaped enlistment; only Carroll, the eldest, was in uniform in Virginia. Lucille, on her part, had left the family home and moved to Philadelphia with her husband.

With Lucille gone, Eunice had lost her only real friend, her only confidant, the only one – except for Mazzy and her father, but that was different – who had known how to listen to her complaints or her dreams for the future. Who was left now to understand just how isolated she felt with her music? She couldn't share those doubts with her teacher, or her father who had such faith in her. Both of them would have reminded her how fortunate she was, how inappropriate it was to complain with all that was being done to help her and her future.

At age eleven, Eunice dedicated all of her free time to playing the piano, her life devoid of the leisure usually allowed to girls of her age. The minute she came home from school and finished her homework, she would practise for hours or run to her classes at Mazzy's. During her breaks she could hear the neighbourhood children playing, a pleasure denied to her for reasons everyone knew. The little prodigy would one day become 'the first black American concert pianist'.[20] The altar her childhood was being sacrificed upon. A master plan for which she had to give up the pleasures of girls her age: friendship, a carefree life, games. This would carry on into her teenage years, leaving her deprived of friendship until she enrolled at the conservatory, where students become competitive rivals.

At just eleven, this exclusion made her feel like 'some kind of freak'.[21] How could she fail to notice the distrust in the other children's eyes? After all, solitude is odd, the praise you're smothered in and the hopes placed in you unnatural, making you into a circus animal, taking away your childhood. Who or what could she turn to, except her piano and sheet music? Those at least wouldn't let her down. Alone with her keyboard, Eunice felt protected, unveiling herself little by little. You had to surrender for this friend to deign to call, otherwise he would turn away from you. You had to be open to decipher and understand the meaning entrusted by these scores.

Mozart, Liszt, Bach; portraits of white faces from other centuries hung on her bedroom walls. As the months went by, they had become close friends. Eunice had learned who they were and what they sought to express through this music Mazzy had given her as though it were a treasure, which is exactly what it was. Eunice had come to understand what it was these genius composers used to create beauty. She treated them as game companions, invoking them, whispering her secrets or just speaking to them, trusting her instincts as when forging an intimate relationship with a stranger. With them, she developed her own personality and secretly managed to escape this world.

Hours spent memorizing scores, every nuance, every pause, rehearsing the same exercises and arpeggios in every possible scale.

When she finally emerged from those hours of solitude she would wander through the house, waiting for her mother to return in the hope of finally managing to attract her attention. Something between them had broken on that day at the town hall. Mary Kate seemed to be ignoring her, avoiding her. Locked in her shame, she no longer offered her daughter the least affection. Was she aware of Eunice and Mazzy's exclusive relationship, that this white woman was now a spiritual, even surrogate mother to her? Did she see that her friendship with Mazzy had drawn Eunice from the black world into the white; that she'd been changed by what she'd discovered? Did Mary Kate feel her daughter was already eluding her? Perhaps she didn't deem it appropriate to show affection to a child on the edge of puberty. Whatever the reason, a rift had widened between them; they'd become two strangers, linked only by the projects nurtured by a mother for her child's blessed gift: 'I couldn't recall the last time Momma had taken me into her arms, or kissed me, or told me she was proud of me,'[22] the pianist would write. Her distress was exacerbated, perhaps, by the image of the ideal household Miz Mazzy and her husband seemed to embody; by comparison, her own family no longer seemed all that perfect.

Then suddenly this loneliness dissipated with the arrival of the Waymons' new neighbours, the Whiteside family, who were Cherokee. Eunice fell in love with Edney, their eldest son, at first sight. She'd often see him when she went to her classes at Mazzy's. He was a handsome boy – pretty features, a strong body, ochre skin and cropped jet-black hair. The first time they met, Edney was shirtless; he was helping his father cut the overgrown grass in their yard, gathering it before burning. He looked beautiful in the sunset. Eunice scurried along, praying that he hadn't noticed her, but the boy planted his pitchfork in the ground at his feet and greeted her. She felt a tremor in her chest, shyly returned the greeting, her cheeks on fire. She carried on walking, not once turning around; then, once she'd reached the top of the hill, as though taken over by some unknown power, she looked back, sneaking a glance at the Whitesides' garden. The boy was still standing there, watching her. Grinning, he waved at her. She felt her heart explode, and ran.

They met again; first by accident, then came the first dates. Every afternoon, Edney would wait for her, sitting on a clump of earth, playing with blades of grass. The first few times, she feigned not to hear him when he called out to her, asking her name. Then one day he spoke her name – how had he found out? – and burst out laughing. He jumped out onto the road, caught up with her at the top of the hill and offered to walk her to her destination. At first she said no, then, on his gentle insistence, agreed. And so they became 'the baby couple'. The news of the young prodigy falling for an Indian spread quickly. This racial mix didn't bother anyone in those areas, in fact it was widely accepted by whites and blacks alike. And so the Whitesides met the Waymons, everyone got along wonderfully and it was agreed that one day their children would marry. But for now their romance was forced within the boundaries of strict social mores.

Edney and Eunice would meet every Sunday at four in the afternoon, under their parents' watchful eye. Then as Eunice grew up, this surveillance loosened, allowing the beginnings of flirtation.

In the meantime, the Waymon family had expanded. Frances was born in April 1942, then Samuel in 1944. John Irvine had left home soon after his coming of age. In town, rumour had it that he'd left as the result of a major disagreement with his father, but that topic was taboo in the family. Dorothy had grown into a pretty young girl; Harold had been declared unfit for service and had left to study at university. Every now and then, they'd hear from Lucille in Philadelphia.

John Divine had given up his job as a foreman shortly before Samuel was born and taken on all sorts of odd jobs since: gardening for whites, waiting at receptions and working as a handyman most of the time. The strong-willed, ambitious character of ten years before was now reduced to juggling precarious jobs, like the little shop he'd opened downtown to sell sandwiches at lunchtime.

'After forty-five years of believing that if he worked hard and trusted in God then, black man or not, he would advance in society, Daddy was reduced to acting the friendly black butler, like the ones we saw in the Hollywood movies every Saturday morning at Tryon's (segregated) picture house.'[23] John Divine was wounded in his pride. How could a man like him see his dreams shattered just like that? How had he got there, breaking his back for a few dollars a day, doing jobs he knew were degrading? His wife and his older children earned much of the money that allowed the Waymons to survive and he experienced his situation as a failure.

Since childhood, Eunice had always heard that to move upwards in society, there was no choice but to work hard. But in that case, what was to be learnt from her parents' social downfall? A mother who'd spent her entire life praising God and who was now reduced to cleaning other people's homes? A virtuous and hard-working father with no steady job? What was there to learn from that? That a stroke of bad luck was all it took to make you reconsider your ambitions, provided it didn't drown you in misery first.

Mary Kate knew this. Even though she was incapable of showing affection to her daughter, she did everything she could to keep Eunice's talent safe from those destructive forces. She'd spent a long time talking about Eunice's future with Mazzy and Mrs Miller. Mazzy'd said there was nothing left for her to teach her pupil, but one thing she was certain of: Eunice had extraordinary musical talent and it would have been a crime not to enable her to continue her studies in a specialist school. The three women were moved by the same ambition: to make Eunice Waymon 'the first black American concert pianist'. Bitterly, the pianist would write: 'It was ironic that Momma's ambition was so tied to race when she spent the whole of her life trying to ignore the reality of her colour.'[24] Perhaps she saw in her daughter an instrument of her vengeance and that of her race.

The place they decided on was the Allen High School for Girls, a boarding school in Asheville, about fifty miles from Tryon, a protected environment where a close eye was kept on the students (young teenagers might fall pregnant!). The teaching there was excellent and the staff were all white. The piano teacher, who happened to be a good friend of Mazzy's, was called Joyce Carrol. Eunice spent three years there, in full board accommodation, only returning to Tryon during the school holidays. Her education was paid for with money from the fund.

Eunice Waymon enrolled at Allen High aged twelve, in September 1945. After a childhood spent in isolation, she would for the first time forge friendships with other girls and learn about companionship. They'd chat about movies and boys, tell each other gossip and secrets and learn the latest dance moves.

The discipline that reigned there was tough, but this didn't bother her; she was determined to do all it took to honour the faith that her mother and Mazzy had placed in her and so she subjected herself to a Spartan schedule. She'd get up at four every morning and practise until eight. After breakfast came the day's classes. Right from the first term, her grades were excellent. She took piano lessons with Joyce Carrol twice a week, accompanied the choir every Wednesday and played in the school orchestra. Then on Sundays she would get up at dawn to play in church.

Thirty years later, when Nina Simone decided to place Lisa Celeste, her only daughter, in a boarding school, she might have been trying to reproduce the same pattern. Boarding school had been a positive experience for Eunice, so when she herself became a mother, she probably thought that her child would feel the same. Sadly, this didn't turn out well.

During the few weeks' annual holidays, Eunice went home to see her family, noticing that despite her siblings' obvious envy, her mother continued to ignore her. Only John Divine showed her any warmth, bombarding her with questions about everything: her teachers, the setting, the food, her new friends, her piano lessons of course. He asked her to play a sample of what she'd learned on the family pedal organ, but she said she'd rather give him a whole recital. Then she ran to Miz Mazzy to show her the progress she'd made. Mazzy was astounded: her protégée played to perfection.

On Sunday, at four in the afternoon, Edney came to see his girlfriend. Watched over by a chaperone, the young lovers eyed each other longingly, having spent the year writing each other passionate letters. In her careful handwriting, Eunice poured out her love to Edney, evoking the happy days they would soon be spending together, their wedding, but also the progress she was making at the piano, her dreams of going to the conservatory, the career as a concert artist she was being promised by everyone... Edney never brought up his loved one's career aspirations, simply telling her in letter after letter how much he wanted to marry and set up home with her, how she would be able to live with him in Tryon as soon as she finished her education.

Three years went by and Edney's letters grew more sporadic. Eunice came home to see him the weekend after he missed a Sunday visit, and he confessed that he'd been seeing a friend of hers. 'You're not home and I miss you too much.' He was eighteen, Eunice sixteen. They decided to break up, both of them still virgins.

Eunice graduated top of her year in June 1950. The whole Waymon family travelled to see the graduation ceremony. John Divine, Mrs Miller and Mazzy all beamed with pride. John Divine gave his daughter a letter from Lucille containing her elder sister's warm congratulations. Mrs Miller brought her a copy of the Tryon newspaper that announced the 'little prodigy's' success. Only Mary Kate remained silent, as though that moment was nothing but a formality, the expected fulfilment of an agreement sealed years before. In the distance, Eunice glimpsed Edney, who'd come to Asheville with his parents to applaud her.

A decision had been made. Miz Mazzy was convinced that the only thing that would yield the girl the career she dreamed of was to study at the Curtis Institute in Philadelphia. Everyone agreed that she could spend the first weeks of summer preparing for the scholarship exam at Curtis, which was scheduled for August, at the Juilliard School of Music in New York. At the end of the graduation ceremony, she was awarded a grant to study there for two months.

As young graduates poured out of the room and their parents carried on their conversations out front, Edney came to find Eunice and asked her to follow him into a vacant room. He threatened her: 'If you go to New York we'll never see each other again, it'll all be over between us and I'll marry your best friend.' But what choice did he think she could make? On the one hand, those years of hard work, the hopes her family, Mazzy and her community had placed in her – what now seemed a certainty of becoming what the two women had decided for her and she believed in too, 'the first black American concert pianist'. And on the other hand, Edney's love, already stained with infidelity. What could he offer her? Marriage. Returning to Tryon. The promise of a life that might indeed be sweet, but without depth or ambition, repeating the mediocre life cycle her parents had inherited.

Her reply was curt: 'I want to go to New York.' Edney went crazy, pushed her backwards, threw himself on her and tried to take her by force. The young girl fought back, hitting him, screaming for him to stop. At last he got up, ashamed of his own violent impulse. He threw her one last glance as though terrified by what he'd done and walked out of the room. She ran after him in the school hallway, caught up with him, begged him to calm down and listen to her. There was nothing he could do to make her come back on her decision, she explained. She'd worked too hard all those years to just give up like that, she said. She had to see her plans through, to fulfill her destiny. Edney was in tears; no one had ever cried for Eunice Waymon before. She took out a photo from her purse, like the one that would one day feature on the back sleeve of her record *Here Comes the Sun*. The picture of a model young girl in the midst of adolescence, obediently gazing at the camera, her hands crossed on a table top. No matter how hard you look, nothing in this girl's features – her shining eyes, posture, her smile – gives any hint of Nina Simone, who would be born from this chrysalis. She gave him the picture. He placed it on the family piano, and a few months later married that other young black woman, Annie Mae.

The few times the pianist would come across her former boyfriend's mother in Tryon, she would always hear: 'Why didn't you marry my son? You must take him back.' Her answer was always the same: 'Maybe I'll come back in a few years.'

She did come back, in fact.

The Juilliard School was one of the most prestigious classical music conservatories in the United States. The foundation it was born from was set up in March 1920 by Augustus D. Juilliard. 'He expressed the wish for his inheritance to be devoted to promoting music in America. The partners in the foundation drew up a plan that would benefit both American musicians and their audiences.'[25] Located on 120 Claremont Avenue (between Broadway and 122nd Street), each summer the Juilliard School offered a six-week preparatory course where students from elsewhere could come and prepare for the entrance exams for the music school they had chosen. Nina Simone always claimed to have spent a whole year there, but it was really just one summer. She took the course scheduled from 3 July to 11 August 1950, along with 780 other students.

Eunice signed up on 29 June 1950 and paid $155 in admission fees from the fund. The Juilliard School provided no accommodation for its students, only classes, so Eunice stayed with a preacher friend of her mother's, Mrs Steinermayer, in a house on 145th Street in Harlem.

She was seventeen and seemed like a scared little country girl. Never before had she been out of North Carolina. The minute she got to her new neighbourhood, its noise and bustle frightened her.

In the early 1920s, Harlem was home to 150,000 blacks, making it the country's largest African-American community. The arrival of this population, mainly from the South, had gradually pushed the European immigrants (Irish, Italians, Poles, Jews...) who lived there out of the neighbourhood. Many black writers, jazz musicians and other artists came and found shelter in Harlem, and it became 'the capital of black American culture'.[26] All sorts of cafés, clubs, cabarets and dance halls cropped up, among them the Cotton Club and the Savoy Ballroom. And just like in Kansas City, this nocturnal fever drew in gangsters.

Far too frightened by the tales of drugs, violence and prostitution she'd heard about Harlem to risk wandering its streets, Eunice wouldn't venture out into the neighbourhood, sticking to the commute between 145th Street and Claremont Avenue, which she did by bus. Still, she was dumbstruck by what she saw along the way: the grocery and clothing stores, the music that seemed to be wafting out of everywhere, the tall buildings that tickled the clouds, the feeling of pride that emanates from this city.

Classes started on 3 July and were due to end on 11 August – with a short break to celebrate the 4th of July. Each day, Eunice attended the Juilliard School from eight in the morning to four in the afternoon, except on Sundays. She spent those six weeks in New York in constant alert, never making friends with anyone, concentrating on her classes. She was the only black student on the course – though others had attended Juilliard, such as Miles Davis. Eunice prepared for her scholarship exam at the Curtis Institute with Dr Carl Friedberg, with five fifty-minute classes a week over the six weeks.

When those classes came to an end, the Eunice Waymon Fund money had almost run out. She knew that the hopes placed in her were huge, crushing even, and that it was essential for her to pass the Curtis exam. No one even imagined that things might turn out differently, to the point where the Waymons had even moved to Philadelphia – joining Lucille and also Carrol, who had moved there after his military service.

Philly was in full bloom. In just a few years, black neighbourhoods had filled up with countless new arrivals. Numerous black families had fled the violence of the South after the recession and hauled themselves up to the ghettos of the major industrial cities of the North. Philly had also become an important centre of the American music industry, home to all sorts of labels, clubs and musicians looking for gigs.

On 12 August 1950, Eunice travelled from New York to Philadelphia by bus. The Curtis entrance exam was scheduled for the following week, with the lucky winners starting there in September.

Before the exam, Eunice spent close to seven hours a day playing the piano, rehearsing the pieces set by the Curtis examination board to exhaustion: one by Bach (prelude and fugue), a sonata (Mozart, Haydn or Beethoven), one romantic piece (Schumann, Liszt, Chopin), a modern piece from the early twentieth century (Debussy, Ravel, Prokofiev), then finally a concerto with an orchestra. The jury would grade her on her technical abilities and artistic merits, determining whether she had personality and managed to express it through her instrument. 'When she was preparing for the Curtis entrance examination,' Mary Kate Waymon recalled, 'I saw Eunice spend seven hours at a time trying to memorize nineteen pages of music. And I saw her cry.'[27]

One morning during the last week of August 1950, Eunice Waymon got her father to walk her to the corner of 8th and Locust Street, near Rittenhouse Square, in downtown Philadelphia.

To this day, what happened that morning remains a mystery. Nina Simone never once mentioned how the examination went. Was she too nervous? Did she play beneath her abilities, or simply make mistakes in her interpretations? What record did the Curtis Institute keep of this exam? None is left today. Whatever occurred, on the way back, for the first time in her life, Eunice began to have doubts.

2

FROM RENUNCIATION TO REVELATION

DESTINY came in a letter from the head of the Curtis Institute, deposited in the Waymons' letterbox that morning in 1954. The whole family sits down around the kitchen table and stares at the envelope. Whatever it is that lies within holds rare powers, capable of rewarding the tenacity of a mother, the efforts of a daughter and the hopes of an entire family. Because there is nothing more certain than the fact that once accepted at the Curtis Institute, Eunice will follow the path that has been defined for her since she was a child. So what if this is a rejection? God forbid. All eyes are on the prodigal daughter, the prodigy who, shaking now, digs her fingernails into the envelope, trying not to tear it open, delaying the moment she will have to face her verdict. Only the sound of paper crumpling between her fingers disturbs the silence. Eunice Waymon carefully puts down the torn envelope, unfolds the letter, scanning it. They are searching her face in silence and watch her features fall apart as she reads the letter through gritted teeth, no one saying a word. There is no need to ask about its contents; they understand as soon as Eunice meets their gazes, looking up from the tattered piece of paper, and brings her arms in along her waist. As she stares into nothingness, she whispers that it's impossible, then slowly holds up the sheet for whomever to see, and says: 'They turned me down.'

John Divine puts on his glasses, takes hold of the letter and, his mouth slightly open, reads those same lines several times over. His little girl, with her great, God-given talent has been pushed away from her destiny and there is nothing anyone can do about it. The letter is passed around the family table, everyone taking hold of it in turns, without a single word to the stunned girl.

'Rejected.' It is now Mary Kate's turn to read the final word that stands out from the hollow sentences spelling out rejection. Eunice will not go to the Curtis Institute. She will never become the first Black American classical concert artist. Never. The only dream they ever shared has just been crushed. If it wasn't for her mother staring at her as though questioning her about her mistakes, demanding explanations or even a remedy to this failure, Eunice would just grab the letter and stamp on it. Almost fifty years later, Tryon's golden child would continue to dwell on the humiliation she was subjected to that day: 'I still haven't gotten over it,' she said, 'and I never will. It felt as though my teachers, my community and my parents had all betrayed me.'[1]

Eunice preferred silence to the Waymons' words of comfort. She ran into her room, shut the door behind her, sat down on her bed and spent hours crying all the tears in her body.

Bitterness gave way to stupor. In the days that followed, she had to face awkward silences but above all, pick someone to blame for her failure. Suspicion slowly wormed its way into Eunice's thoughts and she suddenly found herself casting reproachful looks at her mother and those close to her. Could it be that White Miz Mazzy and Mrs Miller set up the fund just to shed their good Christian guilt, giving the little black girl charity to relieve their conscience?

Her brother Carrol had raised her suspicions. 'Eunice, couldn't you have been rejected because of your skin colour?' There was no need to labour the point, the young woman believed him at once. As though in a flash of consciousness, she became aware of the racism that had surrounded her since childhood. Suddenly she was able to decipher the traits of behaviour that made blacks into the servants of whites: she could see her mother cleaning the houses of families from Tryon's middle class when she was just a child, her father breaking his back for a few dollars paid by a greasy hand. 'Nobody told me that no matter what I did in life the colour of my skin would always make a difference. I learned that bitter lesson from Curtis.'[2]

Sylvia Hampton, her English biographer, thinks that until the Curtis defeat, Eunice had been sheltered from racism by the love of her family and the support of the Tryon community. The curtain had suddenly dropped. This overprotected young girl now had to accept her failure and submit to a life no one had prepared her for: anonymity and slavery in disguise. The failure was made public, spread through the streets of Philadelphia, and within a few hours reached Tryon and the Good Samaritans of the Eunice Waymon Fund.

At that precise moment, the special bond between mother and daughter was stretched beyond repair. Mary Kate couldn't stand watching her pace around the house, looking for a solution that didn't exist. She would never forgive her. What good were all those prayers if the only reward was this slap in the face? And how could she get her revenge now, for her, her family, her race?

From that day on, regardless of the way the young pianist's life turned out and whether or not she achieved her goals or found a job, like her mother had demanded of her, nothing would ever erase this scar, and from that moment Eunice and Mary Kate lost one another for good, neither of them proving capable of alleviating the other's disappointment. What was there left to say? That it was deeply unfair? That they should have prepared themselves for it? Those were things both of them knew.

Mary Kate declared that this was God's will, that they had to bow down to it: 'If your childhood was sacrificed like this, it was to prepare you to suffer and perhaps to overcome this humiliation.' Angered, Eunice began to see her mother under a different light, and for the first time she began to feel distrust towards her. Was it possible that Mary Kate secretly rejoiced in her failure? Eunice began to blame her for turning away from this project they had built together, for meekly accepting fate.

Many years would pass before the pianist understood that her mother was looking towards the future, that her attitude was ruled by her own disappointment and that all she wanted was to relieve her daughter of the grudge she herself bore and the scars that had marred her life. Renunciation for protection. This was unacceptable to this young girl of seventeen.

Now was the time to bounce back, to show some dignity, to give up the piano which repulsed her anyhow. Eunice had to settle for finding a job and accept her fate, a life of dullness. Any job would do, provided that it brought money to the family, those were the instructions. A friend of Mary Kate's told her about a photographer in Philadelphia who was looking for an employee, nothing extraordinary, just some 'stupid' job she said, which consisted of doing the shopping, drip-drying films... A steady job without any appeal. Yet Eunice feigned interest in an attempt to reassure her mother, perhaps to get closer to her.

Carrol, her brother, was encouraging her to resume her piano studies; he tried to reason with her, to push her forward. He promised her they'd find some money, that there had to be a way. Hearing this over and over again, Eunice began to realize just how much she missed the piano, even physically. Carrol managed to convince her to go back to it without much of an effort. There was no way this girl could follow the norm and settle for a menial, ordinary job, lying low for the rest of her days. No one born with such talent is meant to remain anonymous, not when you're one of the chosen, a body gifted with a purpose. Eunice felt this power within her and Mary Kate knew this. The only thing this mother was wrong about was which calling was her daughter's true destiny. Eunice began to look for a solution to this hitch; she'd understood that she had to carry on studying and perfecting her skill until a new opportunity arose, but in order to see this renewed quest through, she needed to find a guarantee of financial independence, a job that would bring her as close as possible to her goals: earn enough money that she could send a share of it to her family every month as custom dictated – and dedicate the remaining crumbs to piano lessons, her goal being to sit the Curtis Institute entrance exam once more the following year.

Eunice Waymon wouldn't back down; it was either 'the Curtis or nothing', as she would later write in her autobiography. Still, assuming that she would indeed get in, her admittance to the prestigious institute still wouldn't guarantee her a successful career as a classical concert artist. There was no set path, nor any diploma providing guarantees of any kind, but she intended to get her revenge for the insult she had suffered, to prove to her community, to her family – to her mother especially – and to the jury, to all the teachers and pupils of the conservatory, that nothing would make Eunice Waymon deviate from her goal. That no one would push her aside and that nothing would stifle the talent that lay within that body of hers, no matter how black.

It is surprising to see that back in those days, with the exception of Carrol, her family seemed to have given up on the projects they'd been working towards for almost a decade. Surprising also to realize now that Eunice never actually was this young naive, fragile woman she would later like to evoke. The Curtis revealed her true nature, that of a warrior for whom music was the weapon of choice, but right then, she didn't know that the obstacles that would truly reveal her were yet to come. At just seventeen, hope was still free, and Carrol had shown her a way she had never suspected existed and never even considered: independence.

There was a little money left in the fund that had been set up for her, enough to enable Eunice Waymon to sign up for a few weeks' classes with Vladimir Sokhaloff, a renowned piano teacher who would have been her teacher at the Curtis. Sokhaloff would play a key part over those years – it was he who suggested to her to let 'the black part of her' speak – though he said he'd never seen any genius in his student. Interviewed by Frank Lords for *The Legend*, his film about Nina Simone, Sokhaloff declared that his pupil had been turned down by the Curtis because other candidates had proved to be better than her. That was all. Was it really? In 1950s America, could anyone believe that a young black girl, the only one to sit the entrance exam to one of the country's most renowned conservatories, had been impartially graded by a white jury? Could one reasonably imagine that a girl like her, who displayed 'a certain talent but no genius', would be chosen over a white student with similar abilities? It took another three years for the Supreme Court to decree educational segregation as unconstitutional through the 1954 Brown v. Board of Education decision.

Still Eunice Waymon, eighteen years old, persevered. She was going to regain the self-assurance required to believe again, despite the slap in the face she would one day call 'her first violation', that she would indeed become 'the first black concert artist, no matter what'. Perhaps she was fooling herself.

Her job at the photography lab bored her to death and at any rate it didn't bring her enough money to pay for her classes with Sokhaloff. She quit and found another job with Arlene Smith, a singing teacher who was looking for a pianist to accompany her during her classes. The work was unrewarding and badly paid, not even a dollar an hour. Still, Eunice got something positive out of the months she spent with Mrs Smith, first of all practically, since she got fed by a cook at lunch, but mostly in artistic terms as the classes allowed her to familiarize herself with the songs in vogue with young whites, 'each one of them worse than the other', as she struggled with them. Her ear was flawless, a memory she would soon put to use, just as she would remember the notions of singing and technique taught by her employer. Those things were the reason why eight hours a day, five days a week, she would put up with those children who screamed more than they sang. Arlene Smith paid her accompanist $50 a month, which barely represented the minimum wage in those days. Eunice gave half of her earnings to her family and invested the rest in piano lessons. She did however manage to save a few pennies.

On the horizon of this insipid life she could once again see her dream begin to rise, though dimmed and affected by deprivation and constraints. Five hours a day playing the piano, church every Sunday. Every now and then, to break up the monotony, Eunice would go and see a European movie in the cinema, and then she would go back – early – to the family home. No friends, and of course, no lover.

Early in 1954, Eunice had saved enough money to be able to afford the rent on a small studio in Philadelphia, on the corner of 57th Street and Master. Nothing exceptional, a bare room on the street, definitely not the cosiest of nests, but more than enough to provide a bedroom at night and a studio during daytime. At last, aged twenty and after more than a year spent working for Arlene Smith, Eunice Waymon was going to start working for herself, taking a substantial share of her former employer's clientele with her. The two women had never been friends – a decent employer-to-employee relationship, but nothing more. They fell out. Eunice left with eight students she'd snatched from Arlene, certain of her abilities as a teacher after months partaking in those private classes. There was a lot in it for Eunice. Though she charged a quarter of her ex-employer's rates, as she didn't employ anyone herself, she managed to make ends meet. Her rent, private lessons with Sokhaloff, what she gave the Waymon family, everything was covered.

At the end of the working day, when the last student closed the door of Eunice Waymon's studio behind him, the little room became a sanctuary, the sound of the hideous pop songs sung there all day long echoing for a few hours still before silence finally set in. No visitors, few signs of the family, only Sheba her dog for company. In her memoirs, Nina Simone would speak of an old acquaintance from North Carolina with whom she spent one night during those monastic years and to whom she lost her virginity. Then came Ed, a young black fellow she'd met at the Philadelphia church choir and had a fling with. Nothing too memorable. Soon he was gone and the young woman would only hear from him through the boy's mother, who was a Baptist pastor in Philadelphia and a peer of Mary Kate Waymon's.

After this lightning-quick affair, did Eunice ever think about Edney Whiteside? How does one face such isolation, in a tiny studio, without drowning in despair? She must really have felt like there was no way out for her to undertake something that might seem progressive or even radical for a young black woman raised in the countryside in the 40s and, moreover, of Baptist faith: every single Thursday in 1955, Eunice went to see a psychoanalyst, Dr Gerry Weiss.

On Weiss's couch, this inexperienced young woman who carried the weight of a still-raw trauma obstinately brooded over the same topics, over and over again: her crushed ambitions, the humiliation she'd felt, her desire for revenge and her will to succeed. Three years had already gone by since the Curtis episode, but she hadn't lost her faith and continued to prepare with Sokhaloff for the next entrance exam at the Philadelphia music academy – an exam she would never end up passing.

After one year, Eunice decided to break off her psychoanalysis. In the light of later events, it might seem odd that this psychoanalyst never spotted any signs in his patient, but who might have guessed what magma boiled inside this girl? Let's take a look at her, not so pretty, very reserved, no particular grace in her movements, no self-assurance, one might think. Definitely a lot of character though – you would need some to be that persistent. At least she knows what she's worth, at least she's fighting for her ambitions, sacrificing her youth and any fun girls her age usually allow themselves. Of course she was aware of that and she suffered from that situation or she wouldn't have squandered her dollars with this Dr Weiss. Simple and tragic as it might be, she simply knew no other way. She was still Pastor Waymon's daughter, the one constantly expected to excel in everything without making waves, quietly, virtuously. How do you change a path you've travelled for twenty-two years?

It was a high-class prostitute who would eventually introduce this socially inept young woman to the ways of the world. Faith Jackson was a well-known character on the streets of Philadelphia. This strikingly beautiful black woman who went by the name of Kevin Matthias took Eunice under her wing, invited her to parties, introduced her to her friends, and above all she told her a thing or two about men. In her autobiography, Nina recounts a few juicy tales of times spent with Faith. Men coming round to Faith's to play erotic fetish games when Eunice was there or Faith following her 'punter' with a wink to her friend as she looked on in outrage. With Faith, Eunice was suddenly propelled into a world previously unknown to her and one can easily guess how fascinated she was by the things she discovered there: the power some women are capable of wielding over men, these men's follies and what they were prepared to do, say or pay to get what they wanted.

Little or nothing is known of how Faith and Eunice met. But in the summer of 1954, Faith invited her young friend to follow her to Atlantic City, New Jersey, one of America's gambling hot spots. As her financial survival was so precarious, Eunice could only take the days off when she was sure she could find work there. She learned that some

Atlantic City bars paid pianists up to $90 a week. Serious cash; almost three times what she earned teaching classes in her studio. One of her students got her the phone number of an agent, who within a few days had found her a job as a pianist at the Midtown Bar & Grill. She took the job without really knowing what she was getting herself into and began to prepare for her trip without saying a word – obviously – to the Waymons about the existence of her prostitute friend.

July 1954. When she embarked on this two-month summer tour with Faith Jackson, little did 21-year-old Eunice Waymon suspect the metamorphosis she would undergo on the stage of a dingy dive. 'First and foremost, I was a pianist. I only became a singer to earn money,' she would later say. 'I was scheduled to become a classical piano star, but I had to take a job in a nightclub. As soon as I got there, I was asked whether I could sing. I said no but they demanded that I sing if I wanted to keep the job. So I sang, and this is how my career in show business started.'[3]

Nina Simone was born in a moist New Jersey watering hole, its floor littered with sawdust to mop up spilt liquor. A dump just like hundreds of others, its air thick with cigarette smoke. The amazement on this reverend's daughter's face was plain to see as she reached the Midtown Bar & Grill and saw this run-down shack, just two streets from the seaside walk, but this kid was tough, and she had no choice. She took a deep breath as she walked into the long, narrow room, heading towards the back where a piano awaited, perched on a tiny stage behind a few tables and chairs. Harry Steward, a short white man with a cigar butt clamped in his mouth, stood behind the bar, probably wondering who this girl was. In any case he must have thought she was OK, provided that she knew how to play and was willing to get up on this measly stage. He showed her the piano. Decent enough. Above it, a leaking air-conditioning unit dripped onto the stool. Eunice pointed it out to Steward who proceeded to grab a bucket and open up an umbrella which he wedged above the stage. Chewing on his cigar, he looked at her and said: 'Come back in an hour.' Eunice nodded and left. She must have weighed up her options: there was no way she could go back to Philadelphia. She'd rented a room for this job, had no classes planned in Philly for the summer and no savings for Sokhaloff's classes come fall. She'd just have to swallow her pride and take this lousy gig.

All shame set aside, she came back to the Midtown Bar & Grill at the agreed time, dressed as though this were in fact a classical recital: a light muslin dress, her hair gathered in a severe bun, minimal make-up. She walked across the room, brushing against the customers' cheap suits, and sat down on the stool in deadly silence, all eyes on her. This audience knew nothing about classical music and all it took was one look to work out that the only accompaniment they required was to the dance their drinks did as they filled them up only to empty them again. To give herself courage, she imagined she was in Carnegie Hall or at the Metropolitan Opera, and launched into it. She played with her eyes shut, forgot about them, her lips tight, trying not to choke on all this smoke. Eunice did what Nina had always known how to do, the reason for her incarnation in this black body: she surrendered to the music, releasing those last four years of her life, freeing herself from the present time and place.

She combined classical pieces, evoked Bach, bits of hymns, sprinkling the whole thing with gospel and popular tunes. She let each piece unfurl and sometimes span over half an hour.

Every two hours she was allowed a fifteen-minute rest. During her first break, she heard in the silence as she walked towards the bar a mixture of violence, racism, amazement, alcohol and lust. She moved close to the bar and ordered a glass of milk. Around her, she heard greasy chuckles. Not one person even spoke to her, yet several people eyed her upside down or mocked her even. Such courage from this girl to endure those minutes and finish her drink, all the while fixedly staring at some non-existent spot just to keep any sign of male attention at bay, avoiding glances above all... Then came the time to get back up on stage. She faced the keyboard, ignoring the clicking sound of the air-conditioning that splashed her instrument as it dripped, filling up the water bucket at her feet. This was her first contact with a public towards whom she would for ever feel some level of distrust, perhaps even thinly veiled contempt.

The sound of a voice tore her from her meditation: 'We're closing! Out! Now!' Now that the Midtown was empty of its clientele, she went to see Harry Steward at the bar. She wanted to know if it had gone all right; he chewed on his cigar, praised her playing and asked her why she hadn't sung. 'Well tomorrow night you're either a singer or you're out of a job.'

She went home exhausted. Where on earth was Faith? Probably in the arms of some punter. No one to tell about this first night, her initial fears and how they had dissipated. No one to confide in about this revelation: that despite the mediocrity of the setting and the bar's clientele, she'd actually enjoyed herself. And now Steward wanted her to sing. How could she say no?

She went back to her hotel room. After counting the few dollars she'd earned and getting rid of the smell of tobacco, Eunice Waymon took off her make-up. She looked at herself in the mirror: the woman she saw in her reflection at that moment was Nina Simone. Nina Simone was not just an alter ego, a stage name for the pastor's daughter to hide behind. Eunice has always been Nina. She never was a good, submissive child; she wasn't the naive girl Nina Simone would later claim to have been. And her story begins here in Atlantic City, a few steps from the ocean, her feet in a puddle of sawdust.

Eunice became Nina Simone, so that her mother wouldn't find out she was playing and singing what she called the music of the Devil. She decided on this cover right from her first night at Midtown Bar & Grill. Should the rumour ever reach Mary Kate Waymon's ears and whisper to her that her prodigy daughter's talents were being wasted on drunks in some unworthy dive, she might never have got over it. Eunice would have been disowned for committing such a crime: turning her back on God and devoting herself to the Devil's music.

Are names innocent of meaning or are they actually written somewhere in a stroke of fate? Does adopting them affect the destiny and the actions of those who take them on?

Eunice Waymon became Nina Simone, a mask that over the years eclipsed her birth name. Nina for *niña*, 'little one', a nickname given to her by a Hispanic lover who nothing more is known about. Simone for Simone Signoret in *Casque d'Or*, a movie the pianist had seen and been impressed by in Philadelphia. Nina Simone, with a stress added on the end, a sophisticated 'e' pronounced with a lingering end vowel.

Granted, Eunice had come up with a punchy stage name – stainless, exotic, mysterious even. Those passing by the poster nailed to the Midtown's door might have been tempted into slowing down, pushing open the door, coming in to lean on the bar and order a drink while listening to the young black woman, this girl dressed in her Sunday best, for a while.

'As a child I used to sing at church with my mother and sisters,' Nina Simone would explain. 'But I always sang low and I didn't know that I could give it feeling with such limited means. My advantage was a perfect ear and that I knew how to play within my range, because my tessitura and my voice are pretty restricted. When the club manager asked me to sing, I picked the few tunes that I knew and I sang and played them within my own range.'[3] On her second night at the Midtown Bar & Grill, Nina Simone made the jump into unknown territory, adapting and putting into practice what she'd been taught by Arlene Smith. She discovered the possibilities of her voice, her range, her tone. She took some liberties with the lyrics of the songs she sang, sometimes improvising when she had to link two tunes, yet it all felt like a spring that flowed out of her, effortlessly, as though this singing had always been within her, waiting to be revealed. A voice, two rough octaves that would have to be polished night after night, but the core was already there, warm and menacing, deep and silky. Just two octaves, when Ella and Mahalia had three or even four, yet this voice was now taking its first steps with a new-found freedom, this richly hued contralto put to use with a quality in expression that would soon prove truly captivating. Though she would one day sing of thirst for love, sorrow and anger, back then, the girl still knew nothing of those feelings that impact lives and all she did was to channel the vague emotions that came out of her as she became acquainted with this stranger called Nina Simone.

What went through the minds of those who heard her on her first night in Atlantic City? Couldn't they see this young black woman hiding in the shadows behind her keyboard, too tall, her face pockmarked with acne scars, severe-looking in her muslin dress, too distant to be likeable? This girl who produced beauty almost despite herself, could they see, those patrons devotedly soaking up liquor, that this was a child seeking to be revealed? Might just one of them have said: 'Is it just me or is there some kind of electricity in the air here tonight? Who is this girl? I like that tune...'? Who was this child who'd felt like she was dying just a few months before, crushed by the rejection of an academy no one had even heard of around here? Those barflies would have had a tough time naming the music this black girl played, yet it seemed natural for it to find a place between those walls, as much for her as for them. Yes, Lord – she felt a strange feeling stir in her belly and tingle along her spine, as though something had come unstuck. At ease at last, open, overcome with waves of conflicting feelings; pleasure tinted with an old sadness she couldn't bring herself to leave behind, rushing through her. A new dialogue had begun, her singing, guided by the piano. Her eyelids shut, she found herself marvelling at how she didn't even need to intervene in this exchange.

There is no one left now to evoke that first night, but we do know there were no standing ovations for Nina. Polite applause at most, a few guys whistling, thinking it was the most direct way to show their appreciation. Some cheering then, so that the pianist would give an encore. The screams would come, in that same bar, as night after night she honed her skills and self-assurance. Then the audience's devotion would be complete. But at that precise moment, as Atlantic City was filled with vibrations from all its dives, its whores, the pleasures of gambling, liquor and the violence all these entailed, Nina Simone's virgin music searched to find its balance with one last song.

A few weeks later at the Midtown Bar & Grill and the music brought by this woman is beginning to feel cultured, rich and versatile, in sync with racial America's bumpy history. An art where classical, pop, and religious music collide, a framework combining skill and variety. The summer of 1954 hasn't even passed, yet what is being weaved here holds the promise of lasting another fifty years.

The clientele is different now. Party-goers, the kind you never used to see around here, show up at the Midtown, mostly beatniks and students, music lovers too. The rumour that there's a young black musician in town, that the things she plays are one of a kind has spread though the streets, along Pacific Avenue, sneaked into every joint. Drawn by a shared curiosity, they've spread the word and now all meet there, elbowing their way closer to the stage. Night after night, they've discouraged the toughest barflies, shoved them out of the way and taken over the Midtown Bar & Grill. Some even go up to Nina when she allows herself a break. 'Hello, I came here yesterday. I really like your music, keep it coming.' She blushes and mumbles a thank you before scuttling off to her glass of milk, her piano and stool. When she sits down to play, there is silence, a silence she, Nina, has achieved. In this second-rate bar, at the core of a town burning with sleeplessness, she manages to make them go quiet right from the first note. No one stirs, barely daring to whisper their orders to the barman as she stands on stage, something quite unheard-of around here. Careful not to let this girl kill off business.

September 1954. The end of the season. Eunice folds Nina Simone's clothes into her bag and makes her way back to Philadelphia with Faith. She reunites with her family, deposits some cash in the Waymons' urn, no one questioning her. She settles back into everyday life, her classes with Vladimir Sokhaloff, singing lessons to those hopeless whites, her dog, her studio, European movies, church on Sunday, otherwise only loneliness, or almost. Faith would give the occasional sign of life, some old friends calling in on her then vanishing after tea, and that was pretty much it. A life of routine which some days, when there was nothing going on, seemed like a slow death.

Even though it continued to be widespread in public places, segregation was declared unconstitutional in American schools when Eunice Waymon was twenty-one. In 1953, in Montgomery, Alabama, one year after the Republican Eisenhower was elected President of the United States, Martin Luther King, a young newly-wed pastor, took over the reins of the Dexter Avenue Baptist Church. In 1955 he received his PhD in theology. In March that same year, Claudette Colvin, a black factory worker, was arrested for violating the segregation ordinance on a bus on the Montgomery City Lines. In December, on that same line, Rosa Parks, a black seamstress, exhausted after a hard day's work, was arrested for refusing to give up her seat on the bus to a white passenger. Four days later, the Montgomery City Lines began to be boycotted and a year later, as President Eisenhower entered his second term, the NAACP (National Association for the Advancement of Colored People) was banned in Alabama. The NAACP, a national body originally founded by W.E.B. Du Bois in 1909, defended coloured people fighting for their interests, defining itself as a biracial integrationist movement that fought against lynching and exclusion. The NAACP based its actions on mediation, pressure groups and litigation.

After a year of boycotts fronted by the pastor Martin Luther King and the NAACP, on 21 December 1956 desegregation was declared on Montgomery City Lines. This victory for the black community was a precursor to the great upheavals that were about to shake up the United States.

July 1956. A bleak year behind her, Eunice Waymon returned to Atlantic City to perform at the Midtown Bar & Grill for the summer. There she was reunited with her faithful audience, made up of a bunch of students who within a few weeks turned Harry Steward's joint into the place to be and a meeting point for music lovers. They'd show up in waves in the evening, quietly sitting down in the sawdust to listen to the black pianist. Among them was Ted Axelrod, a white beatnik who was crazy about jazz and dropped in to see Nina every night. They got to know each other little by little and became friends. Theirs was an unambiguous relationship, mainly based on their shared love of music. He invited the young woman to his apartment in Atlantic City, opened up his record collection to her and played her some tunes, suggesting songs that she might include in her repertoire. One of them was a version of 'I Loves You Porgy', from George Gershwin's opera *Porgy and Bess*, sung by Billie Holiday.

Adapted from the novel by DuBose Heyward, *Porgy and Bess* was first performed in Boston in 1935, a love story set in a black neighbourhood in South Carolina during the Depression. There isn't a glimmer of hope in Gershwin's masterpiece, but it was a resounding success with the white public. Later, several generations of black artists, including Louis Armstrong, Ella Fitzgerald, Billie Holiday, Miles Davis, Oscar

Peterson and Ray Charles, would borrow songs from Gershwin's opera, propelling *Porgy and Bess* into the ranks of America's monuments. In 1969, Janice Joplin, a rock singer who was fascinated by Ma Rainey and Bessie Smith, covered the song 'Summertime' on her first solo album, *I Got Dem Ol' Kozmic Blues Again Mama!*, thus introducing the tragic tale of Porgy's love for Bess into the white pop music stratosphere.

Nina Simone would herself sing 'Summertime' a few years later, on a crowning night at the prestigious Carnegie Hall in New York. But that night at Ted Axelrod's place she discovered 'I Loves You Porgy', sung by Billie Holiday. She hardly knew Billie's repertoire, but she took in her supernatural voice, staring at the record on the verge of tears as it spun while the singer told her story.

Eunice/Nina might have laughed out loud that night if Ted had told her she would be singing 'Porgy' for more than fifty years, right until her final concert! That this song would make her fame and become her trademark. She might have found the thought grotesque, being so versatile, with this insatiable hunger for the new she had felt ever since Ted had offered to introduce her to jazz and some kinds of American popular music. Sing the same song for fifty years, why bother? And this job as a club singer was nothing but a stint, wasn't it?

A few days later, Nina Simone, now aged twenty-two, an African beauty, her svelte figure clad in a pale muslin dress, the intensity of her gaze underlined with kohl as her only make-up, her hair gathered in a bun, would sing 'I Loves You Porgy' for the very first time as the audience fell silent. She'd simply launched into 'Porgy' without any prior rehearsal, trusting her ear to dictate the chords, the tune and even the lyrics. She instantly felt like this song had always been within her, as though it was written in her genes, to the point where as the years went by, she would always manage to find new hues and corners she didn't even know existed every time she sang it. Right until her final years, 'Porgy' would take her back to that night in the summer of 1955 where, pure still, almost a virgin, brimming with hope she immersed herself in the discovery of what lay within her.

The season was coming to an end and for the first time in her life, Eunice Waymon had made some friends, men mainly, and white. But the time had come to return to Philadelphia, where a predictable life and anonymity awaited. Teaching kids who sang like crows. How depressing, and on top of that she now had some stranger living in her own body. Yet if Eunice Waymon, the troubled one, was thirsty for revenge, Nina Simone on the other hand was hungry for recognition, ready for risks and struggles.

Back in town, deeming that not only were her lessons not lucrative enough but that they would never open up any opportunities for her, Eunice decided to send her students on their way ('Just go back to Arlene!') and try her luck in the clubs of Philadelphia. She got in contact with the agent who'd got her the job at the Midtown and got a gig at the Pooquesin, a high-class bar and restaurant. Then came another contract, at the High Tigh Club. She got decent wages, but the patrons were far too busy reading the menu and paid no attention to her. Even when she played 'Porgy', not a single person looked up from their plate.

Frustrated not to be reprising her Atlantic City success, filled with the remorse any girl would feel when lying to her mother and unable to tell her family where the money she gave them every month came from, terrified at the thought that Mary Kate Waymon might one day discover its true source, and at the last tired of having to hide when she thought she was in fact being brave, Eunice decided to tell the Waymons that she worked in clubs around town: 'I want to make enough money to continue with my studies; I am very careful, I never drink liquor and you can be sure that I don't talk to men, I just want to give myself a chance.'

Mary Kate Waymon didn't say a word. She didn't let her shame and regret show. So now her daughter was playing the Devil's music, spending her nights working in godforsaken places where men loiter and liquor is sold, where sex and oblivion are traded. It was no good, no good at all.

None of the Waymons supported the girl's decisions. Her mother's bigotry clashed with the yearning for emancipation of a young woman asserting her choices. Nothing of the kind had ever been witnessed under that roof. Eunice had always been obedient, just as she'd always sought to show herself deserving of the trust her mother had showed her. They were now both locked in a silent confrontation and this wasn't a house where one vented one's feelings or stood up against Mary Kate. So awkwardness was left to set in and anyway, no one felt up to calming down this feud that was tearing what was left of the women's relationship to shreds. No one to remind the others that every month and for many years to come, their stomachs would be filled for the most part through money earned with the Devil's music.

So what about John Divine? He had witnessed the scene yet he didn't budge. From his chair he looked his daughter straight in the eye, waited for his wife to leave and beckoned Eunice to come closer. John Divine knew the reality of life spent touring, the disappointments the job can bring, the dangers lurking for those encouraged to spend too long in this line of work, the risks to young women like his daughter, unaware of the music business's traps. The father warned his daughter against life as an artist, reminding her of the hopes that had been invested in her and the talents God had bestowed upon her.

Over the course of 1956, Eunice Waymon divided her time between her classes with Vladimir Sokhaloff and her commitments with Philadelphia clubs. A new summer began, bringing her back to Atlantic City for the third time. As she arrived at the Midtown Bar & Grill, she found Harry Steward behind the bar. He was pleased to see her return, since the pianist's presence on stage was a guarantee of a full house every night; but this was no longer the place for Nina, who now preferred more professional, comfortable, even exclusive settings, convinced that those were the key to success. But for now she would have to make do with plodding on at Steward's.

Wearing the same muslin dress and hairstyle, with her strict make-up and severe stage demeanour, she once again regained her residence. The same characters as the previous year crammed in, searching for a few inches of space in the compact crowd to listen to the black pianist. Among these was a face Nina hadn't noticed before. A handsome white boy, who came up to her at the end of one of her concerts. He approached her cautiously, as one would an animal in the wild, and introduced himself as Don Ross. Another beatnik, she thought as she looked him up and down, noticing his scruffy shirt, his paint-encrusted fingernails, dirty shoes and dishevelled look. Don said he was a painter and assured her that he'd come to see her every night since the season had begun, even that he'd heard her here the previous summer. He said he'd dreamed about her, which made her laugh. She giggled and from then on made sure that their eyes didn't meet. This didn't stop Don Ross from inviting her to join him for a seaside walk and a drink in a café. She declined and told him she'd see him the next day. As she said goodbye, he gently pulled her towards him and kissed her cheek as he wished her goodnight. She went home, the young man's scent lingering on her skin. It had only taken an instant for her defences to fall. Her thoughts were with Don Ross as she slipped beneath her sheets. He'd be there tomorrow, he'd promised. She tried to get some sleep, tossing and turning a hundred times, unable to find a comfortable position, then sat cross-legged in the dark thinking of how she would have liked to feel him near her.

As promised, Don Ross came in the following night, and the night after that. As the weeks went by, this self-proclaimed beat artist who was really just a fraud slipped into Nina Simone's life, then into her bed, 'without any fireworks' but alleviating her loneliness. His being white made no difference to her, her family or her meagre entourage. Even though the boy would soon prove to be devoid of any ambition or talent, a sloth interested by little more than nightclubs, liquor and reading beat poetry, at twenty-three Nina Simone needed a man in her life. And even if this man turned out to be a burden – and she soon had an inkling that he would – then so be it! He was gentle and kind, even in bed. He made her laugh and was completely in awe of her. Nina was aware that she'd bet on a lame horse and that her story with the guy wasn't the ultimate thrill, but she had plenty of time to make up her mind, she thought, and if need be, she could take up other offers.

There were plenty of men who came and paid her compliments every night; some of them tried to woo her and she could tell from their attentions that this was the prize for her local success – Nina Simone was now a celebrity reigning over a few blocks of Atlantic City – and gave it a great deal of importance. How could she remain indifferent to this love, this flattery, attention and recognition? These aren't things one turns down and Nina meant to savour her success, moderate as it was, far from the stages and audiences she played to in her dreams.

Having moved back to Philadelphia with Don Ross amongst her belongings in September 1956, Nina Simone saw her career take shape thanks to Jerry Fields. This New York-born agent with a fine reputation had been drawn to the Midtown Bar & Grill by a rumour: 'There's a young black woman who plays classical, pop, gospel, well, some kind of jazz thing in this joint in Atlantic City. She's amazing.' He was blown away. Fields convinced Nina Simone to come work with him, promising her that she'd earn more than anything she'd known up until then, even mentioning the possibility of making a record in New York. But for that he demanded exclusivity. She accepted and soon offers were flowing in for gigs in East Side clubs and the north of New York State, New Hope more specifically.

This was the first time that Nina played outside the boundaries of Philadelphia and Atlantic City. During her first stay in New Hope, she met a guitar player: Alvin Schackman, who worked with Burt Bacharach, an American composer whose star was on the rise and who, among other things, had written hits for Marty Robbins ('The Story of My Life') and Perry Como ('Magic Moments'). Nina and Alvin met through third parties who asked them to jam, 'just to see'. Though reticent at first, Nina let herself be convinced and reluctantly invited the guitarist to come and join her. As Alvin grabbed his guitar, some telepathic communion seemed to take place between them, as though they'd already spent years playing together.

From then on, Nina and Alvin became almost inseparable. Al would be there through every struggle and every key moment of Nina's life. Alvin would become one of the few defining influences on Nina Simone as both an artist and a woman. He would be her closest friend, her support, her director whenever the pianist's repertoire needed readjusting due to stage restrictions. Alvin, the white brother who would often sit in the front row through both success and failure.

Over the second half of 1956, they worked together, quickly achieving a complete and intuitive mutual musical understanding.

Closeness began to rear its head, soon followed by the first hints of trust. During their stint at the New Hope Playhouse Inn, Nina and Al recorded a demo which included mainly vocal, piano and guitar versions of 'I Loves You Porgy', 'Since My Love Has Gone' and 'Lovin' Woman'. Jerry Fields, who was in charge of managing the band, sent her to Syd Nathan, a colourful character who managed King Records, a label that'd specialized in rhythm and blues since 1945, based in Cincinnati.

Short in stature and tyrannical in temper, Syd Nathan, a former furniture salesman, managed his business with a grip of steel, never hesitating to physically threaten employees or artists. Still, this tyrant who was nicknamed 'Little Caesar' had a special flair. He knew what kind of music the black American community that had migrated to Northern cities from the South since the Depression wanted to hear and buy, and so he built King Records on the foundations of his Cincinnati record store, at first a myriad of micro-labels, signing up some of the best American R&B artists. One of the most famous was James Brown, then backed by his band, the Famous Flames. For King Records, in 1962 the future 'Godfather of Soul' made one of the greatest live albums ever: *James Brown at the Apollo*.

After several entries in the R&B charts, thousands of miles of his Dantean tours and $450,000 in profits in 1963, James Brown realized that he'd been swindled by Syd Nathan and filed a major lawsuit against him. 'Mister Dynamite' was one of thousands of artists who were conned by the music industry. This has been a feature of the history of black American music and there are countless and sometimes horrifying tales of the frauds that were committed. In his book *I Feel Good: A Memoir of a Life of Soul*, James Brown spoke of his legal battle to recover his master tapes from King Records, how long it took and how harrowing it was, though ultimately successful. In his wake, other black artists of the 50s and 60s would take their turn in trying to regain ownership of the songs they'd written and recorded for a producer or a label that meant to hang on to them. '[I]t was seen as the acquisition of power in the community of our culture,' James Brown wrote, 'a threat to the mainstream status quo'.[4]

It's with Syd Nathan that Nina Simone recorded her first album, and was first ripped off by the music business.

At the beginning of the winter of 1956, Jerry Fields told Nina that negotiations were under way with Nathan. Then a recording session was scheduled in New York. If it turned out well, the record would be released on Bethlehem Records, a division of King Records. One morning a few days later, without warning, Nathan called in on Nina Simone at her home in Philadelphia. When she opened the door, she saw Little Caesar standing in front of her, a box filled with the scores of songs he wanted her to record at his feet. They'd never met. For him, Nina Simone was just another artist, just starting out, who would do anything to get ahead in show business. A starlet who can be bossed around, who complies, asks for nothing and costs nothing.

But this one was of a different calibre. Some character who saw no particular glory in being a singer. This girl wasn't thrown at the thought of making a record and she couldn't have cared less about the charts. What motivated her completely eluded a pragmatic man like Syd Nathan; 'That's out of the question,' she told him. 'I don't record songs on order. I'll only come and make records with you if I get to choose my own songs.' She spoke those words in the dry, hard tone that would make her reputation. Syd Nathan took his cardboard box and walked back to his car without a word as the door shut behind him. He came back in the afternoon. When she opened up the door, she saw that both the cardboard box and bossy attitude were gone. Nathan told her she'd have free rein. So a recording session was scheduled. For the following day.

Twenty-four hours was all the time she had to come up with a list of songs and read the contract drawn up by Bethlehem. What was the matter with Jerry Fields that day? Was it sheer incompetence or a lack of time that prevented him from reading and understanding that this contract stripped Nina of her rights? Especially considering that Syd Nathan's reputation required no introduction. He could at the very least have been cautious. Signing this paper meant giving up ownership of all material recorded. Whether the record was a flop or a success, whether it was released once or a thousand times over, Nina would have to make do with a single cheque and performance rights. The clause stating that she waived her rights to the recordings was written there, black on white, yet Jerry Fields gave the go-ahead.

In the studio Nina Simone was introduced to two session musicians. Jimmy Bond, the bass player, was twenty-six years old and already boasted a sound track record in the music business, first with Charlie Parker, then playing for a young Chet Baker, then Ella Fitzgerald. Then came the drummer Albert 'Tootie' Heath, who was from Philadelphia and immersed in the hard bop scene; he'd recently worked on John Coltrane's first solo album for the Prestige label. Despite the absence of Al Schackman, who was on tour with Burt Bacharach, the pianist was in excellent company.

She'd come in with fourteen tracks, all of which were recorded. For the most part, they were faithful but abridged versions of her Midtown Bar & Grill repertoire: 'I Loves You Porgy', 'For All We Know', 'You'll Never Walk Alone' and the 'Plain Gold Ring' bolero she'd borrowed from the harpist Kitty White; a swing piece, 'Love Me or Leave Me', the ballad 'Little Girl Blue' and 'He Needs Me', recorded by Peggy Lee. Her first album was mainly made up of cover versions (except for two instrumental tracks, 'African Mailman' and 'Central Park Blues', which she wrote during that thirteen-hour studio session). In those days, only a few female 'jazz' artists could claim to be both vocalists and composer-songwriters, and like many of her peers, Nina Simone was primarily an interpreter. For the first years of her career her repertoire consisted mainly of cover versions of major hits or songs written for her. Only in 1963 did she start to introduce her own compositions.

Fourteen tracks in total, all captured in single takes, with barely enough time to choose the next song before moving straight on.

If there is one track that stands out on this album and speaks volumes about the budding art of Nina Simone in 1956, it has to be 'Good Bait', a cover of a Count Basie hit. With the support of the Heath and Bond duet – first-rate assistants who showed a remarkable understanding of the climax the pianist sought to achieve with the track – Nina was able to create a complex instrumental structure where the main theme is brought in as in classical music. Then come the bass and percussion, supporting Nina Simone's piano in a lighter, swingier mode. She lingers on the notes, waiting for the moment to take the piano into a syncopated rhythm, almost like a commentator, adding colour and a bit more impulse. She moves into the tempo's curves and corners, now ahead of it, now behind, and making the rhythm follow her phrasing... then dives back into the core of the tune, extracting its very essence, dramatizing her phrases and asking to be left alone for a few moments, long enough for a digression, finding her bearings perhaps, only to regain the momentum needed for the finale, suddenly gathering the solemn tones of Rachmaninov and Debussy's flow. In a poignant finale, the bass and percussion come in to carry the pianist, honouring her instrument's last sigh.

The last track played in this marathon was 'My Baby Just Cares for Me', a song made popular by Count Basie and which Nina deemed 'one of the slightest I'd ever recorded'.[5] Of course, 'Good Bait' and 'Plain Gold Ring' are in a different class, yet it's to 'My Baby Just Cares for Me' that Nina owes her greatest commercial success, despite failing to fully benefit financially from her hit.

In December 1956, after thirteen consecutive hours spent in the studio, Nina Simone, exhausted, signed a contract tendered by Syd Nathan. A contract which thirty years later would deprive her of one million dollars.

She took her $3,000 check, caught a cab to the railway station, got back to Philadelphia and slept for twelve hours. When she woke up, and for three days straight, she played Beethoven to cleanse herself of that day spent recording pop.

3

SOMETHING INSIDE HER COMES ALIGHT

TWO MONTHS had passed since the New York recording session and still no word from Bethlehem regarding the record's release. Nina didn't care. With the $3,000 she'd pocketed, her needs were covered and she was able to pay for her piano classes with Vladimir Sokhaloff up front. On his part, Jerry Fields attempted to appease promoters by telling them that his protégée had just finished making a record for Syd Nathan, that no one knew exactly when it would be released, but that in the mean time, Nina was available for concerts. Fields was soon able to arrange several gigs in New York clubs. He submitted those offers to the pianist, who decided to accept them all, frightened at the thought that her luck might run out. She saw those contracts as an opportunity that would serve her ambition: 'To get myself known in the clubs of NYC and reapply to the Juilliard.'

She hardly cared that a rumour that sang her praises as a pianist and singer was gaining momentum around the clubs of the East Coast – a rumour that was partly being fed by sidemen like Jimmy Bond and Tootie Heath – Nina Simone obstinately clung on to her dream. She kept hearing flattering comments that her differences and her beauty would raise her to pop music stardom, but to her this situation was but a provisional one and her goal incorruptible: 'classical music or nothing'. Yet Nina lacked sound contacts in this closed universe; she probably knew that at twenty-four it was already getting late for her to be entering the music business and that the New York club scene would not accommodate her career aspirations for very long. Her destiny awaited elsewhere, she kept telling herself. On other stages, with another audience, for whom she would play another kind of music. She was wrong.

In the spring of 1957, Bethlehem Records released the album *Little Girl Blue*, its sleeve adorned with a hastily drafted yet glowing review by Joseph Muranyi. In the sleeve notes, the critic placed Nina Simone at a crossroads between several different musical paths. He made a few slips that would soon prove tough to erase: the two years the pianist was meant to have spent at the Juilliard School when she really spent two months there; her alleged interest in the great figures of jazz – Louis Armstrong, the pianist Sarah Vaughan (her only serious rival) and Louis Jordan – even though right from the start of her career, Nina kept a careful distance from anything branded 'jazz'.

The record sleeve shows a dignified Nina Simone posing on a bench in Central Park (or, depending on the version, sitting by a pond), staring straight ahead, braving the cold in her green sweater (the picture was taken in December 1956, the very day the album was recorded), a forced smile across her face (when she isn't downright sulking, as on the other version). A record sleeve just like hundreds of others seen on jazz and R&B records of the time, none of it highlighting the young woman's individuality except perhaps a few words from her that Muranyi quoted in his notes: 'I believe that my love of progressive sounds stems from my training in classical music.'

Several specialized magazines gave positive reviews of *Little Girl Blue*, emphasizing Nina Simone's skills as a pianist. But for them, this was one more fashionable 'jazz' record among many others, except, admittedly, for that special touch and deep, attractive voice.

Nina Simone found her record sitting in Jerry Fields's office, but several weeks after its release there was still no word from Bethlehem. The pianist carried on touring the clubs in town (the record would end up being re-released with the title *Jazz as Played in an Exclusive Side Street Club*, drawing on the artist's growing status on the New York scene). Still, there was no 45-inch single release in the pipeline, and without the additional boost of a single being played on local radio stations and reaching a wider audience, nothing truly conclusive seemed to be taking off. It was basically as though the record didn't even exist. Nina had her own ideas when it came to promoting it. She tried to reach Syd Nathan several times but he refused to speak to her, never providing any kind of explanation. Was he already betting on a different horse or did he simply not care about the fate, good or bad, of Nina's record? Regardless, without any support whatsoever from Bethlehem, this album and along with it the pianist's career seemed destined to oblivion.

The one person who would turn things around for *Little Girl Blue* turned out to be a white DJ from Philadelphia, Sid Marx. He was an influential DJ whose radio show, dedicated to rhythm-and-blues-related news, called the shots on the scene. He had fallen in love with Nina's version of 'I Loves You Porgy'. Marx began to play 'Porgy' on every single one of his shows and up to four times in a row, thus offering its performer a heaven-sent springboard. This impulse made waves, with some listeners calling up the station to find out more about the song and its singer. The craze spread, and soon other DJs in town began to air 'Porgy' on their shows.

In 50s America, DJs were in charge of both presenting and programming their own shows. They were the one solid link between the music industry and the public. Some of them were all-powerful, setting trends, making or breaking people's records, even their careers. Sid Marx was one such person. The influence those key players had on the public, the record industry and the press even allowed them to launch new artists. Without them, success on a large scale was impossible. Without their support, one might at most hope for a glimmer of regional fame.

Soon after the release of *Little Girl Blue*, Sid Marx met Nina Simone in Philadelphia. He told her how much he loved her version of 'I Loves You Porgy' and encouraged the young woman to talk Bethlehem into releasing this song as a single, swearing that it was bound to be a hit. So she started hassling Bethlehem again. As one might guess, Nathan giving in had less to do with the pianist's repeated phone calls than the enthusiasm of radio DJs who were all in awe of Nina's cover. Anyway, she had won the battle. Nearly six months after the album release, the single 'Porgy' followed, with the ballad 'He Needs Me' on the B-side. Sid Marx's predictions were confirmed: in 1959, 'I Loves You Porgy' by Nina Simone shot its way up the national R&B charts.

Faced with this success that he hadn't really banked on, Jerry Fields summoned his artist and proposed that she leave Philadelphia and move to New York. This, he said, would be the opportunity to capitalize on her hit, to make the most of her sudden fame and to get into the music business, since its nerve centre on the East Coast was Manhattan. The small-town Tryon girl harboured bitter memories of her months spent in Harlem as a teenager. She remembered people being rude, the filthy streets and latent violence. Still, Nina knew that her career and her future projects were at stake. She resigned herself to the idea, told her family – who had barely said a word on the release of her record – of her intentions and her imminent move to New York, and of her marriage to a white man too. No reaction still.

Nina Simone did not want to live alone any longer, and even less to face the adventure she was about to embark on without someone by her side, so after two years of a lacklustre relationship, Eunice Waymon married Don Ross at the Philadelphia civil registry office. Her family wasn't present, as no one had informed them of the wedding date. A member of the registry office staff 'who was passing by'[1] agreed to be the couple's witness – and right after the ceremony ended, the twosome left for New York and moved into a tiny Greenwich Village apartment rented by a friend of Ted Axelrod's, the man who had introduced Nina Simone to 'Porgy'.

So why did she agree to marry Don the Beatnik, when he would have followed her to New York regardless, no questions asked? Nina must have asked herself the same question many times over as she came home exhausted after a whole night's work, only to find her man lying at the foot of the bed, either blind drunk or high on marijuana, barely able to talk about poetry, jazz or art. But the worst thing for this young woman who had been saving every penny for close to ten years was that this man was spending her money whilst proving utterly useless at earning any. She could have dumped him just a few weeks after their wedding, but with no friends in New York and no immediate career prospects despite her hit, she refused to fall back into solitude, even if it meant having to bear this ball and chain of a husband. So she concentrated on her career, took on every club gig she was offered, working relentlessly and, hiding her wages from Don, spending her savings on the trips to Philadelphia she took once a week to attend her classes with Sokhaloff. Indeed, despite the loneliness that continued to claw at her and the lovelessness that shrouded her marriage, her dream remained, intact still. Being admitted to the Curtis. A career as a concert pianist.

But there were more pressing matters to deal with. Recent bad experiences with several club promoters had made her realize how powerless she was against the vultures who ruled the business. She desperately needed an accountant, a manager – a team to advise her and help her avoid bad payers. That wasn't included in the cut Jerry Fields took from each of her fees. He merely took care of finding her gigs, which was something he was genuinely efficient at; since her move to New York, Nina had been performing on stage non-stop, yet her financial situation remained too precarious. She had Don to support, rent to pay, food to buy and the money she sent to her family every month as well as her classes with Sokhaloff which cost her an arm and a leg... She couldn't make ends meet. She slept badly, was plagued with worries and felt constantly exhausted. Nina would have liked to take a break, but that was obviously out of the question. She had to find the money somehow; anything would do as long as it brought in the cash. Nina Simone, with a hit in the charts and her first record release under her belt, playing five club gigs every week, took a job as a maid with a white New York family. Several times a week she would do their cleaning, fold their laundry and wash their dishes. Modest wages.

She thought to herself that she'd gone back to square one, that she'd never fallen this low and that she would never manage to get back on her feet. Eunice Waymon was repeating the pattern her mother had followed before her, more than fifteen years before, when John Divine had fallen ill and finding money had been an emergency.

She kept her second job a secret of course – What? A classical concert pianist in the making does not do the cleaning! But she stuck at it for a while. She hid that job from Don too. She didn't trust him one bit; he would have ridiculed her or, worse, told all and sundry that 'Porgy''s Nina Simone washed laundry for the white middle class! One night, as she came home with a fifteen-hour shift behind her, having smoked several cigarettes on a street corner just to delay the moment when she would once again have to face this guy she had made her husband, Nina found Don lying on the floor of their studio – drunk. She flew into a blind rage and all of her resentment came pouring out. She blamed him for her despair, perhaps even the mess her career continued to wallow in: 'Look at what you're making me do! Look how low I have to stoop to support you!' But he just lay there motionless, staring at her in his drunken stupor, with only pathetic, hollow words to offer her: 'Don't worry...'

Something in Nina then gave for good and this was when she learned to drown her sorrows in alcohol. She started by tentatively accepting the drinks she got given at the end of her sets in New York clubs. One thing led to another and she began to welcome this liquor that lightened the load of a hard day's work, even taking a few bottles home with her, more and more often.

Such strength she must have had to find within herself, and in liquor perhaps, to tell Don to leave, to pack up his belongings, and rise to the challenge of starting over! Choosing solitude once again. Moving. Getting back into studying the piano, working relentlessly, making her way up. This anger, thus channelled, might turn her luck around, she told herself.

A few months after Nina's arrival in New York, in 1959, Jerry Fields introduced her to an attorney: Max Cohen. Cohen was a man with a sound reputation, benevolent, and a fine connoisseur of music. As they met, he told her how dazzled he was by her talent as a classical pianist. He told her how he admired her technique, the breath of fresh air she brought to the music of the times. He made her feel at ease, winning her over. He encouraged her to carry on studying and offered to take her business into his own hands. Max Cohen became Nina Simone's first true friend in New York. Thanks to him, she came to uncover the Bethlehem skullduggeries surrounding her album, the meaning of the terms, and most of all, the consequences of the contract she had signed. She was flabbergasted. What was she to do? Show up on Syd Nathan's doorstep and make a fuss? It was too late for that. The punches she dreamed of throwing at him wouldn't have changed a thing. But Max Cohen convinced Nina Simone that her first attempt would bear its fruits. Hadn't she managed to get her name to the top of the charts with one single record? Hadn't her music been airing on East Coast radio stations for several months already? It was inconceivable to him that the pianist's career might stall there and then. He managed to talk her into persevering.

A few weeks later, following a chance meeting with Joyce Selznick who worked as a talent scout for the Colpix label, a subsidiary of Columbia (and who happened to be the cousin of the movie producer David O. Selznick, to whom we owe *Gone with the Wind* and Hitchcock's *Rebecca*), Nina Simone saw herself being offered an opportunity for revenge. Still, she made no secret of the revulsion she felt for this business and the thought of giving it any more of her time and career. She would soon be repeating the same mantra in every interview she gave, in every conversation: that her ambition, her goal was – and this wasn't subject to negotiation – to become a classical concert pianist. 'If someone had walked up to me in the street and given me $100,000 I would have given up popular music and enrolled at Juilliard and never played in a club again.'[2]

Joyce Selznick had been following Nina Simone's career since the release of 'Porgy'. She had already attended several of her concerts in New York clubs, had inquired about the artist's links with Bethlehem, knowing that the contract only covered one album. When the two women met, Joyce asked her to join Colpix with a multiple-record deal. Max Cohen negotiated the terms of the contract and in 1959 Nina Simone signed a ten-album deal.

The first of these was *The Amazing Nina Simone*, along the lines of *Little Girl Blue* though highly orchestrated, which aimed to install Nina Simone in the public consciousness. One of the album's tunes lingers especially in people's memories: 'Solitaire', a Duke Ellington cover recorded in New York under the guidance of Hecky Krasnow and Bob Mersey.

The Amazing was released in the spring of 1959 and immediately hailed by the critics. Nina Simone's victory would have been complete if Syd Nathan hadn't had wind of the contract binding the pianist to Colpix. A few weeks before the release of *The Amazing*, without a word of warning to the singer, Bethlehem released an album made up of tracks from the *Little Girl Blue* session that hadn't made the record. It lined up the songs 'He's Got the Whole World in His Hands', 'For All We Know', the instrumental track 'African Mailman', which was the first ever recorded trace of a reference to Nina's African origins, and 'I Loves You Porgy', featured just like it was on the previous record. This underground album, on whose B-side Nathan recorded eight tracks by Chris Connor and the pianist-vocalist Carmen McRae, was released as *Nina Simone and Her Friends*, a somewhat ironic title given that the young woman had so few of those.

Nina Simone came across the record by chance, one afternoon, in the window of a Greenwich Village record store – a misadventure that was to repeat itself several times over the course of her career. Filled with rage, she told Max Cohen, who told her there was nothing he could do from a legal point of view. The contract she'd signed stripped her of all her rights except performing rights, but at least the enemy had a face.

Indeed, Nina Simone would soon have other problems, like the expansion of the pirate record market. Like other artists (from Dylan to Zappa), unbeknownst to her and on several occasions during her career, Nina would be recorded while playing in concert. Once released, the records didn't yield the performer a thing, not even royalties. Still, despite their dubious nature and mediocre quality, those illegal records provided unique historical references that allowed the discovery of rare snapshots, facets even, of those musicians in action. Like Nina Simone in concert in Philadelphia in 1957, long before her first official album, with *Starring Nina Simone*. This pirate record, which circulated underground for quite some time – fetching up to $130 a copy – was released in the early 60s, riding the wave of Nina's success with Colpix and revealing the early hallmarks that would make her name as a concert performer over the following decade. You can already hear her haranguing the audience, commenting on people coming and going in the club, her extended rendition of 'Don't Smoke in Bed', a song by Billie Holiday, followed by a little ballad ending on a bolero beat. The pianist's authority is present, her playing clear, with the drama and lightheartedness of swing that reached their perfect equilibrium in *The Amazing*. In 1965, Nina filed a lawsuit against those responsible for the record's release.

By 1959, Nina Simone's career was soaring. Neither promoters nor the public could get enough of the black pianist; people would smother her in praise as they discussed her style, her choice in repertoire veering alternately towards folk, classical music and Broadway tunes. Everyone loved this character in whom they sensed both sensuality and brutality. The scene was already saturated with talented singers and pianists (among them Sarah Vaughan and Carmen McRae) but none of them had this animalistic side, this unpredictable temper that asserted itself as she gained self-confidence.

Indeed, she now knew it was her name that drew customers to the clubs where she performed, and she fought for promoters to start paying her accordingly: rather than flat fees (musicians would get paid the same amount whether the club was empty or full), they'd have to give her a cut of what was made on the door. And she insisted on choosing her own songs: 'Hell, they weren't paying me enough to tell me what to play.' As the sky grew brighter, Nina Simone took an increasingly strict attitude towards music business representatives – label managers, promoters, club managers – never compromising, arguing about everything, even resorting to physical intimidation to get what she wanted. Why wear gloves when dealing with those she despised? She hated 'the cheap crooks, the disrespectful audiences, the way most people were so easily satisfied by dumb, supid tunes'[3]. There she was, biting the hand that fed her, fantasizing about a classical career she'd never really embarked upon, only glimpsing it through her classes with Sokhaloff, her short time at the Juilliard and her audition within the walls of the Curtis Institute.

The first woman since Faith Jackson to come into the pianist's life was Bertha Case, a literary agent Nina met in the summer of 1959 in a New Hope club. They met again in New York, where they discussed Nina's career and her recent struggles with Bethlehem. Nina told her she was urgently looking for a manager and Bertha offered her services, despite her complete lack of experience in the area. Nina agreed without even consulting Max Cohen, 'because I wanted someone around'.[4] In view of the typical traps and rules of survival in the business, their partnership was doomed before it started.

This wasn't the last unfortunate choice Nina made about her entourage and her career, errors in judgement that would later prove instrumental in her downfall. This lack of discernment, a boon for sharks, gold-diggers and freeloaders, would be the source of many personal and professional tragedies.

Later in 1959, once Bertha Case was out of the picture, Jerry Fields took over his protégée's career decisions, and Max Cohen, her first mentor, took charge of her rise to fame. He didn't mind getting his hands dirty, as when he bet he'd manage to hire out the Town Hall, a famous New York theatre near 6th Avenue and Broadway, where Nina did indeed perform on 12 September 1959.

This legendary classical venue gave Nina the opportunity to propel herself outside the sphere of popular singers, and above all, a chance to show her true worth. Artistically, a solo piano performance in a place like that was a bold gamble for someone who had thus far been labelled a 'jazz' artist. Max Cohen decided to make this event one to remember and summoned the press and pontiffs of the music industry to introduce them to the new star of the New York club scene in her finest attire. For most of them, this opportunity to savour *The Amazing Nina Simone* in the conservative comfort of this hall rather than a dirty side-street club was too precious to miss.

On the day of the concert, Nina felt a heavy weight on her shoulders. For the first time, she was unable to display her trademark nonchalance as she went on stage. The name of the Town Hall was stamped in gold on her musical dreams and she couldn't tread those boards without considering the significance of this moment that spelt out her accomplishment and recognition. Respectability at last.

Colpix announced their intention to record the concert and to release the album in its wake, making it Nina Simone's first legal live record. She didn't know it yet, but except for a few studio recordings, her live albums would turn out to be the very best of her discography. Why? Because this woman gave off a strange energy, electrifying the entire room and hypnotizing the audience. Those talents, now just beginning to shine through, would reach their pinnacle over the coming years, mesmerizing her audiences and giving her music a special touch that sometimes bordered on the supernatural.

On the afternoon of 12 September 1959, Nina Simone paid her first ever visit to the corner of 123 West 43rd Street. She walked into the Town Hall, sat down on the piano stool with her back to the heavy curtain that swept across the stage; she slowly took in the silence of the place, breathing in the old theatre's powdery scent, memorizing every nook, every row of seats.

Then she stood up and walked down to the front row. Feeling almost intimidated, she allowed herself a little daydream before moving to the dressing rooms to put on her stage outfit: a long white gown draped over her left shoulder, hugging the curve of her lower back and gliding down her legs all the way to her ankles. White satin pumps on her feet. Nina stood next to the stage curtain, impressed by the crowd that seemed to gravitate backstage. Max Cohen was schmoozing with music label bigwigs; he introduced her to several critics and Broadway actors. Don Ross was there too; even though they'd broken up months before, he and Nina still hadn't got divorced. A few days before the concert, she had called him and asked him to come. Feeling alone in seeing this dream of hers come true, Nina needed the nearness of a familiar face. The Waymons on the other hand didn't make the journey. They had been told and she had offered them tickets, but her mother had declined without a word of explanation.

From her hiding spot in the wings, Nina Simone observed the comings and goings in the room, watching as elegant guests, among them intellectuals, Village artists and members of high society, trickled in. She watched as men in dinner jackets, women all dressed up and wearing heavy jewellery took their seats quietly, elegantly, without a drink in their hand or shouting, whispering and politely greeting one another instead. She was aware that tonight, the audience filling the rows of the Town Hall wasn't unlike that of a classical concert. Cohen whispered words of encouragement to her before she walked onto the stage, as a stage fright unlike any she'd felt before gripped her stomach. He said: 'Good luck Nina. This is your chance. This is your big night.' Someone announced 'The amazing Nina Simone!' She made her entrance under a torrent of applause, approaching her piano in slow, stately strides.

At twenty-six, this was Nina Simone's first time performing on the stage of a venue devoted to classical music and respectable popular events. Only a few people knew that the pianist now taking a seat behind her instrument was the equal of most of the musicians who had come and been applauded here before her. This girl was more than just a seasonal trend or a hit performer. She was different.

She felt happy on the Town Hall's stage. Everything was falling into place. She had weighed up all the songs in her repertoire and opened with 'Black Is the Color of My True Love's Hair', a traditional Scottish Appalachian song that would later be covered by Donovan (she substituted 'yellow' for 'black' in her own rendition, which was closer to the original folklore). It told the story of a girl who waited in vain for her lover to return. During the course of her career, Nina would come to make 'Black Is the Color' her own, eventually stripping it from its folkloric roots and imprinting it with her own trademark style.

Colpix's recording of the Town Hall concert provides a taste (the record only features an edited version) of the range of songs she performed. Accompanied by Jimmy Bond and Tootie Heath, the pianist gave a concert where swing ritornellos ('Exactly Like You', borrowed from Billie Holiday) would alternate with sober ballads ('The Other Woman'), menacing instrumentals where she allowed her technique to shine through ('Under the Lowest', 'Return Home'), and a few Broadway classics including a version of 'Summertime' that swayed between vocal and instrumental, taken from *Porgy and Bess*. This interpretation of 'Summertime' is a prime example of the precarious balance Nina Simone sought to achieve in the early 60s, oscillating between refinement, a theatrical sense of drama and gentle melancholy. Before the finale, choking as she thanked the audience, Nina played a suspended version of the classic 'Wild Is the Wind', a song penned by Dimitri Tiomkin and Ned Washington and made popular by Johnny Mathis the previous year. Nina now took her turn in making the tune her own and would some years later record it in a deeply moving orchestral version. Many artists covered 'Wild Is the Wind' in her wake, like David Bowie, Cat Power and Jeff Buckley, but each one of them pledged allegiance in their own interpretation to the one who had propelled this melody to the edge of tragedy.

For the time being, Nina Simone's music remained without trace of savagery or sexuality. This freedom would come to impose itself naturally over time as the musician's fame grew. Then, beyond music, her insolence, preaching and the involvement of the audience were what would come to constitute Nina's trademark live touch.

That night in September 1959, in New York, after a concert rated as 'classical' in Broadway terms, the woman who had harboured dreams of becoming a concert pianist since her childhood experienced a triumph that lived up to her fantasies. The following day, the press hailed her a star and a new sensation, the *New York Times* going as far as describing how she had eclipsed veterans like Horace Silver and J.J. Johnson with whom she had shared the bill. Those in the business all emphatically agreed that it had been a long time since they had last seen such a dazzling young artist. Look at this woman, look at her stage presence. It was hard to picture her playing in some Atlantic City dive, earning the respect of a bunch of barflies. Watch this girl, remembering in minute detail the etiquette dictated by classical discipline. There was also the matter of this woman's physical beauty. Her features might indeed be bold and she might fail to meet classical beauty standards, that much is true, yet something in her glows as she strokes the piano keys.

A new star was born – of the kind the press hungers for. Max Cohen exulted and his protégée soon noted the change in attitude in those who crossed her path as she wandered though the Village. In just one night, the black Cinderella who until recently dragged her heart and her art in a satchel through the streets of Manhattan had been crowned the new queen of Greenwich. People recognized her in the street, Cohen's phone rang off the hook, and she would be offered gigs all over the country and on her own terms. Journalists full of trepidation demanded interviews, something to feed their paper with, and they were truly spoilt. Indeed, Nina would turn out to be a boon for the press, having not yet morphed into the harpy who would hurl a teapot at your head in return for any questions deemed inappropriate. No, she was still this model young woman (despite the occasional murderous glance), giving calm replies, articulate in expressing her thoughts and who held both herself and her art in high regard.

The anxious young woman was long gone. How did she who dreamed of glory and the recognition of her classical talents handle this success she'd so yearned for and which had burst into her life so suddenly? Could she be resigning herself to abandoning her dreams of a career as a classical concert pianist? Had she just grasped that this destiny would never be hers? Or did she in fact realize that she was, from that day on, actually living her dream? A different one, granted, and under headings she abhorred: 'jazz', 'pop', or any other easy label the press could come up with to pigeonhole her. What did it matter if no one else in America played popular tunes where classical and piano-bar music collided with blues and spiritual folk and pop? She could be this person. And those African roots that twisted and wound their way around the stage when she played the instrumental 'Return Home'... Of course there wasn't a single critic to be found who would fail to mention her playing style. One reporter spoke of 'classical intensity', even 'majesty'.[5] But 'jazz'? Not for Nina. Yet the label would prove tough to shed. Despite the times she lashed out at them, her threats, insults even, the critics wouldn't back down. To them, what she played was jazz. Period.

But in America, at the dawn of the 60s, anything black fell into the 'jazz' category. So what if jazz implied a certain ideology, behaviours, language and a highly typical way of moving, let alone playing? Listening to this woman just once, hearing that Town Hall live recording was all it took to feel obliged to find her a more suitable shrine. 'Jazz' was the first misperception, comparisons were the second.

'Porgy', 'Summertime', 'Fine and Mellow' and 'Exactly Like You', all these songs were already part of Billie Holiday's repertoire. Billie had died in July 1959. The first ever jazz artist to have reached an audience way beyond die-hard aficionados, Billie Holiday changed the art of singing for ever. Her death, too premature to allow an accurate perception of her true impact, left a substantial void in American popular music. After the Town Hall concert, many were the critics or vocal jazz lovers who still mourned Billie Holiday and saw Nina as her natural successor, something that later began to annoy said successor despite herself: 'What made me mad was that it meant people couldn't get past the fact we were both black: if I had happened to be white nobody would have made the connection.'[6] Those were things Nina said when times got bitter, after a long journey across the desert during the 70s and 80s. But in 1959 she felt honoured to be linked with Billie.

Colpix released the Town Hall concert recording at the end of 1959. They got a distribution deal in Europe and the album was released in England. Nina Simone had only officially been in the music business for two years, but after Town Hall her career truly took off and her reputation soared; everyone remembered 'Porgy', and gigs came pouring in.

Greenwich Village, the New York neighbourhood Nina lived in, was a hot spot for American artistic, political and literary effervescence. Its few blocks formed a melting pot of artists, intellectuals, poets, musicians, cinematographers and headhunters for the music industry. At the beginning of the 60s, a white politically tinted movement had begun to blossom in Greenwich. Its heralds bore names like Bob Dylan and Tim Hardin, and among them were the black folk singer Richie Havens and the tremendous Odetta. Their audience was made up of young white folk fans who right then were also rediscovering blues and its pioneers, a whole swath of American culture that had so far been ignored by their generation. Jazz, blues and folk were terms that came to represent shelter, spaces for anti-segregation. The Village was also the epicentre of the black literary intelligentsia. Authors like James Baldwin, Langston Hughes, LeRoi Jones (author of *Blues People*) and the poet Lorraine Hansberry would gather there. It was also the place where John Coltrane would launch his solo career, aged thirty-three.

Indeed, the Village was one of the epicentres of the American jazz scene, a status it owed to its two main clubs: the Village Gate and the Vanguard, which Max Gordon opened on the corner of 178th and 7th Street in 1936. The Vanguard's legend is for ever associated with the path of Leadbelly, a black singer who came and made it his residence from 1941 onward. A convict who had done jail time for murder, Huddie Leadbetter aka Leadbelly was discovered whilst locked up in prison, by John and Alan Lomax who were ethnomusicologists sent by the Library of Congress to record folk and traditional songs from the southern US. Released by a stroke of good luck and under the Lomaxes' protection, Leadbelly became a leading figure of original folk music. His impact on American popular music was considerable, from Woody Guthrie to Pete Seeger, Bob Dylan to Kurt Cobain.

A November afternoon in New York. A metallic blue bathes the city. The Village Vanguard is accessed through a narrow red door. Tunnel-like stairs lead to the entrance of a room steeped in darkness. Some guy appears out of nowhere and comes up to me. 'What do you want?' 'Lorraine. I have an appointment with Lorraine.' 'In her office, right there behind the bar.' I knock on the door of a narrow, damp room flooded with a harsh light. A woman is screaming down the phone: 'It's sold out. That's it. Are you doing this on purpose? I'm telling you it's sold out.' She hangs up and turns towards me. A lean woman of medium build, dressed in an elegant suit, her permed hair gathered in a beehive, Lorraine Gordon's voice as she questions me is authoritative, hoarse, damaged by decades of all-nighters. 'Who're you, darling?' 'I have an appointment, madam.' 'Oh yeah, the Nina Simone guy. Say, darling, you seem awfully young to be wanting to talk about ladies. Do you even know anything about them?'

You don't mess around with Lorraine Gordon. Max Gordon's wife wanted to keep the Vanguard true to its founder's ideals and nothing here has changed in more than sixty years. Oh, maybe a touch of colour here and there, and the furniture has been replaced of course, new pictures have come to adorn the walls of this little room of which it is hard to believe, once you take a seat on a wooden chair in the back row with your back against the wall, facing the stage, that it might have contained whole chunks of the history of black music in the United States. All the greats have passed though these doors. Miles Davis, John Coltrane, Dizzy Gillespie, Charlie Mingus, Thelonious Monk, Albert Ayler, Sonny Rollins and Bill Evans. All of them have played here, up on a tiny stage where the bass player and drummer have to play stuck to one another just to avoid falling off, where the frontman can almost touch the front-row customers with his musical instrument. One can easily guess just how the tension would rise on nights when a sold-out Vanguard turned into a smoked-out sanctuary with temperatures reminiscent of hell. All it takes is to sit down with Lorraine – still eyeing me with that laserlike stare – to feel the vibe, the electricity in the air. As we get acquainted, Lorraine lowers her guard and I discover a wonderful storyteller who is in no hurry whatsoever to answer the phone – 'Let it ring!' She'd rather evoke her first nights at the Vanguard, where she'd once come down as a teenager to listen to Leadbelly. They'd got on well and she'd spent a while 'with this fascinating guy', drinking in his words until morning as he told her the craziest of stories. Then there was Max Gordon. Love at first sight. Lorraine would never leave this place again. While Greenwich saw its jazz clubs gradually disappear and one of New York's golden eras vanish for good, to this day Lorraine Gordon continues to embody one of its last living memories.

'When Nina Simone came to perform at the Vanguard towards the end of the 50s,' Lorraine Gordon says, 'there were always stand-up comedy shows before every concert. This is where people like Bill Cosby, Woody Allen, Dick Gregory and Richard Pryor cut their teeth.' Here also (partly at least) that Nina Simone's reputation as a temperamental diva was born. Late arrivals on stage, a fiery temper that saw her alternating between yelling at her audience and inviting them to join in with her, wild rides that drained the musicians that accompanied her. Then, of course, the music. The music, since some of the most beautiful of 60s American music was written in tiny, damp venues like the Vanguard, and, just a few blocks away, the Village Gate. What a shame that Nina never released an album recorded in this club, even though from Sonny Rollins's *A Night at the Village Vanguard* in 1957 the Vanguard found itself among the first places to make the fame of the artists that performed there for jazz lovers through live recordings.

The Village Vanguard became Nina Simone's base camp. By then, her tours already stretched far beyond the East Coast circuit, taking her as far as Washington's Casino Royal, the Pittsburgh Town House, Chicago's Blue Note and Philadelphia's Showboat, where she performed in October 1959, practically on her own doorstep.

After this concert, Nina heard that her sister Frances had just given birth to her first child. Nina stormed out of her dressing room in her stage outfit and make-up, jumped into a cab and rushed to the hospital. She marched into the hall, but stopped in her tracks when strangers ran up to her: 'Are you Nina Simone?' In the dead of the night, right in the middle of a Philly hospital, she was being hassled to the point where she, Frances and the baby had to be moved to a room away from prying eyes. As the two sisters faced one another, Frances saw Eunice, now a star, in a new light. 'So you've made it. You finally got what you were preparing for when we were children.'

In less than a year, something had shifted. Nina was caught up in a flurry of tours, non-stop gigs, records in the making and endless solicitations. Money had become as much a source of happiness as the audience's applause. Bethlehem sent her a $10,000 royalties cheque – performance rights only. A substantial amount, enough for her to drop everything and at last dedicate herself solely to her classes. With that kind of money, goddammit, she could hire Sokhaloff's services by the year! But this no longer came into the equation. Nina was aware of how hard the last three years had been, how close she'd come to quitting before she eventually got to where she was. Perhaps she somehow felt that she had actually fulfilled her goals. Performing, cash, a career, recognition, success. She had achieved far more than she'd bargained for. Now was the time to live! To make the most of this cornucopia and of the gratifications her new status brought her. To show her mother that she'd been wrong and that her daughter had at long last become an artist. Did Nina really believe that this wealth and seeing her name on the playbill of renowned theatres would affect the way Mary Kate saw her daughter? She sent a handsome part of Bethlehem's cheque to her family, along with a letter that explained where the money came from. She waited for some kind of thank-you note, for a word from her mother, yet nothing came.

Now aged twenty-seven, Nina Simone moved into a six-bedroom furnished apartment on the twelfth floor of a 13th Street building with views over Central Park, a large bathroom, carpet flooring, walls decorated in pastel hues, with a piano in the living room, a live-in maid and friendly concierge. The trappings of success.

There was only one thing missing from those status symbols, so without so much as a driver's licence, she bought a steel-grey Mercedes convertible with red leather seats, matching luggage and a matching hat. Nina would spend hours driving around the Village. This was glorious: it even resembled happiness, the exciting life she'd always dreamed of and which classical music might never have given her. For a girl like her, of her age, this was what an exciting life looked like: heaps of cash and the guarantee of earning more still. Fame and respect. The lust of men, too, as they waited for her backstage or in her dressing room, declaring their love and passion, proposing marriage, sometimes stealing a kiss. And flowers, lots of them, so many that it got dull. More kisses, the occasional embrace, scribbled words requesting a meeting in some 5th Avenue apartment. Late afternoon telephone calls inviting her to dinner, a drink, a date in the park, anything to get her to lower her guard and agree.

A thrilling life indeed, with new friendships, the assurance of never being alone anywhere, even if some of her new 'friends' had their own selfish motives. For Nina Simone, excitement meant evenings when Natalie Wood, Lauren Bacall or Rod Steiger squeezed into the Vanguard to hear her play or walked over to greet her at parties. The elite of New York flirting with her, telling her that she was one of them; Allen Ginsberg who praised her at the end of a lecture she hadn't understood a word of, asking her whether she'd liked his poems and Nina too ashamed to admit it had all gone over her head. Black writers like James Baldwin and Langston Hughes who came into her life and fell in love with her soul, taking on some big brother role and lending her books, opening her mind to culture, poetry, and politics.

Those gigs she'd played in dives where she'd earn a pittance were now a thing of the past. A single concert in a decent venue now equalled two weeks spent sweating blood in the bars of Atlantic City. Pictures of her in the papers, tame at first, getting wilder as the months went by and she asserted herself. One interview after the other, sold-out concerts. Frank Sinatra throwing a fit after a show upon hearing that Nina had been in the audience and had left before the end, when he'd have wanted her to join him on stage. At that moment, she had the chance to choose the ending to her own story. What did she want? To return to the Juilliard, go back to her classes with Sokhaloff and resit the Curtis entrance exam, or to enjoy the opportunities and new friendships her budding career had to offer? For the first time, she was spoilt for choice, and she picked the most thrilling path of all: the well-trodden road to pop stardom.

Among Nina's new friends was the black singer Odetta. Born in Birmingham, Alabama, Odetta Gordon grew up in Los Angeles and displayed an extraordinary voice from her early childhood. Like Eunice Waymon with Miz Mazzy, Odetta owed her career to a sponsor, Harry Burnett, who paid for the teenager to continue her singing lessons. Odetta moved to New York in 1953 and joined the local folk scene, carving out her reputation in clubs like the Blue Angel, where she was spotted by Pete Seeger, then Harry Belafonte (who at the time was just about to take the South African singer Miriam Makeba under his wing). The songs on Odetta's first album were rooted in tradition, including 'House of the Rising Sun', which Nina would later cover, 'Nobody Knows You When You're Down and Out', and the amazing a cappella 'Another Man Done Gone'. The record revealed her as an extraordinary mezzo-soprano and pushed her to the forefront of the folk scene. Listening to songs like 'Bald Headed Woman' (very similar in sound to the 'Come Ye' Nina would sing a few years later) and 'Fare Thee Well', one might be led to think that Odetta was partly responsible for Nina Simone's initiation into the roots of American folk.

The two women became friends and often met at Rienzi's Coffee House, where they'd chat over ice cream and coffee, putting the world to rights in endless conversations. Nina talked about her career, her doubts and regrets, as Odeta listened on, serene. Indeed, behind all those badges of success, Nina Simone was a tortured soul. She'd been divorced from Don Ross in the spring of 1960, and ever since then, she'd kept on falling prey to anguish. She had it all, yet she was suffering from some chronic inability to be happy. Despite the offers she received, there was still no man in her life, and no manager experienced enough to handle her growing fame. No one to entrust with the reins of her career or the strings of her purse.

Nina was terrified at the thought of running out of money, and this fear pushed her to accept every gig she got offered. Her life had turned into an exhausting whirlwind of airports, hotels, bad food, one-night stands and sleepless nights. She had to keep up this relentless pace – she couldn't ease off. She was committed, and Jerry and Max encouraged her to hold on. Her biggest fear, that she might once again find herself in need, that her luck might run out, was what kept her on track. Throughout 1960, Nina Simone played five shows a week, roaming the country from New York to San Francisco, from New Orleans to Chicago. This frantic race brought a new theme to the heart of her complaints: sheer weariness.

In the summer of 1960, her efforts were rewarded when 'Nobody Knows You When You're Down and Out', her cover of a classic by the blues singer Bessie Smith – a suggestion of Odetta's – got into the Top 30 R&B chart. Jerry Fields and Max Cohen rejoiced, Colpix was pleased.

Nina Simone's career took a decisive turn when on 30 June 1960 she was invited to perform at the prestigious Newport Jazz Festival. A seaside resort in Rhode Island State, Newport had since 1954 played host to a festival whose impact on the US jazz scene was critical. It was an honour to be featured on the bill, even though its commercial by-products made it the target of harsh criticism from dissidents like Charles Mingus and Max Roach who retaliated by hosting a rival event: Newport Rebels.

Nina Simone got up on the Newport stage, flanked by Al Schackman, the bass player Chris White (who'd worked with Dizzy Gillespie) and the drummer Bobby Hamilton. The titles the quartet played included 'You'd Be So Nice to Come Home To', a Cole Porter cover, 'Trouble in Mind' (a blues tune that would get into the Top 20 R&B chart in the winter of 1960), a version of 'Porgy' by Dorothy Fields and Jimmy McHugh and the sparkling 'Little Liza Jane'. The magic worked. Once she'd got the audience's undivided attention, Nina Simone was able to launch into a track that must have sounded like a UFO to the Newport audience's ears: 'Flo Me La', a term that meant 'walk' and which, according to her, accompanied the Yoruba warriors' marathon marches. Was this something she'd picked up from James Baldwin or from Langston Hughes, with whom Nina had got involved? Had she caught those words during one of her writer friends' African lessons? 'Flo Me La' was the first song where Nina Simone deliberately asserted her African roots, where the drums ousted all the other instruments, making up the backbone upon which the musicians were invited to build their digressions. 'Flo Me La', a war cry, the affirmation of an identity asserted by a musician in her quest for freedom.

The Newport concert was a resounding success. Satisfied cheers and a worn-out audience. Back in Manhattan, Nina heard that after her concert there had been some violent clashes between members of the audience and security, shenanigans that led to the Newport municipality cancelling the event.

But the time had come to think about the next step, another festival, this one in Newark, where Nina was scheduled to play during the summer, just a few days before her first television show.

In September 1960, at the end of a harrowing summer tour, the pianist felt exhausted and in dire need of a break. Jerry had however confirmed her for some engagement at the New York Basin Street East club. At first she grumbled, then gave in when Jerry Fields argued that this gig was very well paid. So there she went, dragging her feet and knowing full well that the Basin was a place where the crowd typically paid little attention to the music, preferring a drink and chat instead. On her first night performing there, she threw a fit with Jerry backstage and threatened to quit. 'Listen Nina, you signed a contract for a number of shows, there's no going back on it or we'll lose money.' Reluctantly, Nina Simone returned to the Basin for a second night.

From the stage, she spotted her hairdresser in the audience. He was sitting at a table with Johnny Mathis's sister and a handsome, light-skinned black man. The stranger was tall, must have weighed around 180 pounds and looked dashing in his double-breasted suit. She noticed that he wore a silver chain with an African pendant around his neck. During her break, Nina came down to greet her hairdresser and his guests. He introduced her to Andrew Stroud and she sat down opposite him, devouring the quiet, self-assured man with her eyes. She asked him what he did and he pretended that he was a bank clerk. That was a lie. Maybe he was hoping she would find him out as he stretched out the mystery a little while longer, or perhaps he meant to make her feel at ease. Indeed, telling her of his true profession just like that, in a club when they'd barely met might have sent the young beauty running.

But she believed him. 'At long last, someone who isn't involved in the music business,' she mused. She was utterly absorbed by his conversation, making play with her bad manners and munching potatoes out of Stroud's plate; she listened to him as, sweetly, he commented on the first half of her concert. Then, as she got up to get back on stage, he held her back, grabbing her arm. 'Andy. Call me Andy,' he said.

At the end of the show, Stroud asked Nina whether she'd join him for a drink in Harlem. 'Harlem? Are you sure about that?' Nina remembered the neighbourhood from her student days. She remembered feeling intimidated by its atmosphere. Pimps, whores, cops, noise, speed, the scent of violence. She trembled at the offer, fumbling for an excuse, but Stroud was already helping her get her coat on. They left the Basin and he gently nudged her into his car before whisking her off to his own turf. Little did she know that Andy Stroud was actually a well-known Harlem figure. He knew every tiniest corner of the neighbourhood. Stroud was a cop; he had been a police inspector in the 26th Precinct for fourteen years and Harlem was his district. He dealt with drugs, murders and extortion and everyone here knew who Andrew Stroud was. Even the local tough guys feared him and there were rumours going around town regarding his methods. Some said that he'd flung a guy off a roof. That he took bribes, turning a blind eye to some dealings in exchange for a share in the profits. That night, as the twosome walked into a bar, some guys fled on the spot. Nina saw this then noticed the butt of a revolver sticking out from Andy's belt. She didn't ask any questions, she'd already fallen under his spell. There was something special, intense, electrical, and dangerous about this guy and his total self-assurance. She was watching him. He still seemed in total control of the situation. He had a natural authority, charisma. Andy Stroud embodied the African vision of manhood and power she felt attracted to. They agreed on another date, the next day. She soon found out who this man really was and felt a shiver down her spine when he told her: 'I'm a cop.'

Despite his apparent control, Stroud felt intimidated by the star. He'd felt shaken up, seduced as she'd winked at him between two verses at her concert the other night. Stroud's everyday world was all muck and violence and there she was, entering his life, this elegant woman known all over New York, to whom all and sundry promised the brightest of futures.

Less than a week after their first meeting, Andrew Stroud was assiduously courting Nina Simone.

When he walked her home after their first date, he whispered to her how he'd like to come in and perhaps share a drink. The diva coyly declined, telling him it was too soon. She kissed him on the cheek, his manly scent making her feel dizzy. At last she shut the door, only to hear Stroud playing with a set of keys. 'I get in wherever I like, you know.' The lock gave a few clicks before the door opened. She stood there, open-mouthed and he politely said 'Goodnight, Nina' and left. What an act. It was irresistible. Over the following weeks, Stroud would send Nina flowers every day, jewels, a diamond even. 'This guy's a cop, where does all this money come from?' But she never asked, for fear of breaking the charm. It hardly mattered to her in the end; never before had she felt so drawn to a man or come across one so shrouded in mystery.

Her fears were well founded. There were things about Andy's past Nina was better off not knowing. Andy had already been married three times; he knew about women and he knew how to play a girl like Nina. The fact that she was a star even made things easier for him. He'd guessed how much pressure and stress she was under and how crushingly lonely she felt. He gradually made his way into her life, becoming her lover, her knight in shining armour and her confidant. He now waited for her after her concerts, looked after her, listening to her as she told him about her disappointments, classical piano music, her mother, Bethlehem Records, how tough this job was, her never-ending tiredness. He listened to her like no one had ever listened to Nina Simone before, with his undivided attention and absolute devotion. He turned out to be the lover she'd been yearning for. Andy was sensational in bed, and in his arms Nina felt like a woman. She glowed as only a woman in love can.

Now there was talk of getting engaged and the couple made their relationship official in the winter of 1960. Andy was introduced to the star's close entourage, meeting Jerry, Alvin, Max, and soon thereafter, the Waymon family.

In February 1961, the only thing still missing from her life was a word of pride from her own mother. Nina was in love, she was wealthy and seemed irresistibly drawn to the top. And to crown it all, she was scheduled to perform in her fiancé's neighbourhood, at the Harlem Apollo Theater, the ultimate and legendary venue of black American music. This was where Sarah Vaughan had been discovered during one of those unforgettable Wednesday night amateur sessions. James Brown, Duke Ellington, Louis Armstrong, Lionel Hampton and Billie Holiday (and more recently D'Angelo and Lauryn Hill), dozens had established their legend here, out of the hundreds who had trodden those boards, feeling the same apprehension she felt now. Indeed, the Apollo's audience was well known to be a merciless one. There is no playing at that venue without feeling the pressure. Even the Reverend Al Green, perhaps the greatest soul singer alive, admitted upon his return to 125th Street in Harlem in October 2004 to feeling intimidated at the thought of the concert that awaited him.

So, a merciless audience? Yes, that was almost a tradition at the Apollo, and when Nina Simone got up on the stage, it seemed as though a boxing match was about to start. This artist who was known to be pitiless towards her audience was coming to play in the most uncompromising of all black American concert halls. Was it to remind her where she was that the audience was so rude to her? After Nina 'stopped playing and gave them a quick talk about manners',[7] three Harlem ladies got up, walked to the stage and threw coins at the pianist's feet, then left without so much as a backward glance. Backstage hysterics ensued. Andrew, taking her in his arms, whispered to her that she'd been amazing, but Nina felt humiliated and never played at the Apollo again.

So what? The Village Gate, another major New York club, awaited her with open arms. Located on the corner of Bleecker and Thompson and founded by Art D'Lugoff, a major Greenwich figure, the Gate spent thirty-six years as the 'number one club in one of the world's first cities of jazz', according to the *Village Voice*. Opened in May 1958, the Village Gate owed its success to its artistic policy as much as to one golden rule: booking compulsory. Aretha Franklin, John Belushi, Chuck Berry, the Byrds, Miles Davis, Woody Allen, Dizzy Gillespie, John Coltrane and even Jacques Brel played there. Norman Mailer gave lectures within its walls and it was there that a young Bob Dylan, finding temporary shelter in an apartment in the club's basement in 1962, composed 'A Hard Rain's a-Gonna Fall'. Folk, jazz, opera, blues, anything went provided the show was good. In the 60s, those walls even hosted *Oh! Calcutta!*, Kenneth Tyana's infamous nude revue.

Art D'Lugoff offered Nina Simone several weeks as a headliner, which of course she agreed to. Being the star performer at the Village Gate was akin to a new award, but above all, 'Art treated performers as equals,' she said, 'as people worthy of respect,' whereas others saw musicians as mere employees. 'One of the reasons I hated clubs so much was the way owners made you feel, as if they were doing you a favour letting you play... Often, out on the road at some hole in the wall, I would find myself fighting to get paid at three in the morning'.[8] Those things were unheard-of at the Village Gate. To Art D'Lugoff music was sacred and he had the utmost respect for musicians.

In Frank Lords's film *Nina Simone: The Legend*, Art D'Lugoff talks about the pianist's repeat performances at his club: 'Whenever she played for us, the atmosphere was electric, thrilling. You never knew what she was going to do. She'd start out with Bach and slip in the weirdest musical arrangements. She aroused the audience like no one else in the world could. To me, that was her strength. That's what makes me care about her. Because as you know, she isn't easy to get along with. Every night she'd show up so late for her first concert that it was already time for the second one to start. One night we understood why bodyguards were needed. A woman asked Nina for an autograph. She signed it, handed it to the woman, who then said: 'Thanks, Miss.' Nina replied: 'Is that it?' The woman was in shock: 'What else do you want me to say? If we're done, take back your autograph.' Nina got hold of a bottle and tried to hit her with it. That's what bodyguards were needed for at Nina Simone's concerts. To protect the audience from her!'

It's a precious glimpse of the years Nina Simone worked with the Village Gate, her reputation as a temperamental and unpredictable diva and the memorable concerts she played. The Gate became Nina Simone's headquarters.

She went back there to play several shows in the spring of 1961. D'Lugoff had scheduled a young black comedian, Richard Pryor, as her supporting act. A few years later, this young man would be dubbed the black Lenny Bruce, and a decade after that the everyday racism at the core of his sketches would make him one of the most controversial and adored people in American comedy (with shows like *That Nigger's Crazy* and *Bicentennial Nigger*). On his first night, in the wings, Pryor was petrified with stage fright and Nina was the one to comfort him.

When he finally got up on the stage, things were being set up for a French singer who'd recently arrived in New York: Charles Aznavour. Few present at the Gate that night would have known who he was. A singer-songwriter who'd long been part of the Edith Piaf bunch, Aznavour had got out of it and moved to New York on a whim with two demos in his luggage, hoping to get them heard by the label owner Howard Richmond and to attend a few shows. During a recording session, he got a visit from Art D'Lugoff, who'd discovered him in Truffaut's *Tirez sur le pianiste* (*Shoot the Piano Player*) and had fallen in love with the song 'Tu t'laisses aller' ('You're Letting Yourself Go'). Art wanted to offer him a residency at his club, and to convince him, he said: 'There's this amazing girl playing here right now, Nina Simone.' Aznavour had never heard of her. In his memoirs, *Le Temps des avants* (*Past Times*), he tells of his arrival at the Gate and his shock as he saw the young musician's show: 'quite impressive, the lady played the piano as few can'.[9] Upon being introduced to Aznavour by Art D'Lugoff, Nina arranged to meet him a few days later to listen to his songs. A few years later, she would record two of them: 'Tomorrow Is My Turn' and 'You've Got to Learn'.

Finding myself in Charles Aznavour's office to ask him a few questions was an experience in itself. After several letters and the intervention of his record label, I'm summoned to Paris for a fifteen-minute interview and get on the first train. The master, seated in a leather armchair, looks straight at me as I take a seat. 'So, Nina Simone...' Freewheeling, he replies to my questions before I can finish asking them. He describes that conversation with Art D'Lugoff: 'He mentioned this girl, Nina Simone, who was all the rage in his club, so I went to see her that same night. I felt like I'd been winded. She was sensational and her show was a hit, the audience couldn't get enough of her. What struck me was the way she played the piano. Nina played with a man's touch. She had extraordinary harmonies and especially that way of singing which was wildly different from that of her peers. Most of the time, when you listened to a jazz singer in the 60s they'd sound like Sarah Vaughan, but with her it was different. She had her very own way of articulating her lyrics, giving words their full weight. Often those who sing jazz sing the music, but Nina Simone sang the lyrics at the same time she sang the music. After her concert, we got introduced backstage.'

I'm squirming with excitement in my seat. Relaxing a little, I ask him: 'What kind of woman did Nina Simone come across as during this first meeting?'

'Hard work!' He laughed. 'She always wanted something. It was always strictly music-related, always had something to do with the job, which in fact she was completely immersed in. She said to me: "You came to hear me, and now I'd like to listen to what you do." I gave her the few records I'd brought with me. She had no idea who I was, even though back then Aretha Franklin had said that I was the only soul singer in France. That was the key word: *soul*. In the United States someone who sings waltzes can be considered a soul singer. Someone else had told me: "What I like about you is that there is space between your sentences." I am close to jazz without making jazz. What I do is swing. That's what touched Nina Simone when she listened to my records.'

I ask him about the two Aznavour tracks Nina would go on to record for Philips: 'I guess she liked the melodies,' he says. 'Some years later, she confessed that she hadn't recorded them quite the way she should have, but what was interesting about her covers was that although she was classically trained, she moved in a musical world where musicians tend to have hang-ups with regard to classical music and that was one of the main things that made her different, added to the fact that she was a natural when it came to music. Nina Simone lived her songs.' I ask him to tell me more about how Nina adapted and interpreted his two songs, but Charles doesn't even let me finish my sentence. No need to. 'She just completely made them her own, gave them her own twist, her own touch. It was just like when Ray Charles sang "La Mamma". He made it his own. That's what's interesting with those artists; they take on your song and give off the impression that they're the ones who wrote it. That's what I find interesting. I think that that's where the survival of what we songwriters do lies, in this hustle and bustle. Some performers fare better than others; Nina Simone did it with pure genius!'

He pauses. I barely dare breathe. 'You know,' he says, 'if people call it soul music, it truly is because this music comes from the soul, from some faraway place, from the time when their ancestors were slaves, perhaps even before then.' Silence again. 'There's this sound that black American artists have, that peculiar way they have of pronouncing the lyrics. You get the feeling that they're giving the audience their guts, but at the same time, that they're isolating themselves as they sing. When Nina Simone played, she was all about her song and her piano. The audience only came third on her list of priorities. She used her body to communicate with the audience and the connection happened all by itself, with her heart beating right on the stage.'

Aznavour glances at his watch: my fifteen minutes are over. I apologize and beg him to allow me one last question. He glances at his watch again, as though telling me to hurry, as I ask him about that night at the Village Gate. He breaks a smile at last before he begins: 'I'll always remember this song she used to perform, "Brown Baby". Beautiful. Nina loved long introductions, getting into the song only once she'd tamed it, with no layers. Nina Simone didn't make a conscious effort to get a hold on the audience; they were captivated anyhow. There was this magic when she played on stage, but this was a gift she displayed in everyday life too. Something overwhelming. I remember her stopping her limousine in the middle of New York to shout out to me in the street. As she got out, she reminded me of an animal, warm-hearted and... yes, that's it, overwhelming.'

This animal joined Aznavour in a New York studio a few days later and came out having bought two of his songs.

After *Live at Town Hall*, Nina took advantage of her stint at the Village Gate to record another live album, which Colpix released in 1962. Accompanied by the flawless trio of Al Schackman, Chris White and Bobby Hamilton, a team that had already proved its worth at Newport, Nina made a record that was both intimate and glowing hot. It included an anxious and particularly noteworthy version of the folk song 'House of the Rising Sun', which Bob Dylan, then a young songwriter on the rise, covered in turn on his first album, released in March 1962.

Nina kept this traditional in her repertoire all through the 60s. Concert after concert, she transformed 'House of the Rising Sun' into her secret weapon, performing it in so many different ways that it soon became a compulsory part of her shows. She soon heard that in Europe, the English band the Animals' cover version of 'House of the Rising Sun' was a hit too. In the midst of the 'British Invasion' of the United States, this band, led by the singer Eric Burdon, even got its version of the song to top the American charts. There was talk of the band getting grief for conveniently revamping Dylan's song to get a hit. The Brits vehemently denied this, pledging their allegiance to

Josh White, the magnetic-voiced legend of Piedmont blues, yet no one mentioned the Nina Simone track. But they soon would.

On 3 July 1961, Nina played 'at home', in Philadelphia. She showed up sick, fainted in the dressing room and woke up in hospital. When she came to, Andy was there. How had he found out? He drove down to Philadelphia to watch over her every evening, spending the night in hospital by her side only to leave for New York again in the morning.

The doctors thought she had either non-paralytic polio or spinal meningitis. Meningitis. The same disease that had afflicted her brother. She remembered when as a little girl, she had told her father that they should 'get rid of' Harold because he was going to 'hold us down'. She was paying for it now, she thought. This voice inside of her kept saying: 'I told you it wouldn't last; I told you you'd be punished.' She was terrified at the thought of ending her life in a wheelchair, seeing her career and all the rest fall apart. After a second lumbar puncture, Nina's state finally began to improve. Andy swore to her: 'When you get better, once you get out of here, we're going to get married.' She wept with joy.

Seventeen days after her admission to the Philadelphia hospital, Nina Simone and Andrew Stroud returned to New York together. They were engaged to be married and Andy was officially introduced to the Waymon family, whom he'd already crossed paths with several times in the hospital's corridors. Mary Kate adored her future son-in-law. She probably saw her daughter's union with this strong, reliable young man as a step towards the respectability she'd lacked. John Divine stayed silent throughout the couple's visit, keeping his distance from Andrew Stroud, hardly bothering to say goodbye to him as he left. Misgivings of some kind. The fear of seeing his favourite daughter belonging to another man perhaps, or the fact that Andy had already been married three times. But Eunice told him she was in love, and that she felt that with him she could build the life she'd dreamed of. He kept schtumm.

Nina and Andy got engaged in August 1961 and picked a small Harlem club to celebrate. As soon as he got there, Andy sank into a sombre mood. Although he usually didn't drink much, he started on white Puerto Rican rum. There was nothing Nina could do to cheer him up but she wanted to savour her happiness and for the whole room to know that she was engaged. As the night went on, a fan recognized her, came up to her and handed her a piece of paper which she slipped into her pocket. Andy saw this, stood up and asked her about the note. Nina explained about the fan, a harmless note, nothing more than that. He didn't believe any of it and began to yell at her. She burst out laughing at his jealousy. Andy stormed out of the club. She ran after him and seeing him looking for a cab, caught up with him and took him by the arm, calling him 'honey'. He turned around and hit her. Eventually, a cab stopped. Andy forced his fiancée inside and continued to beat her. He beat her 'in the cab, on the pavement outside my apartment building, in the lobby of the building, in the elevator up to the twelfth floor and along the passageway'.[10]

When Nina finally made it into her apartment, she was covered in blood, with open wounds on her face. Andy was out of his mind, screaming like a madman, pushing over the furniture. Bruised and battered, Nina explained to her fiancé that there was no reason for him to get so worked up but he began to question her. A cop, drunk with pointless rage, interrogating his fiancée and punching her when her answers didn't suit him. He made her say all sorts of nonsense. She panicked and told him about letters Edney had written to her when she was at school in Asheville; Andy pulled out his gun and held it to his future wife's temple, ordering her to go and find them. She took them out of a safe and obediently handed them to him. He tore them from her hand, ripped them up, tied her hands behind her back and made her sit down on a chair. Andy Stroud forced Nina Simone to read out several passages aloud, asking her questions, beating her the way he would have beaten an uncooperative suspect at the police station. This went on for five hours. He finally freed her from her ties, led her into the bedroom and raped her. On the night of her engagement she was taken by force. She screamed as her attacker moved on top of her, letting her go only when he was done. At last, his trousers around his ankles, Andrew Stroud fell asleep.

Nina Simone spent two weeks hiding her swollen face at a friend's apartment in New York. No leaks, no one knew of her whereabouts. Gripped with fear, she thought that Andy being a cop, he would manage to find her. She was right. The minute she set foot outside, he cornered her in a café. He paled as he saw the wounds on his fiancée's face, blinking in disbelief, as he said: 'Who beat you up like that?' 'You did.' He denied it adamantly; he stared at her, searching his memories, unable to grasp what he'd done. He told her that he didn't understand, that he wanted to marry her.

She remained cold as ice: 'You're sick,' she said. Nina demanded that he go and see two psychiatrists. She was scared, she wanted to be sure, thinking that a seed of violence lay in him and that he would do it again.

The psychiatrists' conclusions diverged, one of them advising Nina not to marry Andy, the other talking about temporary insanity. She hesitated. Nina wanted to have a family. She wanted to be a good wife and mother. He swore that it would never happen again, cajoled her, winning her over. He told her they'd buy a big house, that she could spend some time decorating it, picking out furniture, that they'd have a real life as a family. Not once did he mention money; that would have been out of place and he'd have had to explain how, with his meagre cop's salary, he would fund such lovely projects.

How does one say no to such a vision when one's life is nothing but a succession of clubs and tours? Andy. Her man. Someone to share her success with and build a future, a home... And who was she to turn him down?

Andrew Stroud married Eunice Waymon on 4 December 1961 in her 103rd Street apartment. The bride wore white and held a bouquet of fifteen white roses in her arms. Andy's five brothers, Nina's sister Frances, the two psychiatrists, Al Schackman and Ted Axelrod were present during the ceremony. Though invited, Mary Kate and John Divine chose not to make the journey and stayed in Philadelphia.

4

'I KNOW WHAT THE WORLD HAS DONE TO MY BROTHER'

THROUGH the porthole, Nina Simone saw the immense tropical forests spreading out before her, their colours extending to the horizon. With James Baldwin standing at her side, she pressed her face up to the glass, trying to engrave every nuance on her memory, right down to the tiniest detail of the amazing sight before her. The plane chartered by the ASAC (American Society for African Culture) came to a halt on the tarmac at Lagos airport on 20 December 1961. Despite the restlessness breaking out among the musicians, organizers, journalists and others, from the cabin Nina could make out the sound of drums around the airport. Finally, the aircraft's door was opened and, following Baldwin, Alvin Schackman, Langston Hughes and the pianist Randy Weston, she descended, dazzled by the intensity of the pale light.

Two weeks after her marriage to Andrew Stroud, Nina Simone had embarked on her first African journey at the invitation of the ASAC. That organization was responsible for the Festpac that was held the year before in Dakar, where the choreographer Katherine Dunham had been the guest of honour. For this second event in Lagos, in honour of the opening of the new cultural centre, the ASAC had gathered together prominent African-American artists and intellectuals.

Although initially intimidated by the proposition, Nina Simone had agreed to travel to Nigeria on the advice of her friends Langston Hughes and James Baldwin. Baldwin had become the great hero and poet of Harlem following the publication of *Harlem Quartet* and more recently of his manifesto, *The Fire Next Time*. Trying to convince her, Jimmy Baldwin had repeated over and over to Nina: 'A revolution is taking place in Africa. We are their representatives in the USA and we should grasp this opportunity to understand how our African brothers are taking charge of their own destiny.'

It was a topic that was stirring the Village's intellectual circles. An irrepressible wave of independence had swept West Africa since Ghana gained autonomy in 1957. Thereafter, the entire continent had been overtaken by a fever that saw seventeen African countries take their destinies in their own hands in 1960 alone, leaving colonial status behind to become independent states.

As she disembarked from the aircraft onto Nigerian soil, Nina Simone heard the drums take hold of and fill the air. The American delegation was received by Nigerian political representatives in traditional dress. For the little girl from Tryon, as for many of the movement's militants, that moment represented a consecration. Here she was in Africa, for the first time, and with Hughes and Baldwin at her sides she was walking in the land of her ancestors. The majority of black Americans would never experience this sort of moment; it would remain just fantasies of returning to the motherland, in songs celebrating a God that, despite their removal from their people, their roots and their language, had not abandoned them to fate.

Apart from what she had learned from Baldwin and Hughes – an education still in its infancy compared to what she would soon learn from a new mentor – until that moment Nina had never had a clear vision of her position as an African living on American soil. She was just starting to be aware of her condition and the fight that she would lead in just a few years to 'proudly assert [her] race'.[1] Although musically pieces like the instrumental 'African Mailman' or the hypnotic 'Flo Me La' tended towards a romantic vision of African rhythms as imagined by her black American brothers, she had never politically or philosophically expressed her desire to form a link with the land of her ancestors. Yet here, thrown into a world she had no control over but that welcomed her like a dignitary, a member of a diaspora dreamed of by those Nigerian politicians as a circle of distant cousins asserting their pride, Nina Simone felt 'the spiritual relaxation any Afro-American feels on reaching Africa... it wasn't Nigeria I arrived in – it was *Africa*'.[2]

Something was stirring in her that, coupled with the teachings of her mentors, would turn her world upside down in a matter of a few months, a few years, a few blows and misfortunes, and lead her towards a new level of awareness of her identity.

Outside Africa, New York was the perfect place for Nina to be at that time. Surrounded by James Baldwin, LeRoi Jones and Langston Hughes, the three most prominent black intellectuals in the Village since the 1950s, she had already been initiated into the ideas of Pan-Africanism. She also received instruction in an unknown history of America, Africa's history. Through her lessons, she learned of the enslavement of her ancestors by white Protestant colonists in America, how Africans had been shipped to the Americas, in what conditions and to what end.

A veil was lifting from her. She remembered the little girl she had been, the child gifted by God who, to save her from the destruction going on outside, had been hidden from the violence committed against her race. Who'd been taught submission as a method of survival; who'd been passed the slave mentality. '[T]he Waymon way was to turn away from prejudice and to live your life as best you could,' she noted, 'as if acknowledging the existence of racism was in itself a kind of defeat.'[3] Only submission to the system and hard work remained as the keys to their hopes.

She listened to her teachers' lessons and saw the lies of her mother and the Church and the whites' deceitful words blown away one by one. Because, in just a few months, Nina Simone learned of all of the violence and deceit perpetrated by America, everything it had tried to hide from its black livestock, the misdeeds it had committed trying to restrain them by force for four hundred years. But now, Langston said, but now a wind of revolt was rising in that land, the 'place of the crime'. A wind that was rising in Alabama and blowing through to the avenues of New York, that was pushing from all over the South and was resonating in grey Chicago. Baldwin prophesied that the fire would spread yet further, swearing: 'I know what the world has done to my brother and how narrowly he has survived it.' What would be the price of revenge now? Fire.

As Baldwin observed her, she didn't dare whisper her response, as war was a path that she could not yet envisage. Nina was on the front line, selected by a handful of black intellectuals whose impact on the community, as well as on the white community which was prudently reading the condensed version of that literature, remained secret. He knew they needed a spokesperson who would add a common touch to their political rhetoric, to represent their ideas. This girl could be just what they needed. After all, had this black pianist not been selected by the ASAC to represent black Americans in Lagos? Was the entire country not watching her career? Was she not considered to be like Duke Ellington, Sarah Vaughan, Billie Holiday and Miles Davis, one of the great black American music creators? In short, was Nina not the perfect example, both physically and artistically, of the very essence of noble, dignified, sophisticated Africanness, and above all, American?

The Lagos concert took place in a city-centre stadium before a human tide whose like Nina had never seen. The cultural shock that she went through, and the certainty that the forces surrounding her were benevolent and familiar, grasped her like a revelation. She was a member of an ancient line. She would later learn, in very dark times following a mystical experience, that her ancestors came from a land at the heart of the ancient kingdom of Dahomey: Ghana. But for the time being, a certainty was growing in her: she felt that she carried a tradition that had been relocated but whose spiritual essence remained intact. Nina Simone was a soul on a mission. The concepts that Jimmy had taught her confirmed her intuition: she was to perpetuate and defend (by any means necessary?) her race, her culture, the thread coming from that land, which had survived the Atlantic crossing to come into being in America, in her.

Christmas 1961. The Strouds' car sweeps down 125th Street, passing run-down houses before coming to more renovated buildings as they approach the Hudson. They cross the river and pass East 138th Street. From the window, Nina Simone can see abandoned buildings followed by a series of social housing projects. The car is headed straight for Park

Avenue, the entrance to the Bronx from 175th Street. From Webster Avenue, the car passes the Botanical Garden, then Williams Bridge, before driving past a cemetery. A couple of miles later, it crosses a sort of no man's land, then the pianist, dozing in the passenger seat, wakes up as they reach the block that separates the middle-class suburbs east of the Hudson. The car comes to a stop at a light above which a sign indicates their arrival in Mount Vernon East. Starting up again, it heads down Main Street and passes another sign with black letters on a white background bearing the town's coat of arms and motto: 'Proud of our past, building our future.'

The car now enters a maze of residential streets lined with trees. There's a feeling of the countryside – a pretty suburb with lines of discreet villas. The car turns down a thoroughfare that will become Malcolm X Boulevard a few years later, but for now it is Nuber Avenue. Andy parks opposite number 406, a large white house. Exhausted by her twelve-hour journey from Lagos, Nina gets out of the car and looks up at the elegant villa: a three-floor bourgeois residence with a 1.5-hectare garden. All around, fir and cedar trees border her new house's plot in the grey winter light. At the end of the garden sits an old, abandoned garage. In just a few weeks, she will turn it into her workshop, installing her piano on the upper floor. Andy will hire builders to freshen the walls, to insulate the roof, pull up the roots that were eating away at the exterior walls. They will get rid of the profane graffiti on the wooden door, the word 'blood' that some neighbourhood teenager must have scrawled with red paint. Later, Nina would decide that that had been a sign.

From the street, Nina could see a large veranda. Nanny appeared at the window, two of Andy's sons hiding in her skirts, staring at the strange woman holding their dad's hand. Despite the cold, Nanny opened the window and shouted out: 'Look who's here! Your father and your stepmother!' The children didn't say a word, watching their father climb the steps to the house followed by that woman. The mistress of the house greeted the Jamaican nanny, then, without even a gesture to Andy's two boys, followed her husband into the house.

The Strouds set up home in Mount Vernon hot on the heels of their marriage. The house was purchased for $37,000 in cash, a sum that Andy considered very reasonable, even a very good deal. Nina let him get on with it and provided most of the money because she was so happy to see her desire to start a family come true at last. It had been such a long journey from the sad surroundings of Tryon to here! The life they were destined to lead seemed ideal. Even the three children that Andy had from previous marriages weren't an obstacle. She would end up bringing them round and even managed to get herself adopted by them. At weekends, the reconstructed family enjoyed Mount Vernon's surroundings, going on long bike rides in the mornings, crossing the forest next to the town, having picnics in clearings and barbecues in the garden. That was happiness, a just reward, the fulfilment of an idealistic dream.

While his wife was in Nigeria, Andrew Stroud had all of her furniture brought over from her New York apartment and arranged in the Nuber Avenue house. He had also bought all sorts of brand new furniture to decorate the three rooms on the ground floor and the enormous living room, as well as a few things for the garden. Andy had insisted on hiring a gardener and a live-in maid, Nanny, a Jamaican who looked after his children at the weekends and the inside of the house the rest of the week: housework, cooking, washing and parties whenever the young couple decided to throw one. Nina had insisted on the house remaining open to friends, and Max Cohen, Jerry Fields, Langston Hughes and Alvin Schackman would come to visit from time to time, slowly getting used to the new, luxurious surroundings far from bustling New York life.

John Divine also came to visit his daughter when his health allowed. Nina hadn't spoken of his absence at the wedding. In fact, she pretended to ignore his frosty attitude towards Andy, excusing the distance he kept from her husband as paternal jealousy. Meanwhile, Andy tried to avoid all contact with the old man whenever possible and made do with measured politeness, no doubt tired of dealing with the contempt of a father-in-law little inclined to civilities.

John Divine arrived from Philadelphia by train and Nina went to fetch him from Grand Central in Andy's car. He stayed with them for several days, and sometimes, when Andy was busy in Manhattan, he allowed himself the one-on-ones he loved with his favourite daughter. Mary Kate? She would only come on very rare occasions. Only when Nina's daughter was born, at birthdays or special events. And her excuses for declining her daughter's invitations were always the same: very much consumed by her ministry, her responsibilities at the church, her tours in North Carolina. At the beginning of the 1960s, Nina's only source of sadness was her mother's stubborn refusal to take part in her new life, because she was convinced that, despite her career and the outside signs of her success, Mary Kate still did not approve of her choices, her life, even of her marriage and friendships.

Nevertheless, her daughter was on her way to becoming a respected personality, promoted by major figures within their community.

That was no mystery to anyone in the Village. Nina Simone was under the wing of Harlem's two great poets: James Baldwin and Langston Hughes. These leaders of black American intellectual life had taken note of her and were initiating Nina in the history of her own culture. They were the ones who had contacted the Lagos festival's organizers so that their protégée could take part in the trip. Langston and Baldwin observed Nina's reactions in Africa, her uneasiness faced with the culture that she was discovering, her attraction to and instinctive understanding of the musical codes and rituals with which all three had been confronted. They noted the intensity she had shown during her concert in the Nigerian capital. In that moment the two men understood that the art and personality of this woman were perfect for their cause, that on stage she might even be able to embody its essence. Did they see the necessary strength in this woman for her to become the messenger? Back in New York, they continued with their friend's political education; the recent disruption that had taken place in the USA gave their teachings a particular resonance.

One name had been on everybody's lips in the black community since 1955 and the beginning of the Montgomery transport boycott: Martin Luther King, Jr. That young Baptist pastor had made the State of Alabama bend after a year of boycotting, when a court ruled racial segregation on Montgomery public buses illegal. For many, Dr King had achieved a great feat; for everyone he was the leader that the blacks could follow to shake off injustice and humiliation. Had he not declared: 'A people without the right to vote is a people without power'?[4] For everyone, at the beginning of the 60s, that man was the leader of the ranks, who would lead the black people towards obtaining the right to vote, an essential condition in their hope to play a role in American society and an enormous step towards autonomy. That's why Martin Luther King had faced the opposition directed at him.

However, white terrorism appeared at the very beginning of 1957. During the night of 11 and 12 January, a series of attacks had wrecked Montgomery's black neighbourhoods and four black churches had been damaged.[5] On the morning of the 27th, twelve sticks of dynamite where found in front of the Kings' front door in Montgomery. From that moment on, the leader of the black community would have to confront his destiny, he would no longer have any respite.

He went to Accra for Ghana's declaration of independence by President Kwame Nkrumah in March 1957, becoming aware of the ravages of colonization and the similarities between colonialism and racial segregation and white supremacist ideology.[6] He realized that African-Americans had much to learn from their African cousins who had been able to resist the Europeans and who, profoundly marked by Marcus Garvey and W.E.B. Du Bois's Pan-African thinking after Nkrumah, had been able to triumph against the oppressor. Marcus Garvey was a Jamaican journalist who in 1917 had created the Universal Negro Improvement Association in Harlem with the aim of repatriating the black population of America to Africa. 'All black people across the globe, in America and in Africa, are part of a single race,' he taught, 'a single culture, and have to be proud of the colour of their skin. All of Africa must be independent and united: Africa for the Africans!'

Upon his return, Martin Luther King would declare 'the time has now come to raise our heads' because when men fight for justice and their rights, God is by their sides. In 1958 in Miami, he made his potision clear in a speech: 'We want the right to vote now. We do not want to be fed liberty from a teaspoon for another hundred and fifty years.'

On 23 June, black leaders met with President Eisenhower. Until that time, with the notable exception of Booker T. Washington after the First World War, few representatives of the black community had been allowed to meet with the head of state.[7] That was a historic day, marking a change in the balance of power. Martin Luther King and his delegation were given the opportunity to express to the highest powers in the land the need for blacks to be integrated into American democracy. On 3 September, King attended the trial of his loyal trail companion Reverend Ralph Abernathy, who had been accused of being a white woman's lover. Dr King was arrested for loitering when trying to enter the courtroom to support his friend. He was seized and arrested by police officers in the glare of photographers' flashes. However, King had understood that his stays in prison were a way of mobilizing his community's attention and the sympathy of 'progressive' whites. For him, going to jail was an emancipating, liberating act. He was irreversibly committed to this fight; he knew that no one could control the flow of events, but that the only possible route allowing him to become fully absorbed by them was non-violent resistance, because 'nonviolence feeds an atmosphere in which reconciliation and justice become possible'.[8]

Martin Luther King was tried on 5 September 1958 by the judge who had presided over the court that found Rosa Parks guilty. The same Rosa Parks whose arrest three years earlier had set off the Montgomery campaign. The sentence came down: the pastor was sentenced to a fine of $10 plus $4 in legal fees and fourteen days in prison.[9] 'I have come to see that America is in danger of losing her soul and can so easily drift into tragic Anarchy and crippling Fascism. Something must happen to awaken the dozing conscience of America before it is too late,'[10] King declared.

A few weeks later, in a department store in New York, the mentally disturbed Izola Ware Curry stabbed King with a letter opener, which brushed his heart. After an operation in Harlem Hospital, he needed three months of convalescence before he was well again.[11] On 2 February 1959, he flew off to Delhi with his wife, Coretta King. In India he met Nehru and Mahatma Gandhi's disciples. During the trip, he came to understand that India had been on a long journey since its independence in 1947. It was in India that he became aware that his sermons based on love and self-sacrifice would not change society. He realized that love was not enough to combat political power, that a step into action was required, but that only non-violence could achieve a meaningful result. He finally understood that he had to draw up the masses against injustices, and that he would only be heard by economic and political authorities by bringing all his weight to bear on the electoral chessboard.

In February 1960, when Martin Luther King's protest sit-ins were taking place in Greensboro, North Carolina (a phenomenon that would soon be taken up across the South), he was accused of tax fraud by the State of Alabama. Tax fraud, America's favourite weapon against dissidents. Had Marcus Garvey's ambitions not already been wiped out using this weapon when he had just bought lands in Liberia and was planning to repatriate his people there?

But Martin Luther King scorned his legal troubles: people were already emulating his way of working. In April 1960, a black student union inspired by King, the SNCC (Student Nonviolent Coordinating Committee), was established. In a few months, it would play a central role in the movement's seemingly unstoppable push. Reverend King's calls were heard, his impact on the black community was unparalleled. Public enemy number one for some, King was also a leader worth cooperating with – his voting instructions for the presidential election of November 1960 may have been decisive.

'In the United States,' the rock writer Greil Marcus told me, 'the Republicans are the party of Lincoln, who fought against slavery. That's why the majority of blacks voted Republican at the beginning of the century. It wasn't until Roosevelt's arrival in 1932 that the black community gave its vote to the Democrats. Until then, the Democrats were the enemies of the blacks' freedom in the USA and only the Republicans had fought for their rights.' In June, Reverend King was officially received by the Democratic presidential candidate, John Fitzgerald Kennedy.

Nixon was defeated by a small margin on 8 November 1960 and it was under Kennedy that the first freedom rides would take place in the southern USA, pacifist marches for liberty that were welcomed by the most reactionary states with a flood of violence. However, under pressure from these actions, desegregation was proclaimed in interstate transport. A few months later, in 1962, James Meredith would become the first black student to enrol in the University of Mississippi.

A black social revolution was under way. Dignified, proud, stubborn and non-violent. In this new chapter in America's history, the black community could hope for an unstoppable step forward towards obtaining their civil rights. 'We Shall Overcome'[12] became the battle hymn when John Edgar Hoover, the FBI and Southern authorities appeared to be putting everything in place from the wings to wreck the movement at the beginning of 1962.

In January 1962, Nina Simone's prayers were answered. She was pregnant. Andrew Stroud greeted the news with enthusiasm, praying for it to be a girl. The couple swam in their new-found happiness, so much so that Andy gave up his job with the police to devote himself to his wife. After months of patiently listening to her complain that she had no one to trust at her side, he became her full-time manager, with a plan mapped out for her career. He'd learned a lot from sitting at the foot of the stage every night during his fiancée's stint at the Village Gate, observing all the business dealings. One evening, Andy told his wife he wanted to leave the police, saying that living in two different professional worlds would harm their marriage, and that in any case he didn't want that life any more. He explained that he could help her a great deal, that in fact he was already well versed in the world of show business and that her dealings weren't all that different from the business he'd been confronted with during his career as a cop in Harlem. Stroud knew the world of the night well, and he knew exactly how to get what he wanted. Andy wasn't the type of guy that a promoter could impress. Better yet, he knew more than anyone about club gangsters and their intimidation, physical threats, blackmail and violence. There was no late payer that could get round him, no negotiation that he couldn't win. Furthermore, before he became an inspector, Andy had graduated from university in management, and by taking care of Nina's interests he'd also be looking after his family. She was thrilled to accept his proposal. Andy didn't have to insist. Blinded by her love and impressed by her man, Nina put her husband-manager forward in January 1962.

From the very first few weeks, Andy took his role very seriously. He met with the bigwigs at Colpix and scrutinized every contract, completely immersing himself with Max Cohen in the nitty-gritty of the music business to understand how it worked. Andrew Stroud built a new strategy for his wife's career. It was at this time that Jerry Fields disappeared from the scene; we can't be sure whether Andy fired him or whether Fields realized that the wind had turned against him and it was time to leave with his head held high.

So Andy was her husband and manager – a system that can be found here and there throughout the history of music. It was the same with Maria Callas, wife of Giovanni Battista Meneghini, an Italian industrialist who became the manager of the 'first artist of the century'.[13] After her separation from her husband, Maria had these bitter words: 'He wasn't a husband, he was a businessman. He wanted to profit from my glory. That's why we're no longer together.'[14] Nina would follow in Maria's steps.

For now she was pregnant and surely needed some room to breathe, concentrate on her pregnancy, take advantage of the tranquillity of the Mount Vernon house. But Andy didn't see things like that. Maybe he knew that Nina could aim higher that what Colpix, whose influence was limited to the USA, had to offer. He wanted to step up the pace and reminded Nina that her contract with the record label required her to deliver a new album for the beginning of 1962. The album would be *Nina Sings Ellington*, a homage to Duke, a true monument of American music whom she was soon to meet. The album was released during Nina's eighth month of pregnancy. In fact, Andy had her working until the final six weeks before she gave birth. The couple's entourage was shocked and reminded Andy that for Nina to keep working with the same intensity so late in the pregnancy was risky to her and the baby's health. Nevertheless, Andy found the right words and told his wife that it would be crazy not to concentrate on her work in spite of her pregnancy, that the months to come would bear the fruits of all of those years of effort. That their goal was now within reach. Just inches away. She listened to him.

On 12 September 1962, three years to the day after her first concert at Town Hall, Nina Simone gave birth to her daughter. The baby was born late and the labour was difficult. Andy was overjoyed. In remembrance of his daughter who had died a few years earlier due to accidental poisoning, he gave the child the same name: Lisa Celeste. So the girl's fate was foreshadowed, promising a life worthy of Greek tragedy.

Nina rested in a New York hospital for three weeks before the Stroud family returned to their Mount Vernon home, where Rose Steward, a wet-nurse hired to feed and take care of the child full-time, was waiting for them. Despite Nina's begging, Andy refused to let her breastfeed their daughter. Nina, the loudmouth of the town, the terror of any venue she performed in, had become a submissive wife to the demands of her man. Andy was now in control of every aspect of her life. He was the husband, the father, the manager, the business executive. Andrew Stroud was the embodiment of the image of the African male's virility and authority. The man who gives his wife orders, who takes decisions and makes choices for her without her having any input. This power mechanism within their marriage obviously affected Nina's career, which he was currently running. Whenever, despite everything, she tried to make him loosen his grip, contradicting his choices or bringing up her constant tiredness, Andy would remind her that it was no longer just her career that was in play. That they were a business, that the decisions that had been taken were in the interest of her career and family.

Andy surely didn't realize, so transfixed as he was with his task of managing, but Nina's relationship with music had changed. Resting at the hospital, she came to understand just how deeply Lisa's birth had shaken what used to be certain. Classical music had quietly left her life. Her dreams of being a concert performer were now far away, once more out of reach. In any event, she knew that she no longer had either the time or the motivation to regularly work on her piano. 'That intense young black girl who once burned with an ambition to play in front of an orchestra at Carnegie Hall was now a wife and mother with a career to take care of and employees and their families to support.'[15] Because Andy had been busy. He had set up a publishing company in his wife's name, hired a secretary, an assistant, was in regular contact with Colpix and was getting to know the music business's ins and outs.

In January 1963, after their first Christmas in Mount Vernon, the Strouds embarked on a cruise to Acapulco, just the two of them. That would be Nina Simone's last holiday for ten years; coming back to New York, she started preparing her great stage comeback, planned for spring.

The comeback took place on 12 April 1963 in Carnegie Hall. In the 'hall of halls' Nina returned to her public, but above all, she reached an artistic turning point. That evening saw her mourn her classical music dream and the death of the variety singer that she had become in the eyes of the public after *The Amazing* and *Live at Town Hall*. The artist treading this stage was different: a pianist freed from her demons and a woman who had been profoundly marked by motherhood. With classical music now out of her life, her career took up a path that would lead Nina to bloom and win growing success.

At Carnegie, Nina played a mix of popular pieces reinterpreted using her classical training. John S. Wilson, a *New York Times* columnist, wrote the following about this pivotal concert: 'Miss Simone seemed totally absorbed by the atmosphere of the moment. She has a way of being so relaxed and loose that as she performs her pieces she is able to cross through several degrees of dramatic intensity at will. Miss Simone has a very developed sense of the dramatic and of contrast, as when she plays a popular song with a primitive, repetitive and sensual rhythm. She's a highly talented animal on stage, with a great sense of how to give a show, that is why even when her ideas are not a success – which can happen – it is interesting to follow the wanderings of her audacious imagination.'[16] She opened with a mournful bolero: 'Black Swan', in which, at the pinnacle of her art form, she purged her music of all tricks, retaining only the basic colours, carrying her naked melodies to the limits of drama. She played the instrumental themes from *Samson and Delilah* and *Sayonara*, opening the latter with a whispered invocation to a mysterious force. She also played songs from her albums, including 'If You Knew', 'The Other Woman', and Duke Ellington's 'Cotton Eyed Joe'.

Nina Simone's concert at Carnegie Hall was a triumph, extended a few months later by the release of a record through Colpix. With this live album, the pianist would enter a new phase in her career: the richest phase, mixing artistic urgency and audacity.

But after her successive triumphs, she had to deal with a life of routine. Andrew reminded her every day: 'We have to capitalize on your success, never allow you to fall out of the public eye, you have to be everywhere, on tour and in record stores.' It's undeniable that his pugnacity and acute understanding of business – as well as his faith in Nina as an artist – helped her break through a decisive turning point and confirm her art with authority. Nina Simone would recognize this fact during the last years of her life: 'Without doubt, Andy was the best business man I ever had.'[17] Stroud had a very clear vision of business, his manoeuvres and methods. He was an intelligent guy who worked furiously, concentrating all his efforts on his wife's career – could Nina hope for better? And she didn't contradict his decisions. Not yet. When Andy told her that she had to think long-term, that she should commit to a major promotional tour across the entire country, she set out straight away on an eight-month journey covering nearly every large American city. Promotion, interviews with journalists, meeting fans, a concert every evening, a hotel, bad food, then the next day the same thing all over again somewhere else. Nina came out the other end exhausted. She was barely back in Mount Vernon and had been able to enjoy just a few days of rest and a few rare moments of time shared with her daughter when Andy was setting her a hectic new schedule: a new studio album, rehearsals, tour, special gala events, TV appearances, interviews... and the build-up of fan mail to go through...

Sometimes she would crack under the strain, complain about not having enough time with her daughter Lisa, about not having seen her New York friends in ages, about not even having the time to visit her father in Philadelphia any more. On these occasions Andy would calm her down, using his diplomatic talents to best advantage and promising her that one day they would live like royalty and not have to work any more. There was that blackboard in the kitchen in Mount Vernon on which Andy had written 'Nina will be a rich black bitch by...' and a changing deadline. That made her laugh, but above all, she let herself be convinced. Because, if money was their promised land, for Nina it was also a guarantee of the Waymons' family love. From the first months of their marriage, it had been agreed that a cheque would be sent to Nina's parents once a month. John Divine didn't have a regular job any more and Mary Kate was looking after the home on her own. However, those cheques would not win the young woman her mother's love. She still did not accept Nina's choices, had not encouraged her success and refused to support it. Though she continued to ignore her daughter, she accepted her money anyway. But from that to expressing any sign of gratitude...

Overloaded with work and obligations, and feeling increasingly cut off from the world, Nina also began to realize that life at home was wearing her out. Had disenchantment set in so early? There's a photo that must be from around this time. Andy, in the foreground, stares straight at the camera with a mean look; Nina, by his side with straightened hair, looks absolutely mad with rage. She's holding baby Lisa in her arms. Two of Andy's sons sit at the end of the bench. One of them sports a show-off smile. The photo was taken in their garden, probably at some point in 1964, and the least we can say is that Nina doesn't exactly look to be enjoying a gentle life.

After two years of marriage, the Strouds already had no life together as a couple and few memories that were not linked to Nina's career. Something was stirring in her. Her crises of doubt were back and she was tired, nothing could shake her tiredness. Her marriage had become a source of unhappiness and she was never a woman with Andy, she was always an artist. The professional side of things had encroached upon their marriage so much that it was suffocating it. Their sex life was minimal or non-existent. Andy would disappear for days at a time. He'd come home late and she would ask him questions; he just didn't answer. Her nerves would get the better of her but he remained stubbornly silent. Each time she would lose, and start crying. Finally, spending so much time away from her daughter, she was not the best mother. She would later tell him: 'I wasn't able to bring Lisa up right.'[18]

Andy didn't see anything wrong, he was too busy running the company he had created around his wife, and that company was doing very well. Several business organisations had been set up and held the earnings from concerts, royalties, publications, different contracts. The last tour had earned comfortable profits. Andy opened a permanent office in New York, on 5th Avenue, where a press rep, business administrator and a few other assistants were on the books. Max Cohen was still taking care of legal matters. By 1963, thirty-seven people were making their living through Nina Simone, so when she threatened to take a break because of exhaustion despite his better judgement, Andy made sure to remind her that she was 'responsible for an entire team'. Feeling guilty, she got back to work.

Nina was dependent on him for everything. Andy signed contracts in her name, received payment of her cheques and royalties. She didn't have the time or the interest to follow her business affairs closely. In fact, she had no idea how much she was worth and didn't even have a bank account in her own name. Whenever she needed money, she had to ask her manager of a husband for it.

Still, there was no reason to be worried: Andy had made Nina and co. a flourishing business, and that would go on. After all, she lacked nothing and her schedule was full for the next twelve months.

It was because of the Montgomery bus boycott, the result of which was a US Supreme Court ruling declaring segregation on the state's buses illegal, that Nina because aware of the power of collective action for the first time. Her friends Langston Hughes and James Baldwin had taught her about the issues at stake in the fight for civil rights, but she had never imagined that she would play a role.

Throughout her life, few women figured in Nina Simone's entourage. But it was a woman who made her dive into the action at the beginning of the 60s. Lorraine Hansberry was a figure in the intellectual life of the Village. She was the first black author to meet Broadway success. That came in 1958 with the play *A Raisin in the Sun*, which spoke of the different conflicts within a black family and for which she received the New York Drama Critics' Circle Award, the first time this award had been given to such a young woman, and black to boot. This committed intellectual, close to Martin Luther King, was to become Nina's last mentor.

The two women met in the Village at the end of the 1950s. They struck up such a strong friendship that Lorraine became Lisa's godmother. She lived on the banks of the Hudson, about ten miles from Mount Vernon. Meeting Lorraine was decisive for Nina Simone. History doesn't record how Andy Stroud took this friendship, but what Lorraine was preaching seemed likely to extend a shadow over the projects that Andy had built up for his wife's career. Deeply committed to the civil rights movement, Lorraine sought to instruct Nina Simone in the condition of blacks in the USA. She spoke to her about revolution, politics, Marx, Lenin, class struggles and civil rights. 'Lorraine... saw civil rights as only one part of the wider racial and class struggle. She... told me over and over that like it or not I was involved in the struggle by the fact of being black'.[19] That was the decisive argument.

Lorraine taught Nina about their race's history from the very beginning. She had her read about the great African civilizations, highlighting the fact that they existed when Europe was still deep in the 'darkness of ignorance'. She taught her about Egypt, about the kingdom of Dahomey, the 'Black Sparta squeezed between the Yoruba tribes of present-day Nigeria and the Ewe tribes of Togo'.[20] Nina learned that slave trafficking between the west coast of Africa and America had lasted for four hundred years. Four hundred years of round-ups organized by whites, sometimes with African and Arab complicity. That 'Millions (the estimates differ – fifteen to thirty million people) were captured and shipped under horrendous conditions across the Atlantic. . . in the course of such a journey (which lasted two to three months) nearly half the slaves routinely died of hunger, asphyxiation, or thirst... Those who survived were later put to work on sugar and cotton plantations in Brazil, in the Caribbean, in the United States, building the riches of that hemisphere.'[21] That that traffic hadn't officially ended until the second half of the nineteenth century. She also learned how hope had survived despite the violence.

Lorraine told Nina the story of Nat Turner, a rebel slave at the head of a band which, in 1831, spread terror in southern Virginia. During their escape, they massacred fifty-seven Quakers. Once captured, Turner was hanged in public on 30 October. Yet his blood could not redeem the first trauma felt by white society on their own land, and with just cause. White America's repugnance towards considering Africans as human beings had excluded the eventuality of such a drama. Since Nat Turner, the ghost of a murderous black, choosing freedom despite his assured death, has haunted white Americans to this day.

Turner's bloody escape resulted in the creation of a concentration camp like society in which each white in Southern territory controlled 'their' black. The black population was no longer allowed to assemble in large groups and their presence in churches was strictly controlled. Reading and writing was prohibited, leading to organized and underground disobedience.

When, in 1859, the ship *La Clotilde* unloaded its slaves for the last time in the port of Mobile in Alabama,[22] the South seemed ready to sink into interracial violence. Humiliated by its rout in the American Civil War, appalled by the adoption of the Thirteenth Amendment to the Constitution on 6 December 1865 ('Neither slavery nor involuntary servitude, except as a punishment for crime whereof the party shall have been duly convicted...'), the South stoked up and directed its hate against a black population judged responsible for the defeat. According to LeRoi Jones, 'Two hundred years of bending to the will of the white man had to leave its mark... indelibly on the very foundations of the new separate black society.'[23]

Soon, under the presidency of the ex-general Ulysses S. Grant, elected in 1868 in place of Andrew Johnson, who was considered incompetent and devoid of charm, the 'carpetbaggers' invaded the South. These white immigrants from the North were profiteers without scruples. They exploited the ex-slaves' naivety, pitched the blacks against the whites, took control of the Southern states, bought devalued properties and stole public money. Their rise to power would allow a visceral racism to appear, taking the place of the paternalism shown by the slaves' former masters,[24] the Uncle Tom syndrome about which Abiodun Oyewole, leader of the black activist group The Last Poets, declared: 'I hate to say it, but Tom was a good idea at the beginning. He lived with the master, was trusted by him, he had the keys to the house. The real Tom shared the same religion, the same clothes, the same customs as his master but he knew he was African.'

With the arrival of the carpetbaggers, brutality took on a new face in the South, that of secret societies composed of ex-Confederate soldiers such as those who swelled the ranks of the Ku Klux Klan, to which the lynching and death of four thousand blacks was attributed between 1866 and 1914. Their goal? '[F]righten Negroes into abandoning their newly won rights, particularly the right to vote, and in a great many cases these attempts succeeded.'[25] Faced with this horror, a large number of Southern blacks accepted the idea that the only way for them to survive was the submission and segregation imposed upon them. During this period, the South became the 'scene of the crime',[26] a militarized territory where the law was used to institute a racial segregation regime that seemed 'normal and unavoidable'.[27] By the Jim Crow laws, 'the blacks of the South were submitted to complete political and educational discrimination... Jim Crow attacked almost all aspects of black social and professional life.'[28]

Systematic lynching appeared, organized programmes like Sunday activities. More than 150 happened every year between 1882 and 1901.[29] These are the 'pastoral scenes' that Billie Holiday sang about in 'Strange Fruit'. ('What's a pastoral scene, Miss Holiday?' 'It's when Quakers cut off your balls and put them in your mouth, that's what it is!'[30])

But the rumour grew, whispering in her gravelly voice, that the Underground Railroad, a secret train organized by smugglers, would remove the blacks from their nightmare and take them to the North, to Chicago or Detroit, where an industrial future was fast developing that promised a job and a better life for all. ('It seems a white hit a black up there in the North, so the black laid in at him, he quickly got the better of him, and it seems no one did anything.'[31]) The Underground Railroad echoes in the blues songs Charlie Patton and Robert Johnson recorded in the 1930s. For the bluesmen, it represented what outer space would symbolize for the jazzmen of the 60s and then their funk (George Clinton and others) and techno descendants: a symbol of freedom, a synonym of hope, a bridge leading out of pain and perhaps a way to save your skin. From Son House to John Coltrane, the Underground Railroad became engraved in the black American awareness as an exit from the horror.

The girl who was brought up sheltered and protected from the fears of her community's destiny was now, thanks to Lorraine, discovering a history she knew nothing about. James Baldwin taught her that 'As all of American society places black people's existence in question, we have to place the existence of that society in question. In response to absolute oppression, [I] call for absolute revolt.'[32] As, he said, 'A people from whom everything has been taken away, including, most crucially, their sense of their own worth, will do anything to get it back.'[33] Including revolution. Including descending into violence when no other solution will do.

On 12 April 1963, when Martin Luther King and other pastors were arrested and imprisoned in Birmingham, Alabama, where they had come to protest against segregation in public buildings, Lorraine called Nina Simone. Her argument was decisive: 'What are you doing for the movement while its leaders are in prison?' That night, Nina was performing in Chicago. For the first time, while King was writing the Letter from Birmingham Jail (in which he once again set forth the importance of non-violence and the motives that had pushed him to organize the campaign in Birmingham),[34] the pianist placed her status, her repertoire and her art at the disposal of the movement to which she was irresistibly drawn.

After the Birmingham campaign – which saw schoolkids join the movement's ranks in May and a series of confrontations between the protesters and police forces, reinforced with fire hoses and police dogs – a biracial agreement was signed on 10 May between the Southern Christian Leadership Conference (SCLC) and the authorities. The agreement aimed to put an end to discrimination in public institutions, increase job offers for blacks and free the protesters who had been thrown in prison.

On 11 May a bomb exploded in front of the Reverend A.D. King's house, Martin's brother, then a second explosion devastated Martin Luther King's headquarters at the Gaston Motel. As a reprisal, black students rioted in Birmingham. Two hundred and fifty police officers were summoned to restore order.

On 20 May 1963, the Supreme Court declared Birmingham's segregation ordinances unconstitutional. From that moment on, for King, the battle was to 'keep up the pressure on the Kennedy brothers, whose priority was to maintain racial peace to the detriment of equality'.[35] He proposed a march aimed at pressuring Washington into enacting a civil rights law. The march, planned for August 1963, would be about jobs and freedom. On 11 June, confronted by Governor Wallace's refusal to apply desegregation in the University of Alabama, President Kennedy publicly stated his intention to present a civil rights bill to Congress: 'The events in Birmingham and elsewhere have so increased the cries for equality that no city or state or legislative body can prudently choose to ignore them... We face, therefore, a moral crisis as a country and a people.'[36]

The South's response wasn't long in coming. In the hours following Kennedy's declaration, Medgar Evers, the local secretary of the NAACP, was assassinated when a bullet was fired into his head on the steps of his home in Jackson, Mississippi. During the trial of Byron De La Beckwith, accused of the murder, the state's governor entered the courtroom and walked up to the accused to shake his hand. Beckwith left the court a free man. He would be condemned to life imprisonment at his third trial in 1994.[37]

The murder of Evers was but the first in a long line of political assassinations that would soak the country in blood until 1971. The targets? The movement's activists, whites and blacks alike, but also politicians and those working to achieve desegregation in the Southern states, with the Kennedy brothers on the front line.

It was Medgar Evers's assassination that made King decide to officially announce the project of a march on Washington from Birmingham on 20 June 1963. Two hundred and fifty thousand protesters were expected. King wanted 'to make a forceful demonstration of non-violence and mobilize the population beyond the black community',[38] and thus demonstrate that the civil rights law was something that white Americans and religious groups wanted too.

Tensions began to appear between the NAACP and the SNCC, and Kennedy began to fear that things would get out of hand. The march on Washington took place on 28 August 1963 in an electrified climate. More than 250,000 people, a quarter of them white, responded to the Reverend King's call. America's television channels broadcast the event live, offering America the spectacle of a multiracial protest peacefully invading the capital's gardens. Martin Luther King appeared to read his speech, but chose to digress to a topic he had already used during the previous months, notably in Birmingham in April, then in Detroit two months later: *I have a dream.* The power and sentiment of King's words, the historical significance of that day, that immense crowd stretched out before him from the Lincoln Memorial to the Washington Monument, it all came together to provoke an emotional shock of an intensity never seen before. '[W]e will be able to speed up that day when all of God's children – black men and white men, Jews and Gentiles, Protestants and Catholics – will be able to join hands and sing in the words of the old Negro spiritual: Free at last! Free at last! Thank God Almighty, we are free at last!' Because, Martin said, armed with such faith, 'we will be able to hew out of the mountain of despair a stone of hope'. His ovation was enormous. The impact it had on American society was unprecedented.

Standing behind his lectern, Martin Luther King reeled off the demands his community were making of white America: A civil rights law and a school desegregation law, a public employment programme for blacks, a minimum wage of $2, a council of federal judges to investigate employment discrimination. Because, for the black leader, the economic exploitation of blacks and the respect of their economic and social rights had become just as important as political equality.[39]

After his speech, in the eyes of Hoover, the powerful head of the FBI, King became 'the most dangerous Black for the future of the country in terms of communism'.[40] The champion of non-violence had just signed his own death warrant.

Nina Simone was thoroughly disgusted to hear of Medgar Evers's assassination on 11 June 1963. That murder affected her like a detonator. She had watched King's declaration on TV during the great march on Washington at the end of August, and felt guilty about not joining the protesters – all of her time was taken up preparing a new series of concerts at the Village Gate that were due to kick off on 20 September. When, on 15 September, she learned that four little black girls – Denise McNair, eleven, Cynthia Wesley, Carole Robertson, Addie Mae Collins, each fourteen years old – who were getting ready for a service in a black church in Birmingham had been killed by a bomb, and several other children seriously injured, she was overcome by shock. 'Birmingham is becoming *Bombingham*, a citadel of racism and hatred.'[41] Governor Wallace sent his troops in to calm the anger of the black community which had descended upon the streets. A young black man was killed during this intervention. A few days later, the city of Birmingham failed to send a delegation to the funeral of the four bombing victims, not even a bouquet of flowers or a few words of condolence.

Nina was rehearsing in her studio, fitted out on the first floor of her garage, when she heard of the attack and the events that followed on the radio. She also learned that a gang of young white guys had pulled a black off his bike and beaten him to death in the middle of the street, in front of everyone. She was stunned. Hatred washed over her. When Andrew Stroud came to get his wife from her studio at the end of the day, he found her down on the ground on all fours busy collecting scraps of iron.

'What are you doing?'

'I'm making a gun!'

She had been taken over by an uncontrollable need for action and violence: 'I had it in my mind to go out and kill someone,' she explained, 'I didn't know who, but someone I could identify as being in the way of my people getting some justice for the first time in three hundred years.'[42]

On 15 September 1963, Nina Simone crossed a line, crossing over for the first time into the space where her music became a way for her to take part in the fight. Despite Andy's attempts to keep her away from political commitments, she plunged head first into the fight for civil rights. Nina wrote that from that day on, she knew that she would dedicate herself 'to the struggle for black justice, freedom and equality under the law for as long as it took, until all our battles were won'.[43] But what if that victory was never achieved?

On that day, as she sat at her piano, a melody surged from deep within her. In an hour, she composed her first anti-establishment song: 'Mississippi Goddam'. She wrote that 'it erupted out of me quicker than I could write it down'.[44] After that, with a few rare exceptions ('Come Ye', 'Be My Husband'...), all the songs that Nina composed throughout her career would be protest songs for the fight.

'Mississippi Goddam' displayed Nina Simone's talent for creating metaphors about terror in her music. One of the most direct songs she ever recorded, setting aside all mannerisms to take the listener's breath away and go straight through the threatening end: 'You don't have to live next to me, just give me my equality.' Otherwise...

Otherwise she would take up arms and obtain justice herself. And if she couldn't manage it, destiny would take care of America: '"Mississippi Goddam," to me, is a prophetic tune. I believe that America is going to die'. Would it be killed or commit suicide? *'C'est la même chose!'*[45]

In 1968, during her second European tour, Nina Simone declared to the English weekly *Melody Maker*: 'I was beyond angry when I wrote 'Mississippi Goddam'. I was violent. But I'm not constantly violent. Normally I'm like everyone else. But I know that my people need me, and I won't let them down.' Because, beyond the song's nature as a firebrand (notably rejecting non-violence and patience in fighting the battle), 'Mississippi Goddam' represents Nina Simone's full entry into the fight. A fight that would last several years and turn her, from then on, into the movement's singer. 'Mississippi Goddam' was performed and recorded in public at the Village Gate for the first time a few days later. The single was then very quickly released by Colpix. The news began to spread, the song was even the centre of debate among black intellectuals. It sold well, except in the Southern states, which boycotted or censored it because of the offensive 'Goddam'. In a few states the single became known as 'Mississippi XXX'. Some South Carolina retailers even returned their stock to Colpix, having carefully broken each disc in two.

Driven forward as one of the civil rights movement's figures, and having become in the space of one song the muse of a generation of black activists, Nina saw her life's path accelerate. In a few weeks music and politics completely filled her existence, whereas before 'Mississippi Goddam' she was a mere singer submissive to the schedules imposed by her husband-manager. She was now an angry, lucid woman: 'The first thing I saw in the morning when I woke up was my black face in the bathroom mirror and that fixed what I felt about myself for the rest of the day – that I was a black-skinned woman in a country where you could be killed because of that one fact.'[46]

If Nina was plunging, in this way, into the movement, it was also because the career she had built for herself was not enough. Her entry into the fight was that little girl from Tryon's revenge, that little girl who was slapped down by a white music school; the daughter of a mother who spent her life bowing down to injustices; the daughter of a father who almost died of fatigue when his family's survival depended on his work. It was also Nina the mother's entry into politics, a mother who had a frightened look on her face about a world that seemed destined to crush her only daughter. She was an artist screaming for revenge for the suffering endured by her people, now wielding her music like a blade, demanding compensation.

Far from romanticism, Nina's entry into the fight was also that of a woman who had always lived her life on the sidelines of various groups. For several years activists in the black struggle, young people who hoped to see themselves in her, who told her of their admiration, who pushed her to join them in fighting for equality, asked her to become their voice, to speak in their name. They told her that her art was unparalleled, that they adored her for her music, her personality and her strength. The SNCC's activists told her that her music was always present in their meetings right across the country. That in a way, her music had become their soundtrack. They even told her that the only things ever stolen from their offices were her albums! In 1962, when SNCC activists from Howard University, Washington, went to Nashville for a conference, they found that their colleagues from Tennessee also had Nina Simone albums and for the same reasons.

She would be told that in 1964, during an SNCC meeting organized in Atlanta, the Mississippi delegation had suggested pushing the meeting back two weeks to tie in with a Nina Simone performance at the Magnolia Ballroom, and it was agreed. They met, debated and then all went together to hear Nina Simone play. She was flattered by these revelations, honoured to be included in this fight despite herself, to learn that many saw her as a 'committed and anti-establishment' artist.

A married woman wracked with doubt, limited by a restrictive husband, pursued by regrets at not having become the artist she expected to be, Nina Simone found in the movement the key to achieving her independence. She also found in it a sense for her life, a path that allowed her to make her art part of history.

Ideologically, Nina Simone felt close to the SNCC, whose position had slid towards a radical concept of the fight: 'By any means necessary.' She was convinced: 'I knew a time might come where we would have to fight for what was right'.[47] She was ready for that eventuality and had turned her concerts into a veritable platform for the movement. On stage she appeared as an African queen (bulky silver jewellery, braids gathered into a high bun, a silk tunic or a heavy white wool dress), a warrior calling people forward to the armed fight, interrupting her performance to ask how many members of the SNCC (pronounced 'snick') were present. She aimed to incite her audience, to convince them of the validity of taking up the fight.

So far, Nina believed that the music she performed was of an unimportant sort. In her opinion, 'The world of popular music was nothing compared to the classical world'.[48] It wasn't necessary to work as hard and it took so little to make the generally ignorant public happy. When the album The Amazing was released, she had already stated that 'we give them everything they want, the same lyrics and melodies that they already know',[49] thus agreeing with the writer Tristan Tzara, one of the founders of the Dada movement: 'You only like and only listen to what you already like, you bunch of idiots!' he declared at the beginning of 1916 on stage at the Cabaret Voltaire in Zurich. And what a strange coincidence that Nina would echo these words in, 1963, the year that Tzara passed away in Paris.

Nina's artistic change was progressive. Each of her records, each of her appearances on stage opened a little further a musical spectrum whose root remained the dramatic colours of classical music, blues and folk. In her worry to represent the tormented times she was living in as closely as possible, she became the beautiful side of protest songs, delving deeper into her African roots and fighting towards the repertoires of European composers such as Brecht and Kurt Weill. During her last concert at Carnegie Hall, she realized that non-elitist yet sophisticated music could allow her to touch people's consciences. Her music became the vehicle of a goal that was more important than striving for classical perfection. She was dedicated to the fight for her people's freedom, she said, to her historic destiny. Serving a cause, Nina believed that her music and her concerts had taken on a 'value'. She set herself the goal of making her concerts likeable to everyone, understanding that mentalities would change through the movement, but also with the aid of white sympathizers.

Over those years, her music became the exact reflection of those changes, the perfect soundtrack of the events tearing America apart: 'An infusion of pop, gospel, classical, jazz, folk and ballads' that Nina had baptized 'Black Classical Music'. That shocking formula, like 'Black Power' (a term that had yet to appear), aimed to hit white consciences and transmit the 'community' pride of black artists and fighters.

The singer of cross-genre music, the movement's muse, embodying the voice of the oppressed, Nina Simone could finally respond to the reproaches her mother had thrown at her: 'Why do you sing all over the world when you could praise God?' 'To defend the dignity of my people.'

Andy couldn't understand any of it; he was was too busy worrying about his company's health to put any effort into the fight or even to encourage his wife down that path. Maybe he simply wasn't made that way. Up till now he hadn't intervened in his wife's artistic choices. He doubtless understood that she would not accept any incursion in that area. In the future, she would credit him for a handful of songs, most of no great interest, and history records that he was flattered by it. However, the artistic freedom that Andy had conceded to his wife became a subject of discord when Nina released 'Mississippi Goddam'.

Until then she had been an artist who took part in her community's fight, but hadn't taken on the American establishment head-on. But there it was. 'Mississippi Goddam' left no room for doubt. It was a direct song – of which there were very few at the time – denouncing the hypocrisy of the government and American public opinion. 'Everybody knows about Mississippi Goddam!' she sang. And yes, everyone did know. But Andy didn't see anything good coming from a fuss like this. He knew that, over the long term, uproar wasn't good for business.

Since the controversy around the release of 'Mississippi Goddam' and the radicalization of her positions, Nina had become a government target. The CIA had her under surveillance, two agents had even come asking questions at the Juilliard School and the Curtis Institute. They had interrogated Professor Sokhaloff, asking him if he had any proof of a 'rebel uprising' by his ex-pupil. Obviously he didn't.

Nevertheless, government surveillance was soon to be extended because of Nina Simone's friendship with an exiled South African singer living in the USA: Miriam Makeba.

Miriam Makeba began her career in 1952 with the Manhattan Brothers, one of South Africa's most popular groups. In 1956 she released her first great success in the Zulu language, 'Pata Pata'; in 1959 she appeared in *Come Back, Africa*, an underground anti-apartheid film that won her an invitation to Europe. That was where she met Harry Belafonte, that unique black American film and singing star, the idol of women like the hard women of the ghetto. Bob Dylan called him 'a fantastic artist, sang about lovers and slaves – chain gang workers, saints and sinners and children... Belafonte is one of those rare individuals who exudes grandeur, and you would like that to rub off on you. The man inspires respect. He could have chosen an easy path, but he never did.'[50]

Belafonte took Miriam under his wing and brought her with him to the USA. In America, she would become a tireless denouncer of the segregationist regime in South Africa. She would be linked to Marlon Brando and invited to sing at Carnegie Hall for Kennedy's birthday, would publicly denounce the Pretoria regime in 1960 and give a speech in 1963 that would create a lot of interest in the United Nations and lead to her being prohibited from residing in South Africa: 'I call on the

United Nations to use their influence to open the doors of prisons and concentration camps in South Africa, where thousands of my people, men, women, children are currently being held.'[51] An icon in her own country, and a figure in the fight for equality respected by blacks the world over, a magnificent singer who entered the American chart in 1967 with a new recording of 'Pata Pata', Miriam Makeba joined the fight for civil rights in the United States.

The exact conditions of the first meeting between Nina Simone and Miriam Makeba are not clear. According to Nina, they met in the New York club the Blue Angel at a Miriam Makeba concert, while Makeba wrote that the first meeting was at the Village Gate in the presence of Harry Belafonte, Duke Ellington and Miles Davis.

Miriam approached Nina and said that she had heard her music at the end of the 50s on the radio in Johannesburg. Nina was flattered and the women got on well together. Miriam was 'very African', as Nina would write, meaning that she was very relaxed, direct and warm. They would find common positions in everything: politics, cooking, alcohol, men, clothes, and music too. But above all, Miriam was already a legendary figure in the blacks' fight for equality. She would tell Nina about her people's fight in South Africa, the similarities between the conditions of oppressed Africans and those of black Americans: 'I'm living in a new country, but I found the same racism here. In South Africa we call it apartheid. Here, in the South (of the United States) you call it Jim Crow.'[52] Finally, she spoke to her about the crush she had on a young black leader born in Trinidad and brought up in the Bronx who was part of the new generation of students fighting for civil rights and was en route to becoming one of the SNCC's leaders: Stokely Carmichael.

'He was tall, lean, had beautiful skin, bright eyes and a wonderful laughing voice,'[53] Nina wrote. He became a champion off the back of a speech breaking with Martin Luther King's non-violence policy. In so doing, Stokely became a threat to the moderate wing of the movement and the government alike. In 1968, Miriam said this about the man who became her husband: 'He's brilliant but full of passion. That passion makes him angry, and that fury makes him say things that most people take as threats.'[54] And they were right to do so.

Stokely, questioned on television about the movement's advances and the emergence of Black Power, was asked about the message he wanted to send to his people. His response was terse: 'I want to tell them: You would be better taking up arms!' On Miriam Makeba's advice, Nina attended a meeting in a Philadelphia church where Stokely was to give a speech: 'The only problem with non-violence is that we've never been violent. We have always been too non-violent,' he said that night. After his speech, Stokely designated Nina the 'great civil rights singer'. So, at the moment of truth before a gathering of black leaders, she felt inexorably pushed towards fulfilling her mission.

But Nina only had part of her energy and part of her time, because even though she was tempted to respond to all of the requests – that was her nature after all – Andy made sure that he refocused her, giving her life a rhythm in which recording and touring was always going on at breakneck speed.

Despite that, the pianist knew how to stay on the front line and participate in the great stages of the fight. In 1963 she performed with Johnny Mathis at Miles College in Birmingham, at what was the first major non-segregated concert in the South. Threats had been received from white extremist groups. Both the audience and the artists were worried. 'It was a dangerous time. We met many people who were after us,' Nina wrote. 'I was excited by that. I felt more alive than now because I felt needed. I could sing to help my people. It became the mainstay of my life. That's what was most important to me. Not classical piano, or classical music, or pop music, but the music of civil rights.'[55]

Nina Simone had joined the battalion of American artists involved in the fight. Of course, it would be wrong to pretend that she was the movement's one and only great voice. As Solomon Burke, a giant among the giants of soul music, indicated to me: 'All black American artists at that time were involved in the movement in one way or another.' In his recent autobiography, James Brown wrote: 'It was impossible to be on the road at that time without realizing what was happening and without taking part.'[56]

Sam Cooke – without doubt the most important soul singer in history, the inventor of the genre and a decisive influence on black

American music in the 60s – recorded the song 'A Change Is Gonna Come' in 1963, a song said to be influenced by Dylan's 'Blowin' in the Wind'. It was the first great civil rights hymn and propelled Sam Cooke to iconic status. Other songs would follow and take over from Sam Cooke's masterpiece: 'Respect Yourself' by the Staple Singers, 'Back Stabbers' by the O'Jays, 'The World Is a Ghetto' by War, 'Respect' by Aretha Franklin, 'Keep on Pushing' then 'People Get Ready' by the Impressions, 'Power to the People' and 'We the People Who Are Darker Than Blue' by Curtis Mayfield, 'Ball of Confusion' from the Temptations, 'The Klan' by Richie Havens, 'Say It Loud – I'm Black and I'm Proud' by James Brown, 'What's Going On', Marvin Gaye's masterpiece, 'There's a Riot Goin' On' by Sly Stone... The list is just too long. All these artists – who, on the whole, were happy to perform rhythm and blues music aimed at entertaining their audiences for the first part of their careers – would chronicle what was happening, sometimes placing their work, sometimes just a single song, at the service of a cause and thus inciting their audience to take a position in the light of what was happening.

When I interviewed the American writer Greil Marcus in Paris, he recalled a poster he had seen after the death of Ray Charles, advertising a civil rights movement concert in Georgia in 1963. 'The poster was dominated by Ray Charles's name,' he said, 'it was written much bigger than Martin Luther King's. There were lots of other names on the poster, but Ray Charles was put forward as the face of the movement. But Ray Charles wasn't someone who had taken radical political positions in the struggle. He never turned his music into a grandstand for civil rights. Nevertheless, for many American blacks, Ray Charles was perhaps the community's most important artist. He created his own fate, invented his own identity, he brought his *joie de vivre* and his knowledge to millions of people. Didn't that make him the face of civil rights? Didn't the civil rights movement want to see blacks fulfil themselves? Isn't that what Ray Charles did?'

At the time, however, the media and a fringe of activists had taken up the chant together, raising Nina Simone to the heights of the artistic wing of the struggle, to the status of 'the great civil rights singer'. Those journalists who never really knew what box to put Nina and her music in – or how to deal with her ever more common mood swings during interviews – had perhaps found an appropriate label for this unusual artist.

She dived straight into that role, both on stage and in life. From then on, people expected Nina to rage, take aggressive positions, offer up her anger at the slightest opportunity. Was she so wrapped up in her role that she couldn't see its limits? She no longer hesitated before interrupting an Off-Broadway play if she thought the two black actors' roles were humiliating, or halting her concerts to launch into sermons for civil rights, forgetting that her audience was mainly there to listen to her music.

But events were rushing on and everything was getting confused.

On 22 November 1963, following a summer that saw riots break out in Chicago and Philadelphia, President Kennedy was assassinated in Dallas. Lyndon Baines Johnson succeeded him in office. In 1964, while Nelson Mandela and seven other members of the ANC were condemned to life in prison in South Africa for sabotage, treason and conspiracy,[57] the SCLC's campaign was just beginning in St. Augustine, Florida. On 21 June, three Mississippi equal rights activists disappeared. Their bodies were found in August. In July 1964, President Johnson signed the Civil Rights Act, making segregation illegal throughout the United States.

The Gulf of Tonkin incident happened a month later, pushing Congress to authorize Johnson, who was re-elected on 10 November, to send the American army to Vietnam. On 7 February 1965, North Vietnam was bombed. Military escalation followed, symbolized by the deployment of 3,000 marines. 'The conflict in Vietnam is a war where "a people of colour" have been attacked by one of the most powerful countries on the planet. Blacks provided a disproportionate part of the combatants in the conflict, enlisting due to the lack of any other solution for their future. Oppressed at home, black soldiers are going to practise oppression abroad,'[58] Martin Luther King declared in defiance of Johnson's policy and sent a telegram to the President demanding the end of hostilities. Johnson did not listen.

On 10 December 1964, while in hospital in Atlanta, Martin Luther King, *Time* magazine's Man of the Year 1963, learned that he had been awarded the Nobel Peace Prize. He shared out the $54,000 prize with the organizations fighting in the movement. In January 1965 in Alabama the Selma campaign began; on 1 February King was jailed with other marchers. On 10 February 1965, Sherriff Clark ordered his troops to attack the school pupils protesting in the town's streets. With their leaders outside the town, the police attacked lines of schoolchildren with their batons, making them run until they were exhausted.[59] The scene brought back terrible memories of the forced marches of captured slaves. Finally, on 21 March 1965, Dr King headed the march from Selma to Montgomery. The violent atmosphere had reached a peak. The dissensions between the different factions leading the fight were reaching a point of no return. Nevertheless, there was still hope. On 15 March, in a televised address to Congress, President Johnson assured the civil rights movement of his support, ending his speech by taking on one of the civil rights slogans: 'We shall overcome.'

Martin Luther King was at his zenith. The march from Selma to Montgomery was his last great success. Despite an attempt by local police to put down the march, seriously injuring sixty protesters, 3,200 activists joined the pastor and rallied in Selma, passing battalions of soldiers, police officers and whites bearing Confederate flags as they marched. As they entered Montgomery on 25 March 1965 and headed towards the government buildings, the demonstrators' numbers had swelled to 25,000. 'Blacks in Alabama came to exercise their right to protest like any other citizen of the country.'[60] Jim Crow had been destroyed.

On 25 March 1965, Nina Simone cancelled a series of appearances at the Village Gate to participate in the large concert organized following the protest in Montgomery. Andy Stroud, Al Schackman, Langston Hughes and Art D'Lugoff were by her side.

The authorities were informed that a delegation of artists were en route to Montgomery. They sent bulldozers and trucks to block the runway at the airport. The plane that Nina and her team were travelling in was forced to land in Jackson, Mississippi. There they found a single-engine aircraft and managed to reach the St. Jude school on the outskirts of Montgomery. A stage had been erected on empty coffins at one end of the football field. It was raining, the ground was a huge mud pit where 4,000 people were waiting, soaked to the skin, to hear the artists who had come to take part: Harry Belafonte, Leonard Bernstein, Nina Simone. The atmosphere was electric, even paranoiac. A rumour began to spread among the activists that white racists were planning to attack them.

When she came on stage, Nina was confronted with an exhausted audience. She felt her energy intensify and gave an a cappella performance, accompanied only by Alvin's guitar. The audience responded with singing and prayers.

Then the team was led to the hotel and settled into the last available room. Five mattresses had been placed straight on the floor. They were warned: 'Don't get too close to the windows, we're worried that snipers may be waiting.' Outside the building, federal police officers armed with rifles had been charged with protecting the artists playing at the concert.

Despite the success of the Selma-to-Montgomery march, Martin Luther King's influence would start to decline. If non-violence had allowed progressive changes to take place in the South, it didn't meet the reality in the North. In Chicago and Detroit, in the Watts ghettos (where the riots broke out in 1965) and in Newark, economic hardship had worsened and the blacks had been the first victims. Challenged by his own camp, confronted by a violence logic advocated by the SNCC (with Stokely Carmichael at the head), considered a 'bourgeois moralist' by his opponents, or worse, an Uncle Tom by the movement's radical fringe, the Reverend King would see the situation get away from him.

Despite her affinities and links, Nina was not officially part of any doctrine and reached her own conclusions: 'In the whites' world, the blacks always lose. That is why the idea of a separate black nation, in America or in Africa, was defended. I did not believe there was any fundamental difference between the two races. Those who are at the top will use all means necessary to maintain their position, and if black America was in that position of strength, it would wield racism to oppress the whites, just like they did against us.'[61]

Nina did not believe in a pacifist solution; she was convinced that there was no hope of harmony between whites and blacks. In her opinion, the birth of a new society was at stake, and to achieve it, profound changes would have to be provoked in American society. In her view, a black revolution was unavoidable.

Nina's ideas were growing close to those of the Nation of Islam, an organization founded in Detroit in 1932 by the enigmatic W.D. Fard (or Fard Muhammad), which aimed to help black Americans discover their true identity: the sons of Islam, the lost members of the tribe of Shabazz. Since Fard's death in 1934, the group had been led by a mysterious figure, considered a divinity by his disciples: Elijah Muhammad. According to James Baldwin, the mission that Elijah Muhammad had set himself was 'to return "the so-called Negro" to Islam, to separate the chosen of Allah from this doomed nation'.[62] Elijah Muhammad denounced the whites' diabolical nature and prophesied the imminence of their downfall, arguing that God himself was black, and that as a result all blacks belonged to Islam, that they were the chosen ones and that Islam would one day govern the world.

The Nation of Islam advocated the separation of the white and black races. For that they required an official representative, a spokesperson whose stature and spirit embodied the threat that the organization wanted to bring to bear on America. That person was Malcolm X. Along with Marcus Garvey and Martin Luther King, Malcolm X was the most important black leader of contemporary history. If Garvey was the instigator of African unity and the Reverend King the architect of desegregation in the United States, Malcolm X, the heir of Garvey's work, was the champion of black nationalism. He embodied the Nation of Islam's independence and self-defence programme, affirming his distrust of whites. From the mid-1950s, thanks to Malcolm X's mystical rhetoric and his aggressive discourse, the sect's aura had grown exponentially in black ghettos, swelling the ranks of their army and pressing to play a central role in the armed struggle that they foresaw.

The son of a Baptist activist in Marcus Garvey's Universal Negro Improvement Association, Malcolm Little was born in Omaha in 1925. Following the death of his father, who was possibly murdered by whites, he was snatched from his mother and placed in an adolescent detention centre. Taken in by a white woman, he grew up in Michigan and become the very incarnation of the 'good Negro' that America was wild about. He worked in various jobs in Boston, where he straightened his hair and went out with a white girl. In 1946 he was arrested for burglary and sentenced to ten years in jail, which he served in the Charlestown prison. There he was converted to Islam by a Nation of Islam activist. Charismatic, eloquent, brilliant, Malcolm joined the organization upon leaving prison and embraced its separatist thesis, adopting X instead of his 'American' name in 1953. 'Since slave times,' he explained on a TV programme, 'the master would give the slaves working on his property his own surname. X in mathematics means an unknown. To the extent that we have been cut off from our history, our past, our culture, our land, we should use an X, an unknown, until we go back home.' In 1953, Malcolm X became the assistant minister in the Nation of Islam's Temple No. 1 in Detroit, the very temple where the group was born. The following year, by which time the sect had more than 100,000 members in the United States, Elijah Muhammad entrusted him with the task of building temples in New York and proposed him as the organization's official representative in America. With Malcolm X's arrival the Nation of Islam put its political strategy into practice. While the organization born in Detroit at the beginning of the 30s had never been a threat to the American system, by the beginning of the 50s its ranks had taken in thousands of members and it could now attack the very foundations of American society.

In the face of racist violence, the black Muslims of the Nation of Islam used the logic of self-defence, a categorical break with the Christian non-violence policy defended by Martin Luther King. They drew on the social and moral dissatisfaction dominating the black ghettos 'because, Elijah Muhammad said, by making things the worst they can be I will only ever have contributed to the destruction of land that I abhor'.[63] By cutting out King, the Nation of Islam argued for abstention from voting and called for the United States to be partitioned, demanding that the Southern states – the slave states – be handed over to the blacks. White America was shaken. In his essay *The Fire Next Time* (1963), where he described his meeting with Elijah Muhammad, James Baldwin wrote:

> Let us say that the Muslims were to achieve the possession of the six or seven states that they claim are owed to Negroes by the United States as "back payment" for slave labor... then the borders of a hostile Latin America would be raised, in effect, to, say, Maryland... the white people of the United States and Canada would find themselves marooned on a hostile continent, with the rest of the white world probably unwilling and certainly unable to come to their aid.[64]

The Nation of Islam's policy of destabilizing power, represented by black America's most famous figures – including the boxer Cassius Clay, who on the day after his victory over Sonny Liston in 1964 announced his membership of the Black Muslims and took the name Muhammad Ali – had dazzling success in the ghettos. 'The Nation of Islam made Islam appear like the only way out of that dire situation,' James Baldwin noted. 'Those living in ghettos saw the Nation of Islam as children of Islam, disciplined men who weren't breaking any laws. Real (and seductive) demonstrations of force came from that fact and attracted a large number of ghetto inhabitants.'[65]

But why was the Nation of Islam's doctrine managing to affect black Americans now when their leader had been repeating the same message for nearly thirty years? According to James Baldwin, Elijah Muhammad 'has been able to do what generations of welfare workers and committees and resolutions and reports and housing projects and playgrounds have failed to do: to heal and redeem drunkards and junkies, to convert people who have come out of prison and to keep them out, to make men chaste and women virtuous, and to invest both the male and the female with a pride and a serenity that hang about them like an unfailing light. He has done all these things, which our Christian church has spectularly failed to do.'[66] But representing such a threat to a society that was still a concentration camp society came at a price: blood and war, through the death or crucifixion of its leaders, or, worse than death, treason.

Proposed as the organization's spokesperson, Malcolm X placed himself at the centre of the media's attention, becoming a public figure serving a doctrine that openly affirmed its wish to turn America's violence against it ('It is criminal to teach a man not to defend himself when he is the constant victim of brutal attacks,' he said). In the white psyche he became the very incarnation of the black threat. Challenged in his own camp because of his growing popularity – which Elijah worried would overshadow his own authority – in 1963 Malcolm X was ordered to make no further public declarations following the outcry caused by his comment that the assassinated Kennedy 'never foresaw that the chickens would come home to roost so soon'.

Replaced at the head of the organization by Louis Farrakhan, Malcolm left the Nation of Islam and founded his own organization in New York, its goal 'to eliminate political oppression, economic exploitation and the social degradation suffered by twenty-eight million African-Americans'. He wanted to bring blacks of all religions together, and moderated his views. He also created alliances with other black leaders and even accepted the external help of whites. He returned from a pilgrimage to Mecca completely transformed, convinced that 'the true practice of Islam could heal societies of the scourge of racism'. Having become El-Hajj Malik El-Shabazz, Malcolm continued with his action, refining his thinking, attempting to attract new members to his organization. 'Let us practice [brotherhood] amongst ourselves, and if others wish to show us brotherhood, we will accept to do the same unto them. However, I do not believe that we should seek to love those who do not love us.' Malcolm X's last few years, demonized by the press, bankrupt, a target of both the Nation of Islam and the white establishment, were those of a haunted and threatened man. On 14 February 1965, a fire gutted the house in Mount Vernon where Malcolm was living with his wife Betty Shabazz and his four daughters, a few blocks away from Nina Simone. On 21 February 1965, he was assassinated by three members of the Nation of Islam at a meeting in a ballroom in Manhattan.

Why was he killed? One less source of competition among the Muslim factions, according to the American press, given the fact that Malcolm X was openly denouncing Elijah Muhammad's sect: 'All those determined activists have been paralysed by an organization that is not active in any fight. An organization that is only a threat to itself.' Malcolm X was no longer limiting his fight to America, but had broadened it to a general rebellion, of 'the oppressed against their oppressors, the exploited against those exploiting them'. Indeed, there are numerous theories declaring that at the root of his assassination was a vast conspiracy through which the hand of the Nation of Islam was guided from afar by the white establishment; after all, had Malcolm not declared just a few months before his death that 'From 1965 we will be engaged in all levels of politics'?

Nina never met Malcolm X, but she often heard him preach in Harlem at the end of the 50s and then a few months before his death. The day after his assassination, she joined the Committee of Concerned Mothers, a mutual aid group that collected $8,000 to help the widowed Betty Shabazz.

Although she had always felt respect towards Martin Luther King – to whom she had been introduced by Lorraine Hansberry – Nina felt philosophically closer to Malcolm X's political ideas and had taken up his teachings herself: 'You've got to understand... down there they don't need a reason to kill a nigger. They just do it. It doesn't matter if you're minding your own business. If the white man wants to have him some fun, hanging's a sport for him. I know Martin [Luther King] says we need to be non-violent, but there's times I just want to get a gun and shoot somebody, just to get it out of me, you know.'[67]

Nina Simone felt close to the Nation of Islam's separatist ideas, but she would never join, despite the arrival in Mount Vernon of the sect's new head: Louis Farrakhan. One night, during a one-on-one discussion, he tried to convince his hostess about Islam. She made advances on him, but he dodged them, preferring to continue with his rhetoric into the small hours of the morning. 'So he didn't manage to convert me and I didn't convert him,' she would write in her autobiography. In 1975, after the death of Elijah Muhammad, Farrakhan would create a new Nation of Islam, in the same line as the teachings of its founder, but showing itself to be more extremist and openly anti-Semitic.

It wasn't a black revolutionary who would become Nina Simone's 'man of destiny' – 'The man,' in the words of the Ivory Coast writer Ahmadou Kourouma, 'we have to follow to truly fulfil ourselves'.[68] Instead, it was a Dutch businessman weighing three hundred pounds who she met one night, collapsed in his seat at the Village Gate: Wilhelm Langenberg. There are many legends about this story: a run-down reveller, a ruthless businessman whose business sense was only equalled by his huge appetite. But above all, Langenberg, alias Big Willy ('the boss' in slang), was, along with Irving Green, the owner of the major Dutch record label Philips. What made him come in? She nearly shrieked when the stranger declared: 'I'm Wilhelm Langenberg and I've come to take you back to Holland so you can be on the Philips label. I own it.' He explained to her that he had been so dazzled by 'Mississippi Goddam' that he listened to it fifty-two times in a row! He jumped straight on the first plane to New York to offer her a multi-album deal: it would be an excellent contract, the best she could ever hope for, with the promise of international distribution and the money that goes with it. Big Willy was introduced to Andy, who he seduced with talk of Nina's career, facilities, trips to Europe... Neither of them had visited Europe yet. A guy fresh off a plane is offering thousands, offering a contract with such favourable conditions that such a chance might never appear again. Opportunities like that don't come along every day. Nina signed.

The last Nina Simone album Colpix released, without telling her, was *Folksy Nina* in 1964, basically made up of songs recorded at the April 1963 Carnegie Hall concert. Two years later, again without informing Nina, Colpix released the tenth album agreed to in their contract: *Nina with Strings*, a collection of unreleased and available work and other hits to which string arrangements had been added.

Nina Simone's career with Philips began in early 1964. During the three years it would last, the pianist was the only artist to deal with Wilhelm Langenberg directly. Big Willy became a friend, a guide, a guardian angel to her. That man understood the artist's suffering and her role as an activist in the civil rights struggle in exactly the way that Andy understood nothing. 'I guess I loved him,' Nina wrote about her Dutch accomplice; 'he was the greatest friend a person could have.'[69]

In a very short space of time, between April 1964 and August 1966, Nina Simone would record a series of mythical albums for Philips; albums that would propel her career onto the world stage. Her art had reached its peak: subtle, arrogant, moving, charming, violent and mystical all at the same time. Big Willy believed – and he was right – that the best records Nina had made so far were live albums. He wanted to push his protégée forward in Europe, but first he wanted to test the market with a live record. The resulting album was sophisticated and essentially made up of ballads. Eventually, the time would come to release a more personal studio record.

That live album was recorded in New York on 21 March and 1 and 6 April 1964, a very close likeness of her stage show. For the audiences that were just discovering her it was a perfect introduction, for fans it was a beautiful phase in the evolution of Nina's talents. More direct, rougher, more brutal that the concert recorded at Town Hall, a complete break from the sophistication of *Nina at Carnegie*, this first record for Philips was a taster of a radiant and unpredictable artist. *In Concert* was made up of classics ('Porgy', 'Plain Gold Ring', 'Mississippi Goddam'), blues standards ('Don't Smoke in Bed'), newly composed songs ('Go Limp', the advice given to protesters during police assaults), but the memorable and unexpected track that set Nina apart from other active singers was 'Pirate Jenny', a song from Kurt Weill and Bertolt Brecht's *The Threepenny Opera*.

Like Bob Dylan, Nina discovered 'Pirate Jenny' in Marc Blitzstein's adaptation of *The Threepenny Opera* performed at the Theater de Lys in the Village in 1963, and just like him, she was struck by the incredible cruelty of that amoral tale, 'a nasty song, sung by an evil fiend',[70] composed in 1928 by Brecht. She may also have been seduced by Brecht's personality, a Marxist, anti-Fascist irreverent artist who had been banned in his own country for a long time.

'Pirate Jenny' tells the story of a masculine, bitter woman 'consumed from within',[71] employed as a maid in a grotty hotel in the heart of a nightmare port. The song is continuously interrupted by evoking a Black Freighter approaching slowly in the distance. While singing, the maid cooks, washes floors, and makes the beds of the smug gentlemen staying at the hotel. She repeats: 'you'll never guess to who you're talking'. These gentlemen don't take any notice, but they become her prey. Soon the Black Freighter arrives in port and all the buildings collapse except the hotel. That makes the gentlemen wonder, 'Why do they spare that one?' But it's too late. At midday a mass of sailors invade the docks, chain people up and take them to the maid, radiant in her cruelty. They ask her if the gentlemen should be killed now or later. In a deathly silence she answers: 'Right now, that'll learn ya!' Learn them what? For being snobby, for having made the staff slave away in exchange for a miserable tip without a second thought, for representing power. And exactly that, power, is turned on its head. But who is this woman who boards the ship leaving behind a landscape of destruction?

In the first volume of his *Chronicles*, Bob Dylan writes that he would never have had the idea to write (or even known that it was possible) songs like 'It's Alright, Ma (I'm Only Bleeding)', 'Mr. Tambourine Man' and 'Hard Rain's a-Gonna Fall' if he hadn't heard 'Pirate Jenny'. A song of unprecedented hostility, without compromise, a piece that demands that the artist presents their character with absolute assurance, giving the listener an experience as raw as life itself.

Nina would only rarely play that song. It's not because she wasn't satisfied with it: on the contrary, she would later declare that she was particularly proud of it: 'It's a real theatre song. I sang it at Carnegie Hall for the first time... That was a real challenge for me. It's a song full of hate. I don't sing it on stage any more, it's too hard, it saps too much energy.'[72] That song of hate and cruelty, 'Pirate Jenny', was Nina's first incursion into the repertoire of Weill and Brecht, her first direct borrowing from European music, and one of the strangest pieces in her work. The song revealed her theatrical sense, in a twisting path that no other artist of the time would have dared to take. Who else would have had the guts to take on such a monument? Listen to Nina's performance of 'Pirate Jenny', above all, listen to the silences she creates between each of the death threats uttered by her character. No one in Carnegie Hall moved an inch. Did the good people of high society present that night feel directly threatened by Jenny? They would have had good reason. Nina/Jenny didn't spare them. She even went so far as to explicitly threaten them. 'I'm counting your heads, no one will sleep tonight!' she screamed. Her anger must have followed her audience all the way to their beds that night.

That first Philips record had everything, the full range of qualities and colours present in Nina's music. Her virtuosity, the power she gave her words, the balanced fusion of genres, her sense of drama, her beauty, and her ability to hypnotize her audience.

At the beginning of 1964, she was in perfect control of that effect, which she had discovered during her summers spent in Atlantic City. It seemed that that power had always been there, hidden, waiting to be revealed. A real spiritual current flowed from her as she played; those watching could feel that she was in a state of grace. 'It's like being transported in church; something descends upon you and you are gone, taken away by a spirit that is outside of you.'[73] She had the power to move the audience and take it along with her to another level of consciousness. 'What happens is profound, very profound,' she said. It was the feat of a magician able to exercise a magnetic power over her audience, to captivate them, dominate them and hold them in the palm of her hand.

She always followed the same ritual before each concert. She would go to the hall in the afternoon. Standing on the stage, she would look out at where and how the audience would be sat. At what distance. How the rows were set out, how the speakers had been positioned. She would choose the microphones best suited to her voice, and finally she would close herself off and rehearse for a few hours. Then she would join her musicians. She never gave a definitive set list before each concert, preferring to wait to the very last minute. She would walk out on stage, create an atmosphere with her first song and maintain it with those that followed, all while trying to forget the audience, to play for herself, to have a good time until she could feel the emotions coming to a peak. Once she felt that the energy had invaded every member of the audience, that everyone had become an extension of herself, she would stop to judge her impact. Complete silence. She would hold them.

Following a concert in which that magic had worked, Nina declared to Sylvia Hampton, her English biographer: 'The spirits of my African ancestors were there. I could feel them and they really took hold of me... I could see them moving about. I know they got the spirit this time. Shit, it was everywhere, man. Yes, it was deep, man.'[74] She explained the phenomenon as follows: 'I just let the spirits take possession of me... But you know, I expect people to respect me. What I do demands so much of me that they must respect what I do. Sometimes, I sit at the piano and it's as if my hands were playing on their own and I'm just happy to go along... it's like electricity going through me and out into the place. They can feel it, man.'[75]

Everyone I've met who knew Nina Simone intimately, on stage or off, insists on one particular point. Her hypnotic powers were real. In a few months she would be given the title 'high priestess of soul'; a title that would not be usurped.

Nina Simone's gifts were revealed from her first nights at the church revivals. They were of another world, other shores, crossing the ocean to take over her body. The musician George Clinton said one day that 'Once the Spirit takes your body over, you can't get away from it.' If the Spirit chooses you, if you are selected, if it gives you enough powers to fulfil the mission it entrusts to you, you will have no rest, no peace, until you achieve what it demands of you. You become a *houngan*, a messenger, like Charlie Parker, Bob Marley, John Coltrane...

Should we believe that Nina Simone was a *houngan*, charged with propagating the Spirits's wishes? I believe so. Can we reasonably believe that the little girl who struggled away on a terrible piano in the Tryon countryside and who, more than twenty years later, managed to hypnotize an audience with her music, was accomplishing the mission entrusted to her by a Spirit, whatever its name was? I believe so.

In certain West African cultures, when you are given something, you are expected to repeat the gesture. Gifts aren't selfless or one-way: acts of kindness to you demand that you return the favour. That is how exchanges are perpetuated.

Can we believe that, granted these powers which she used often, so much so that she would lose them in the end, Nina used the Spirit to her own ends without it ever seeking payment in return? Was the spirit ever compensated for the power it gave? What could it have asked for other than her life, her *raison d'être*, her soul? Did Nina Simone pay a high price? Was her peace the price she had to pay for her powers?

There is a photo of Nina while staying in Europe taken by the Dutch photographer Gerrit de Bruin. Gerrit would soon appear in Nina's life and would prove to be one of her Good Samaritans. But not straight away. So, a photo, a picture among about ten others, all lined up. It shows Nina working on a poetry project for black children. Her hair up in a headscarf, she's wearing heavy silver earrings, and her whole appearance seems to have a gypsylike style. In one photo she's concentrating on something, in another she's staring straight at the camera, further on she's deep in thought. Finally, a picture shows her staring at a point in space that it seems only she can see. She's staring at that point, that shape, and her eyes show madness. She seems caught up, subjugated. She has allowed herself to be penetrated by an invader, seconds before being transported to another world.

Nina Simone's crises would become her nightmare, and that of her entourage, in a few years. Most of those who shared her life at that time speak of psychological imbalances, of psychiatric illness that had nothing to do with magic, mystics, the *loas*. The secret would be carefully kept by insiders, members of the family. Admissions would be made that Nina was ill, juggling the terms used without really knowing which were most appropriate: cyclothymia, depression, schizophrenia. A neuronal dysfunction would be mentioned, a mineral deficiency in the brain, as the diva's sudden changes had to be explained, the attacks that could make her sink into a deep silence or into blind violence.

These symptoms would worsen over the years, until they devoured her at the beginning of the 80s, but they were already there in the mid-60s. They had been building since her childhood, lying dormant in her body, waiting for the right moment to break free, and, little by little, progress by taking advantage of a series of events that would weaken her soul, just like the cancer that devoured Lorraine Hansberry.

Lorraine passed away on 12 January 1965 at the age of thirty-four. The blow was terrible for Nina: 'When she was getting ready to die she asked for me,' she would write. 'I went down to the hospital with a record player. I played "In the Evening by the Moonlight" for her, and she raised her hands in front of her face and said, "Nina, I don't know what's happening to me. They say I'm not going to get better, but I must get well. I must go down to the south. I've been a revolutionary all my life, but I've got to go down there to find out what kind of revolutionary I am."'[76] A few days later, the pianist played 'In the Evening by the Moonlight' again in New York at her friend's funeral. Did the two women agree a pact during their last few moments together? Did Nina promise Lorraine to become the revolutionary that her friend was pushing her to be? Shortly before her death, the poet was working on a new piece entitled 'To Be Young, Gifted and Black'. Nina borrowed the title, planning to write a song in Lorraine's memory, a hymn to the movement's glory.

But that project would have to wait, as at the beginning of 1965 it was a grieving woman who stepped on stage at Carnegie Hall for the second time in her career. Thanks to the great resources provided by Philips, Nina structured her concert in two parts. First, accompanied by her musicians, before being joined in the second part by a large orchestra mostly composed of strings. Her dream was coming true at a bitterly sad time. Nina Simone was producing at that time 'the most beautiful music in the world', just like Ellington and Bird before her, and like Coltrane, Miles and Mingus after her. She was producing against prevailing winds and tide. Each chord was an ode to resistance, a declaration of war aimed at white power. Her blues carried physical threats, her ballads were poisoned with toxins, her standards were torch songs, carrying hope and galvanizing her troops.

The Waymons, who weren't present at their prodigal daughter's first coronation at Carnegie, travelled to New York from Philadelphia. John Divine and Mary Kate were accompanied by Miz Mazzy, and both women agreed that, from the very beginning, they knew she would be a great success. Other members of the Waymon family also made the trip, and even some of her brothers and sisters. After the concert, glowing with pride, John Divine went to see his daughter in her dressing room. Her mother, however, didn't say anything. She sat in a corner, allowing her silence to maintain the emotional distance from Nina. Perhaps the two women had been distant for too long to get past the silence. However, when she finally left, Miz Mazzy told Nina that while she wasn't there, Mary Kate had confided in her how proud she was of her daughter. But she couldn't take the step to tell it to the stranger that Nina had become – the person who so needed to hear it – not even just once.

The next day, John S. Wilson wrote in the *New York Times*: 'Miss Simone... is often an innovative artist, with a great deal of talent in depicting humour. She controls every facet of the development of the pieces she chooses, creating a series of cameos whose superimposition is fascinating. She is one of those very few stage artists able to hold the audience in the palm of their hands.'[77]

That concert at Carnegie Hall was followed by her second set of studio sessions with Philips, the first having produced the album *Broadway-Blues-Ballads*, in which 'See-Line Woman's irresistible groove stood out. But the record that Nina recorded under the direction of the arrangers Hal Mooney and Horace Ott had all the makings of a masterpiece. The album was *I Put a Spell on You*, which Philips would release in 1965.

The record borrowed its title and first single from the song by Screamin' Jay Hawkins. An atypical blues figure well known for his escapades (people have stopped counting the number of risks he took), his theatrical extravagances (he began early concerts by coming out of a coffin) and his strange outfits (zebra stripes, polka-dot shoes, voodoo fetishes), on stage Hawkins screamed and shook: 'I just torment a song. Frighten it half to death.'[78]

The context in which Nina Simone recorded 'I Put a Spell on You' makes her intentions clear. An obsessive lament, a ritual bewitching and a love song to death itself, its lyrics repeat: 'I put a spell on you / cause you're mine / You better stop the things you do / I ain't lyin' / No I ain't lyin' / You know I can't stand it'. While this song seems to push the singer towards exasperation, the final stage before death, Nina threatens her lover 'I love ya!', as if trying to stun her prey before sacrificing it: 'I love you anyhow / and I don't care if you don't want me / I'm yours right now / You hear me / I put a spell on your / because you're mine.'

It was during the recording of this second studio album for the Dutch company that Nina adapted 'You've Got to Learn' and 'Tomorrow Is My Turn', the two songs she bought from Charles Aznavour during their meeting in 1962. This album, her longest, shows a remarkable richness and contains a new version in French of 'Ne me quitte pas' by Jacques Brel, a radical choice that according to Philips was aimed at opening the doors to French-speaking territories. In her autobiography, Nina explains how she discovered the song, and it has to be admitted that her version is the only one to come close to Brel's: 'I was in New York, listening to the song without understanding a word of the lyrics, but each time Brel sang "Ne me quitte pas", I broke down in tears. I learned the song phonetically with a teacher and I repeated it over and over for three years before daring to sing it.' Later, she would sing it many times, including her last concert in Paris in 2001. 'Ne me quitte pas', with 'Porgy', 'My Baby Just Cares for Me' and a handful of other songs, would become the pianist's classics, songs that would mark the collective consciousness, eternally linked to both Nina as a person and to her work.

'Gimme Some' and 'Take Care of Business' are credited to Andy Stroud (whose talents as a composer had not been seen up to that point; people say that his wife gave him the rights to these songs as a gift). The sophisticated masterpiece *I Put a Spell on You* contains one final misleading sentiment: 'Feeling Good'. The changes coming for Nina would defy this song.

On 21 February 1965, Nina learned of the assassination of Malcolm X by three members of the Nation of Islam. His death was like a bomb going off in black American society. New organizations would appear, drawing inspiration from Malcolm X's words, but the assassination of the black leader foretold violence that was going to wrack America.

The death of Malcolm X strengthened Nina's conviction that the civil rights fight could not be won without taking up arms. It was not a piece of news to her but a tragedy that struck her life. What did Andy say about the shooting? What did he say when he saw his wife shattered by Malcolm's fate, the fate of Betty Shabazz and her children, now dependent on the generosity of compassionate neighbours? But above all, what did he think of the forces that were pushing his wife irresistibly towards taking a greater role in the movement? She confided in him that she wanted to give it all up, 'go down South, become a revolutionary and return each and every blow!' He tried to reason with her, assuring her that she knew nothing about politics, that it was men's business, that she should concentrate on her career, not allow herself to become distracted, bogged down in a fight whose outcome was uncertain.

Was Andy Stroud that Uncle Tom who was only worried about his business, as was often reported, or did he believe that the danger for those who became blindly involved in the real fight was too great?

Whatever the answer, his talents as a manager are irrefutable. The business 'Nina Simone' had become one of the most profitable around. During 1965, his wife recorded 35 songs. Philips divided them up between four albums that were released between June 1965 and September 1966. Preceded by an efficient promotional campaign, the single 'I Put a Spell on You' saw her enter the British charts, and almost instantly, the pop group the Animals covered the song, making it popular across Europe. In a few years, her bassist, Chas Chandler, would become Jimi Hendrix's manager.

Hot on the heels of this success, Nina was preparing her first European tour. Logically, the first step was England, where the Strouds went accompanied by Lisa. Andy had finally arranged a few days of rest for them in London so that his wife could relax after a trying year. They spent their first few days as tourists, having a good time, going for bike rides around the streets of London and shopping on Bond Street. Those were some of the last intimate moments for a couple that was now united only by work. Her successful London concerts were followed by her first appearance on British TV, on the music programme *Ready Steady Go!* As they were leaving England to win over France, the first Nina Simone Fan Club was coming into being in London, thanks to Sylvia Hampton and David Nathan.

They would become Nina's English family. In a few years, their role in her British career would even become essential.

In France, Nina was invited to the Antibes Jazz Festival in August 1965, where Duke Ellington was headlining. Nina and Duke knew each other; she had even dedicated an album to the master's songs. It is said that her performance in Antibes was so intense that Duke wrote the song 'La Plus Belle Africaine' for her as a tribute. And he was quite right, because Nina was at the peak of her beauty: tall, slender, elegant, with her hair tied back in braids with a silver ribbon, she was the very incarnation, in appearance and in her mannerisms, of black beauty.

The two concerts that Nina gave at Antibes would lead to one of her very first interviews in the French music press. Issue 212 of the monthly *Jazz Hot* features a full-page interview with Nina Simone by Michel Delorme and Maurice Cullaz. Cullaz would become the head of the Jazz Club de France and would save Nina from a bad move in the 80s when, in incredible conditions, she would flop in Paris. The article gives us an insight into her first French festival appearance. She surprised the audience in Antibes with her material, even singing 'Au clair de la lune', along with a selection of American folk songs: 'If I hear something I like, even if it's difficult to learn, I know that I'll sing it one day,' the pianist said.

But above all, in this interview Nina insisted on how she wanted to represent her people wherever she performed: 'I feel a very strong connection to my roots, my art is anchored in my people's culture and I'm very proud, it's a useless pride because I should not have to proclaim that my people's music has to be listened to. That shouldn't be necessary, but from the moment it is, I'm one hundred times prouder, one hundred times more aggressive in doing so. Because of the lack of respect that has gone on for hundreds of years, each time I travel to a new country, I feel I have to include songs in my set that proudly affirm my race; and do not be mistaken, whether I'm singing a ballad or a lament, it's the same, I don't want people to forget who I am.'

Later in the interview, answering a question on the obvious differences between her two performances in Antibes, she responded that 'time goes on, it can't be stopped. Whatever we do, it's time that counts, and not action. When I sing it's a moment of my lift that's flowing by, I'm not playing a role, I'm living. Every moment is different from the one before, it's the same thing in music, why should it not be the same for two different concerts on different days and at different times, in different atmospheres... That's what happened. The audience had to get to know me on the first night, on the second they knew what to expect from me, I had nothing left to prove and I was more relaxed.'

In autumn 1965, the Strouds went back to the USA. They had barely arrived and Nina had to throw herself into another American tour booked by Andy, with headline dates in Philadelphia, Chicago and Los Angeles. The previous two years were still weighing her down. Between the concerts, the studio recording, her involvement in the movement and her role as a mother (which she had never really been able to fulfil), Nina got little rest. She felt unusually vulnerable, depressed, and she began to drink during this new American tour. When asked about the drinking by Frank Lords for his film, Mary Kate Waymon said of this period that her daughter had become a 'draught horse. She wasn't respected, she was used, she was abused...' The pressure was never-ending, the work rate was furious and the rewards few and far between. Singing upset her, the melodies would haunt her for hours, disturbing her sleep. Overworked, unable to control her increasingly violent anxiety attacks, cut off from the world, frustrated at not being able to participate fully in the fight's advances, confronted by Andy's lack of understanding... all of these factors would lead her to a breaking point.

But would Nina Simone's art have reached the dramatic intensity that it achieved without this psychological instability? Without this impossible antagonism between her career and political involvement, between femininity and violence, between motherhood and disorder in her love life? Her inability to deal with these dilemmas would soon set her on track towards a tragedy. She would become a heroine confronted by incompatible forces, seeking serenity on the one hand and on the other desiring vengeance. That duality would soon contaminate every layer of her being and seem destined to tear her apart.

What appeared at the time to be anxiety attacks would transform in the months to come into irreversible turmoil. The only beneficiary would be Nina Simone's art. One of the pianist's masterpieces bears the mark of the coming madness: the album *Pastel Blues*. Hidden under Nina's peaceful, radiant pose on the album sleeve, the album contained all the problems of a haunted artist.

Pastel Blues was recorded in New York during the spring of 1965 with one of the best teams that had ever worked with the diva: Al Schackman supported by the guitarist Rudy Stevenson, the drummer Bobby Hamilton and the bassist Lisle Atkinson.

The album is a skilful balance between covers of American folk ('Nobody Knows You When You're Down and Out', already performed by Odetta, and 'Trouble in Mind'), the a cappella number 'Be My Husband', credited to Andrew Stroud, a heart-rending cover of Billie Holiday ('Tell Me More and More and Then Some'), an idol about whom Nina said: 'That voice touched me profoundly... In fact, I had to spend an entire day getting used to it, it was the strangest voice I've ever heard.'[79] Finally, two firebrands, two masterpieces complete this record.

Nina knew that her obligations wouldn't let her dedicate herself entirely to the movement, that Andy and her record company would prevent her from diving into the fight body and soul. Nina knew that music was still her only weapon, that each record had to contain grains of anger, that she had to include messages in her records, viruses designed to show her commitment to the movement.

The first of those two shots is 'Sinnerman', inspired by a gospel song whose chorus goes on for ever: 'Oh Sinnerman, what are you going to do / when the world is on fire and bleeding?' Nina adapted the song, retaining only the original's main chorus. 'Sinnerman' remains a gospel song aimed at God. She says: 'Oh Sinnerman, where you gonna run to? / You run to the moon / moon, can you hide me? / You run to the sea / sea, can you hide me? / You run to the sun / sun, can you hide me? / The Lord says: Sinnerman, the moon is going to bleed / the sea is going to sink / the sun is going to freeze.' So the Sinnerman who cannot find refuge anywhere turns to God: 'Lord can you hide me?' God answers him: 'Sinnerman, you better pray.'

It would be impossible not to link her choice of this song to her participation in the movement. Nina suggests that there is no way out, no cure for distress, all that can be done is pray to God. 'Sinnerman''s arrangements, structured around a repetitive, obsessive chorus, led by a rhythm evoking a crazy path towards freedom, inevitably lead the listener to think of death during the bridge when hands clap as if to hasten the condemned man's escape. It is too late to atone for his sins. 'Sinnerman' shows all of Nina's art of climax, where during one specific C major chord she seems to place a gun on the table, ready to fire. A song about despair, disenchantment, disillusionment in the face of a situation that offers no alternatives but flight or prayer. The end of the song leaves no doubt as to the option chosen by Nina (was she the condemned person?). War. Chaos. In one sense, 'Sinnerman' is a preparation for the last song on the *Pastel Blues* album, without doubt one of the most important and subversive songs ever sung by Nina Simone at any time in her career: 'Strange Fruit'.

Recorded on 20 May 1965, during the same sessions as 'Sinnerman', 'Strange Fruit' is considered one of the songs that changed the world. By covering this anti-lynching ballad, unique within American musical history and previously immortalized by Billie Holiday, Nina threw a bomb into a political and social environment that had sunk into violence.

In his book on the history of 'Strange Fruit', David Margolick features the statements of a certain Vernon Jarrett, who witnessed a lynching in the South: 'There were stories of white people fighting among themselves for the dead man's fingers or toes, or pickling his penis and keeping it in a jar in the local barbershop. Or stories of white people putting on their Sunday best to attend lynchings, or even their uniforms from World War I or the Spanish-American War, as if racism was real patriotism: "I am a real American. I lynch black folks. I keep them in their places."'[80]

In *The Fire Next Time*, James Baldwin noted: 'Just as the pogrom is not an accident in Jewish history, but its crystallization, the exasperation of an endemic situation, lynching, hanging and burning are nothing more than white people's true feelings towards black people taken to the limit.'[81] The American Congress has never managed to pass an anti-lynching law in the United States, where between 1889 and 1940 around 3,800 people were lynched.[82] H.L. Mencken wrote that lynchings often took the place 'of the merry-go-round, the theatre, the symphony orchestra'. Lynching is a recurring theme in literature, theatre and black art, but with the notable exception of 'Strange Fruit', the topic had not appeared in music. 'Strange Fruit' thus has to be considered a historical document.

The song was written by a white communist Jewish New York teacher, Abel Meeropol, under the pseudonym Lewis Allan. According to David Margolick, Meeropol may have been inspired to write 'Strange Fruit' by a double lynching that took place north of the Mason–Dixon line, the historical boundary between the North and South.

Billie Holiday was the first singer to perform the song, in 1939. She was twenty-four, had spent most of her life in Northern cities, had never seen a lynching and didn't feel affected by the trauma. Despite everything, Billie began performing 'Strange Fruit' at the end of her concerts, and it soon became a ritual. When the audience heard the first few notes of that crepuscular ballad, they knew Lady Day was bringing her performance to a close.

> Southern trees bear a strange fruit,
> Blood on the leaves and blood at the root[83]

When Billie Holiday's recording of 'Strange Fruit' was released, supporters of anti-lynching legislation called for copies to be sent to Congress, where Southern senators were preparing to torpedo the latest bill.[84] The legend of 'Strange Fruit' began here. The black activist Angela Davis wrote that the song had 'put the elements of protest and resistance back at the center of contemporary black musical culture';[85] Charles Mingus stated that 'this sort of music is there to tell the White world that they have acted evilly towards the Blacks'.

Nina Simone was the only important artist who dared to cover 'Strange Fruit' in the 60s, surely because performing it meant too high a personal investment. The song devours its performer, demanding that they somehow give the feeling of having been lynched themselves. It was impossible to play anything else afterwards.

When *Pastel Blues* was released, the Strouds and their only daughter (Andy's two boys had gone back to live with their mother a long time before) left for Holland on Wilhelm Langenberg's invitation. A series of concerts and television programmes were awaiting Nina, with the promise of a family Christmas as the key. After three years of marriage, the Strouds were already exhausted. Little sex, no signs of affection or comradeship, the couple's communication had broken down. The only thing remaining was Andy's ambition for his wife's career.

A few days after arriving, they attended a 'memorable' New Year party given by Big Willy in his home. The party lasted two full days. As was the case each year, hundreds of guests crossed the Atlantic to take part. Nina would make the journey every New Year for eight years.

5

'HELL IS RIGHT BESIDE ME'

THE STROUDS returned from Europe in early January 1966 and immediately set off for Chicago, where Martin Luther King had recently moved. Nina was to give a benefit concert there for the CORE (Congress for Racial Equality), a militant black organization that worked to obtain social reforms. The CORE had joined forces with the SNCC to develop Black Power in black neighbourhoods and recruit militant youths.[1]

Upon landing at O'Hare airport, Nina heard that she was about to be awarded a distinction by the CORE for 'her work for the movement', that the presenter of the show was an old acquaintance of hers: Sid Marx, the DJ who had contributed to launching 'Porgy' on Philly's airwaves, and lastly that Stokely Carmichael would be giving a speech before her concert. In the past few months, Stokely had become a champion of Black Power, a designation intended to give the black man back his pride in the face of a system christened 'Amerika', a reference to the tragically notorious K of the Ku Klux Klan (the SNCC saw white America as still tolerant of those outbursts of racist violence). A few months later, in May 1966, this new rising star of the black struggle would be elected head of the SNCC; under his lead, the union would take on a tougher stance, renounce non-violence and begin to preach self-defence and armed conflict.

For Nina, his presence carried a symbolic value. She, having so often felt frustrated by not being able to partake in the major steps of the struggle, was now being invited to perform at a political summit that would prove to be a landmark.

There was another person worth a mention in the audience that night; he was a civil rights militant and a follower of Malcolm X's theories: Huey Newton. In Oakland, California, in October, Newton would instigate a revolutionary nationalist movement with Bobby Seale, based on armed self-defence, inspired by the theoretical legacy of Malcolm X and which would reprise Stokely Carmichael's Black Power slogan ('Power is the only thing that people respect in this world and we have to obtain it no matter what the cost'[2]): the Black Panther Party.

The Black Panthers embodied a certain black American revolutionary romanticism. A lot of black kids from the ghetto identified with those rebels who claimed the right of their people to carry a weapon. They felt like heroes, ready to challenge the government, to fight or even die for their ideas if need be. But the Panthers, who might have been nothing more than an armed group playing on its community's desire for revenge, also championed social action, setting up canteens, nurseries and free clinics in black ghettos and providing the community with legal aid and healthcare. They also set up so-called 'liberation schools' that taught black history. These initiatives were largely ignored by the press, who preferred to talk of the organization's darker side.

To the West, the Black Panthers were a convenient symbol of black revolution: an army under the disguise of a 'legitimate' political party, whose uniform, a black leather jacket and black beret, rang loud in people's minds. Greil Marcus reckons that this revolutionary organization was 'in many ways very traditionally

American, close to populists, with similarities to the Irish gangs seen in New York in 1860. The Panthers would say: "Society despises us. We are going to show them that we are just as capable as anyone else, perhaps better, even." There was no comparison between them and what the Nation of Islam stood for. Despite its radicalism, the Black Panther Party had a strong desire to form part of American society. They wanted to free blacks from their situation versus white America, but ultimately, their goal was to free the country from its racism. What they by no means represented was a sectarian movement that only concerned the black community.'

The Black Panthers were very vocal indeed when it came to defending themselves from accusations of racism, and intended to fight an internationalist popular struggle. Bobby Seale wrote:

> The Party understands the imbedded racism in a large part of White America and it understands that the very small cults that sprout up every now and then in the black community have a basically black racist philosophy... We do not fight racism with racism. We fight racism with solidarity. We do not fight exploitative capitalism with black capitalism. We fight capitalism with basic socialism. And we do not fight imperialism with more imperialism. We fight imperialism with proletarian internationalism... we believe our fight is a class struggle and not a race struggle.[3]

While setting up their organisation in October 1966, the Black Panther Party brought together the black, nationalist, Pan-African ideology of Marcus Garvey ('The Negro should not have but one nation'), the internationalism of Martin Luther King and his support of all colonized people, and the partition theory preached by the Nation of Islam and Malcolm X. Lastly it positioned itself as a socialist movement aimed at bringing down capitalism, which it deemed to be a source of racism and injustice.

The CORE joined Stokely Carmichael and the SNCC on the path to Black Power. Soon the Black Panthers would bring the final touches to the emerging new face of the black struggle. Reverend King, however, found himself in a vulnerable position. He knew that the major industrial cities of the North had not benefited from the struggles and changes of the South; no movement worth mentioning had seen the light of day, whether supporting the SCLC's campaigns or beginning any in-depth political work for the underprivileged black population.[4] Convinced that it was his duty to rouse the people from the ghettos that were plagued by unemployment and discrimination and overlooked by the municipality, King started a crusade against poverty and the dreadful housing conditions his community was subjected to. His goal was to make blacks understand that they had the power to take their destiny into their own hands, to take action to improve it and achieve the American dream of opulence and equal opportunities.[5]

King moved to Chicago in January 1966, determined to set up a tenants' union and to instigate a campaign against the use of derelict rental housing and for the improvement of some of the most dilapidated buildings. But soon, the cost of the operation proved too high. The noticeable drop in funding devoted to King's initiatives by middle-class citizens had weakened his organization. In addition, the Vietnam War now mobilized many of his white sympathizers. Eventually, King was faced with the logic of a city that made for unfamiliar territory. Chicago was not the South and the mobilization of blacks was no longer effected by churches alone. The population wasn't used to protest marches and was less sensitive to the liberation movement. Moreover, King's actions were being countered by Richard Daley, the mayor of Chicago, who fully intended to keep Chicago's black community under his own command.

The Chicago campaign was doomed to fail, and after that, King would no long be the irrefutable unifier of various militant bodies within the movement; for the younger generation, Nina Simone included, this role now belonged to the SNCC and the Black Panthers. The flag of the struggle was no longer that of non-violence; it was now Black Power.

As we have been able to see, Nina was in favour of a clear distinction between the struggle and whites. Just like Stokely, she felt that it was best to avoid glorifying the participation of whites and insist on calling for more support from the black community.[6] Like him, she believed that it was necessary 'to give up any hope of a collaboration [with whites] and declare that blacks had to work with blacks in order to become infused with a sense of their own existence'.[7]

If there is one song by Nina Simone that brings to mind this move away from submission and towards violence, it has to be 'Four Women'.

Yet in many ways, with its four verses and lack of chorus, 'Four Women' also constitutes an accurate biography of Eunice Waymon's career – her submissiveness until the invention of her alter ego Nina Simone, this creature's first steps until the emergence of her desire for revenge and the fulfilment of her mission.

'Four Women' was recorded on 30 September 1965 in New York, and just as the first signs of psychological trouble began to show. After waiting almost a year on Philips's shelves, the song was eventually released on the album *Wild Is the Wind*.

By the fierceness of the lyrics, the dignity and the infinite sadness in its interpretation, 'Four Women' might easily fall into the same category as 'Strange Fruit'. The two songs share the same power, the same minimalism, the same quality in writing put at the service of a dreadful denunciation. In a way this is a lynching of the soul where Nina explores the feelings of four black women whose skin colours range from light to darkest, 'something that has a profound effect on their concept of their own beauty and self-worth'. Nina paints a harsh picture of the submission of the black American woman, enslaved to her own beauty and birth to survive. Nina seems to say that as long as black women fail to accept their Negroid beauty rather than judge it by white standards, they will never break free from their subservience.

A feminist anthem if there ever was one, 'Four Women' is also Nina's exploration of all those masks and faces, having herself been each one of those four women in succession. The first brings to mind Mary Kate, or perhaps the woman Eunice would have become if destiny hadn't torn her way from her life as a child prodigy with a sacrificed childhood: a black woman fallen prey to pain, an African woman trapped in a world that demands her destruction. The second woman is mixed-race, beautiful and lost in limbo, between two worlds that would never welcome her, and Nina seems to want to send us back to her crushed ambitions of becoming a concert pianist, seemingly never in the right place, a victim of every duality, every antagonism. She next evokes the woman she was only yesterday. Obedient, quiet, willing to let herself be damaged by the whims of men, in exchange for the promise of money and a better life. Andy's masculine shadow looms over the figure of this 'sweet thing' he manipulates, satisfying her one day, only to abuse her the next. As Nina writes 'Four Women's final verse, she is this last black woman consumed with anger, who demands amends and is willing to kill. Too much suffering endured, the impossible weight of her ancestors' history to carry on her shoulders. Everything about her condition brings her back to her desire for revenge :

> My skin is brown
> And my manner is tough
> I'll kill the first mother I see
> Cos my life has been too rough
> I'm awfully bitter these days
> Because my parents were slaves
> What do they call me?
> My name is Peaches

When it was first released, 'Four Women' was banned by several black American radio stations that considered this song an 'insult' to black women. Later on, several feminist groups tried to appropriate 'Four Women' and make it their anthem, but Nina systematically refused: 'I aspire to the same as any ordinary woman,' she asserted. 'Four Women' was a confession, an autobiographical summary of Nina Simone's experience and she couldn't be doing with any appropriation, criticism or censorship. Is it even possible to censor such a self-portrait, even if the image it projects is openly violent or even obscene?

Nina would write that 'by the time the sixties ended I'd look in the mirror and see two faces, knowing that on the one hand I loved being black and being a woman, and that on the other it was my colour and sex which had fucked me up in the first place.'[8]

An old scar had reopened since the terrorist bombing in Birmingham and 'Four Women' probed the depth of the wound. It told of all the despair, vagrancy and servitude of a woman removed from the world, standing on the edge of the troubles her race was caught up in. A woman and a mother also, deprived from any kind of family harmony. Her talents funded by her husband; her motherhood obliterated by professional obligations; Nina's life was no longer anything but a frantic race against time. Still, she'd built herself a kingdom, precious despite its narrow boundaries, something she could hold on to when her disillusions took hold. She said that travelling, performing and trying to be a mother was 'like a juggling act at times, but it's the road I've chosen. Sometimes I think it's too hard trying to do it all, but then I remember all the hard work I've done, and I look at Lisa and I thank God!'[9]

There was one more trouble to add to this list: the feeling of being uprooted. Andy had signed a major deal that tied Nina to RCA for a total of ten albums. She would no longer be working with Big Willy, who was tactful enough not to argue and to respect her manager's decision. Nina would only get one more chance to see her Dutch mentor.

Nina Simone made one last album for Philips. Others would follow, however, mainly consisting of previously made recordings, released by the company in an attempt to cash in on the terms of the contract and Nina Simone's still intact popularity.

During the month of December 1966, Nina divided her time between the RCA recording studios and a New York rehearsal studio. That month, her exhaustion reached the point of no return without anyone around her showing the slightest hint of concern. She had become the draught horse her mother spoke of (though Mary Kate was too wrapped up in her own respectability to think of bridging the gap with her daughter and giving her comfort) – pushed into producing records, into getting up on stage, cheered and given flowers only to be put back in her cage and for the circus to start all over again the next day. There is a photo, taken during the recording of 'Backlash

Blues', that was made into an oil painting picked out for the sleeve. The picture shows Nina seated with her back to her piano, staring at the floor absent-mindedly, a lit cigarette dangling from her fingertips. The photo screams of solitude. RCA would use it for their promotional campaign, probably thinking that they'd got themselves a personal, intimate picture there that showed Nina's humanity. At the top, spelt out in bold lettering, it read: 'Is it too late for us all?'

No time to dither. Andy had scheduled an American tour for his artist wife with the comedian Bill Cosby, due to start the minute she finished promoting her record. But Nina was somewhere else altogether. For weeks now, she had gone to sleep only to wake up feeling exhausted. At night she was haunted by melodies, hearing snippets of speech or even voices whispering in her bedroom. Panicking, she'd turn on the light, looking around but there was no one there. Later the voices would return. During the daytime she'd sometimes black out, or suddenly become agitated and lose her rag for no apparent reason before sinking back into deep silence. Unable to ignore the situation any longer, Andy finally began to worry. Never before had he seen her in such a state and he did the best he could to try and soothe her by talking about the blackboard in the Mount Vernon kitchen. 'One day my Nina will be a big black woman loaded with cash!' There was no reaction; she was gone, lost in some daydream. Something inside her had given way and Andy was scared for his business. What if she was too run-down to perform? The money they stood to lose if she couldn't play! And what would Bill Cosby say? Performing alongside a superstar of his calibre was too good an opportunity to miss.

His wife had sunk into a deep depression and he couldn't even see it. Something inside Nina had died and all he could think about was that night's performance. Right in the middle of the tour, in Baltimore, he found her in her dressing room, clad in a white gown, applying foundation to her hair. 'I was having hallucinations; I thought that I had to be the same colour all over, so I put make-up on my hair. Brown make-up, so that my hair would be the same colour as my skin. I thought I had to get on a laser beam with Andy, I thought I could see through his skin, that he was my nephew, not my husband. I told him we had to leave Baltimore as fast as we could to get onto the laser beam. I was hallucinating but I was too tired to understand that I was.'[10]

She continued to suffer similar bouts until the end of the tour. Her hallucinatory attacks, which could last up to several hours, were interspersed with calmer periods. Did Andy even contemplate halting the tour? No. He made Nina play every night, right up to the final date, in February 1967. Late arrivals on stage had become the norm and the pianist now made mistakes, when she didn't seem to be playing on autopilot.

Back in Mount Vernon, she slept for three days and three nights straight. Andy, Max Cohen, the musicians, everyone knew, yet the code of silence prevailed. It was inconceivable for the RCA guys to get wind of the fact that Nina was sick, as this would have compromised the deal they'd signed, the commitments they'd agreed upon and Andy didn't want that, so things were left as they were. Not one person even suggested that she see a doctor.

Two months touring, preceded by two months in the studio. In the mean time, all hell had broken loose in America, as Nina was now discovering after months of absence. On 7 June 1966 the militant James Meredith, the first ever black student to enrol at the University of Mississippi under the protection of the federal administration in October 1962, had been shot and injured as he marched from Memphis to Jackson to urge the blacks of Mississippi to register to vote. This had become a national matter and fuelled general feelings of anger. The NAACP and Stokely Carmichael's SNCC became divided, the former wanting to organize multiracial protests to demand new civil rights legislation, whilst Carmichael wanted the march to be all-black and protected by a black armed militia, siding against Lyndon Johnson and the Democratic Party. These were positions that were untenable for Martin Luther King.

On 16 June, Stokely was arrested. Upon his release, he declared that 'every courthouse in Mississippi should be burnt down tomorrow'. On 26 June, following several days of tensions between the SNCC supporters and King's, the march reached Jackson. Carmichael let loose with a furious speech: 'In this country we need to... build a base for power so strong that we'll bring whites to their knees every time they provoke us.'[11] His speeches were condemned by the press and the moderate wing of black activists, but he didn't care. In December, the SNCC expelled whites from its ranks and division took hold within the movement.

But public opinion was diverted from the movement towards the war in North Vietnam, where 84,000 American GIs were fighting.

After giving his first public speech on his opposition to the Vietnam War in Los Angeles, Martin Luther King fronted an anti-war protest in Chicago in March 1967. In April, in New York, he once again denounced the absurdity of the conflict ('the greatest purveyor of violence in the world today: my own government'[12]), although according to polls, 75 percent of those surveyed declared themselves in favour of this intervention.[13]

The activist H. Rap Brown, who was close to the Black Panthers ('so bad that Congress passed a law against him'[14]), took over the leadership of the SNCC in May, replacing Carmichael who was being threatened by the FBI, which considered that he had 'the necessary charisma to be a real threat'.[15] In June, the boxer Muhammad Ali, a member of the Nation of Islam, found himself stripped of his world title and his boxing licence and sentenced to five years in prison for refusing to fight in Vietnam (he was later released on appeal). 'I ain't got no quarrel with those Viet Cong, anyway. They never called me nigger,' he had said.

On 12 July 1967, violent racial riots broke out in the ghettos of Newark, New Jersey, followed on 23 July by bloody unrest in Detroit's black suburbs and inner-city neighbourhoods. The government ordered the rebuilding of white property only, abandoning black areas to their fate in a manner reminiscent of the ghost town of Benton Harbor. And guess what happened to be the song that everyone chanted in the streets during the Detroit riot? Was it 'We Shall Overcome'? Did they hum 'Young, Gifted and Black', the civil rights anthem Nina Simone had composed as a tribute to Lorraine Hansberry? Greil Marcus answered this question for me: 'During the riots of 1967, what the Detroit rioters sang was "Dancing in the Street" by Martha and the Vandellas, a Motown band. The same song was heard during other riots, in Newark for instance. Was this a song intended as the voice of the civil rights movement? Probably not, but the population had made it into a banner of their revolution; it spoke of their wishes, it said they were important and that they existed.'

The Los Angeles Watts Riots of 1965 – possibly the greatest racially motivated rebellion in American history – were described by the songwriter Randy Newman as 'the biggest thing that ever happened, the greatest shock I ever got and the greatest ever injustice in this country. I've always felt like the racial situation was worse here [in LA] than anywhere else.'[16] And with cause: while whites had no trouble finding jobs in LA, especially in the building and aeronautical sectors, black unemployment had soared to 20 per cent in ghettos, bordering on 30 per cent in Watts.[17] Also, LA's town planning in those days had forced minorities far out from the city centre. The Watts Riots bore witness not only to the seriousness of racial tensions but, in broader terms, the decline of the American city as a whole. This riot would be the one best remembered in American minds, its ghost re-emerging with every episode of racial violence (the beating of Rodney King, for instance). 'And when protesters made it out of the riots safe and sound, they saw the collapse of their community, the dead, those who'd been arrested, their streets on fire,' Greil Marcus told me; 'all that remained was their sense of honour, the feeling that they'd instigated something that had got the whole world's attention, and that this world now had to take it into consideration and fear it. Long before the Detroit riot, all of this was happening to the tune of "Dancing in the Street", a song that spread a positive and exciting message and that might have been heard as follows: "What do these riots mean? They were all about dancing."'

By the end of the summer 1967 riots, the face of Detroit had changed for ever and soon the city sank into financial crisis. The mottos on the city's flag mean 'We hope for better things' and 'It will rise from the ashes'. Motor City had sunk into darkness, never to recover.

In September 1967, Martin Luther King started the Poor People's Campaign, aimed at Washington. Its goal? The redistribution of wealth and financial power in order to reduce social injustice.[18] The idea was to bring black America's poor to the Capitol and to get them to stand

Nina in her crochet outfit at
Newport Jazz Festival, 1967. *Corbis*

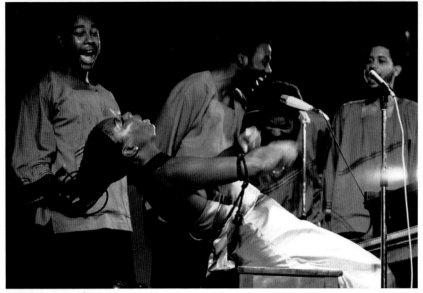

In full swing at the 1er Festival Culturel Panafricain at the Théâtre de l'Atlas, Algeria, 1969. *Magnum Photos*

Reading a story book to her two-year-old daughter Lisa before departing by jet for London from New York City, 1965. *PA Photos*

A publicity shot of a young and glamorous Nina in the 1970s. *Getty Images*

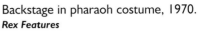
Backstage in pharaoh costume, 1970.
Rex Features

Looking out from the stage in Dallas,
Texas, 1971. *Getty Images*

Shooting the
audience her
trademark gaze
of intimidation,
1977. *Rex Features*

In concert at Palais des Glaces in Paris, 1982. *Rex Features*

Performing at Ronnie Scott's
Club in London, 1984.
Rex Features

Capturing the crowd at the annual Jazz festival in Antibes Juan les Pins, 1988. *Rex Features*

In African head-dress at Les Rencontres internationales de D'Jazz de Nevers, 1992. *Rex Features*

Presented with a special award by Sinéad O'Connor for her lifetime achievements in music at the 1999 Heineken Hot Press Awards, at the Hot Press Irish Music Hall of Fame, in Dublin. *Rex Features*

Her most coveted stage: performing at the JVC Jazz Festival in New York's Carnegie Hall, 2001.
PA Photos

Lisa (centre) and Myriam Makeba (right) leave the church after Nina Simone's funeral ceremony in Carry-le-Rouet near Marseille, April 25, 2003. *Corbis*

Nina, 1994. *Corbis*

outside Congress 'to paralyze its political activities'.[19] Reverend King intended to force the Congress to vote in laws that would guarantee minimum wages, jobs and allocate a national budget of $30,000,000 to the fight against poverty as well as start work on 500,000 homes yearly for low-income households.[20] Should Washington decline to hear his request, King intended to organize boycotts on a national scale.

He knew that he was being targeted by the FBI. The Bureau viewed the pastor as the enemy, and in an attempt to destabilize and discredit him, members of the Bureau flooded the press and the various groups that made up the movement with documents, often anonymous or fake, that compromised Martin Luther King, including a notorious phone transcript suggesting loose sexual morals. During the final months of his life, King was devastated by dreadful political and psychological pressures. This government with which he'd been trying to open up a dialogue for the past ten years viewed him simply as a dissident.

In October 1967, Nina read in the press about the anti-war campaign. Millions of protesters, both black and white, had invaded Capitol Hill in an unprecedented demonstration of power to try and push back Lyndon B. Johnson's war policy.

Nina hadn't taken part in this protest and she had missed out on the marches that had criss-crossed the country over the past few months. For all the people who told her she was their muse, she never got involved in the action, as her professional obligations stopped her from fully living out her commitment: 'there was no way I could know such closeness and community,' she would later lament, adding: 'I was different. I had no community at the back of me, I was a national star and my job was to go wherever I was needed. I had no home town waiting... when I needed to recharge my batteries... I was rich and famous but I wasn't free... I had to plan months, sometimes years, ahead. So I felt part of the struggle, yet separated from it. I was lonely in the movement like I had been lonely everywhere else.'[21] Everywhere else indeed...

Her circle of friends was shrinking. Those who hadn't died or gone into exile were finding it harder and harder to communicate with this diva at her wits' end, a woman who little by little had become quite egocentric. Her family? Just a gap where an omnipotent husband, set on making her forget about her 'whims', had turned her into a recluse; her brothers and sisters had kept their distance from her ever since Philadelphia. Locked in her ivory tower, alone with her wrath and unable to be a mother for lack of time, she said, but also because of her failure to bond with Lisa, Nina sank into solitude. John Divine seemed to be the only one who continued to understand the troubles that raged inside her. This loving father was the only one left who would listen unconditionally to his favourite daughter's distress. He was the one to comfort her, to try and show her that not everything was as dark as it seemed, that the career she'd built was the proof of exceptional success. That great things were still to come. That people worshipped her, and that no matter what, she was still his beloved daughter. His favourite. He knew how to soothe her even when her crises were at their worst, but those moments of peace regained never lasted.

Deeply frustrated by her situation and unable to recharge her batteries or take a step back, Nina tried to counter her isolation by taking more and more aggressive stances. She'd indiscriminately pick up the ideologies of the most radical political groups and would try and convince her audiences that the time had come to join the armed struggle: 'There was a general feeling among us that the time for revolution was ripe, and if we didn't work all out to make it happen we might not get another shot at it for years.'[22]

The black writer Toni Morrison, winner of the Nobel Prize in Literature and author of works devoted to the history of African-Americans, asserted that 'Nina Simone was fundamental to me and to my generation. I only met her a few times. She was indestructible. Incorruptible. She even scared me a little. She would tell us to take up arms! She would tell us to forget about Martin Luther King and non-violence, that it was time to follow the Black Panthers, to join the revolution. I had to confess to her that I wasn't ready to take up arms and that I'd rather take up my pen. She'd get mad; I guess she wasn't ready to take up arms either because she channelled it all into her music. She was several women rolled into one. I loved her... There's really just one thing for me to say: Nina Simone saved our lives.'[23]

'She was several women.' Toni Morrison's words ring true. They bring us back to the four characters in 'Four Women', their inability to find a way out of their dooms. We come back to the antagonism that was at the heart of Nina's music, at the crossroads between classical music and blues.

If you listen carefully to her music, you hear within it two opposite people, two beings with nothing in common, as though trapped together and forced to share the same means of expression. An artist leading a double artistic life, unable to find her own place anywhere.

Nina was a prisoner of this antagonism. And how could she resolve her obstinate commitments to the movement when she couldn't fully take part? Did her engagement all come from her political conscience or was it a matter of holding on to the one thing ever to give her collective legitimacy? Indeed, the movement had brought her the new feeling of belonging, and one can easily understand how painful her self-questioning could feel now that she was isolated and cast side.

Yet all she could do was sing, record and perform on stage, no matter what. That was the one territory where she could deliver her message and serve the cause she wanted to surrender herself to. Perhaps she dreamed of one day becoming a beacon for her people – that was the only path that could relieve Andy's pressure and her career's duties, that could justify her feeding that ravenous machine.

And this woman, already close to the edge, now had to embark on yet another marathon project: her first English tour. A new challenge which, in her current state, seemed insurmountable.

The Strouds arrived in London on Sunday 9 April 1967 at eleven in the morning. This two-week tour coincided with the release of Nina's first album for RCA, *Sings the Blues*. In three days between the end of 1966 and early 1967, she'd recorded a set of ballads, swing numbers, laments and the subversive 'Backlash Blues', an anti-Vietnam War manifesto built around a poem by Langston Hughes, her late friend. Facing the British fans and reporters crowding to interview her, the pianist waxed lyrical about the fever that consumed America, the importance of the fight and what was at stake. Europe knew very little about those events. Nina positioned herself as a spokeswoman for her community's struggle: 'in America they want to keep us down, shut us up and a whole other bunch just want to bury us!'[24] This was a far cry from the reasons that had brought the British to see Nina Simone.

The English tour came to Bristol, where, inexplicably, only thirty tickets had been sold. Andy and the musicians were concerned. How was the pianist going to react? Would she feel insulted by the small audience and get mad, as she now did at the slightest aggravation? Against all expectations, Nina kept her nerve, got up on the stage without making a fuss and once seated at her piano, asked the audience to move closer to the stage. She played 'I Put a Spell on You', 'Take Care of Business', 'Ne me quitte pas', 'Day and Night', 'Do I Move You', giving a remarkable performance in the deserted venue. The next day, in Portsmouth this time, she did it again for an audience of about 100.

A few gigs later, the team returned to London on 23 April where, before the climax of her tour at the Royal Albert Hall, she was scheduled to play at the Ram Jam Club in Brixton. Nina was impatient, repeating to whoever would listen that she was going to play 'for [her] people'. The only problem was that the one song that had brought this Jamaican audience in was 'My Baby Just Cares for Me'. Nina hadn't played that song in years. She thought it insignificant and had banned it from her repertoire, but the audience didn't want to know. They weren't interested in listening to 'Day and Night', or to 'I Put a Spell on You', not even to 'Porgy'. They screamed and shouted until she stopped.

What Nina Simone didn't know was that 'My Baby Just Cares for Me' had become a hit with Jamaican sound systems and all over the Caribbean.[25] In the mid-60s, King Records, Syd Nathan's record label, had used its influence to acquire Prince Buster, the king of ska's catalogue, on the recommendation of James Brown, who'd become a ska convert whilst touring the Caribbean. Nathan had exported part of his catalogue to Jamaica, where sound systems were on the constant lookout for new sounds in the style of the blues beat that was popular on the island in the day. Unknown to Nina, 'My Baby Just Cares for Me' had been a huge hit in Jamaica, and was soon covered by local ska artists. 'Young, Gifted and Black' would meet a similar fate and be covered reggae-style by Bob Andy and Marcia Griffiths, a sensational singer who was a member of the I-Threes, the trio who sang backing vocals for Bob Marley and the Wailers.

Exasperated by this fervid audience who couldn't have cared less about her arpeggios, she screamed: 'Just shut up! I won't sing this shit. I don't even remember the lyrics!' Andy showed up on stage and handed her a bottle of gin. Livid, shooting defiant glances at every member of the audience, she grabbed the gin, drinking straight from the bottle. The promoter came and found Andy, fearing a riot. From the Ram Jam's boxes, you could hear the crowd chanting 'We want "My Baby Just Cares for Me"!' She put the bottle down on her piano, and without so much as a glance at the audience, she launched into the first notes of 'My Baby Just Cares for Me', not even bothering to hum the tune. Right from the first chords, she could hear them roaring with glee. She stopped suddenly and harshly asked the audience: 'Are you happy now? Is that what you wanted?' The room still at long last, she carried on with her set as though nothing had happened, finishing with the ballad 'Since I Feel for You'. That night, she'd met her match. Wasn't this just the kind of clash she wanted in order to earn respect and stir things up?

Back to the States. It was summer and Nina got invited to perform at the Newport Jazz Festival. She heard that there had been riots in Tampa, Cincinnati and Buffalo, with fourteen people critically injured. Newark and Detroit had been set ablaze and thirty-six protesters killed. Though she'd barely landed, it was once again time for her to pack her bags for Las Vegas where a week's worth of gigs awaited her at Caesars Palace: 'That was a joke – playing a city almost entirely segregated and stuffed full of gamblers and whores. I lasted four days... then walked out.'[26]

Plagued by insomnia, tears, constant exhaustion, feeling lonely and worn out, she turned to alcohol more and more frequently. Andy tried to put a brake on her binges, all the while signing her up for an insane number of gigs: 'You've got to keep building your career; it's too soon to relax.' The way Nina saw it, Andy was selling her shows too cheap, and he was aiming too low, making her toil like a 'beast of burden'. Nina now cast a new eye on her manager husband and this outlook gave rise to a new attitude towards him: more aggressive and uncompromising.

'He didn't get Nina,' said Sam Waymon, an organist, singer and the brother with whom Nina had forged a privileged bond. 'He didn't understand the artist's complexity or her madness. Confusion, joy, happiness. How someone can love what they do one day and hate it the next.'[27]

The diva didn't need any encouragement: 'Andy was a leech; just a week into our marriage and all I'd dream of was to see him walk out the door.'[28] It's a claim very like Nina, probably exaggerated, yet there is little to go on to shed light on their private relationship. It's known that their sex life had dwindled into nothingness, that the Strouds had stopped making love around the mid-60s, Andy telling anyone who'd listen that his wife was his 'sleeping pill'.[29] Nina would write in her autobiography that in the bedroom Andy's attitude was neither tough nor dominant, and one might guess that Mount Vernon must have been a haven for them, a sanctuary from the violence – insults, threats, punches – that ran rife in their life on tour. Yet it was thanks to this routine of concerts that Nina so abhorred that Andy managed to preserve his wife's mental balance. On this matter, Lisa Stroud said that 'when my father was around she had a certain schedule, which kept things balanced'.[30]

In September 1967, Philips decreed Nina Simone the *High Priestess of Soul*, with the release of a record collated from the cutting-room floor and songs captured live in 1966. Amongst those songs was 'Come Ye', a ballad and prayer to the African race sung a cappella with minimal percussion backing: 'Come ye ye who would have peace / Hear me what I say now / I say come ye ye who would have peace / It's time to learn how to pray'. And 'Brown Eyed Handsome Man', a Chuck Berry cover, the gospel song 'Take Me to the Water' and the nostalgic 'I'm Going Back Home'.

In its wake, RCA released the luxurious *Silk & Soul*. On the sleeve, Nina appears as 'la plus belle Africaine' as prophesied by Duke Ellington. Her hair in a bun threaded with silver and pearls, a tender and melancholic look on her face, silhouetted on a background that brings to mind blood more than silk. The album was recorded on 13, 15, 21 and 29 June 1967 in New York, in RCA's studio B. In the credits, Gene Taylor, the bass player who would accompany her on her next European tour, and an authoritative drummer, Bernard Purdie, who'd already been seen playing with Curtis Mayfield and Aretha Franklin.

Among the pretty pieces on *Silk & Soul*, let's mention 'It Be's That Way Sometimes', written by Sam Waymon, the scathing 'Go to Hell', a precursor to Mayfield's 'If There's a Hell Below, We're All Going to Go', and 'Consummation', the favourite song of Louis Farrakhan, the Nation of Islam's new leader. And last, a hymn to civil rights, 'I Wish I Knew How It Would Feel to Be Free':

> And I wish I knew how
> It would feel to be free
> I wish that I could break
> All the chains holding me

Solomon Burke was one of the few male artists who dared to cover 'I Wish I Knew How It Would Feel to Be Free'. When we met at the Grand Hôtel in Montreux in July 2004, I asked him about this cover he'd added to his repertoire in the 60s: 'I would have loved to have written that song,' he swore. 'I was fortunate enough to play with Nina Simone during that period, to rub shoulders with her, and I was one of the few artists whose company she agreed to on stage. I felt honoured to know Nina, and what a gift the Lord gave us in her! The things I learned from her! She was a genius. Nina was also a role model; her elocution was perfect, her personality and charisma knew no equal. She was up there with Dinah Washington in terms of power. The first time I heard that song, "I Wish I Knew How It Would Feel to Be Free", I was blown away. That one, and also "Young, Gifted and Black". My God! When Nina played, she gave it her all. When I recorded that song, I tried to draw inspiration from everything I learned by Nina's side and to infuse it with my own feeling.'

The song 'I Wish I Knew How It Would Feel to Be Free' was naturally picked up by civil rights militants and included among their war anthems. Back then, no one even suspected that the year ahead would be one that saw those hopes systematically destroyed.

1968. The year that marked the point of no return. In February, Nina Simone performed at Carnegie Hall to a standing ovation. A new live album was in the making, which would be recorded at a concert played in the framework of the Westbury Music Fair on Long Island. On 4 April, as Nina walked into the Westbury studio to rehearse, she heard the news on the radio. Martin Luther King. Shot like a dog on the balcony of room 306 of the Lorraine Motel in Memphis, at 6.01 p.m., local time.

Non-violence was dead.

An unprecedented wave of riots unfurled across the country. Thirty-eight rioters were killed and the press reported over 20,000 arrests.

During our meeting in London, Abiodun Oyewole, a member of the black activist group The Last Poets (widely considered the first hip hop group), told me of the immense anger that had overwhelmed him when he heard of the death of Martin Luther King: 'When King's assassination was announced, it made me feel absolutely furious; even though we agreed with Malcolm X, even though I disagreed with the ideology of non-violence that Martin Luther King preached, I felt profound respect for what he was trying to achieve. I knew that I'd never allow anyone to call me a nigger and just passively sit there and take it; and I saw Dr King do that, on television. He exuded such dignity and I just couldn't believe that some scum could have murdered a man like him. I felt devastated, it made me want to be a merciless warrior, a Mau Mau. Our community experienced Martin Luther King's assassination as a deep offence.' Or as James Brown, who performed in Boston that same night, wrote, 'Dr. King's murder looked to be the place where Black people were going to draw the line.'[31]

The black Moses had been killed and his assassination marked a turning point. Though Martin Luther King had managed to push back ignorance, racism, and repression, he'd failed to eradicate them. His death triggered shockwaves across the country: Washington, Baltimore,

Kansas City and Chicago were ablaze. His assassination also signalled the explosion of the movement. Something had given. Violence called for more violence, spiralling out of control. King's death was a blind and desperate act that showed America's true face. From then on, there was nothing left to prevent flocks of black youths from turning radical and joining revolutionary organizations united around Black Power.

On the subject of Dr King's assassination, Nina declared: 'He was becoming too strong, you know, they couldn't let him live. The people were finally getting the message, and they had to shut him up. But, you know, they can try to kill me – I know they want to – but I'm not going to be quiet, *no way!* I'm not scared of them. They think killing us will stop us, but even if I die someone else will keep on telling them the truth. I'm hurting inside, you understand... They killed Martin, man, just shot him dead like a dog. This is too hard, sometimes it's just too goddam hard.'[32]

President Johnson proclaimed 7 April a national day of mourning. But all black artists scheduled to perform on that day went ahead with their concerts. James Brown in Boston, Nina Simone in Westbury, both of them finding the weight of mourning and the emotional load too crushing. This was the first time that Nina performed 'Why? (The King of Love Is Dead)', a song written by her bass player Gene Taylor, a funeral tribute to King. The song begins with a long instrumental introduction; it digresses, whispers, prays, condemns and salutes Martin's memory: 'I dedicate this show to the memory of Dr Martin Luther King, as you obviously know. This song was inspired by him and written for him... As for today, what will, happen today, in our cities where my people are rising up? They're living in abandon, and even if I were to die right this second, I want them to know what freedom is! What will happen now that the King of Love is dead?'

You could feel the depth of Nina's sorrow and despair just by listening to her. Early in the concert, she played the ballad 'Sunday in Savannah'. In a gentle, soothing voice led in by a long piano introduction, she expressed her gratitude to the audience for making the journey on that night of mourning. 'We're happy you came and surprised to see so many of you here. We didn't expect anyone tonight and you know why... Everyone knows and there's nothing more to say, you know why... We hope to be able to give you... Something. Tonight, on this very special night, at the strangest of times in 1968. We hope to be able to give you something... Something... What you want, what you need...' The Westbury concert was recorded by RCA and released under the title 'Nuff Said! As though Nina were proclaiming that the time had come to quit the dialogue, to take up arms and to join the revolution. The album was nominated for an Emmy Award. This was one of the best concerts Nina ever played, and a historical testament, captured at one of the most tragic times in American history.

Within a few months, black leaders would be forced into exile or silence, sidelined by the government, all to the relative indifference of public opinion and white liberals tormented by a Vietnam War that occupied everyone's minds. Anti-war movements had formed. Some of them, like the white activists of the Weather Underground, wanted to bring the war to American soil by attacking representations of power. They followed the Black Panthers, opting for terrorist acts that targeted symbols of power and going underground.[33]

The FBI had infiltrated all black organizations. In Louisiana, Rap Brown, who'd taken over the reins of the SNCC from Stokely Carmichael, was sentenced to prison for carrying an illegal weapon. Before the trial, the judge had privately said he was 'going to get that nigger'. Released on bail while he awaited his appeal ruling, he decided to go underground. Stokely Carmichael, watched and persecuted by the government, chose to go into exile and sought shelter under the protection of President Sékou Touré in Conakry, Guinea, with Miriam Makeba. 'With the Vietnam War, student protests, the riots in the ghettos, everyone is scared [in the States]. Everyone lives in fear of a major black upheaval. The government is afraid that Stokely might become the leader of this rebellion. The FBI wouldn't leave him alone. And just because he was born in Trinidad, which used to be a British colony, he was banned from all the countries of the Commonwealth, meaning about thirty countries. All this because he might have caused those people to rebel.'[34]

The police sowed terror in the community, waging a relentless war against the Panthers. Seale was thrown into prison in 1969. Newton was trapped by the role he had been given by American society. He ended up drugged and was beaten by a gangster in the middle of the street in Oakland who wanted to show his strength. 'Look how strong I am, I beat Huey Newton.'

Nina watched the collapse of the movement and felt betrayed. Black leaders who hadn't chosen exile had taken refuge in university careers or in social action programmes. 'I felt sick at my own naivety,' she said. But despite the collapse, she continued to take increasingly radical positions, even going as far as to shout down her white audience during concerts. Weary, that white audience began, little by little, to turn away. Despite that defeat, the spilled blood, trampled souls and dreams, Nina remained obsessed with the armed struggle. In her opinion, the war had to be fought no matter the cost and despite the fact that its leaders had been eliminated. In truth, she had been kept far from the crossfire, hadn't fought in the streets of the ghettos. And her contribution seemed slight now that all was lost.

She would later write: 'If I had had the choice, I would have been a killer, without doubt! I would have taken up arms, I'd have gone down to the South, and I would have fought violence with violence. Blow by blow if I'd had the choice. But my husband told me that I knew nothing about it and he refused to teach me. When I obeyed him I was left with nothing more than music. But if I had had the choice, I probably wouldn't be sat here today, I'd probably be dead. I would have used arms, I am not non-violent. I don't blame whites for what they did. They were slave-drivers. That what they were, they were slave-drivers. If the blacks had had the opportunity, they would have had whites as slaves, yes!'[35] She also said: 'We didn't achieve what we had fought for. If we had, we wouldn't be where we are today with only five black mayors in the United States, we would have had half of the United States for ourselves, a separate state. That's an idea I support. America is full of prejudices and discrimination. And blacks will never have their rights until they have their own state. They should have led an armed revolution. A lot of blood would have been spilled, but I believe we would have a separate black state today.'[36]

However, is it right to claim that all blacks in the United States were committed to the fight for their rights at the time? Certainly not. The abundant black literature produced during the 60s and 70s provides a prism through which we can see a more insidious, darker reality, the reality of life in the black ghettos. That alternative literature, scorned upon publication in the United States, uses straightforward language to depict life in black society. It states that, far from the manoeuvrings of the movement, the black community also included individuals ready to harm one another. This can be understood by simply reading the books of Iceberg Slim, Donald Goines, Charles Perry or Clarence Cooper.

Let's take Donald Goines for example, the author of sixteen novels in the 1970s. Like the characters in his books, he led a life as a pimp, spent a few years in jail, and ended up shot over some dope. His writings are a cold, documented, authentic description of drug addicts, of the daily life of seedy pimps in the ghetto. Raw, precise stories that stink of danger and urgency, in which we follow Kenyatta, a character whose two ambitions are to 'clean drug dealing out of the ghettos and bring down all racist white cops'. This is far from the black intellectual scene formed in Harlem in the 50s, far from the Harlem Renaissance of the 20s and 30s, far from the dazzle of Baldwin, LeRoi Jones or Chester Himes.

Strangely, one of the biggest best-sellers of the post-war period was written by a black pimp: Iceberg Slim.

Born Robert Beck in Chicago in 1918, Iceberg Slim began his initiation into the world of dealing at eighteen years of age and set out to build an empire with women and drugs, until his fall and a prison sentence of ten months' solitary confinement in Cook County Jail in 1960. Afterwards, he dedicated himself to writing, recording unvarnished and without looking for redemption his memories of his twenty-five-year reign as the 'world's greatest pimp'. His first book, *Pimp*, covers his rise and his daily life as a pimp: What was it like running a prostitution business? What problems did he encounter? But beyond that, *Pimp* tells of the rise of a black man who became powerful and free, flouting the law and applying white America's profit logic, until he was trapped by its rules. *Pimp* was published in 1969 by Holloway House, a small Los Angeles publisher specialized in salacious reports on Hollywood. This first novel achieved unprecedented success in the ghettos, selling two million copies. The *New York Times'* refusal to carry advertising for the novel in its honourable pages changed nothing. The book held up a frightening mirror to the black community, showing the implacable mechanism of its obsessions, its deviances and its ordinary violence. A mythology, an aesthetic, a ghost of the black gangster defying the laws set down by the government was born with *Pimp*. Twenty years later, the traces it left would become apparent in the birth of gangsta rap. Because without Iceberg Slim there would have been no Ice Cube, no Ice-T, no Snoop Dogg and no 50 Cent.

In fact, this literature was judged indecent at a time when black leaders were fighting to bestow a positive and virtuous image on their community. Here we are far from the slogan 'Stand up and be counted', far from Curtis Mayfield's call for union, far from the debate confronting self-defence with non-violence. Here, everything overflowed with filth, misery and despair. And what were Iceberg Slim, Donald Goines and Clarence Cooper saying? That it's not just the whites who are responsible for blacks' hardship. That it's more complicated than that. To tell their tales of ordinary crimes, excess and disillusionment. But this picture of ghetto reality didn't come into the black institutions' perfect model. You couldn't shout 'Black is beautiful' and read *Welcome to hell* without questioning your certainties. The leading lights of the black community didn't want to hear the truth about its weaknesses, and white America didn't wish to recognize the existence of a new generation of black writers holding up a mirror, the authors lapsed into obscurity.

However, the figure of the 'Bad Nigger', as opposed to that of the 'Good Negro' as theorized by the writer Nik Cohn, continued to haunt America, even catching up with it. That happened on 16 October 1968 at the Mexico Olympic Games when the black athletes Tommie Smith (who had just broken the world and Olympic 200 metres records with a time of 19.83 seconds) and John Carlos (who came third) gave the Black Power salute on the podium: raised fist in a black leather glove and lowered head. The image went around the world. The two athletes explained that the freedom sung of in the American national anthem was only available to whites. The International Olympic Committee forced their suspension and banned them from the Olympic Village.

To protest against the absurdity of the war, Nina Simone decided to cover 'Ain't Got No/I Got Life', a song from the musical *Hair*, with which she would reach number 45 on the British charts. Straight on the heels of that release Nina embarked on a European tour, her first sold-out tour. RCA insisted on the pianist harvesting the laurels for her hit and Andy Stroud set up a two-month tour whose highlights were a London concert, a performance at the Olympia in Paris and then the new Jazz Festival in Montreux, Switzerland.

Other American and British artists had by now interpreted many of the songs in Nina's repertoire, achieving notable success in Europe. Following 'The House of the Rising Sun', the Animals had climbed to the top of the charts with 'Don't Let Me Be Misunderstood', Shirley Bassey had a hit with 'The Other Woman', Alan Price had tried 'I Put a Spell on You'...

Despite the increased fame these covers brought Nina, they disgusted her. She thought the public didn't know where the songs came from: 'This list started to get me down after a while, especially when some of my audiences thought I played those songs because they were familiar crowd-pleasers, as if I only covered other artists' hits like some second-rate cabaret singer.'[37] Nina had some cheek to be upset, as most of her own repertoire was covers. But perhaps she reckoned to be able to do what her rivals couldn't: give those songs their full value.

First stage, London. The Strouds arrived at the Mayfair Hotel in the West End. Since her last tour, Nina had further affirmed her allure as an African queen. Sexy knitwear dresses, heavy silver jewellery, hair drawn back in a bun and encircled by a metal crown. She was on edge but still resistant. Despite everything, she remained deeply committed, asserting her Africanness in everything she did. But perhaps she was also losing herself in her role. It was dressed like this that she appeared on *Top of the Pops* and then on *The David Frost Show*, two beacons of British music television. Emotions rose when, her face grave, the lady began 'I Wish I Knew How It Would Feel to Be Free'.

Then she played at the Palladium and the Royal Albert Hall. Before the concert, an argument with Andy broke out in the dressing room: 'You think I'm a machine, you're just like all the rest. You just want me to perform, you don't give a damn.'[38] Their relationship seemed broken: 'Andy was a good manager, but not a good husband,' she would later tell her friend (and president of her British fan club) Silvia Hampton. 'There was never any passion between us. We had neglected our relationship so much that we never spoke about our feelings, our hopes, all we ever did was fight... Without doubt I expected more of Andy that he was willing to give.'[39] He only took decisions as her manager now, having abandoned his role as a husband long before.

In 1968, the Strouds' relationship reached a point of no return. The main problem was that they'd been working together too much and for too long. That and the lack of sex, Nina's frustration at not feeling loved or desired, fed the feeling of imprisonment that haunted her. Logically, a couple going through an emotional desert like that separates. But Nina had become dependent on Andy on every level. For a long time he'd decided on every detail of her existence – with the notable exception of the safety valve provided by her involvement in the movement. Perhaps he let her continue with her activism for that reason. At least she still kept the hope of enjoying some sort of freedom...

Accumulated tiredness, commercial pressures, artistic worries, growing doubts about her ability to seduce, the movement's collapse, never-ending tours, her role as a mother that she hadn't been able to fulfil, her body starved of sex and her disintegrating marriage, all of these factors contributed to pushing Nina over a line after which the consequences seemed irreversible.

Little by little regular violence took root in her marriage. Everybody who spent time with the couple in those days felt that it took infinite patience to put up with the diva's increasingly violent tantrums. Andy was at the centre of the storm. He was both the husband who no longer satisfied his wife and the manager responsible for her endemic tiredness. Whenever she went through these rages, Nina zeroed in on him as her target. She would try to provoke him, insult him, question his virility or his honesty in public. She would push him into a corner until he exploded and answered her back. He hit her, she hit back blow for blow, and everyone who witnessed these outbursts of violence retains a traumatic memory of them. There were numerous scenes of this kind, and they terrorized the Strouds' entourage and wove a self-destructive knot within the marriage. '[Y]ou don't know what he's doing to me. I'm telling you, man, if you find me dead, he's the one. You better take him out of here or I might just shoot him dead. I mean it, man.'[40] Escalating violence that inevitably led to divorce.

After their separation and until the last few years of her life, Nina would continue to depict Andy as a monster whose sole interest was power. We have to draw nuances from each of their viewpoints and recognize that he had an impossible role. In reality, Andy Stroud knew that his wife needed rest. But he was caught between the record label's demands (after all, he wouldn't get two chances to manage someone like her), tours, and the need that Nina Simone felt when her audience was calling for her. The stakes at hand, RCA's pressure on Andy's shoulders, and Nina's nervous fatigue affected their marriage and Nina's mental health.

The secret was kept till the end, and revealed in these terms by Sylvia Hampton, Nina Simone's London friend, in her biography of the artist, *Break Down & Let It All Out*. The chronic psychological problems that appeared around 1967 and 1968 were due to 'a medical condition that created an imbalance in her brain. Her mood swings were nothing more than symptoms of this imbalance.'[41] Sylvia Hampton concluded: 'being around her at that time had become incredibly difficult'.

Although she had managed to control her attacks till now, she was exhausted, overloaded, exploited, dominated, cheated: the pain worsened and her bouts of anger refused to subside. Whenever she plunged into torments, only Andy had a hope of pulling her out. But as he became the enemy against whom Nina focused all her aggression, he gradually stopped being able to soothe his wife. Her rages became so violent, so uncontrollable that the story seemed bound to end in drama: 'Goddam it, you don't give a damn, you just want me to be a work horse. Nina sing, Nina play, Nina smile. Well I'm sick of it, you hear me, man? You can't keep working me to death. I've had enough. I need a rest, man, and you'd better let me rest or you'll be sorry, real sorry.'[42]

These crises began, little by little, to dominate her life, poisoning her. Everything had become a touchy subject, her music, her tiredness, the colour of her skin. When she appeared on *Top of the Pops* in 1969, the stage manager asked Nina's manager for her to change the black dress she was wearing. The set was black. Black dress, black skin, black set for a black-and-white broadcast: no chance of seeing anything on the screen but the pianist's teeth. This nearly caused an incident. Sylvia Hampton, who was with Nina that day, told the stage manager that she refused to take the suggestion to Nina. How could she tell a woman on the edge of a nervous breakdown and whose great battle was pride in her race that she was too black and had to change her dress? The set dresser put up a white background and Nina never knew anything had happened.

But there were incidents like that every day. And the results were often far from happy. Nevertheless, the European tour had already begun and the stakes were high. There was no question of going back. The Strouds flew off to Dublin, Cardiff, Edinburgh... In Holland on 8 June, the forces of destruction caught up with Nina Simone: Robert Kennedy had just been assassinated. She was stunned. It would never end. But there was no time to think, she had to leave for Rotterdam, and then Paris.

I learned something quite unexpected about this first time in Paris. Afterwards, I tried to confirm it with people who were close to Nina Simone over those years and each time their eyes opened in wonder, as they simply said to me: 'How do you know about that?'

Nina Simone was not alone in Paris. Of course, Andy was there with her, the musicians accompanying her on tour, but also a young Haitian woman who was none other than Nina's 'intimate friend': Marie-Christine Dunham, the dancer and choreographer Katherine Dunham's adoptive daughter.

Katherine was the black American Isadora Duncan. Raised in Chicago, the daughter of a Canadian mother and a black American tailor father – whose ancestors, she said, came from Madagascar – Katherine Dunham gave her first performance at eight years of age, to raise money for the Methodist church in Joliet, Illinois. Her career was launched in 1941 when she played the role of Georgia Brown in *Cabin in the Sky*, the first musical with an all-black cast ever produced on Broadway.[43] Thereafter, Katherine Dunham explored all aspects of African dance practised in the United States, the Caribbean and West Africa. She set up a troupe of dancers, singers and musicians who toured by her side across the world and accompanied her in creating shows like *Carib Song*, *Bal Nègre* in 1946 and *Tropical Revue*. Becoming a black cultural icon across the world (from Niger to Morocco, Dakar to Addis Ababa...), Katherine Dunham appeared in many Hollywood films, including *Carnival of Rhythm*, *Stormy Weather* alongside Cab Calloway in 1943 and triumphing in the blockbuster *Mambo* in 1954.

In 1941 she married John Thomas Pratt, the famous theatre designer. After founding the Dunham School of Dance and Theater in New York, Katherine resided in Dakar before settling in Port-au-Prince where she bought Résidence Leclerc, an old colonial plantation that had belonged to Napoleon Bonaparte's sister, which became a centre for the black intelligentsia. Over these years in Haiti, she adopted an orphan: Marie-Christine.

A writer (including *A Touch of Innocence* and *Island Possessed*, her exploration of Haitian voodoo), poet, ethnologist, a living memory in black cultures across the globe, a figure committed to her community's politics in the United States, and, finally, a dazzling choreographer and dancer, Katherine Dunham presented the show *Bamboche!* at the Théâtre de Paris at the beginning of the 60s. She took Marie-Christine with her and they were welcomed by the swells of Paris: the Cocteaus, Jean Marais, Mistinguett, Josephine Baker... While Katherine split her time between New York, Dakar, Port-au-Prince and, soon after, East St. Louis, Illinois, where she set up another dance school in the mid-1960s ('I've gone around the world, and I've never known a place with so much apathy and so little reason to hope... It's a terrible place'[44]), Marie-Christine stayed in Paris, determined to start a career as an actress. We can see her influence in a piece played by Roger Pierre and Jean-Marc Thibaut, and again in *Opération Lagreleche*, performed by Michel Serrault and Jean Poiret, and finally in *Les Enfants de Coeur* by François Campaux at the Fontaine theatre in August 1967.

I've found several studio photos of Marie-Christine during these years. A pretty young mixed-race woman of clear beauty, shy in front of the camera but giving off irresistible charm. But Marie-Christine's career would never take off. She lived in Paris at the Notre-Dame-de-France school in Malakoff, rue Marius Franay in Saint-Cloud, then rue Mahler, in the 4th arrondissement, where she was until at least the middle of 1968. She was living there when Nina Simone came to Paris for the first time in June.

Nina Simone and Marie-Christine Dunham were to have an affair. I don't know how long it lasted, or how it developed. In the future, Nina's taste for women wouldn't be denied, even if none of her homosexual experiences would last beyond initial attraction. It is hard to suppose that Andy Stroud was in the dark about his wife's intimacy with Marie-Christine Dunham, but no one can say how he reacted to the news.

In fact, the relationship was no great mystery. Nina and Katherine Dunham had known one another for several years. In the United States, Katherine was an artist everyone revered, committed to the fight for civil rights just as, later, she would take a public position against 'Papa Doc' Duvalier's dictatorial regime in Haiti. Nina admired Katherine Dunham, a model of intelligence, grace and the very image of black American femininity. Perhaps she met Marie-Christine while in New York or Chicago. We can imagine that the forlorn diva found a confidante in her, a soulmate perhaps, a woman who appreciated Nina for herself and not for what she represented.

In any event, Nina was in good company with Marie-Christine during her first visit to Paris in June 1968. On her advice, she contacted a great young hairdresser who moved in the artistic circles of the time, the night before her concert. His stage name was Robert de Paris. Robert was close to Jean Marais, an intimate friend of the vamp Rita Cadillac and the transsexual Coccinelle. He spent time with stars of the day, from Fernand Raynaud to the young Alain Delon... Robert was a figure in the fashionable life of Paris's Rive Droite, the sort of man who knew everything about even the smallest new things, enjoying his access to that closed world that could help you unearth 'what you're searching for'. Nina called during the day, giving the name Marie-Christine Dunham, and telling him that she 'needed a service' and that she'd come during the day. That afternoon, a black Mercedes drew up in front of Robert de Paris's salon in rue de Clichy.

With her thick, short, masculine hair, fake eyelashes that were almost falling off, not wearing any make-up, Nina made quite an entrance in that little salon, introduced herself to Robert and at once stated what she'd come for. As he always did, Robert tried to get to know her, but in the face of this woman's roughness, he gave up and guided her as best he could. 'I remember a woman with no manners, not expansive or cordial, a reserved woman with a certain shyness about her,' he said.

Nina in Paris in June 1968. Did she know that only a few weeks before the French capital had gone through a revolutionary student uprising? That Stokely Carmichael had even come to meet the anti-establishment students movement at the Sorbonne? That what was going on in the United States was not an isolated phenomenon, but that from Prague to Paris, from West Germany to Italy, from Spain to Mexico, the world had gone through a student uprising and a longing for change, for freedom? Did she know that the fight being led in her country was repeated across the globe, that the uprising was worldwide, that it was no longer about race, but a class struggle demanding change, using weapons and violence if necessary? During her concert at the Olympia, in any event, she didn't say a thing about it.

In the opinion of Jean-Michel Boris, the Parisian music hall's artistic director at the time, 'Nina was nervous before taking the stage at the Olympia.' And she had every reason to be – that venue was world-renowned, even in the USA. The stars of black music had already put on triumphant concerts there: James Brown, Duke Ellington, Miles Davis, the Motown crew, and so on. Nina, who had performed Brel and Aznavour, who had even been invited by Piaf, could not fail to give a concert in this symbolic venue.

She came out on stage in a black dress, like an African princess, her hair styled in braids woven around a metal tube. At first she played solo, upright, mechanically, but she quickly relaxed and let herself go with the flow. Then she was joined by her musicians, who sat a little further back, at the foot of the curtain. Those who experienced the concert remember to this day a skilled artist playing music unlike anything the Olympia knew at the time. That is how Nina achieved her first Parisian success. A standing ovation, two encores and 'I Wish I Knew How It Would Feel to Be Free' to close.

Following this triumph, the Strouds were invited by Bruno and Paulette Coquatrix to the traditional Olympia after-show dinner. I spoke to Mrs Coquatrix by phone and she remembered that 'It wasn't exactly a pleasure to dine with Nina. I admit that I dragged my heels a little. I found her very cold, very distant. She was a little nasty too.' Even Bruno Coquatrix, whose hospitality towards artists was legendary, admits being put off by the coldness of the couple he had invited to his table.

The next day Nina set off for a small town in Switzerland to participate in the second year of an event that would soon achieve international importance: the Montreux Jazz Festival.

If you go to Montreux out of season you'll be struck by the boredom that reigns there. It is true that the town's location is wonderful, built as it is on the banks of Lake Geneva opposite the Alps. Up in the mountains that loom above the town, a few high chalets offer staggering views over the lake and the Alps. The soul of the Montreux Jazz Festival nestles among these high peaks. During the first weekend in July 1968, at the beginning of the marathon two-week event dedicated to all types of music, a man was seen running in all directions: Claude Nobs.

Nobs, who apprenticed as a cook, founded the festival in 1967. Thanks notably to his sense of hospitality, he has been able to bring the greatest names in music of the last forty years to the banks of Lake Geneva. From Miles Davis and Count Basie to Led Zeppelin, from Ella Fitzgerald to David Bowie, from Quincy Jones to Lou Reed and Dylan, all of them, down the years, would accept Claude Nobs's invitation.

When Nina Simone arrived in Switzerland on 16 June 1968 to perform at the Casino de Montreux, she felt at her worst. The concert she gave that night has never been released, but recordings made then of 'Backlash Blues', 'House of the Rising Sun' and 'Ain't Got No' can be found on dubiously legal records from the early 70s. Nina would discover the extent of the pirate market in Europe during this tour.

For her it was straightforward theft and simply mentioning the phenomenon was enough to send her into a rage. She realized that black artists in particular were victims of this industry. She developed a violent line against these practices, judging that small labels were practising large-scale swindling.

Claude Nobs introduced Nina to the audience: 'Here's the high priestess of soul music: Miss Nina Simone.' Sam Waymon, who accompanied his sister at the organ during that tour, gave the sign and the group (Bob Clark – drums, Gene Taylor – bass, Jimmy Young – guitar) opened with an instrumental piece that can be found as an intro on the great live album *Black Gold*. The diva then made her appearance and sang 'Go to Hell' ('Some say that hell is below us / I say that hell is right beside me'). She then moved on to 'Just in Time', the traditional 'When I Was a Young Girl', then 'Don't Let Me Be Misunderstood', 'Ne me quitte pas'... Nina Simone tells that, suddenly overwhelmed by Martin Luther King's death, she dissolved in tears and had to leave the stage, under the cameras' gaze. She also said that her repertoire was entirely made up of anti-establishment songs 'to let people know what was going on in her country'.

The reality is less clear-cut. Having obtained and listened to the original recording, I can say that it not only offers a pretty representative range of Nina Simone's art (from ballads to blues, from traditional folk to protest songs), but is a high-quality, two-hour-long concert that is hardly interrupted by the audience's applause. Lively, open music performed by an artist happy to play with her audience, such as during the jumping 'See Line Woman'. When speaking with the audience, her voice is soft, smooth, an invitation to participate. The extended versions she plays of the jumping 'Ain't Got No' (which ended the first half) and 'I Wish I Know' (which closed the set) are admirable. In certain ways, even though Nina's fatigue occasionally comes through in her voice, the Montreux concert is better than the *'Nuff Said!* live album, even though it doesn't feature the same dramatic tension. Focus on the way Nina directs her musicians, commanding them with authority, guiding them with respect to tonalities, directions, digressions as she sets off on short improvisations. From 'Gin House Blues', she links into 'I Wish I Knew How It Would Feel to

Be Free' and with this change of tone we can feel the spirits setting themselves down by her sides. Accompanied by Sam Waymon on the organ, supported by a remarkable rhythm section, Nina performed a vibrant call for freedom for her European audience ignorant of the American strife. A few images of the Montreux concert are available. During the last part, we see Nina jump up from her stool, stride to the front of the stage, face her audience and invite the spirit to enter her body, then make a dance move that seems to resonate in her like a tremor, and, feverish, return to her seat, her eyes set on a point in space no one else can see.

Nina would often return to Montreux in the future. In the 1980s she would even move to just a few miles away, while in her freefall period she turned up in Nyon and then Geneva in circumstances that remain mysterious. The day after her first Swiss concert, en route to Geneva airport, could she have imagined that she would wind up here again in less than ten years' time?

Back in New York, Nina Simone went into the studio between 16 September and 1 October 1968 to record what she planned to be her masterpiece, and a revenge for her battered destiny. In fact it would be an unloved, misunderstood record, only a partial artistic success: *Nina Simone and Piano*. Nina had dreamed of this record as a statement of her classical talents. Singing and playing without a band, she includes here and there classical themes, such as by Bach and Liszt, that she adapted to a pop repertoire. The record is an artistic compromise between virtuosity and lyrical compositions. It contains some of her classics, such as 'Nobody's Fault But Mine', 'Compensation', and the dramatic 'Another Spring', the chronicle of the solitude of a desperate old woman who regains faith in life when spring returns – an image, trait by trait, of the fate awaiting Nina in a few years.

But *Piano* is, above all, an opportunity to study Nina Simone's game very closely. Through it, she wanted to prove to the world that she was OK in spite of everything, a concert pianist that destiny had placed on the wrong track. The record is stripped down, a meeting between Nina's voice and her piano, with very little space around them. A perfect setting to hear this record for listeners used to classical piano.

In Lausanne I met Céline Gorier-Bernard, a young French concert artist whose talent can be heard in the Jazz Café in Montreux. I asked her to listen to *Piano* and then a few classic songs from the Newport and Village Gate live albums, and to give me her comments. My test was simple: what would a well-trained classical musician hear in Nina Simone's music? Her response was instructive: a slap in the face to those I'd talked to previously, who on the whole said that Nina had 'put herself on a pedestal' and lacked the talent and discipline for a career in classical music. After listening to the records that I had given her, Céline Gorier-Bernard's response was categorical: 'She plays the piano marvellously well. She has the skill of a classical concert pianist. It comes shining through on this record. It's brimming with nuances, her touch and sound are very precise, she doesn't play at all like a jazz pianist. In fact she never even evokes a jazz feeling. Not in the rhythms, or the sound, or the character. Not even in the live so-called jazz albums, like the ones recorded at the Village Gate and Newport. Nina Simone sings jazz, but when she plays, she doesn't accompany what she's singing; she's playing a classical part. At most, where she has to, she plays a few jazz chords then sets off on her classical lines again as soon as she can. Nina Simone never left classical music, she never ventured into jazz. Even in the pure blues pieces, she always plays through her classical sensibility. She uses a range of gestures, linking very short notes and rhythms, that you only find in classical music, never in jazz.'

Why could none of the critics or the musicians who worked with her grasp this essential point? 'Nina Simone sings in a jazzy way,' Céline went on, 'her musicians come from the world of jazz, but behind that façade she's playing classical music. If you take her voice off the tracks, leaving just her piano playing, it's pure classical music. Her playing covers the great classical periods (without quoting them at length): Bach, the rhythms you find in Brahms and Beethoven, the sound impressions present in early-twentieth-century music. When listening to *Piano* you realize that Nina can play everything and mix it all up. She plays like someone who's studied Beethoven, Haydn and Mozart a lot.

Her playing is clean, precise, close to the playing of a concert pianist such as Clara Haskil, a Mozart specialist, very far from the playing of jazz pianists like Ellington, Monk or Bill Evans. Nina does things that jazz musicians aren't technically able to do, but it's really in the sound itself that the essence of her playing is revealed. In fact, it is extremely difficult to play a piece of classical music, with all the different details to respect, and sing another melody at the same time. Nina Simone doesn't stick to the rhythm the way jazz musicians do, she takes time, slows down and speeds up like when you're playing a classical piece. When she improvises, it feels like playing Mozart: a precise, very clear sound. *Piano* is a destabilizing album. It has something desperate about it. Her voice is tormented, hoarse, it's a voice from the street, and she accompanies it with this Mozartlike piano, luminous, elegant, the opposite of her singing. The mixture is troubling.'

Almost as if the opposed figures possessing Nina Simone were expressing their antagonism through her music.

Piano was a commercial failure, and the next year RCA chose to capitalize on the success of a Bee Gees cover Nina played with the album *To Love Somebody*. As well as the title track, the pianist also recorded three Bob Dylan covers (including 'The Times They Are a-Changing'), 'Turn, Turn, Turn!', adapted 'Suzanne' by Leonard Cohen and included the song 'Revolution', which she had co-written with a jazz musician who'd recently become her artistic director: Weldon Irvine, Jr. 'It's about a revolution, man; not just colour, but everything! It's about the barriers being broken down... It's time, honey. People are just so hung up about life, age, sex, how much money you've got – it's all just a mess. We need a revolution to sort it all out and get back to God. You know how lost we are, man – it's sad.'[45]

To Love Somebody sold well, without finding any particular resonance on the American or British charts. At the same time, Philips released a greatest hits compilation.

Meanwhile, Nina performed at the prestigious Lincoln Center in New York on 26 October 1969. The concert was a triumph, saluted by the columnist John S. Wilson in the pages of the *New York Times* the next day:

Each year, as Nina Simone gets deeper and deeper into herself and into her music, new facets of this remarkable performer come into view. During the past ten years, she has evolved from a relatively traditional jazz artist and ballad singer to become a weaver of exotic moods and then a fiery black polemicist. Last year she branched into rock – her own version, of course, for everything she does bears the stamp of her strong, personal style.

Last night a full and enthusiastic house at Philharmonic Hall saw and heard this year's development. The mood material, spun out in the throbbing beat of her sensuous voice, is still there. And so are the polemics. But her stage personality is more open, more free. She smiles and glows as she has never done before. She runs merrily across the stage, looking very Russian in a dark blue belted blouse and trousers, stuffed knickerbocker fashion, into her high black boots.[46]

This concert was recorded and became one of the masterpieces of Nina Simone's discography, released by RCA in 1970: *Black Gold*.

When you listen to this disc, you sense that Nina had never sought so much to communicate with her audience, and RCA had the brilliant idea of leaving in the long monologues before each song. The final version of the record doesn't include the Richie Havens cover she performed that evening, or the calypso version of Leonard Cohen's 'Suzanne'.

The evening was opened by Ed Williams. He introduced the musicians, recited a poem by Langston Hughes, then introduced the diva. She opened with a stripped-down version of 'Black Is the Color of My True Love's Hair', joined by the percussionist Emile Latimer, who in turn played his own version of the song on acoustic guitar, accompanied by Nina on piano. Up to this point, she had never invited a musician to take the starring role in a song. When you listen to the two versions you realize how complementary they are, alternating between Nina's dramatic tension and Latimer's roughness. Then 'Ain't Got No/I Got

Life' in a funky version close to the way it was performed in Montreux, which she finishes in fits and starts, murmuring: 'I say I have my soul... I still have my choice to live, to laugh or to cry, I take all of those choices, I have to stay here and work, and till then... *I got life!*'

Finally, she takes a break and addresses the crowd: 'Good evening, I'm happy to see you. Well, well, it's a full house! It's a good time to introduce you to the beating heart of our organization. The pulse of everything we do is organized around the drummer. Do you really, seriously remember, throughout your life, to listen to your heartbeat? That beat is the rhythm, isn't it?' We hear the first beats of the conga drum and Nina introduces 'Westwind': 'This is a song Miriam Makeba asked me to sing. She's my friend and this is a prayer.' She invokes the west wind, the spirits of bygone days and their powers to save the living. Structured on a minimal, percussive framework, excluding all other colourings, 'Westwind' invites Nina to make her prayers: 'West wind, in your splendour, free my people.'

Then, in an exhausted voice, she warns: 'We are recording this evening's concert, that's why we're trying to give you something that we're too tired to do. I think it's Faye Dunaway who said, in the film *Bonnie and Clyde*, that she tried to give the people what they want. But really, it's a mistake. But soon I'll learn my lessons, and you'll buy even more records because you want to see me!' Energized by the applause, Nina addresses the audience again, as if telling them a secret, and whisperes a question that had been haunting her: 'At certain times in your life, you have the chance to ask yourself what is this thing we call time? You leave for work by it [the clock], you have your lunch in the afternoon by it, your coffee break, you get on a plane, you arrive, and it goes on and on. Time. Where is it going, what is it doing? But most of all, is it alive? Is this thing that we can't touch alive? One day, we look at ourselves in the mirror, we've grown old and we wonder: Where does the time go?'

Accompanied by an acoustic guitar, Nina begins 'Who Knows Where the Time Goes', moving forward delicately, cautiously, with a depth of emotion that from the first bars seems on the point of breaking. Then the pianist really comes into the song, playing strong chords and leading the song towards its climax. You have to listen to this track carefully. A guy at the record label ran a pair of scissors through it. It's impossible to think that the last section of 'Who Knows Where the Time Goes' was performed the way it appears on the record. It's harshly cut together, even the tonality is not good. Suddenly the organ and the drums, which had been relegated to the sidelines, come in and lead a funky instrumental, then it's a new blend and Nina plays the first notes of 'The Assignment Sequence': 'This song is about the breach between lovers, especially married lovers!' She knows what she's talking about. The hall breaks into laughter. She glances towards the wings where Andy is watching.

The concert ends on the civil rights hymn 'To Be Young, Gifted and Black', a song that Nina co-wrote with her artistic director, Weldon Irvine, Jr., in memory of Lorraine Hansberry. 'To Be Young, Gifted and Black' would end all of her concerts from now on: 'It's like a religious song for me now. I can think of nothing more appropriate to end with than this song that was the fruit of a moment of inspiration. It was given to me – given to me to sing one Sunday morning. One afternoon, I called Weldon Irvine, my artistic director – and I told him that I needed lyrics and what ideas they had to talk about, and the next day the song was finished.'[47]

On stage at the Philharmonic Hall, Nina gave homage to Lorraine: 'I miss her more every day... It's the story of her life, Weldon Irvine, Jr. and I wrote this song for her. I think that in a few weeks I won't be able to sing this song any more, because each time I do, I miss Lorraine too much.'[48] She reminded the audience that the song had just come out as a single, that it was addressed to blacks, that its aim was not to attack whites, but simply to ignore them. Finally, she reminded them 'there are twenty-two million black people in this country and I ask a million of them to buy this record!'

'To Be Young, Gifted and Black' says that there are millions of young, gifted, black boys and girls, that the world is waiting for them, their adventure has only just begun and that their soul remains intact even when they feel defeated. The song entered the American R&B Top 10 upon release, helped by a huge promotional campaign orchestrated by RCA, and later boosted by the covers performed by Aretha Franklin and Donny Hathaway.

The company sent radio DJs copies of *Black Gold* along with a second disc featuring an interview recorded with Nina Simone, and a booklet with the interview transcribed. DJs could thus ask questions during their shows, broadcast Nina's answers, and pretend they had her in the studio.

During the thirty-minute interview, Nina answers the questions in a bad mood, repeating several times that she wants the record to sell well. But she did reveal this: 'I'm very proud of this album. There's a lot of energy on this record. There's great communication between the audience and me, which was lacking in some of my previous live albums... That was a magical night. Even though the album had to be edited, that's the way it goes... We wanted to release the concert just as it was, but it was too long... Still, eighty per cent of what happened that night is captured on the album. But you can't always capture the feeling of a concert or the warmth of a moment. That was often the case. But that night, it worked... That's why that night and this record are dear to me.'[49]

At the peak of her stage art, but increasingly affected by a worrying state of physical and psychological fatigue, Nina Simone gave a concert in Newark, New Jersey, in March 1970, the same place where violent race riots had taken place three years before. The audience was entirely made up of blacks. Disgusted by the movement's bankruptcy, the exile or resignation of black leaders, Nina attacked political leaders of all races. Nina Simone's political disengagement began at this concert. But how could she turn her back after so many years lived through and for the fight to gain civil rights?

Her goal was clear: she was at the end, it was vital to release the ballast in all areas, in her political commitment, in her career, and in her love life. Soon came the Newport Festival, after which the *New York Times* would run a headline on her triumph. On the way to her performance, a violent argument exploded between Nina and Andy. She told him that she wanted to take a break from her career, that she needed to rediscover herself, that she needed a few months to breathe. He didn't want to hear any of it and kept using the same reasons: pressure from the record company, contracts that had been signed with promoters, the money they would lose if they were cancelled, and so on.

The concert took place, but on the way back the same subject set off another argument. She tried to convince Andy, to make him see reason, she even begged him, but he remained stubbornly locked into his role as manager. She saw red. She had just crossed a point of no return. Suddenly, everything was clear. She would have to leave Andy for a while, forget this country, its disappointments, her career, and go away to recharge her batteries. She needed an island, some down time, peace. She had been dazzled by Barbados during the Caribbean tour. She had always sworn she'd go back there. Why not now?

Lisa was at Andy's mother's house for a few weeks. When they got back to Mount Vernon, Nina saw her husband set off again for Manhattan, doubtless thinking that by leaving her alone, he'd teach his wife a lesson, that she'd think this over and beg him to come back, to not get angry.

That was too much. She put a few things in a case, shoved the money she could find in her purse, left her wedding ring on the bedroom dressing table, ordered a taxi, went straight to the airport and took the first flight to Barbados.

6

THERE'S NO WAY OUT
OF OUR TROUBLES

SEPTEMBER 1970. Nina Simone arrived at Grantley Adams Airport to take her first holiday in seven years. Cost was not an issue. She had to take advantage of this opportunity. She went down to Sam Lord's Castle Resort, a five-star hotel in Long Bay, a few minutes by car from Bridgetown. Nina slept for twelve hours the first few nights. But she still felt exhausted when she got up, as if her body, used to hyperactivity for over ten years, was reacting strangely to this new idleness. These were dreamless, lifeless nights. She experienced muscle pains upon waking, her neck was strangely sore, her muscles were stiff. But when she got up and finally pulled back the curtains, a view of paradise greeted her: sea and sky mixing in a crystalline blue. Four hundred dollars a night. A fortune! But a little money wasn't going to ruin this moment. Money didn't have that power. She called room service with a hoarse voice. Coffee please. She asked for coffee and fruit juice to be brought up, then she would see.

The next day, Nina woke up at nine o'clock. The night before she was happy just to go back and forth between the hotel's air-conditioned buffet, the swimming pool and the freshness of her room. She couldn't image the heat that would build up in just a few hours, when the sun would be so fierce it forced all living things to seek the slightest bit of shade. The beach was only five minutes away on foot: from the hotel's swimming pool past the carefully clipped hedges, down the wooden steps to the sand and the ocean beyond, where she could choose where to go. Nina bought a swimming costume, a beach towel, sun cream, a pair of white sunglasses that took up half her face. She called a bell-boy, ordered a taxi and, under a porch where some holidaying Americans were strutting about in their linen clothes, she slumped down on a Liberty-print chair to wait for her driver. She sat watching the comings and goings in reception. She saw a woman talking to the hotel manager and who turned her head to stare at Nina from time to time. She read the woman's lips as she whispered: 'That black woman over there, she's not that singer, is she? Yes, you know...' The manager nodded: 'Yes, madam, it's her.'

Sitting in the back of the taxi, she demanded to be taken to 'The most beautiful beach.' The taxi drove for a few minutes and left her at the entrance to Crane Beach, on the island's east side. Delighted, she gave the driver a generous tip. He murmurs a rude thank-you. Stretching out in front of her was a scene like a postcard. A beach of immaculate white sand, completely deserted. She said to herself 'The Caribbean' and, still fully dressed, dropped down and stretched out on the sand. She planned to take advantage of her stay on the island to recover from her fatigue: beach, sun, swimming, walking slowly back to her towel, basking in the sun, diving lessons, back to the hotel, shower, pool, more sun. And an abundance of water to purify her soul from months of filth. Later, reminiscing about her first few days of happy solitude, she would say: 'I was in paradise and America didn't exist, had never existed...'[1] But New York was only a three-hour flight away and the ocean that separated her from America couldn't wash away all her worries. There was too much to be forgotten...

After another day of idleness, she had closed herself away in her room, ready for an early night, when she had a feeling that something in the room had been moved. Had someone been in there? She felt a presence. She came out in her dressing gown and tore down to the reception: 'Someone's been in my room, there's someone up there!' The receptionist looked at her carefully: 'Would you like one of our guys to see you to your room, Mrs Stroud?' He called her Mrs Stroud. He didn't know what he was saying... She demanded that they come to see who was hiding in her room, and where! 'Yes, send someone with me.'

They called one of the staff. 'This is Yuma. He'll see you to your room, as you wish.' She got into the lift with the young man. Black, slender, not bad. How old was he? Twenty-five? No more. She asked: 'Do you recognize me?' The guy looked at her, surprised: 'No madam, no. Should I?' 'Check if anyone has been in my room... I'm sure someone's hiding in there, do you understand?' And she began to get carried away: 'I'm sure, I'm certain there's someone there.' The kid panicked, he'd have held her by the shoulders to calm her down, but his orders were clear: absolutely no contact with clients. She could be a celebrity, and she looked quite dignified, he'd better do as he was supposed to. He opened the room door.

'Would you like to wait for me out here, madam?

'No, no, I'll stay with you.' The guy inspected the room, opening each door with care, every cupboard, he looked under the bed, checked that the window closed as it should, that the lock hadn't been forced. 'No madam, everything's in order. You think someone's been in here?' She stared at him, her mouth wide open, her hands twisted. 'Do you want to stay with me?' The kid's face changed from intrigued to worried: 'No, I can't, you understand...?' 'Then get lost.' Then screaming: 'I said get lost! Out!'

There she was, sat on the bed, staring at the curtains dancing in the warm breeze. She thought she would fall asleep watching the sun go down then sink below the sea. She hadn't turned on any lights since the kid had left. She covered her shoulders with a shawl, and went to get her cigarettes from her bag. There, sitting on a wicker chair on the balcony, she wondered how long it had been since she had made love. She laughed sadly: 'A long time, it's been a long time.'

She thought it over, and what did she see? That her life had been nothing more than a succession of obstacles to overcome, both in her marriage and her career. She'd managed to convince herself that she would triumph. But there she was, a failure. Had she been so blind? As an artist, had she lived up to the expectations of those who had fought for her? Had she been fair with Andy – a good wife, a good mother? So many questions and so few answers. She thought back to the day of Lisa's baptism. Andy by her side, laughing as they cycled through the streets of London. She thought back to the stage at Carnegie, the audience standing to applaud, the flowers thrown on stage and her sudden need to get out of there as fast as she could. She thought back to her young, firm body, offered to her husband on the first nights of their marriage. She thought back to the peace marches, her anxiety as she carried herself with dignity alongside Jimmy, Langston, Odetta, Miriam, Stokely, Lorraine... Over those few hours she felt again that strange fervour that she had when thousands of hearts came together as one. A fist raised, a weapon, a threat to make their rights heard in the hope of an honourable victory.

She felt the shadows glide around her in her hotel room, the faces of people far away, of vanished friends. She had no more strength to face up to the present, nothing to anchor her. The living and the ghosts, the disappeared and exiled, she missed them all; those absent people haunted her. She felt deprived, abandoned. She would have to talk to Andy, put an end to their arguing and find an arrangement, why not find the basis for a new beginning? She had to break this destructive cycle and start again from zero.

But there was more than that. It was strange, she couldn't hear the music any more. It used to be a part of her, in the slightest rustle, the slightest intonation of a voice, it was in her gut, seeping from her pores. But something in her had broken. She felt like a flat battery. She didn't know what to do with the feeling of disgust that filled her. She urged Lorraine's ghost to appear to her and promise her peace. But nothing came to console her.

At the end of September 1970, Nina left Barbados to fulfil a date in San Francisco. Two weeks had gone by and Andy still hadn't turned up. And yet she'd let Max Cohen know the number of her hotel, as she was convinced that her husband would look for her and end up asking their lawyer how to get in touch. Still, she didn't formalize anything, believing that a time apart would be good for both of them, they'd soon be back together again to sort out their problems. But in her mind there'd never been any question of divorce. Before flying off for the West Coast, Nina decided to pass by Mount Vernon to get a few things, check her mail and find Andy.

As she got out of the taxi, Nina knew straight away that something wasn't right. The house had a hangdog look, as if no one was living there. The hedges hadn't been trimmed for weeks, there were no toys lying around the garden, the shutters were down and the letter box was overflowing. Some were postmarked from more than two weeks before. She lingered on the postmarks. Mount Vernon tax office. Her pulse began to race. Something wasn't right. She set down her things beside the front door and shouted: 'Andy!' No answer. She emptied her handbag on the doormat, found her keys and opened the locks one by one. The house was locked up as if its inhabitants had decided to leave for a long time. The front door opened into darkness. The house was asleep. She tried to turn on the light. *Shit!* The fuses must have blown, or maybe someone had cut the power off. It smelled musty inside. She opened the shutters and windows, inspecting each nook and cranny of the house, creeping from room to room as if in a strange place. There was not a trace left of any of Andy's things, not a single piece of clothing, no toiletries, not even any records. His personal papers had also gone. The house hadn't been burgled. All the furniture was in order, her jewellery was in its box where it was always kept. In the kitchen she looked into the fridge: empty. The blackboard had also gone. 'Nina will be a rich black bitch,' you said.

She just couldn't stay there on her own. She made a few calls: *Do you know where Andy is? Lisa?* Nobody knew anything. They all thought he was still in Mount Vernon. She called his office but no one answered. That wasn't normal. It was a Wednesday afternoon. *What the hell is going on? Jimmy, Lorraine? What's going on?* She called a taxi, threw a few things into a big leather bag and took refuge in Manhattan.

Nina would never spend the night in Mount Vernon again.

The next morning she took a flight straight to San Francisco. She looked drawn, as if a few hours in New York had undone all the benefits of her two weeks' rest in Barbados. Alvin was waiting at the hotel, he didn't seem to know anything, welcoming her warmly, hugging her and teasing her: *So you old lazy bones, you been away in the Caribbean for two weeks?* He pulled out of their hug when she melted into sobs. She told him about the wedding ring she'd left on the night stand, that she'd just up and left, about her two weeks in Barbados without sending any notice, her worries about not having received any news from Andy. She told him about the house in darkness, that her husband's things weren't there. She panicked, he calmed her down.

That night's concert was like torture. She played the minimum she was required to and then left the stage, passing Alvin in tears and muttering: 'No encore, no encore or I'll go mad.'

He catches up with her, she gets away from him, he follows her to the dressing room till she shouts: 'Leave me alone, Al! Give me some peace.' He forces his way in and finds her collapsed in a chair. He takes her in his arms. She screams now: 'Where's that bastard gone, where's my daughter, Alvin?' He says the things that friends always do: 'Shh, it'll be OK, I'm here, Nina, calm down or cry if you want to, calm down, everything'll be OK.' He gets a chair and throws a can at a journalist who's watching the scene, missing him, and watches his friend suddenly burst out in laughter: 'Oh! Fuck... Thanks... I don't know where I am, Al, really, I don't know...'

He sat down in front of her: 'Come on, tell me what's going on.' 'Andy and I aren't talking any more, Alvin.' He could have asked her a simple, short question: 'Nina, did you ever talk?' But Alvin Schackman stayed silent and listened to the diva tell of her worries, of the clouds on her horizon, her submission to Andy over all those years, the business that she'd entrusted to him and her inability now to stick the parts of her career back together. She told him it was the first time in ten years that she'd been alone, that she didn't really know what strength had allowed her to get through so many obstacles before she met her husband, her confidence in him when he wanted to take charge of her business, and now her idleness. And now what? Continue her career alone? Beg Andy to come back? 'No, Alvin, I'd rather die than give in to him again.'

'What are you going to do?'

'Go back to Barbados.'

'There's nothing waiting for you there.'

'But I've nowhere to go.'

What could she say to him anyway? Could she tell him: 'I've failed in my marriage, I was an absent mother. I blindly committed myself to a revolution that was crushed, in spite of myself I became the muse of a movement that lost'? Or: 'When I lost my footing my friends and everyone else who swore they'd always be at my side abandoned me too. Those who haven't are dead or exiled. I've lost everything'? Could she tell him about all the vultures that were following her as the smell of death grew stronger? The government crows that wanted her hide like they wanted Stokely, Rap Brown, Miriam, Angela Davis...

But for now, there were more urgent matters. She was broke. She spent $400 a day in a five-star hotel, and in a few days she'd be forced to give it up. She didn't have her own bank account, not even any cash, other than a wad of a thousand dollars that she'd got after the San Francisco concert. Only Andy knew where the money was (almost certainly split between the publishing company, the production company...). She didn't even know how much she'd earned up to that point! No one was answering in his office in New York any more, and no one ever called her here. She had nowhere to go, except the Mount Vernon house. But how could she sleep in the place that had put an end to her dreams of happiness? She'd have to start over. And why not? It wouldn't take much. A man. Someone to look after her. She needed a man, a man's arms, a touch of insouciance, sex, lightness... But she had nothing of that to turn her luck around other than just forgetting.

She had to earn money. The fees she'd earned over the last few shows had barely lasted a few days. Where'd the money gone? She'd thought about it but couldn't understand. It had been months since she'd bought new clothes, or perfume or jewellery. There was no question of staying idle. There were other engagements that had to be honoured, dates Andy had planned up to eight months in advance. And above all, she'd have to find others. But that task seemed impossible without a trusted team. As she didn't know where to begin and no longer trusted anyone outside her family, she headed from New York to Philadelphia. She wanted to speak to her brother Samuel, ask him to be her manager for the next tour, which was coming up soon. She called him from the airport: 'Wait for me, Sam, I'll be there in a few hours. It's important. It's not a favour, Sam. You and the family are all I have left.'

Samuel Waymon, eleven years Nina's junior, had been living in his sister's shadow since he first began forging his career as a musician in the mid-sixties. He had already played and recorded with Nina, contributing to the albums *Silk & Soul*, *'Nuff Said!* and, soon after this, *Emergency Ward*. In the years to come, he'd profit in a small way from these years at his sister's side. He wrote the soundtracks to a few films in the 70s, such as *Ganja & Hess*. In the 90s he would form the Magic Band, a group of veteran rhythm and blues players, and co-write a song for Jonathan Demme's 1993 film *Philadelphia*.

Sam accepted his sister's proposal. However, although he had some experience in the music business as a musician, he'd never been a manager. The responsibilities that Nina was asking him to take on were considerable: he'd have to make sure everything relating to the tour (transport, hotels, concert conditions, payment, etc.) was in line with the promises made by concert producers. Interviewed by Frank Lords, Sam Waymon said that he had only agreed to his sister's proposal to protect her. For the moment, Nina was no longer hearing voices or plagued by hallucinations. This made her problems identifiable and Sam advised her to deal with them head-on.

When Nina arrived, the Waymon family found Eunice in a worrying state. When they heard of the separation from Andy Stroud, they kept quiet and didn't judge her. However, no one seemed shocked at the news. Back at her family's home and on the brink of bankruptcy, Nina realized that they saw her as a stranger, a distant relation. The complicity, the affection, the little quarrels that feed the fabric of daily life – all that had crumbled away a long time ago.

Nina Simone stayed in Philadelphia for several days, completing preparations for the forthcoming tour. She got up each morning at eight, sat round the table with the other members of the family, avoided the living-room piano as much as possible, and took long walks with her father. John Divine admitted that he was not surprised to learn of the separation. In truth, he never liked Andy, he always sensed violence in him and never believed his intentions were sincere.

She confided in him about her fears, her anxiety attacks, her feeling of abandonment. And it was her father who took her by the shoulders and said the words that Mary Kate was incapable of saying: *We love you, stay here as long as you want. Your mistakes are in the past. You have to allow life to heal the wounds.*

At night in bed, worries filled Eunice's head. She wasn't keen to get under the covers, feeling that the room's darkness had become more opaque. There was a presence. She put her dressing gown back on, and decided to join her father and Sam, who were still talking in the living room. She put on some old slippers and headed towards the living room without turning the hall light on. She heard the mumbling of a conversation, and as she drew nearer she could hear her father confidently explaining to Sam that he had always met the family's needs on his own, that he had fed them all these years, through all their difficulties, and that though he was now an old man he'd always looked out for the family.

That was too much for Nina. We can guess at how she must have felt, having sent the family a cheque every month for ten years, only to hear her father claim the credit. She left. She would never see her father again.

It was a broken, disgusted woman, with no way of surviving except to run from gig to gig, who committed to a European tour in spring 1971. Passing through Amsterdam, she met up with Big Willy and let him in on her problems, her separation from Andy. Willy listened. At her wits' end, she even knelt before him imploring him to marry her, he who had always said they'd be married if she hadn't been with Andy. She was ready to offer herself to Willy, but he dodged the question and consoled her, telling her that it's a bad idea, that friends don't marry each other when it's so obviously too late. She spent the night at his house, going over the same stories again: her feeling of having wasted her career, her marriage, her life as a mother. Her dread at seeing her life slip away and her terror in the face of the future, that feeling that something inside of her was broken, that there was nothing left but cold.

It was a night for talking things over, kneeling before Willy, who patiently listened to her. She drank and smoked and finally fell asleep with her head on her friend's knees. She woke up spread out on the sofa feeling numb. Willy was still there, facing her, with a sad smile on his face. He said, 'Morning, Nina,' and offered her a cup of hot coffee. A taxi was called to take her back to her hotel. She was running late and her musicians had to wait for her in the entrance hall, their instruments already packed into a tour bus ready to drive to Rotterdam. Nina and Willy said goodbye.

A few years later, sitting in a dressing room, a Dutch journalist would translate a letter sent by Philips a few weeks before: 'We regret to inform you of the death of Wilhelm Langenberg.' She would feel like the sky was falling on top of her and she would smack the face of the company man who let her into Big Willy's secret: he held shares in an obscure business with the South African government selling boats. It wouldn't be the insult of feeling swindled again that would push her off the rails. After all, Langenberg had always insisted on separating business and morality. The violence in her would break out because she hadn't been able to be present at her protector's burial. She hadn't been able to say goodbye to her friend. The Philips spokesperson would get a slap for his trouble. He'd get over it. Later he'd make use of the incident during formal dinners. The number of people slapped by Nina Simone was now up to twenty or thirty; at best they got an anecdote out of it, at worst they made an international scene.

Back in the USA, RCA advised Nina that her album *Here Comes the Sun* was about to come out. The title track was a cover of a George Harrison song from the Beatles' *Abbey Road* album, released in 1969. Recorded in a week in RCA's Studio B, New York, this album contains little of interest. With syrupy production awash with choir, harp, big chords and terrible reverb, *Here Comes the Sun* began Nina Simone's artistic decline. The track selection, with songs that mostly would have made perfect B-sides, reflects an artist lacking inspiration. Her covers of 'Just Like a Woman', by Dylan, and 'My Way' could have been left in a drawer without depriving music of anything. RCA seemed determined that their artist should record the records agreed in the contract in the shortest time possible. It is true that two great live albums were to come, but they would be released by the company as if trying to get rid of an embarrassing employee. Among the songs recorded and not used for *Here Comes the Sun*, it is worth mentioning 'Isn't it a Pity', a George Harrison cover, a wonder of balance that in the end was included in *Emergency Ward*, the diva's last great live album, released in 1972. It was also the last album that we can tell she had any artistic control over.

If *Here Comes the Sun* can raise any interest at all, it's because of the lack of any credit granted to Andrew Stroud. It had been a long time since he'd not been around. A photo of a twelve-year-old Eunice Waymon can be found on the back cover of the original album, and in her child's writing, a near-quotation from Walt Whitman:

> All music is what awakes within us when we are reminded
> by the instrument;
> It is not the violins or the clarinets;
> It is not the beating of the drums;
> Nor the score of the baritone singing his sweet romanza;
> nor that of the men's chorus, nor that of the women's
> chorus –
> It is nearer and farther than they.

Nina must have found this photo during a visit to her parents' house in Philadelphia, which must have been before the argument with her father, before the flood of legal problems began. It may even have been during the good times, when order and harmony were after a fashion kept in balance.

In the winter of 1971, Nina agreed to join the Free the Army tour, organized by the actors Jane Fonda and Donald Sutherland against America's involvement in Vietnam. The troupe performed at the Philharmonic Hall in New York (where Nina appeared flanked by three percussionists, a cello player and a back-up musician in charge of replacing her at the piano whenever she moved around the stage[2]), then Fort Dix, New Jersey, where a free concert was held on 18 November 1971 to honour the black GIs returning home.

After hours of waiting, Sam Waymon introduced Nina as the 'high priestess of soul'. She came on stage to the audience's welcoming cries, joined by her brother Sam, Lisa (who had finally been returned to her mother), then aged nine, and the Bethany Baptist Church Junior Choir of South Jamaica (a New York gospel ensemble directed by Weldon Irvine, Jr.). Nina went straight into her frenzied gospel version of 'My Sweet Lord', from George Harrison's second solo album *All Things Must Pass*. The only thing Nina kept from the original was the refrain 'I really want to see you but it takes me too long, my Lord!', where George Harrison had flooded his song with 'Hare Krishna, Hare Brahma'. She blended the song with the poem 'Today Is a Killer' by David Nelson. Backed by wall-to-wall choir, Nina shouted herself hoarse, carried by a hypnotic bass line and a swarm of tambourines, percussion and handclaps that helped her call upon that God of mercy who had let her fall and command Him to appear. She told Him of her love, that she had always had faith in Him, but not enough to subject her petitions to divine whim. Sam was there, responding to each prayer – we hear his talent as a singer, relieving her, giving her courage – 'Yes Nina, He has to show himself.' The bridge is sublime, everyone goes quiet while the voices of the choir seem to rise to heaven, until they fall silent – you feel yourself suddenly in the middle of the ocean, all on the same boat trying to slice through the waves and flee the despair flooding the earth. 'I hope it's not too late, that's what I hope, but I'm very much afraid that it is, in spite of everything, my Lord,' she says. And she's off again. Ten thousand hands clap like percussion, and Nina would never have a groove anything like that ever again, she would never show so much authority in the face of her despair. Then, she was finished. But now she was alive, in front of thousands of people who were going mad as the place flooded with beautiful music. It didn't stop, because 'she could feel the presence of that divine being all around her, it was in the air, and in a few seconds it would surely show itself'.

'My Sweet Lord' was an exuberant demonstration of Nina's hypnotic powers on stage. Of course, she had already produced dazzling theatrical displays, that placed their performer on the edge of a precipice. No one comes out unharmed from 'Pirate Jenny', or live versions of 'Four Women', or 'Mississippi Goddam', which very nearly pulled her down into the abyss with them. But here, she produced an unknown beauty as she whispered: 'I have to get out of this chasm, you have to help me, Lord.'

Nina's performance of 'My Sweet Lord' was released by RCA on the album *Emergency Ward*. Two songs were added on the B-side: 'Poppies', recorded on 12 February 1972 in New York, and another George Harrison cover, 'Isn't It a Pity', an acknowledgement of powerlessness in the face of humankind's thirst for destruction. She sings that we should give, give to receive, open our doors and believe in love and compassion as essential virtues for the salvation of our souls. Because beauty is all around us and it is shameful to be so blind. Stripped down, accompanied by a piano playing in clear colours and a double bass, with a grandiose arrangement despite the purposeful austerity of the ensemble, this cover is a masterpiece of fragility. And who cares if, once more, it was a cover? Nina penetrates the song so deeply, she fills it with such despair, such deep conviction, that she makes it her own. ''Cause we're moving too fast,' she sang. 'But some things take so long.' We are lost, we hear in her breath, there's no way out of our troubles.

The Strouds' divorce was pronounced that year, 1972, in Santo Domingo. In her autobiography, Nina stated that they did not take 'the companies, monies owing and debts'[3] into account. As soon as the divorce got under way, she learned of the tax problems for the first time. For example, for several years the government had been demanding tax return forms that had mysteriously vanished. And there were lawsuits in progress for accumulated royalties, certain licensing agreements weren't legal, and the government was threatening to audit the accounts of companies established by Andy Stroud in her name.

She understood that none of these problems could be resolved amicably, and that money was one thing, but soon they'd have to bring up custody of Lisa. The coming battle promised to be terrible. But that didn't matter to her, if she had to she'd take mortal blows. She was determined, she wanted a clear, official, irrevocable separation. At first she had doubts about seeking a specialized lawyer's advice, as she was sure that Max Cohen would manage all the legal issues surrounding the separation in the best possible way. She was wrong.

Once the divorce had been pronounced, Nina Simone felt abandoned. The money she had in cash was slipping away before her very eyes, but having nowhere else to go, she chose to return to Barbados. There she had a brief love affair with Paul, a hotel porter from Trinidad, who had no idea who Nina Simone was. At least, she thought, he wasn't with her for what he could get, he wasn't one of those gigolos who were only interested in getting at her money. With him, Nina would enjoy a few carefree days of motorbike rides, cuddly siestas, strolls along the beach. The young girl in her came back to the surface, tasting the pleasures of a non-serious relationship with a man who was 'kind and gentle, nice to be around'.[4] Soon, Nina told him who she was. She wanted him to know what set she belonged to, so he would show her the consideration her position deserved. 'You know, I'm very famous in America. I'm a singing star.' He didn't believe a word of it, telling himself that she was obviously another one of those married women with a tendency to exaggerate who had come to the island to slum it. He laughed in her face. She let it drop.

One day, in her hotel room, her anxieties resurfaced. Always the same questions, condemned to remain unanswered. Should she pay for mistakes she wasn't responsible for? Why had none of the Waymons got involved in her argument with her father? She wouldn't have given in, but she'd have liked to receive his excuses. Maybe she would have accepted them.

Frightened by the prospect of another night without sleep, Nina took powerful sleeping tablets, but they couldn't calm her anxiety. Fear pursued her into her dreams: fear of tomorrow, of insecurity, vanished money, the shadow of the tax authorities. She knew she couldn't stay in Barbados, clutching to this minuscule plot of happiness, keeping a physical distance from her problems. She'd have to take them on.

Nina returned to the USA, where she was due to play concerts that had been planned far in advance. Even if Andy was no longer there to assist her, she'd have to honour those concerts, pocket her fees and continue like that until her problems were solved. But for the moment her problems remained intact, and even seemed to have grown in her absence. The authorities in Mount Vernon were harassing her about her house, now uninhabited. The ground floor had recently been damaged by flooding. Max Cohen and Ivan Mogull informed her that the tax problems facing her were serious. Following an inquiry, the authorities had accused her of failing to make a tax declaration for four years. Their threats were explicit: they were talking of tax repayments, legal action, seizing assets... But it seemed impossible to locate the tax return forms that the government was demanding. Nina discovered that a fire, whose cause remained unexplained, had ravaged her New York office and that all the documents there had been destroyed. Meanwhile, it was impossible to reach Andy.

And Nina's relationship with her record company was also deteriorating. RCA had never looked fondly upon the diva's political commitments. The time when her album 'Nuff Said! had been nominated for an Emmy was now long gone. The records that had followed, To Love Somebody and Here Comes the Sun, had been commercial disappointments, and despite critical acknowledgement, Black Gold had not achieved as much public success as hoped.

Times had changed. Nixon had withdrawn American forces from Vietnam and the last GIs had come home on 29 March 1972, while the Hanoi government was freeing America's prisoners of war.

A new generation of soul artists had appeared in the USA offering a sort of sophisticated music more in keeping with the times. On 20 August 1972, the Stax label (which had recently moved from Memphis to LA) organized the Wattstax festival at the Los Angeles Coliseum. All profits from the concert were to go to reconstruction of the Watts neighbourhood, which had been destroyed during the last round of race riots. Under the patronage of the Reverend Jesse Jackson, the cream of Southern artists had been assembled: Isaac Hayes, David Porter, the Staple Singers, the Emotions, the Bar-Kays... That time also saw the birth of independent black cinema and Blaxploitation: Sweet Sweetback's Baadasssss Song by Melvin Van Peebles and Shaft by Richard Roundtree. The early 1970s were also marked by Curtis Mayfield's triumphant soundtrack for the film *Super Fly*, the hit 'Papa Was a Rollin' Stone' by the Temptations under the influence of the visionary producer Norman Whitfield, 'Let's Get It On' by Marvin Gaye before his divorce, fall into depression and exile to Europe, the appearance of Cymande and War, Kool & the Gang, psychedelic funk and Parliament/Funkadelic... New female figures appeared, such as Millie Jackson and her foul-mouthed soul music, and Betty Davis, the wife of Miles Davis and mistress of Jimi Hendrix, who offered a sexual, poisonous sort of funk. Disco would soon makes its appearance in Philadelphia (Gamble and Huff...) and New York (Tom Moulton, Loretta Holloway, Gloria Gaynor, Donna Summer...), a genre that brought a new enthusiasm for black American music and placed hedonism at the heart of its priorities. And a little later, from 1974 onwards, a Jamaican-born DJ would appear in the Bronx: Kool Herc. With him, in a few years a black urban culture would be born that would inherit the rhythm and blues and social combat of the civil rights era: hip hop.

Riding 'My Sweet Lord''s wave of success, the album *Emergency Ward* did fairly well in the USA. But she could feel that little by little she was losing the public's attention, already becoming an old-fashioned figure, against the sweeping changes under way in America's musical landscape.

Once again she sought refuge in Barbados, and in the arms of Paul, trying to put physical distance between herself and her problems. A few days spent trying to relax again. A call from Lucille put paid to those efforts. 'Dad is ill, the doctors have diagnosed prostate cancer. He's been admitted to hospital in Shelby, near Forest City where Momma's ministry is. He's really in a bad way, Nina, he can't weigh more than ninety pounds. He won't last long. You have to come back.'

Their quarrel had lasted for quite a while by this point, around fourteen months, but it seemed that time hadn't dulled her resistance. Nina still couldn't forgive her father for lying, for having acted like everyone else. For her, the pact that had united them since her childhood, that had guaranteed her that he would always be by her side, had been trampled on. Is it only in this light that we can measure just how bitter this woman was? After the annoyances, the betrayals, the fatigue, the threats and arguments in her life, there was the shadow of death yet again.

Back in Philadelphia, she let Lucille know she'd soon be arriving in Tryon. She would go along to say hi then stay with Miz Mazzy. What did Miz Mazzy say about all this mess? Powerless, the old lady must have felt her share of guilt when Nina arrived. 'Eunice,' she said, and looked at the black woman stood stooped in her doorway, her features marked with sorrow, her back bent under the pain of coming home again. 'Mazzy.' The two women embraced. Nina hadn't seen her friend since the Carnegie Hall concert in 1965. Now she found an ageing, astoundingly fragile Mazzy. She was still an elegant lady, her kind smile lit up her face as it always had, but something in her had changed. Age, the closeness of death perhaps, or the feeling of having had something to do with her protégée's straying. They sat down in silence with cups of tea, Mazzy trying to put her at ease: *We know all about it, Eunice. I want you to know that we still love you.* It's then a little girl who breaks down sobbing, who says she's sorry, takes Mazzy's hand then kisses her neck and murmurs: *I'm going to be forty soon, Mazzy. I'm so scared, if you only knew.* She picks up her bag. Stares blankly at a point in the room. *Nothing in this house has changed in twenty years, has it? – No. Nothing every really changes here. Our lives wouldn't stand it.*

The days go by. Nina refuses to come to her father's deathbed. When she's not hanging around the family home, she's strolling about the streets of Tryon, saying hello to faces from her childhood, to people who still call her 'Eunice', letting memories come back to the surface and letting her feet guide her to the Whitesides' family home. Then a crazy idea occurs to her: what if she took Edney back? What if, despite all those years without making contact with him, she could find her childhood sweetheart, undo her silences and start afresh?

But Mrs Whiteside, Edney's mother, has now become an obstacle. The woman who, twenty years before, begged Eunice Waymon to come back and marry her son now insists that she leave him in peace.

Nina came back to the Whitesides', respecting Edney's mother's instructions to the letter. She took the photo back and left again without a word, without a single look. In a few months, she would lose the beautiful photograph at Duke Ellington's place one evening.

Nina Simone left Tryon in the second week of October 1972, heading for Forest City to prepare for her concert at Washington's Kennedy Center. The night before the show she learned of her father's death from Lucille. The illness had got the better of him that afternoon. Knocked out by the news, she didn't cry a single tear, as if her heart had dried up from shedding too many. She decided not to go to the burial, not to say goodbye to her father or, in front of his grave, express to him just how deep her regrets ran. While Nina Simone was flying to Washington, John Divine Waymon was buried in Tryon cemetery, at the top of the hill, behind the little Baptist church where, as a child, Eunice Waymon made the walls tremble and called forth spirits.

That night, it was a grieving artist who stepped on stage at the Kennedy Center. Years later, Nina would tell Sylvia Hampton that she still did not understand how she was able to sit at the piano, play for the audience and feel nothing. At the end of the show, she addressed the auditorium and announced her father's passing. She played a song in his memory. This is how it finishes:

> I loved him then and I loved him still, that's why my heart's
>   so broken.
> Leaving me to doubt God in His Mercy
> And if He really does exist then why does He desert me?
> When he passed away I smoked and drank all day,
> Alone. Again. Naturally.

In Philadelphia at the end of October 1972, Lucille, the Waymons' eldest daughter and Eunice's favourite sister, was also claimed by cancer. She had never spoken of her illness and no one in the family was aware of the seriousness of her condition. The doctors had diagnosed a lump in her breast, but hadn't been worried about it. 'Maybe she thought she could stare death in the face and frighten him away, like she could anyone else.'[5] The bad omens were multiplying. Disorientated, murderous and with her heart dried up, Nina took Lisa with her and set off to her refuge in Barbados yet again.

But even the charm of Barbados was wearing off. However, for the first few days she was greeted by the sweet routine of Paul's flirting.

But every little thing pulled her back from her idleness. 'My Happiness' was on the radio one day, and at once she became gloomy thinking about Edney, about that time, long ago, when the song's sweet melody had been their secret garden. It was worst at night when dark ideas fed her insomnia, when she could hear Lisa's breath, sleeping in the next room, not knowing where to turn or how to free herself from her regrets. Everything lost its flavour, even her relationship with Paul, who bored her now. That hotel porter who refused to believe in her fame, and now it was starting to fade. Her fame was all she had left, and this guy insisted in thinking she was lying. 'You want me to prove to you that I'm a celebrity?' Nina asked the hotel's staff who the most important man on the island was. The answer was Errol Walton Barrow. It was the first time she'd ever heard his name.

An ex-Royal Air Force pilot, a London-trained lawyer, Errol Barrow was a national hero. On 30 November 1966 the politician had led Barbados to independence, putting paid to more than three hundred years of British power on the island. The former finance minister and leader of the Democratic Labour Party became the island's prime minister on its independence (his first term lasted until 1976), and initiated a foreign investment policy to promote the development of industry and tourism. An eminently respected and dignified politician who was at the same time a simple man who wished to be close to his people, Errol Barrow was able to do his shopping in a supermarket and then a few days later receive a visit from Queen Elizabeth or Prince Charles at his villa.

But when Nina Simone asked for directions to his residence, she didn't know any of that. It is even possible that she never understood the man's importance, or the extent of his responsibilities, as in her memoirs she doesn't see him as anything more than a rich and powerful man to whom she could have become mistress or even wife.

Dressed as if going to a gala (she hadn't brought more than a handful of clothes in her suitcase), she asked to be driven, with Lisa by her side, to the Prime Minister's official residence. The car park was full of official cars. A reception was being held. Nina saw that as a good omen: the island's press and elite were there. There was nothing better to ensure a bit of publicity.

A butler greeted her on the house's steps, she gave her name and claimed the master of the house was expecting her. She was led through a maze of rooms and corridors, decorated in Victorian luxury, to the conference room. Holding her daughter's hand, Nina made her entrance. Journalists, local politicians and a range of officials all saw her as Nina Simone entered the room wearing her Yves Saint Laurent hat. She was recognized immediately. Cameras started going off and her name was taken up and repeated by the assembled guests. 'It's Nina Simone, you know, that American singer. Yes, she's very famous.' Barrow rose and the room fell silent. He was a good-looking man, distinguished, with dark skin, greying hair, and the slightly stout build typical of men in their fifties. He strode out to greet and welcome her. The photographers called for a picture; Barrow posed proudly next to Nina (Lisa hiding behind her mother's skirt), holding her hand, the smile of a satisfied politician all across his face.

In the photo, Barrow is the image of the ideal man per Nina Simone's criteria. He is breathtakingly elegant, he throws off the aura of a natural leader, but above all, he seems rich. And rich he was. He possessed one of the island's largest fortunes. The anxieties of recent months fell away from Nina in an instant. Pain and sorrow flew away, in their place a new plan that might help her to stay in the Caribbean. What plan? Seducing Barrow, becoming his mistress – a clear and also wretched ambition.

But none of that could be seen in the first few moments. The flashes were still going off as, with a steady voice, the Prime Minister asked his guest the normal questions all hosts ask. 'How are you? Are you having a good time on our island? Where are you staying? Are you sure you want to stay in your hotel? Would you accept our invitation for you to stay in one of our private properties, next to the sea, for as long as you like?' She was absolutely filled with warmth, while Barrow's insistence was now repeated by Dr Esther Archer, the Prime Minister's personal doctor. She accepted with a smile of victory. I may have very little left, but my powers of seduction are still there, she told herself. While the journalists left to inform their editors as quickly as possible about the event, Nina was told that staff would come to collect her things during the day so she could spend that very night in an official residence on Paradise Island.

The name speaks for itself. It was a large house on the beach, with three bedrooms, a large dining room and a garage. The view was sensational. Looking out from an immense veranda, she could see the waves rolling in and washing over the white sand, high coconut trees waved gently by the ocean and the rest was just sun and contentment.

Nina sat on the sand with Lisa, the waves dying gently at their feet. They had watched the breathtaking spectacle of an ocean sunset. Night had fallen and Lisa was already in bed when Errol Barrow came to check that his guest was comfortably settled in. Nina sat with him in the dining room and they chatted. She talked to him about her career, of the rest she needed and had found on the island. She told him she hoped to be able to stay in this dream for a while. 'As long as you want.' He left again but returned the next night, around midnight. He had just come out of his office and wanted to check that she had everything she needed. He lingered, being charming, and eventually left around four in the morning, promising to come back and see her again the next night. Sitting on the steps, Nina asked: 'Are you married?' He smiled and said yes, for almost twenty years to Caroline Barrow, an American.

Nina met Caroline a few days later at the Hilton hotel's beauty salon. Although Barrow was strongly but gracefully pressing his attentions, Nina was warm with the island's first lady.

The singer was in seventh heaven. In only a few days she had managed to pull out of her misery and an emotional idleness that threatened to suffocate her, and here she was flirting with a rich and powerful man whose mistress she had just become. The situation was perfectly to her liking as there was no commitment and no lectures. For the moment. She decided to live this pleasant and carefree affair to the full. But soon an idea would get lodged in her head. Why not become more than a mistress to this man? After all, this sort of opportunity didn't present itself every day. She liked Barrow, he met all her criteria, and above all, Nina knew that with him, her needs would be met. But she didn't tell her lover anything about these plans. She made herself as feline and seductive as possible and tried to snare the Prime Minister by becoming indispensable. Because if her plan worked (and as long as her eminent lover really had fallen for her), it would mean a great deal: no longer being forced to earn money, giving up her career, ensuring herself a happiness of peace and simple pleasures, and at last, playing music for fun.

Towards the end of 1972, after having been away from the island for a while to honour a series of concerts in the USA, Nina was met by the Prime Minister's limousine on getting off the plane. She no longer required a visa or to go through customs: a message had been sent out among the authorities and the official mistress was treated as a VIP on the island. A promotion that involved certain obligations: she had to be available to a now seriously infatuated Errol Barrow, who might arrive on Paradise Island at any time, day or night.

Nina tells this spicy anecdote in her autobiography: when Alvin Schackman came to join her in Barbados the diva asked him to change the locks on the house's doors without informing Barrow. When he came back from swimming, Alvin found the Prime Minister trying to force the door that his keys could no longer open. Nina was in town, completing the necessary steps to import her Steinway (playing the piano looking out over the sea, that was an idea worth some administrative bother) while Al and Errol came face to face, one in his prime ministerial suit and the other in his still-damp swimming costume. Barrow headed for his official limousine in a furious temper, revealing his identity before turning his back on the guitarist. When she returned, Nina learned of the misadventure. The story made her laugh and led her to innocently introduce the two men officially at a reception a few days later.

Nina's amorous relationship with Errol Barrow was going to open the doors to a society lifestyle. She became connected to the Barnes family, a diplomatic couple close to the Prime Minister. Their daughter was called Ilene. Born in Detroit, Ilene Barnes spent her childhood in Surinam before becoming a famous blues artist in the 1990s, recording several notable albums. When I met her in Paris where she now lives, Ilene recalled those years when, as a child, she was often with Nina and Lisa. The two little girls were then ten years old. They met on a beach and Lisa wanted to introduce the girl to her mother. Next Mrs Barnes, a close friend of Caroline Barrow, became friends with the singer. She opened her house to her, often welcoming Lisa, sometimes even for several months when her mother disappeared or left to fulfil some tour in the States. Over a period of three years, Ilene Barnes and Lisa Stroud were brought up together, setting off for two summers in a row to the Camp Bessie Cox summer camp, in Vermont, where they joined Malcolm X's children. Ilene's account is invaluable because it provides us with more information about the relationship between Lisa and Nina over those years.

Ilene remembers Lisa as a young girl who had already grown up, very pragmatic, organized, who had in some ways become her mother's secretary, taking messages for her and seeing to it than nothing came along to bother her. Because Nina was still suffering from anxiety attacks; they could erupt for the merest of trifles and be taken out on Lisa or the first person Nina came across. Lisa did everything she could to prevent Nina's attacks. She made sure no annoyances came along to disrupt her mother's nervous balance, sometimes to the point of absurdity: the little girl always got up before her mother and hurried to make her bed, otherwise she would be scalded. Yet despite her vigilance, uncontrollable attacks could break out at any moment. That's what happened at the North Point natural springs, where, in spite of repeated warnings, Nina wanted to sit on a mound of earth. It was, in fact, a red ants' nest. Devoured by the insects, she made a scene and wanted to sue the owner of the site. One night, in a fashionable mountain restaurant on an old plantation, a guitarist was playing a tune she knew. Nina was humming along while Lisa and Ilene chatted away. Nina began to scream at the two little girls, then she turned on the whole restaurant: 'Shut up!' Who could understand that the great Nina Simone was inspired and that everyone must listen to her? Lisa was used to it, and fell silent. Ilene, however, was terrified.

Her anxiety attacks would multiply as her affair with the Prime Minister deteriorated. Frightened by the lack of neighbours around her beach house at night, she asked the Barneses to lend her their dogs for protection. A harmless labrador and a three-legged poodle were entrusted to her. She make them sleep in a room with the air conditioning on full. Not the best way to protect her, but perfect for freezing two dogs unused to air conditioning. In the small hours of the morning, as they seemed totally groggy, she started shouting at them and had an attack.

Despite her escapades, Nina had become part of high society in Barbados. We know in particular that during her stay she spent time with the American singer Roberta Flack. Of course, relationships with the diva could sometimes be stormy, tense even if we believe the story of the dinner to which Mrs Barnes invited Caroline, Errol Barrow's wife, and Nina, his mistress. If Mrs Barnes was unaware of the adultery that was going on, Caroline suspected.

Had Caroline Barrow really found out her husband's relationship with Nina? In any case, the singer's reputation now preceded her. Even Mrs Barnes, a woman of character, had to make things clear to Nina when she made advances to her husband.

The romance between Barrow and Nina lasted almost two years. The Prime Minister obviously had to be discreet. The two lovers met often in New York, in the apartment Nina rented from ASCAP, the American Society of Composers, Authors and Publishers. They had a good time there, far from Barrow's overloaded schedule and bodyguards standing by while the lovers frolicked.

During these long stays in Manhattan, Nina sounded her lover out, insinuating that he could divorce Caroline and marry her. Errol didn't accept. Nina began to think that the situation would drag on until Barrow had his back up against the wall. She decided she had to impose herself on Errol Barrow's life until he could no longer ignore the fact that their passing affair had given way to an official relationship. Without telling him, she had all her possessions sent to Barbados. One could understand such behaviour from a fool, or even a young woman for whom male psychology remained a mystery. But at her age, almost forty, it was an irreversible blunder. Not only was her target not a mere bank clerk in a bad marriage, Barrow was a politician. So the Prime Minister must have thought: this woman could ruin his career, his reputation and his marriage. And this was only a matter of months before he'd be campaigning for re-election. Perhaps

Barrow had understood the risk he was running by continuing his relationship with this demanding woman when he ordered that her , things be blocked by customs. At the same time, Nina and Lisa were invited to leave Paradise Island to live in Old Trees Bay, another official residence located on the island's east coast.

From that moment on, Barrow did everything he could to detach himself from his mistress and rarely came to visit her. Feeling that she was on the way to losing her man, Nina played the blackmail card to get his attention. She didn't have the situation under control, and we might wonder at such persistence with this man who, from then on, became obstinate. But faced with his lover's determination, maybe the Prime Minister got scared and agreed to indulge one last whim: taking her to lunch in Martinique on his official jet. One day Errol Barrow announced to Nina than they would be flying early the next morning. Rather than capitalizing on this victory and opportunity, Nina spent the night in a Bridgetown club, went home drunk at five in the morning, and when a limousine arrived at seven to drive her to the airport, she refused: 'I'm too tired. Please give the Prime Minister my apologies.' You don't jest like that with a man like Errol Barrow. Already sensitive about his affair and looking for a pretext to break it off, he grasped this impropriety to put an end to it. This final inexcusable faux pas scuttled their relationship. But what did Nina expect? That he would leave Caroline Barrow and marry a woman like her, putting his political career in jeopardy?

Less than two years after they met, Errol Barrow let Nina Simone know that she was kindly requested to leave the Old Trees Bay residence. No alternative was offered. She and Lisa moved into a little bungalow on the grounds of Sam Lord's Castle, the hotel where Nina stayed upon arriving in Barbados for the first time. Back to square one in a way.

In her fine biography, Sylvia Hampton reveals Nina's rage against her former protector: 'You know he was just like all the rest, like all the men I've known he just wanted to use me. You know I was going to live with him. I took everything over there and he thinks he can treat me like shit. Well he messed with the wrong one, honey. I ain't about to let no man treat me that way ever again'[6] We may wonder at her questioning herself so little.

Nina found herself alone again, starting over, living in a bungalow at a Barbados hotel paying prohibitive prices and with no prospect of a future. A sign of her decline or an unfortunate coincidence, two days after moving in at Sam Lord's Castle, a burglar broke into her bungalow. He cleared off when, bouncing from her bed, Nina transformed into a tigress. The next day, Nina told people that the man had even tried to rape her daughter and had Barrow informed. But the elections were coming up and the Prime Minister let her know that he had to be careful. He refused to help and took care to avoid her, while she believed this wouldn't last long and their romance would resume once the elections were over.

But she had other realities to deal with: she learned from Max Cohen that the IRS was planning to go after her, their threats were serious and she was needed in the USA as soon as possible. So Nina Simone and Lisa left Barbados. The only belongings they brought with them were their suitcases of clothes, the rest of their things were still impounded at customs. Upon arriving in New York, Nina learned that her only bank account had been frozen and that the Mount Vernon house, with a value of $37,000 when purchased in 1962, had been seized and sold by the IRS. Only $1,400 was left over once the county and the government had taken their shares. Sylvia Hampton notes that 'The loss of her home in Mount Vernon had indeed caused a great deal of upheaval. It had for a long time been a place where a certain amount of stability could be guaranteed for her and her family, and her daughter Lisa felt the impact fairly heavily.'[7]

With her port in the storm gone, Nina Simone, mired in an emotional and financial bankruptcy, was informed by her record company RCA that a new live album was to be released in 1974, which would be her last record with the company. What humiliation, to be brutally dropped by her record label after ten albums (including a best-of) and some notable successes that had helped fatten the company. Without a contract or commitments, without a manager or a friendly contact in the American music industry (Big Willy was no longer there to console her), Nina Simone found herself at a dead end: 'My record deals expired along with my marriage and I became one more black artist "difficult to place" in the neat world the labels created,' she wrote. For her, her sidelining was also a punishment for her commitment to the movement: 'It was no accident that the most active black musicians couldn't get recording deals with the major labels'.[8]

Nina Simone began a period of isolation from the American music industry. Her last record release of the 1970s was the live album *It Is Finished*. Could there be a title more evocative of her mood? On the sleeve she appears as a wild child sitting on a pile of coconuts. She's wearing a black and red patterned dress; an elegant straw hat sits next to her. Her face is that of a woman resigned. She stares at the camera unsmiling, letting her body express her renouncement.

Made up of excerpts from concerts given in July 1973 at the New York Philharmonic, *It Is Finished* may be regarded as one of Nina Simone's best albums for RCA. The intensity of Nina's concerts, now at the peak of her art, was rarely so truly recorded and reproduced. Revisiting her signature numbers such as 'I Want a Little Sugar in My Bowl' where she plays on the sexual ambiguity of lyrics made immortal by Bessie Smith, Nina is dazzling and aggressive. This record sums up Nina Simone's political and racial involvement between 1963 and 1973. It's a foretaste of the African years ahead and a bitter statement on the movement's collapse and on social breakdown in the USA.

Like 'Pusherman' by Curtis Mayfield, 'The Pusher' is a song that violently denounces drug dealers, monsters distilling their poison among the children of the ghetto. Further on, 'Funkier than a Mosquito's Tweater', 'Dambala' and 'Obeah Woman' foreshadow Nina's departure for Africa and join other African soul gems in her repertoire, such as Miriam Makeba's 'Westwind', one of the highlights of the masterpiece *Black Gold*. Her imminent departure for West Africa (a journey she didn't know she was going to take when these songs were performed) is heard here as a dive into dizzying percussive funk. A bewitching groove which, more than thirty years later, would see Nina being played on English DJs' decks, while for the general public she would remain 'that black pianist graced with one danceable hit', 'My Baby Just Cares'.

You have to listen to 'Obeah Woman' (Obeah is Jamaican ritual magic) to understand her true nature as a sorceress, a witch conjuring the spirits and taking in their powers: 'I'm the Obeah woman, above pain, I can eat thunder and drink the rain, I kiss the moon and hug the sun, and call the spirits and make 'em run.'

And finally 'Dambala', a song inspired by a Tony McKay poem, on which Al Schackman accompanies her on a sitar. Nina sings that slavers in their turn will know what it is to be a slave, that if you're one of them, you won't go to heaven or to hell, but stay in your tomb. Nina prays for Dambala to come: 'the ancient, the venerable father... as of a world before the troubles began... image of the benevolent, paternal innocence, the great father of whom one asks nothing save his blessing... Damballah's very presence, like the simple, even absent-minded caress of a father's hand, brings peace.'[9]

As a last tribute to a musician committed, body and soul, to a now lost cause, 100,000 people had come to honour Nina Simone on 11 May 1974, at the annual Human Kindness Day in Washington. She was introduced by Muhammad Ali, who was preparing to fight George Foreman in Kinshasa, Zaire, in was already being called the 'fight of the century'. During the ceremony, Nina received an honour for her 'contribution to humanity',[10] and played on a stage in front of the Washington Monument, surrounded by symbols of white America. This consecration was marked with the weight of goodbye. Without a record contract, Nina Simone was acclaimed by an audience that had come to declare its love.

In the audience, Mary Kate Waymon realized for the first time what her daughter represented to these thousands of people. This was belated revenge for Nina, who for a long time kept with her a photo taken that happy day. In the photo, the two women face the camera, hugging each other tightly. Mary Kate, dressed in white, allows herself to be embraced by her daughter, radiant at being able to enjoy this moment she had dreamed of for so long. The closeness of their two faces allows us to hope there'd been a kiss, a simple but decisive word from this modest mother to the daughter whose fate had escaped her. I love you. I'm proud of you. Simple words, but words that can save a life. At the end of that day and its six-hour concert, an official dinner was held at the Smithsonian Institution.

11 May 1974. Nina had just made one of her last great appearances in America.

She would have other stop-overs in Barbados, until she understood that she had lost Errol Barrow for good. He won the elections. He remained the island's leader until 1976 and then would triumphantly return to power in 1986 and remain there until his death the following year.

In September 1974, Nina Simone was reunited with her friend Miriam Makeba in New York. Miriam was preparing to leave for Liberia, where she had been invited to sing at an event in honour of President Tolbert. From Monrovia, the Liberian capital, Miriam would then head for Kinshasa in November, where (on the same bill as James Brown) she would perform in a concert to be given before the Ali–Foreman fight. You've nowhere to go, come with me, come home, she must have said to Nina. Nina looked at her with the eyes of a woman of her age. She accepted her friend's invitation: 'All my friends had left the movement, were in exile or had been murdered. I was lost and bitter. Very bitter. I imagined that someone was going to spring out and grab me at any moment, carry me off and kill me. The FBI had a dossier on me. Once the civil rights movement died there was no reason for me to stay.'[11] Perhaps she also wanted to seize this opportunity to escape the IRS.

On 11 September 1974, Miriam Makeba, Nina Simone and the young Lisa Celeste Stroud flew to Monrovia. As the plane touched down on the tarmac, Lisa Celeste thought the official welcome put on for them was because of her birthday. Indeed, on 12 September Lisa celebrated her twelfth birthday in Africa. Her mother made herself the promise of starting a new chapter in her life.

7

THE COMPANY OF GHOSTS

FOR ALMOST a century now, Liberia, a country located on the west coast of Africa between Côte d'Ivoire, Guinea and Sierra Leone, has been enshrined in the black American imagination as a land of salvation and a symbol of freedom regained.

In 1816, a liberal, philanthropic and Protestant association known as the American Colonization Society was founded in the United States, its goal being to help victims of the slave trade return to African soil. Those people consisted mainly of emancipated slaves who had worked on cotton plantations in Virginia, Georgia and Maryland. The members of the ACS, some of whose representatives enjoyed strong support in Washington, thought that 'the best reparation for the injuries of slavery would be the return of former slaves to the land of their ancestors – to Africa'.[1]

Faced with the hostility of the indigenous population, the first organized attempt to bring freed American slaves back to their land of origin ended in failure when the ACS sought to settle them on the coast of Sierra Leone. Diverted by the local people, the American ship reached the coast of modern-day Liberia in 1821. On the beach, the American officer Robert Stockton met the local tribal chief, King Peter. The language barrier and his good intentions resulted in the agent of the ACS to hold his pistol to the king's temple and force him to sell the land of Cape Mesurado at the mouth of the Saint Paul River in exchange for his life, six muskets and a chest of beads. King Peter gave up his land and the settlers won a territory on which the first city of freed slaves was built. The settlement was named Monrovia in honour of James Monroe, the fifth president of the United States. Soon, more colonies were established on the Liberian coast, despite the growing hostility of the Kra and Mande tribes. From then on, each year, ships from the New World offloaded freed African-American slaves at Mamba Point.

It was to the shores of Monrovia, too, the vast land he had negotiated with the Liberian government, that Marcus Garvey, the 'black Moses', tried to bring his people to the motherland aboard ships of his own company: the Black Star Line.[2]

The settling of former slaves 'repatriated' by the American Colonization Society marked the beginning of a utopian project whose outcome, over a century later, would be a bloodbath. These were the beginnings of one of the most foolish and disastrous experiments ever initiated by Protestant America, in the hope of offloading their slavers' guilt.

In 1841, Joseph Jenkins Roberts, a freed American slave, became the first governor of Monrovia. He proclaimed the Republic of Liberia in July 1847 and imposed English as the official language (ignoring the local Pelle, Bassa, Grebo, Krahn and Klao dialects). Both the young republic's constitution and its flag were copied from the American model, and an income-based voting system was instated that allowed some 6,000 former American slaves (less than 1 per cent of Liberia's population) to dominate the country.

This new ruling class, born in slavery, knew only one model of society, the one in force in the plantations of the southern United States. From the second half of the nineteenth century and with US support, those emancipated slaves, now masters, created a new slave society, declaring themselves the only true citizens of the country and implementing a system of ethnic segregation and domination long before the white Afrikaners imposed apartheid in South Africa.[3] When they weren't captured, enslaved and sold on to Guinea, the indigenous peoples were forced to work on farms. One year before Lenin's birth in Simbirsk, in 1869, Liberia's leaders invented the single party with the establishment of the True Whig Party that ruled Liberia until 1980. Forced to sign a series of agreements with Great Britain and France starting in 1892 (aimed at fixing Liberia's boundaries), the country would enjoy the financial support of both the United States and the British Crown, providing allied troops with a military base during the First World War and opening up its natural resources (rubber, gold, diamonds) to major European companies. This was how in the early 1930s the Firestone Tire and Rubber Company won a government concession for a rubber plantation spanning 400,000 hectares, a genuine state within a state. Liberia's prosperity was largely built by forced labour imposed by American-Liberians on the native people,[4] a practice condemned by the League of Nations, forcing the Monrovia government to resign, though sparing the Firestone concessions. Forced labour was officially banned in Liberia in 1936, but indigenous peoples, still without voting rights, continued to be treated as second-class citizens.

The new leader of the True Whig Party who had been in power since 1945, William Vacanarat Shadrach Tubman, strengthened the country's ties with the United States. He opened up Liberia to the American armed forces, creating a base against the Axis and setting up a Voice of America radio antenna a few miles from the capital. Seeking to win favour with the indigenous people, Tubman granted them the right to vote before implementing a programme of schooling for all, followed by a major infrastructure improvement plan. A law prohibiting racial discrimination was voted in, yet nothing changed practically and American-Liberians continued to be the sole masters of the country. In May 1951, during a presidential election where for the first time native landowners were allowed to vote, William Tubman's regime banned opposition parties from representing indigenous peoples. Opposition leaders were eliminated or forced into exile, and Tubman ensured his own re-election. When he died in 1971, after more than twenty years in power, Tubman left behind a prosperous country, untouched by the wave of independence that had been shaking up sub-Saharan Africa since the late 50s.

William Tolbert, who had been vice-president of Liberia since 1951, took over as head of state. Tolbert was 'a walking embodiment of corruption'.[5] He was a man fascinated by money, who exerted his power through violence. During his reign which was marked by repression, imprisonment and the systematic murder of hundreds of political dissidents, Liberia experienced corruption at the highest level. But above all, Tolbert tried to distance himself from the United States so as to bring his country into the independent African community. He focused his government's efforts on maintaining Liberia's financial strength, continued to exclude indigenous minorities and worked to enrich the American-Liberian upper class.

In the mid-70s, dissatisfaction ran rife in Liberia; the country had one of the fastest-growing populations in the world, unemployment was soaring and Monrovia, booming, could no longer contain the flow of families seeking better living conditions. In the space of thirty years, from 1956 to 1986, Monrovia's population grew tenfold, even with no industry and poor communications. The streets were rough, and electricity and running water remained aristocratic privileges.[6] Soon slums began to grow from the outskirts of the city in towards the centre, the last shelters of the most disadvantaged.

Liberian high society ignored the plight of indigenous people. They lived on the coast and ventured into Monrovia but never inland. This upper class numbered only a few tens of thousands, with names like Dennis, Parker, Bright, Tubman, Buchanan and Tolbert. They were Baptists (like their slave ancestors in the southern United States) and their homes were carbon copies of the grand colonial-style houses of the American plantations. Intent on showing off their difference from the indigenous population, despite having the same colour skin, the Liberian elite took great care of their appearance. Their dress code spoke of their nostalgia for colonial splendour, and so, despite Monrovia's scorching heat, women wore wigs and bright hats while men donned bowler hats, gloves and frock coats.

Trying, generation after generation, to stay out of reach of its subjects, this Liberian upper crust had done everything in its power to stick as faithfully as possible to the society of the Babylon that had enslaved their ancestors. Now, aware (and frustrated) that they were an elite ignored by the wider world, they lived in luxury and dreamed of aristocracy and America.

On 12 September 1974, the plane carrying Miriam Makeba, Lisa Celeste Stroud and Nina Simone set down on the tarmac of Robertsfield airport, the biggest in Africa and one of the biggest in the world. They were met by an official reception, thanks to Miriam Makeba's status as African ambassador. The Tolbert administration heavyweights lined up at the foot of the plane and gave them a clamorous reception, with the Liberian flag raised and the national anthem playing loud and proud as they came down the stairs: 'All hail, Liberia, hail! This glorious land of liberty shall long be ours. Though new her name, green be her fame and mighty be her powers.' Makeba was used to this treatment wherever she set foot in Africa, but it was a first for Nina. In New York, before the trip, Miriam told her Liberia was 'a good place to start at for any Afro-American looking to reconcile themselves to their own history'.[7]

Was Makeba unaware of the country's history, or did she gloss over it because of the honours she received? But it's conceivable that *Nina* knew nothing of Liberia, though it could be thought embarrassing if, after ten years fighting with the movement, she should still be in the dark about the history of this land of slavery. Whatever the case, the hopes invested in this trip were immense. This was Nina's opportunity to leave the music business and the United States behind for good, and to discover a long fantasized-about continent. She also hoped to meet some rich Liberian dignitaries; that was one of Miriam's arguments for her friend to follow her to Monrovia. 'The city is full of rich, attractive black businessmen,' she kept telling her. 'Who knows, one of them might turn out to be the ideal husband!'

From Robertsfield airport, Miriam, Nina and Lisa were driven with an official escort to the presidential palace, where a party was being given in honour of the anniversary of William Tolbert's inauguration. The country's elite were in full attendance and eager to meet Miriam Makeba, the only African artist to have truly made it in the United States. They also flocked to greet Nina Simone, already a major celebrity in those parts. She was admired and coveted, not only as a guest of honour but also a curiosity. For those affluent representatives of an African country with its eye on America, it seemed incredible for a black American artist to have taken such a firm stand against the government of her own country. Nina had feared for a moment that Miriam would steal the limelight, but she was soon surprised, then charmed at the thought that those well-meaning people might know of her work as well as her trials and tribulations. Better still, they were well aware of Nina's role in the movement. Everyone praised her records, quoting their titles and discussing the songs. A gentleman named Mr Bright even complimented her on her gig at Carnegie Hall in 1963. She marvelled, 'Really? You were there?' Impassive, the man answered that he spent his whole life between New York and Monrovia. 'Import/export, you see. But I absolutely love your music. You know, your records have been available here for some years now.'

The party went on until morning. When, at dawn, Nina and Lisa were dropped off in the Bassa district, at a large residence facing the ocean, the President's daughter told them that the house was at their disposal 'for as long as they cared to stay'. Little did Nina and Lisa suspect that the coming days would be punctuated with more parties, more receptions, as though they were the sole entertainment of the Liberian elite.

When she got up, Nina saw the pictures of their arrival on the front page of the Monrovia newspaper laid on the dining room table. The article described Nina's career in the United States, her success and her immense fame around the world, and the honour given to the Liberian people and President Tolbert to be able to welcome her with 'Mama Africa', Miriam Makeba. For Africa – largely ignored by the West and still reeling from colonization – those African-American figures (Muhammad Ali, James Brown, and so on) who had made their community's voice heard in their own country were seen as distant cousins turned prophets. Nina Simone was thus treated with the utmost respect. Flattered, she understood that her fame in this country placed her at once at the heart of its elite, and that she would be looked after by the regime for the length of her stay (however long she extended it), and didn't have to work. If need be and if she was asked, she would give a few concerts – why not play in honour of President Tolbert, her benefactor? That would be the least she could do...

During the daytime, heat in the city was crushing. Hot, viscous, moisture-laden air pressed on the inhabitants and slipped into their homes. Leaving the villas or venturing out of the shade was out of the question. But no matter, the pace of her nightly ventures was such that soon Nina was staying in bed till the middle of the day, eating lunch when other people were finishing work, then going off to one of the countless receptions where she was guest of honour. At the centre of attention, with all eyes on her, Nina Simone saw her life take on colours and textures she'd stopped believing were possible. It was a release, a rebirth for this woman now aged forty, to whom Miriam had promised to introduce no less than six men, 'all of them rich and single'.

The first of them was Clarence Parker, a member of a powerful family. He was handsome, very self-assured and direct. He invited her over to his villa for a drink. The walls were covered with paintings of positions from the Kama Sutra. Parker came on to her, and when that didn't work he made his intentions more explicit. With some difficulty, Nina fought off her seducer's advances, but was charmed enough to go with him to a club in Monrovia: the Maze. Although the place couldn't hold more than fifty people, it was *the* meeting spot for Liberian high society. Barely a week into her stay in Monrovia, Nina already knew all the faces there. That night, she drank a bottle and a half of champagne and took to the tiny dance floor. Overcome by some kind of fever and cheered on by her new friends, she let go – kicked off her shoes and pulled off her dress, twirling it over her head while throwing provocative glances at the men who watched her. She threw the fabric in Clarence Parker's face; he brought it to his lips, breathed in her scent and smiled at the American woman lustfully. Nina Simone ended up naked in the middle of the club as the cheers got louder and louder. There was nothing left for her to unveil but her spectators didn't care, they demanded more dancing, more indecency.

The news of Nina Simone's delicious indiscretion went around Monrovia's tiny aristocratic brotherhood so fast that the following night, President William Tolbert himself came to the Maze, hoping to enjoy the show himself. Alas, the American was hiding away at home, exhausted, perhaps happy, perhaps embarrassed.

Much later, in less happy days as she wandered through Europe in search of a solution to her loneliness and other troubles, Nina Simone would write 'Liberian Calypso' in memory of that night. We all have a few of those special nights when drunkenness freed us from some burden and caught us up in the now. In those rare moments when we feel most alive, in tune with our existence, we let go of our sense of propriety to at last surrender to unadulterated joy. Those times leave you wrung out, all senses blown away. Looking back on those instants when we find ourselves naked of politeness, fear or calculation, they illuminate who we are and sometimes bring tears to our eyes as treasured memories can do. Nina gave her precious night of freedom a melody, a memory that for us her audience took on the light accents of Liberian Calypso on the album *Fodder on My Wings*, which she recorded in Paris for Carrère, when in the dull Parisian greyness her memories were all she had left.

Her life much eased by her status as guest of honour, Nina felt right at home in Monrovia. 'Within a few weeks I felt as if I had been living in my house on the beach all my life. Situated where it was, a little way outside of the town centre, its location was just far enough from Monrovia's noise and excitement to allow me peace and quiet whenever I wanted without being cut off.'[8] And far enough from the rudimentary shelters built by the poor for Nina to escape falling prey to any kind of guilty conscience. All her expenses were covered by the Tolbert administration, no one was asking her to play music, Lisa was enjoying school and Nina Simone, as she later wrote, had 'never felt so free, so beautiful and so well-liked'.[9]

There are a few pictures of her from that time. Wrapped in a colourful boubou, Nina looks like a genuine African queen, sublime, svelte, desirable. She radiates a feeling of peace seldom to be found in photos of her. The boubou might only have been fished out for the photograph, since Nina tells us in her autobiography how she went around in a bikini and boots! Current fashion among the Liberian elite veered towards American styles, these descendants of slaves averse to resembling the local population. The long-running trend of dressing like white colonists was no longer deemed proper. They now wore dinner jackets and elegant suits, importing the fabrics from the United States and Europe at great expense and not giving a damn for Monrovia's sticky heat that choked them in their garments. To them it was out of the question to be confused with 'natives', let alone mingle with them on their own doorstep. For the past century, they'd lived crammed into small towns on the west coast, on the outskirts of Monrovia, carefully avoiding the original population, to the point of ignoring the interior of the country.

Nina Simone had only been in Liberia for a month, but her decision was made. This was where she would spend the rest of her days. She needed to take care of things in the United States: 'to arrange for money to be sent to me and to pick up some of my things and let people know where I was'.[10] At least that's how Nina justified her return trip in her autobiography. One wonders how she could take such a risk when her accounts were meant to be frozen and she might be held at the US border by order of the tax authorities – especially since her friendship with Tolbert's entourage would have let her manage her business from Monrovia, inform Max Cohen and pass on her instructions without having to fear the worst. Yet Nina left Lisa with the President's daughter (how that child was tossed about!), travelled to New York, stayed there just a few days before returning to Monrovia, at the end of October 1974, without any problems at customs.

Millie Buchanan, a Liberian friend of Miriam's, met her at the airport. 'I'm taking you somewhere,' she said. Exhausted, Nina didn't ask where. The two women drove into Monrovia, to a part of town Nina didn't know. The area was filled with row after row of basic, low-rise housing; little cabins made out of corrugated iron sheets everywhere, decrepit dwellings, sleepy little stalls, groups of young *bayaye* wandering the streets or gathered in tiny pools of shade. Millie stopped the car in front of an anonymous house and a man in a grey suit welcomed them in. He introduced himself as a witch doctor. In a country where the President himself, and Tubman before him, had their own witch doctors and claimed to have magic powers themselves, it wasn't surprising for a woman like Millie Buchanan to be visiting a tribal doctor. Tubman was said to know herbs that assured his victory at every election, to know everything that happened in his country through the services of spirits, and have powers to turn the bullets of his enemies.

Nina Simone and Millie Buchanan followed the doctor into the house, bare of furnishings except a folding iron table, three chairs and a plastic basin. The man sat on the floor and took some bones from his jacket pocket, throwing them up in the air and studying the pattern they formed on the floor. Without saying a word, he picked them up, threw them back up in the air, and silent still, focused on the shape they made in front of him. He asked: 'Who is this person on the other side who loves Carnation milk?' (Nina had fed it to her father every day for months until his wound healed.) 'Whoever this man is, he's a doctor now and he can help you from the other side, but you must forgive him for something he did while he was here.'[11]

This spirit needed to be soothed, forgiven and kept company for a few days. '[I]f you couldn't forgive someone you became their slave mentally':[12] this was a concept Nina had been familiar with all her life, one she'd heard over and over again during her childhood, because her mother said it was written in the Bible, an idea dating back to the dawn of Christianity. Suddenly she was being offered a chance to escape remorse and destruction: 'You stay in this house for three days. Do not see or speak to anyone. Wrap your hair in a scarf, don't smoke, don't drink and stay in bed with a tin of Carnation milk under your pillow. Act as though your father were sleeping in the bed next to you.' 'If I obeyed the ritual everything between us would be forgiven and Daddy's spirit would be with me again':[13] that was what the man assured her of.

The witch doctor left, Millie found Nina a tin of milk, and she was on her own. When she awoke three days later, she felt a weight leave her and in an instant saw her father again: 'It was a distinct physical sensation, as if I had lost half my body weight in one sudden moment. And the next instant I saw my father: I am not allowed to say how, because the tribal doctor swore me to secrecy, but he was there in front of my eyes for a short while and then he left.'[14]

It's hard to tell what tradition this ritual belonged to; throwing bones and deciphering the omen they announce is common in West African magic. It wasn't Bwiti, in which the sorcerer would have used a powerful psychotropic substance like Iboga. It certainly wasn't Vodun, mainly followed in Benin and Haiti. In Africa there are many 'powers', and we must understand that ritual magic, practised in many regional and tribal forms, remains inseparable from everyday life and deeply rooted in tradition. The field of beliefs and superstition is wide open and in constant motion. The dead hold a fundamental place, and the existence and influence of their spirits within the tribe isn't up for debate. They must be honoured and feared, as the one who opens the door between the living and the ancestors must also be feared.

From that moment on, John Divine Waymon's spirit would watch over his daughter, but what could he do to save this woman from the destructive forces she faced? Maybe it was then that Nina Simone's behaviour, deemed extravagant in the 60s, began to change. Two decades later it would be thought that of a madwoman, the Western press baffled to see the diva talking to walls and assuring people that her father was sitting beside her. In Europe, 'None could appreciate the safety of ghost company,' as Toni Morrison wrote.[15] But here in Africa, spirits have a direct effect on life. In the natural cycles of life and death, both share the land and the living owe obligations to their ancestors; they cultivate their land, carry on their work, culture and traditions, and offer them worship and sacrifice.

Miriam left Monrovia a few days later to go to Kinshasa to take part in the concert preceding the Muhammad Ali–George Foreman fight on 30 October 1974. 'A gift from President Mobutu to the people of Congo. A source of pride for the black man,' according to the poster issued by the Zairian dictator. It's surprising that Nina Simone had not been contacted by the organizers, as American commentators emphasized that 'for the first time in history, the cream of black American and African artists [were doing] something together'. From a symbolic and artistic point of view, did she have a place in this historic event? Certainly, Nina Simone's aura and the combat she'd waged those last ten years should have won her a place alongside James Brown and Muhammad Ali (who had just met for the first time on the tarmac of Kinshasa airport). After all, all three had paid a dear price for their commitment to the movement. B.B. King and the Spinners, who *had* been invited by the event's promoter Don King as warm-up acts, hadn't done so much for their community and the people of Africa. That the artists who were present, even Ali, later faced criticism for their indirect support of Mobutu's government is another matter. But Nina wasn't invited to Kinshasa. She stayed in Monrovia, where she met the one she believed would be the new man of her life, her 'man of destiny'.

C.C. Dennis was the father of a Liberian minister. An aristocrat and freemason, C.C. was one of Monrovia's most prominent figures. Tall, handsome, a widower courted by high-society ladies, he was as rich as he was bossy. This 'Liberian Rhett Butler' stormed into Nina Simone's home one morning, making a racket before yelling that they'd be married within six weeks. Nina was dumbfounded, Lisa hiding behind her. Who was this man who marched into their home unannounced, gesticulating and barking orders? He barely even introduced himself as he told her to pack her bags and be ready to follow him to his house in the mountains the next day. His tone wouldn't suffer any argument. Nina had never met such a man, acting like the lord of the manor, catching her in her silk dressing gown in her own home, and demanding that she become his wife!

What happened after he left? Perhaps once the C.C. Dennis hurricane passed, Nina questioned Lisa. 'What did you say to them for Millie to take me to the witch doctor? Who said I was looking for a husband?' Could Miriam have launched the rumour before she left for Kinshasa? Whatever the case, in a blink of an eye, all of Monrovia knew that Nina Simone was set to marry C.C. Dennis. In the morning, when C.C. Dennis stormed in again, she was ready and radiant, her mind made up. But barely a few minutes into the journey, the charm was broken. That man wouldn't stop talking – shouting, to be accurate. More intimidating still, he knew all about her: that her personal effects were still being held at customs in Barbados, her tax troubles, her divorce, her ailing career in America, even her drinking problem, which she'd told no one about – then again, perhaps she did drink inordinately at parties and that was a detail that fed the gossip.

They drove like that for a few hours before reaching an estate in the middle of which proudly stood what was definitely a small castle. The scenery was beautiful, the property surrounded by a dense forest from which rose the sounds of unidentifiable birds and wild animals. A special atmosphere reigned over the place, as though it had escaped the effects of time. They were greeted by a stooping employee who called C.C. Dennis 'master'. He used the term because C.C. was a freemason, but to Nina it was a painful reminder of the old conservative South,[16] carried on by these sons of former slaves, now turned rulers. What Nina Simone saw should have horrified her, shattered her illusions, and shocked her into standing up to the man and demanding to be driven back to Monrovia on the spot. Yet perhaps Nina felt she was now dependent on this stranger and that her past and present both now rested in C.C.'s hands. Was she aware of her own contradictions at that point? Whatever the case, she kept quiet, because the stakes of staying were more decisive than the loss of her new illusions. She'd left so much behind that she could only accept the rules of the game set by this seductive stranger with his loud promises of an easy life. The charm of the place and the man's aura had bewitched her.

But in order to marry C.C. and climb to the safety of his shelter, she had to give the old man a hard-on. Dennis had made that much clear; there was only one purpose to those few days in his castle. As soon as they arrived at his estate, C.C. disappeared into his bedroom. What was she to do? Follow him? Wait for him to beckon her? She waited. The day passed, and come the evening he came to see her and told her to dress in a silver negligee. She followed him into his bedroom, slipped into bed with him and caressed him while he lay there motionless. She slowly rubbed herself against him, displaying imagination and gentleness, yet C.C.'s sex remained lifeless. The same scene would unfold the following day, again without result. Pushed out of C.C.'s bed, Nina sought refuge in another room. Feeling lost, she burst into tears.

The weekend was cut short; on Sunday morning, C.C. told Nina they were going back to Monrovia. Back at her villa, she thought back on her crazy weekend: 'Life with C.C. was something I thought I could get used to but I needed help sorting him out, getting to be a proper wife in bed.'[17] A proper wife in bed, that fundamental obligation for an African woman. Feeling confused, Nina confided in her 'African momma' Martha Prout. She told her about her weekend, C.C.'s orders, her failure to give the old man an erection, her doubts, her fear of seeing Dennis's promise of marriage ('in six weeks') vanish into thin air.

At that moment, Nina was light years away from thinking that Martha might betray her. Martha who had looked after her daughter, listened to her sorrows and welcomed her secrets since her arrival in Monrovia. Martha, a woman of the world, held in high regard by the jet set, and who was Nina's key to that lavish universe. What Nina didn't know was that her benefactor was in love with C.C., and that since the death of her husband, a former senior official of the Tubman administration, Martha was set on marrying C.C. Dennis. And she wasn't about to let the whims of an American who'd been in town less than two months thwart her plans.

When she got up the next day, everyone knew about Nina's misadventure with C.C. Dennis. Martha had carefully twisted her friend's confession, so the gossip reported that Nina couldn't give a man an erection, and even someone as virile as C.C. had remained unstirred thanks to the American's clumsiness. This would have been enough to discredit most people and force them into leaving town, seeing as her livelihood depended on a tight circle made up of about a hundred chosen few. But for Nina, this offence opened much deeper wounds. She was once again someone who got pointed at, a failure, someone whose wishes couldn't come true without earning her the wrath of some hostile force.

Panicking and with no one to turn to (Miriam was still in Kinshasa), Nina decided to leave Lisa in the care of Dorris Dennis, C.C.'s daughter (!), and go and seek her mother's advice in the United States. Reading Nina Simone's autobiography, and through all the documents and interviews I was able to collect, I've always wondered about that decision. Why would she leave Monrovia and give Martha Prout free rein? Why take the chance of disappearing from C.C.'s sight without a word of warning? Why run the risk of such a hurried departure being misinterpreted? All that to consult with a mother with whom she'd never even talked about men, let alone sex, and who was sure to be horrified by hearing her daughter talk about surrendering to some

African aristocrat just to live a comfortable life. It was a bit of a long shot.

The house in Philadelphia was in mourning, memories of Lucille and John Divine weighing on the living. Yet Nina stayed there with her mother for some time. She made a pit stop in New York and got the low-down on her tax problems from Max Cohen. No one in the music industry had got in touch to offer her concerts or a new record deal. Her music career seemed well and truly over. She hadn't played in public for almost a year. Financially, things were dire. The IRS warned her that they would soon carry out their threats. It was time to go back to Monrovia before the net tightened.

After a four-week absence, Nina came back to her daughter. One does wonder how Lisa could have felt about a mother this fickle – a loving mother, but so self-centred that her only daughter was always a secondary priority. A few hours after her arrival, Nina found out about the new gossip peddled by Martha during her absence: that she'd returned to the States for good, leaving her daughter behind because she didn't love her. The way Lisa looked at her mother didn't lie; the girl had obviously heard the humiliating rumours. How could she even have doubted them? She'd barely spent one day with her mother since they'd been living in Monrovia. Little by little, they had become strangers, Lisa at the mercy of her mother's whims and moods, shipped off to nannies and luxury day care as Nina trotted all over the country. Even then, Nina paid little attention to what she saw in her daughter's eyes. It was too much to bear, she just couldn't stand it. She was set on recovering her honour and marrying C.C.

She tried to contact him but was told he was out of town. Doris Dennis, whose advice Nina had come to seek, told her that her father was actually going to marry Martha Prout in a few weeks. Then she got a message from C.C. saying he no longer wanted to see her. She felt crushed.

Nina would only see C.C. Dennis once more, almost by accident, at a reception. He was dry and obnoxious when she came to greet him, asking her about Lisa (implying she was a bad mother) – Lisa, who she'd left in the care of Liberian friends for some time – but she could read her mistake in his contempt, and that was having failed to give the old man an erection.

Nina Simone lived in Monrovia until 1976. She returned to an ordinary life, stayed in touch with Doris Dennis and fell in love (though the relationship was short-lived) with a Frenchman from the Central African Republic. During the last months of her Liberian life Nina tried to reconnect with Lisa. Their story had been a long series of separations and reunions, and their relationship had got stormy those past few months. Lisa was now a teenager, her character had hardened, and she stood up to her mother to the point where she reduced her to tears or would spend days without speaking to her, refusing to obey her orders or to show her the slightest affection. In those times of crisis, Nina worried about her daughter's education. Lisa had been at the American school in Monrovia for three years. She'd always enjoyed herself there and refused to leave town to follow her mother back to Europe. Surprising as it might seem, Nina was waking up: she worried that the schooling her daughter received was inadequate. She remembered that during her affair with Errol Barrow, he'd advised her to send Lisa to boarding school for three years. That was a lifetime ago.

Set on this new prospect of happiness, Nina decided to pack her bags and take her daughter to a private boarding school in Switzerland, where she'd get a better education. But why Switzerland? And with what money? Wouldn't England have been an easier choice for both mother and daughter? Whether in terms of visas, language, a black British community, friends, the record industry (if Nina ever needed to relaunch her career), it all seemed so much easier in London, a city where Nina had stayed several times.

Switzerland seemed to be the worst choice after three years spent in Liberia. A country so wrapped up in itself, one that played by the book, so white! Yet Geneva was the place where Nina Simone and Lisa Stroud ended up.

But a few days before she was due to leave for Switzerland, Nina met a man: Imojah. A wealthy East African farm owner, he had sought shelter in Liberia after some murky business with his government. It was love at first sight: 'I have never met anyone like him sexually, before or since. He didn't even have to touch me sometimes – just being near him was enough.'[18] After the unfortunate episode with C.C., one can easily understand how she found refuge and unhoped-for relief in this relationship. She was reluctant to leave, and God only knows what Imojah told her before promising to join her in Europe.

On the plane that flew Nina and her daughter to Geneva, Nina cried over her lost dreams, her easy life amidst the Liberian upper crust, Africa or the little of it she'd experienced during her years in Monrovia, a handful of friends, C.C., and last, Imojah.

Four years later, on the morning of 12 April 1980, a group of seventeen soldiers barged into President Tolbert's residence to demand their unpaid wages. Though the soldiers were ready for a fight, there was no one to be seen at the gates of the building, not even a guard to get in their way. Their leader, Master Sergeant Samuel K. Doe, twenty-eight years old and barely literate, was a former *bayaye* – one of those unemployed youths who loiter in African cities – who'd got to Monrovia when poverty forced him out of the jungle. He was from the Krahn tribe, one of Liberia's poorest ethnic groups, who live deep in the jungle. The soldiers got into the President's bedroom and finding Tolbert fast asleep, they took out their bayonets, killed him in his bed, disembowelled him and left his entrails for the dogs. Doe, who was both the highest-ranking and the eldest of the group, immediately proclaimed himself president. He ordered thirteen government ministers killed; they were publicly tied to coconut trees and tortured to death. C.C. Dennis's son met a similar fate and his father burned his castle so that none of his wealth would end up in the hands of the rebels; he died of a broken heart two weeks later. Then came the turn of Monrovia's notables. Yesterday's lords were paraded naked in the streets of the capital under their torturers' blows; the executions were lengthy, to the indigenous people's delight. Both men and women were delivered to the mob, massacred right in the centre of town. This was 'a revolution within the slave world'.[19] To symbolically mark the end of the old reign, Doe ordered the destruction of a monument dedicated to the greatness of President Tubman, then the Masonic temple (one of the largest in Africa) in the heart of Monrovia.

That day in April 1980 marked Liberia's descent into civil war, systematic looting, and devastation. Samuel K. Doe proved incapable of running a country or providing for the population's needs. He filled the state's leading positions with his fellow tribesmen, moving them straight from abject poverty to the luxury of the presidential palace. Chaos set in. Within a few weeks, Monrovia had no electricity, the shops had no goods, fuel ran scarce, most of the major roads that ran across Liberia were closed, border posts were deserted and Robertsville airport was nothing but a memory. American-Liberians fled the country as soon as the coup was announced. Most of the survivors had to grease the palms of soldiers at the border, but many managed to flee through neighbouring Sierra Leone. Though they escaped with their lives, those former masters turned refugees found only destitution at their journeys' end. Forced to run with no time to take any of their wealth, they ended up forming a strange diaspora.

In May 1980, Liberia sank into darkness and Samuel K. Doe (now a self-appointed general) took the leadership of the People's Redemption Council. The president-dictator suspended the constitution, suppressed political freedoms and gave himself absolute power. Opposition parties were gagged, the 1985 presidential election rigged. Doe's regime was characterized by corruption and the systematic violation of human rights. Diplomatic relations with neighbouring countries (Côte d'Ivoire, Sierra Leone, Guinea) and the country's historical 'godfather', the United States, become more and more strained as violence spilled onto the streets and unemployment, inflation and poverty took hold.

Samuel K. Doe knew he couldn't run the country except by intimidation, and that sooner or later he would face reprisals. He surrounded himself with a crowd of brainless guards, all Krahn, and carried on his reign of terror for ten years, torturing or executing many. In December 1989, Charles Taylor, a US-trained economist from the Gio tribe and former close friend of Doe's, declared war on the dictator. In June 1990, Taylor, at the head of an army swollen by the flood of people terrorized by the regime, marched into Monrovia. Their objective was neither to restore democracy nor any ideal of sovereignty, but the pile of money that Doe was supposedly sitting on. Victory was but a few battles away when Taylor's chief of staff, Prince Johnson, split off to form his own army. Liberia became the stage of a war of three armies! Soon Monrovia was reduced to a field of ruins, civilians roaming country roads, doomed to perish as the country's borders remained closed. In September 1990, to pacify the capital, Nigeria sent in troops that were soon met by those of ECOMOG, a peacekeeping force created by ECOWAS (the Economic Community of West African States). Doe went to the port to greet this support. Through the windows of his presidential car he saw the desolation into which he'd plunged the country. Pillaged, Monrovia was deserted even by ghosts. The only witnesses to human activity were bullet-ridden bodies collapsed in the dust. Arriving at the port, Doe was captured by Prince Johnson's army and his bodyguard massacred by other *bayaye* recruits.

Here this mock president-dictator's ten-year rule came to an end. No Western television station would broadcast what every customer in every bar in Monrovia got to watch: President Samuel Doe tortured to death by Johnson and his crew. But the war spread through the whole country, entire regions falling into the hands of warlords bleeding the last of Liberia's people to death. Taylor took power in July 1997, and although civilian deaths during the conflict stopped being counted in 1990, the body count is estimated at 400,000 people. Worse still, Liberia became a source of instability for the whole of the west of the continent. Neighbouring countries like Côte d'Ivoire and Sierra Leone soon burst into flames too, falling prey to the brutal exploits of the warlords, shaken up by internal conflicts that the international community failed to resolve.

What would have become of Nina Simone if she'd stayed in Monrovia? Better still, what would have happened to her had her wish to marry C.C. come true, or if, having settled in the midst of Liberian high society, she had been present during Samuel Doe's coup? She would have been forced to march through the streets of the capital naked, delivered to the mob like Martha Prout, who, some said, was stoned to death by the crowd, along with a dozen other beauties. Nina would have been manhandled, then executed and her body thrown on top of a mound of trash, territory of rats and vultures. Such was the fate that befell Samuel Doe.

8

ADRIFT

NINA SIMONE'S stay in Switzerland is shrouded in mystery. In this country where secrecy is part of the culture, where the obsessive sense of order and discretion in all things can make you nervous if you don't share those virtues, it seems impossible to wholly lift the veil on what really happened during these years. We know Lisa joined the International School of Geneva, La Châtaigneraie, at the start of 1976, and Nina moved into a house in Prangins, a town near Nyon, where she lived without a job and without a purpose.

I have heard some of the strangest stories about these years – that she could be seen wandering like a tortured soul through the streets of Nyon and its surroundings; that she underwent a whole range of medical check-ups at the Genolier clinic, which specialized in oncology, cardiology, surgery and anti-aging treatments; that one night, clearly in a state of some anguish, she grabbed a revolver and fired it into the air from the front steps of her house; that for some time she lived with another woman, Susan Baumann, who was Nina's governess, friend and manager. I have been told disturbing but unverifiable stories about Nina occasionally hooking up with rich and discreet men so as to ensure a comfortable lifestyle... or perhaps merely to survive.

However, what we do know is that Nina was totally out of her element in Switzerland. Could there be a country further removed from Liberia, in terms of its culture, environment and mores, than Switzerland? Probably not. A rich, insular, conservative country, paranoid about immigration, or more precisely the immigration of blacks, Switzerland was the worst possible choice for Nina.

So why Switzerland? Or rather how, as it is impossible to stay in this country without declaring your presence, your purpose and your income. You cannot stay in Switzerland without support when, like Nina Simone, your pockets are empty, your skin is black and your artistic career is already behind you. A patron, a Good Samaritan, was needed to give Nina a helping hand to allow her to stay for a while close to Geneva, where the cost of living is out of the reach of a penniless American. She needed a residence permit; even better, official papers authorizing her to work in the country, as it was from this time that Nina, out of necessity, resumed a career that had been left for dead over three years ago.

One date served as a trial run for her comeback, while showing Nina's psychological state on her arrival in Switzerland. On 3 July 1976, Nina Simone appeared at the Montreux Jazz Festival, together with Sarah Vaughan (11 July) and Odetta, who sang at the casino on the eve of Nina's performance. Nina shared the bill with Al Jarreau and the bluesman Luther Allison in a show where her classics ('Little Girl Blue', 'Backlash Blues'...) were intermingled with new compositions inspired by her Liberian years ('Feelings', 'Africa').

This 1976 concert has entered the mythology of the Montreux Jazz Festival. It was one of the most chaotic, extravagant and explosive events that the festival has ever known. More than thirty years later it exemplifies, for those who took part or caught it on television, the folly, excess and art of Nina Simone. I had the chance to visit Le Picotin, Claude Nobs's mountain chalet whose parties made its owner's reputation for hospitality, to watch the film of the concert. The light dimmed in his projection room, and Nina's face appeared on the big screen in front of me.

Cropped hair, eyelids painted blue, she had a wild look about her in her belted black dress. The only decoration she wore that night was a heavy silver necklace set with a large precious stone. Her silhouette had thickened, but she retained some of her athletic lines. Her bare arms were surprisingly muscular, and during this concert of extremes her movements would be surprisingly supple, giving off a fascinating sensuality.

Nina was visibly anxious as she hit the stage. She appeared vulnerable, shifting between discomfort, laughter and stage fright. Her movements were slow and sensuous. A certain hardness radiated from her, yet her femininity dazzled from the first. After taking their applause, Nina faced the audience and said: 'I haven't seen you since 1968. I decided not to play jazz festivals any more...' But here, of course, it's different. Joined by a percussionist and a drummer sporting large Afro hairstyles, the diva turned to her piano and played 'Little Girl Blue'. She began singing: 'All you can ever count on is yourself, little lady,' then interrupted her song with a cry of 'Imojah!', an incantation to her lover from Monrovia.

She stood up from her stool, with a look of defiance on her face and a hand elegantly placed on her piano, fixed the audience with an icy stare. Full of pride, she seemed to be challenging them. Applause started to ripple through the crowd, after a delay, as if intimidated. Satisfied, Nina sat back down at her piano and lingered on the melody of 'Little Girl Blue'. She asked for her mike stand, which was slowly sinking, to be repositioned. While a festival technician was adjusting it, she addressed the audience: 'You didn't forget me! I didn't think you would!'

With the technician now off the stage, Nina returned to her mike stand, and without any explanation, it sank again. She burst out laughing: 'I didn't even touch it! This thing's got a life of its own!' The hall burst out laughing too. While the technician came back to try and sort out the stubborn prop, Nina digressed on the subject of Liberia and went into a slow performance of 'Backlash Blues'. The audience could sense she was happy to be performing. She moved to the edge of the stage and crouched down on her high heels, taking in the applause, bringing her palms up to her forehead in the namaste sign of thanks.

Next came 'See Line Woman'. Nina danced, letting loose on her audience, sang a few lines then moved on to one of her favourite themes: the crooks who pirated her records. Then she performed a version of 'I Wish I Knew How', going into a long introduction, attacking the song's chords as if to hurt the audience. Suddenly she cried out: 'Oh yeah! The spirit is here!', calling the audience to witness the presence of her ancestors. The audience duly applauded, paying the diva tribute once again. On that note, she swept off the stage.

Claude Nobs appeared in his astounding outfit (curly hair, huge psychedelic glasses, a brightly coloured suit) and gave Nina a bouquet of flowers. She seemed sincerely moved, placing the bouquet on the piano, and as the applause faded and at last fell silent, she seemed suddenly lost: 'I'm tired...' She digressed again, informing the audience that her daughter would be attending school in Switzerland and that she would also like to settle there: 'I'm hoping to stay with you for a while, if I'm permitted.' Suddenly she called out to David Bowie: 'David! Are you there?' Met with stifled laughter, she explained: 'He's a friend of mine and I know he lives nearby, I wanted to know if he was here tonight!' Then she turned and looked at her piano's keyboard. She started to play 'Feelings', which she interrupted to explain that the heavy necklace she was wearing had been gifted to her by Claude Nobs, and that it used to belong to a queen. 'Because I'm a queen!' There was silence in the hall. The audience didn't know how to react to that. An uneasy feeling settled over them. Nina sat down again and resumed the song when she noticed a movement out in the seats. She interrupted her performance once more and stared at a point in the darkness. She ordered a woman who was trying to leave to 'Sit down!' Then louder: 'Sit down, lady!' You could see the anger on her face.

The incident now over, she began playing again as if nothing had happened, before dismissing her own song: 'What sort of state do you have to be in to write a song like that?!' she exclaimed. The concert drew to a close not long after in an atmosphere caught somewhere between disaster and genius.

What other artist would dare let their audience witness such personal drama? Demand their attention while making them uneasy, remind them to applaud, caress them then bite them, sometimes both at the same time?

Nina Simone only played four songs that night, stretched over an hour, but during that chaotic comeback performance she showed her audience the full range of emotions contained in her art. As you watch the film, you can't help thinking about the burnt emotions Nina left behind her, revealing herself as a naked wildcat, torn between blinding revelation and self-destruction. That concert was a snapshot of Nina's psychological and artistic situation upon arriving in Switzerland in 1976 – a dramatist torn between her madness, her excesses, the disaster of her odyssey, and, despite all, hope. The hope that through her art and her proudly asserted dignity, her luck could change again.

Many people assured me that Claude Nobs gave her that date because he wanted to help her out: he was aware of Nina's perilous financial situation upon arriving in Switzerland, and apparently he hired her at the last minute to play three songs (and as a result be entitled to receive an official fee). Willy Leiser, one of Nobs's close collaborators, was Miriam Makeba's European manager at that time – I think that through Willy, Claude Nobs reached out to offer Nina personal and perhaps also financial support. Here is what I was told by a source who wishes to remain anonymous, though I couldn't confirm it: 'Claude Nobs helped her enormously in crossing the desert, as he has helped a number of artists that he literally pulled out of the gutter. He offered Nina a helping hand to get her out of a bad financial fix. Thanks to Claude Nobs, Nina got a flat in Switzerland, first in Prangins and then in Geneva. And residence permits are not easy to get here, especially for people with legal problems at their backs.'

I've been told many stories about Nina, sometimes in roundabout language, but confirming what I had sensed. Yes, Nina was desperate in Switzerland, yes, she was dying from boredom, but that's plain to see in her biography. Yes, she would call Claude Nobs during the day sometimes to have a driver sent to take her to his chalet.

It's not hard to understand Nina's wish to flee the boredom of her house and take refuge, for a few hours, high up in the hills of Montreux where she would be well treated. I know that people can go a little mad in Switzerland, mad from loneliness when a new day breaks and nothing happens, nothing moves, nothing spices up the routine. It's a strange land for those who come to settle here, uprooted and penniless, seeking to break into this region but constantly coming up against forced politeness and its people's unhealthy discretion. From Geneva to Lausanne, from Vevey to Montreux, in winter all is greyness and pale light along Lake Geneva. You have to wait till summer, when the Riviera takes on a Californian feeling and a stifling heat hovers over the streets, replacing the reasonable mildness that reigns for the rest of the year. This is a country where nothing happens after 8 p.m., everyone seems stiff and undemonstrative, and 'If you see anybody at all it's only the same people as you saw yesterday.'¹ Perhaps she thought she would be able to break into the inner circles of the wealthy living between Geneva and Montreux as easily as she had done in Monrovia. But these were inhospitable lands for a forty-three-year-old black American artist soon forced to revive her career by financial obligation, and they offered nothing but loneliness. Depression gnawed at her again, making its home in her flesh.

Lisa suddenly found herself thrown into the closed world of international boarding schools. Going straight from the freedom she enjoyed in Monrovia to the strict rigour of this Swiss establishment, the teenager must have felt abandoned once more by her thoughtless mother. Their relationship was at its worst: too many mistakes, too many oversights to forgive, to start again on a good footing. And Nina's latest fad of giving her daughter the best possible schooling, for her own well-being, only made the conflict between them worse.

Mother and daughter only saw each other rarely, during Lisa's few weeks and weekends of holiday, when Nina came to get her in Geneva. But their relationship had been poisoned. The girl felt caught up in her mother's drifting, and blamed her for it; she felt her mother didn't care about her and had abandoned her in a boarding school. Their arguments became more and more frequent, until Lisa started throwing hateful words in her mother's face. Soon Lisa stopped visiting Nina when her school calendar allowed, and her mother had no idea how to get close to her. We can't help but think that Nina was repeating with her own daughter the pattern Mary Kate had set with her.

Nina was waiting for Imojah. She made up stories, telling herself that that man who had given her the shivers for a few weeks was the love of her life, that he would take a plane from Monrovia and fly to Geneva just for her, come to her door one morning, and that everything would be fine.

Abandoned to her torments, she was again beset by hallucinations, which lasted 'two or three months'.[2] An eternity. Why would she want to end them during her darkest days, when there was simply no one to talk to, no one to speak with about Nina Simone's battered destiny? But her father's spirit was still there. For a while, it was the only presence she had to talk to.

It had been a long time since Nina cut her ties to the United States. Her years in Liberia had taken her mind off her fans, the music business, her friends in the movement, who had now been dispersed or rebuilt their lives. Only Miriam and Stokely reappeared, from time to time. In a few weeks, Nina would collapse, falling into a depression from which she would never fully recover. But now she began a cycle of personal unhappiness in Switzerland. In the suffocating silence that had become her life, she quickly lost confidence – in herself, in her destiny, perhaps also in her nature. Little by little, Nina Simone became that young mixed-up woman once again, that shy girl she had been upon arriving in New York in the late 50s. Something had withered in her, but what? Maybe she thought she had now fulfilled her musical destiny. That the finest hours of her career, from beginning to end – from the Town Hall concert to her crowning moment at Carnegie Hall, from the peak represented by *I Put a Spell on You* (the album and the single) to the firebrand *Emergency Ward* – formed a coherent oeuvre, complete, whole and of an intensity yet to be equalled. She had been honoured by her peers, critics and fans. She imagined herself a Maria Callas, retired from the boards, the confinement of the last few years aside. Perhaps in the best of worlds she would have continued making records, but without the suffocation of life on tour, without being forced to feed the public's insatiable appetite. She was in agreement with Maria Callas: 'Sing? Yes, but just for me, for pleasure. The audience is a monster. It's because of them I'm not rushing to get back on stage.'[3] In spite of everything, the hunger to play the piano would probably have remained, and she could have reached a balance.

But Nina was like Maria, and both had become Violetta, the heroine of *La Traviata*, 'who spoils in front of men before adoring them, because that is what she was born for!'[4] Just like Maria, Nina hadn't married a man, but a manager, swearing like the legendary performer of Norma: 'Today I want to be a woman like any other. With children, a house, a dog... Believe me, I would love to have a normal life. A private life.'[5]

What happens in an artist's heart when they feel they have given what they had to give, said their piece and have nothing more to say? I believe that was Nina's drama. Despite everything, they have to go back to work, without purpose or ambition except to live. Earn money. And to do that, they have to submit to promoters' and audiences' whims. Getting back on stage, 'being applauded, given flowers, put back in your cage', in the words of her friend Gerrit de Bruin.

Nina was broke. On the edge of bankruptcy. Lisa's education was costing a fortune. Who was paying for it? Let's assume Andy was bearing part of the cost; a few charitable souls may also have helped, even if they are difficult to identify. A Swiss friend of Nina's called Susan Baumann took her in when she was at her lowest. No one knows how they met, but according to some members of Nina's 1980s entourage, the two women lived together in Geneva for several months. Susan wanted to become her manager, take care of her merchandising, write a book about her... By all accounts, their relationship was strange and unbalanced: Susan was in love with the out-of-favour diva, and Nina, who never admitted her occasional taste for women, maintained their friendship even though her feelings towards her Good Samaritan were not love. So just what happened between Nina and Susan? It's impossible to know. Those who know do not wish to tell. Likewise, no one dares comment on the often-heard whisper that the two women lived for a time in a caravan in the suburbs of Geneva! What to do with such information? The few people that were close to her who gave me any comment on the subject said only: 'True or not, it's very Simone.'

Since her performance at the Montreux Jazz Festival in July 1976, the word got out: 'Nina moved to Switzerland.' Despite the taste of chaos that appearance left, she received offers to perform. She hesitated for a long time, pushing back deadlines. She had no entourage, band or management. Once again she was suffering from terrible anxiety attacks that kept her at home, made her chew over the past and convince herself that a vast conspiracy had been organized to bring her down. In the midst of this depression and paranoia, Nina was unable to make a decision. But now, on the edge of a financial and mental cliff, she no longer had a choice: she'd have to get back on stage. Meanwhile, lawyers, accountants and record company emissaries were asking her for records of royalty disputes and the companies Andy had set up. And the American IRS was still pursuing her for back taxes from 1971 to 1973! At the time, her only defence was declaring herself stateless and refusing to pay the American government a single cent. She said she owed nothing to a country that had crushed the movement and mired itself in a loathsome war in Vietnam.

Looking to escape her troubles, Nina Simone took the first available flight and returned to Liberia on a whim. She wanted to see Imojah. His memory obsessed her, the symbol of all she had left behind. She wanted to go and find him in Monrovia, ask him, face to face, if he planned to join her in Europe, yes or no, if he was with her, if he would be able to save her. But no, Imojah didn't want to hear about Europe. Of course he had promised to come and see her, and maybe he would have if things had been different, if he had been smitten with her. But he wasn't. As she stood before him, staring at him crazily, he knew he would never go. Imojah was one of those men who hate it when their conquests try to control them. He was surprised and scared when he realized this American had travelled all that way for him. For him? But they had only been lovers for a few weeks. It was good, yes, but it was months ago. He hadn't got in touch, she had sent letters, he hadn't answered, he had hoped she would understand. Yet here she was, trying to get a promise out of him.

Nina was hurt; she'd been counting on this man to rebuild her life. At this stage, she would have settled for anyone to start over with and not be alone any more. Lisa? Lisa was at boarding school. The day would come when she would be an adult and would decide to leave, because that's what children do. Men too, they leave. They abandon you to your loneliness and are astonished that you are worried about them. But that's all you're left with: worry. Sometimes it's the only link they allow you to have with them. Because soon that neglected daughter would join her father in the United States and enlist in the Army (she would be stationed in Frankfurt in the 80s). Nina would claim to be destroyed by her daughter's departure, even though through their years of wandering, from Barbados to Monrovia then on to Geneva, she had been unable to take care of her.

Nina Simone lingered in Liberia, plunging back into her social life in Monrovia, a closed world where nothing had changed over those years. At the same parties, Nina was once again their American cousin, after having been treated harshly by some of them not so long ago. She was once again the centre of attention and received many requests. She was embraced as an old friend. She was invited to events, pressed with questions, then, when people understood her pain and her doubts, they made her laugh and dance, hoping she would feel free. Nina made use of any excuse to stay on in Monrovia. While she was there, she forgot about her daughter, her worries, Europe. Little by little, she convinced herself that she had no reason or obligation to return to Geneva, and week after week, she extended her stay in Liberia.

One night, Nina Simone met a Liberian businessman, Winfred Gibson. She confided her difficulties to him, her doubts about restarting her career. Winfred listened. Of course he understood, he had heard her records, he even assured her he had a few contacts in the music business, particularly in London. He elaborated about his talents, assuring her that he was a good entrepreneur, a ruthless businessman upon whom lady luck had always smiled. Managing the material aspect of things, being inflexible in business and getting what he was fighting for, that was what he was best at. He could help her. Very quickly, he offered his services to manage her career, take care of the business, save her that energy and leave her time to concentrate on her concerts.

She was seduced. She trusted him. Despite the fact that they weren't lovers, he hadn't even tried to get her into his bed. No, in fact he had been very insistent on that point: Gibson only wanted a strictly professional relationship with her. Nina asked her friends about him, and the response was unanimous: Gibson was a talented businessman with an unblemished record.

With their professional association still fresh, the pair decided to head off to canvass labels and promoters in London, the nerve centre of the European music business where Winfred Gibson said he was sure he could negotiate a series of contracts for Nina. They checked into a suite in the Carlton Tower Hotel, a five-star establishment in Cadogan Place in south-west London. Each evening, when he came back, Gibson swore he was sure there were serious possibilities of recordings, concerts, maybe even a tour. The days passed. Nothing concrete was happening. Nina Simone had been in her suite at the Carlton for nearly ten days when the manager asked her to come with him to his office: 'he asked when I was intending to pay the bill for myself and Mr Gibson. I looked at him and said I thought Mr Gibson had taken care of it'.[6] But he hadn't.

That night, the conversation between Nina and Winfred Gibson turned sour. They jostled and swore at each other. They fought and he hit her: 'He rabbit-punched me on the neck and I was unconscious before I hit the floor.'[7] Nina came to in an empty room. She realised she could hardly move and her neck was sore. She crawled over to the night stand, where the telephone was, and pulled on its cable. She dialled 0 and the girl at reception answered. Nina screamed for help. The hotel nurse was sent up and found a black woman lying on the floor unable to move. Injection. Morphine. Sleeping drugs. It was a day before Nina woke up, bathed in sweat and with a sore neck. She called out, but there was no one there. Carefully, she got out of bed. She was dizzy, her head filled with tinnitus. She moved around the room by holding on to the furniture. She moved from the bedroom to the living room and saw that it had been turned upside down. Her cases, her bag, the desk drawers, all had been rifled through. Nina grabbed her handbag, thrust her hand inside, searching. Her money was gone. She began swaying. She called reception again. The same voice said 'Help,' the same response: 'We're coming.' The manager burst into her room. He had just been informed of the incident. Policemen were with him; they examined the suite as Nina was sat down in an armchair. They asked her to explain what had happened. She told them how she met Mr Gibson in Monrovia and how she had come for a series of contracts, insisting: 'He was meant to take care of everything!'

Thirty-five sleeping pills for thirty-five hours out of it. Gone to a place no one comes back from unwounded.

What made her come back? The pipe thrust into her stomach? The images breaking through the night? A voice, a force that dragged her back to the living? But what for? There was so little hope there. It was a call for help, of course. But why should she come back? For Lisa. The hope of a second chance. Was she forbidden from crossing over? Did a voice order her to turn back because it wasn't time, or, on the edge between two worlds, through affection, fear and habit, did she agree to return to the body lying below her? One last time. To see what happens. Or because it was too cold where she was. Because she felt too alone. More alone than among the living.

Her neck was held in a collar, her stomach was sore. The British newspapers learned that an American star had tried to commit suicide in a suite at the Carlton. They cashed in on the story for a few days, but interest soon waned and they moved on to wrecking other reputations.

Psychiatric examinations. Clinical tests. Tablets. Experts. Convalescence near Oxford at a health facility. Low moments for an abandoned woman. Diagnosis: 'Manic-depressive. Cyclothymia.' Prescription: tablets, lithium, rest.

Nina Simone reflected on her life. On what she had left, on what she had lost. She looked for a way out, examining the options available to her a hundred times over. They were scant, almost non-existent. She'd have to make decisions based on need. Stay solvent and keep her reason. Knuckle down and give herself a break. Nina Simone decided to return to performing.

In September 1977, Nina was hired by Ronnie Scott's, a London jazz club to which she would soon return. Once she got started, she performed in Paris, the Netherlands, Belgium and Germany, but without an entourage or a manager Nina was back to the gloom of badly paid concerts given in cheap joints. She was confronted by dirty dressing rooms, shabby organizers and their crude audiences. And she had to really fight to get paid after the shows: 'Promoters and managers rarely show respect for an artist without representation, and Nina was no exception.'[8] She was bound to detest every moment of these shows,[9] particularly because her poor treatment fired her temper again, living up to her reputation as a monster and making her a target for showbiz papers and gossips.

On the cusp of the 1980s, Nina Simone, who had once been feared and admired, was being mocked. Cruelly, it was her reputation as a harpy that brought audiences back 'to see if I was as difficult as the press said I was'.[10] That is where the parallel legends that darken our memory of her come from. People who saw Nina on stage during those years confirm she was a Fury ready to break into storm, crisis or tantrum, someone that people went to see hoping for blood. She was described as unbearable, 'because I objected when people weren't punctual, or didn't take any notice of my instructions for the staging, or didn't tune my piano properly, or didn't pay me the agreed sum at the contracted time'.[11] These aren't unusual demands. Faced with promoters' abuses, she found herself destitute, with her anger as her only protection.

For instance, the story goes that Claude Nobs intervened so she could perform at MIDEM, an annual music industry gathering held in Cannes, one year. Journalists and record company people tried to sabotage her concert, accusing her of throwing her contempt for them in their faces from the stage. She threw back that they were just a bunch of thieves, con men making fortunes off artists' backs, before abandoning them when fashions changed. They were no more than leeches, she said, parasites who had caused her misfortune. And they booed her when she stopped her performance, preferring to return to her dressing room than play for 'those pigs'.

After that episode, for less scrupulous journalists she became a matron worth provoking: and she'd crack, rant and rave and make a scene, a hateful diva. In England, some journalists didn't hesitate before humiliating her, jostling with her, waiting for her in her dressing room without permission, raining their obscene questions down on her, insisting until Nina exploded in a torrent of insults and threats.

With Andy by her side, such annoyances would never have occurred. She understood that she would remain vulnerable until she had someone to look out for her interests. In the middle of that trouble, Nina got a call from Andy. He had found out she was playing again, and wanted to offer her a short American tour. It would be strictly professional between them. He would be her manager, he'd take care of everything, he could guarantee her suitable fees and time in New York to see her friends, to rest. The last night of the tour would be at Carnegie Hall, a concert at the Newport Jazz Festival, which in 1972 had moved to New York following riots.[12] Andy was the man who would assure Nina her return to favour. She'd have to put together a band as soon as possible, the dates had to be confirmed over the next few days. Nina got in touch with Al Schackman; they hadn't worked together for almost four years. She offered him the tour, Alvin accepted; she arranged to meet him in New York in a few days, enough time to get her things in order and buy a ticket.

June 1977: the plane carrying Nina Simone back to New York landed at JFK airport. She passed through customs and headed towards the arrival hall. The atmosphere was unusually agitated. In the crowd, a group of reporters clutched their cameras and notebooks like daggers. Nina wondered if this was for her. One of the journalists recognized her, called out her name; his colleagues threw themselves at her, repeating her name like little barking dogs: 'Nina, Nina!' They quickly surrounded her, bombarding her with questions: 'Nina, are you glad to be back in the country? How do you feel?' She was still being questioned as she was passed a copy of the *New York Times*. She read about her return to American soil in a box on the front page. For a second she was happy, imagining her triumphant return to the country, as reconciliatory words formed on her lips.

'Nina, do you think you'll go to jail?' 'Nina, how are you going to plead?' 'Nina, who will be leading your defence?' That was a shock. Too late, she suddenly understood the trap that had been set for her. Unsteady, quickly taking refuge in her astonishment, she was told she'd have to appear to answer charges of failing to file tax returns from 1971 to 1973. The IRS were claiming a fortune, several hundred thousand dollars. But that was all up to Andy. Throughout those years, he was the one who looked after the business, had managed her interests, her accounts, she hadn't even seen that money since their divorce. Andy had knowingly betrayed her, or did he think the IRS wouldn't notice the income he planned to hide? Whatever the reasons, Nina was legally responsible in the eyes of the law: it was her payslips and the accounts of all of the companies Andy had created in her name that were at issue.

Andy pushed the reporters aside, jostling with them, scattering them, before finally coming face to face with his ex-wife. He welcomed her, seeming deeply sorry for the nasty surprise she'd just had. He took her cases and asked her to follow him to the airport car park. A few journalists ambushed them from behind some cars – then they were gone. Andy was uneasy; he told her everything would be all right and explained she'd have to go to court in New York for three days before the tour began. He assured her there was nothing he could have done, nothing he could have told her, but he'd hired a good lawyer so Nina had nothing to worry about. He put the cases in the boot and drove, in silence, to a city-centre hotel.

A meeting had been set up with the district attorney. She went accompanied by Andy and the lawyer. During the meeting, Nina listened carefully to the deal being offered to her: plead guilty to not filing tax returns for the first two years, and they'd drop the charges for the third year. The lawyer explained it was a good deal, and she'd better take it.

Next, Nina Simone was summoned to appear before the District Court in Brooklyn. The court was presided over by Constance Baker Motley, the first African-American woman to be appointed a federal judge, in 1966. Nina's lawyer pleaded guilty, and judgement was postponed to a later date. But Nina was taken 'down underneath the courts to some kind of holding facility'.[13] There, an ugly white guy with a Southern accent took her fingerprints, as if she was a criminal, calling her 'Nine-ah'. He toyed with her sadistically; terrified, abandoned by her lawyer, she screamed for Andy but he was gone too.

Finally, Andy appeared. He found Nina shattered, curled up, rocking back and forth on her bench, a defeated look on her face, her hair a mess. He apologized for not coming sooner, claiming they wouldn't let him. She asked: 'How long have I been here?', and found it was five hours. She asked when it was all going to end, when she could get out of that cell, get out of that wretched place and finally wash. Andy was silent.

Nina was let out on bail after ten hours of detention. She was informed that the judge would announce her sentence in a few weeks, on 25 June 1977.

The tour with Andy began. On the whole, the welcome she received at these concerts was good but not great, except in Berkeley, where she got a major ovation. But the pressure of the concerts, coupled with waiting for the verdict, was unbearable for Nina. Her only source of joy was the prospect of playing at Carnegie Hall again, this time as part of the 24th Newport Jazz Festival. Andy refused to discuss the legal charges with his ex-wife. There was no more love or trust between them – they were an old, worn-out couple joined together by fate, because all she knew how to do was play and he had never shone so brightly as he did at her side.

What did Andy Stroud do during their years of separation? It's hard to say, as he has stubbornly refused to talk about that period ever since. We know he didn't go back to the New York police. He may have cashed in on his talents in the music business. Officially, he is said to have worked in insurance.

What was left holding Nina and Andy together? Faded glory and the hope of finding it again: its taste, its intoxicating feeling, its comforts. And Lisa. They shared the guilt of knowing Lisa was closed away in a Swiss boarding school. Did they think about her? They did when they accused each other of abandoning her. Finally, money, the reason for all mistrust, and the fraud charges, which weren't going to help their relationship. It was so bad that at one point Andy had a stranger pass Nina her fee after concerts. That was the point of no return.

They went back to New York on 25 June and were informed of the judge's decision. Nina Simone was found guilty and sentenced to a heavy fine. The law never went after Andy Stroud.

singer who had had a national hit a few years before with the song 'Oh Katy'. Very quickly, Nina realized that neither Creed Taylor nor the arranger, David Matthews, was planning to give her any artistic control over the album. Later, she would confide in Sylvia Hampton about her resentment at feeling used yet again: 'I'm not at all happy with [the album]. You know how important my music is. I told them I had to have control over it, man. I don't want people messing with my music, but they just did what the hell they wanted... I hate [the cover], it's not who I am, and they never even bothered to ask *me* what songs should go on to the damn record... It's the same shit that I've been dealing with all my life and here we are twentysomething years later and nothing's changed.'[14] And Nina had reason to be unhappy. The album cover is indeed ridiculous: she's shown in a sophisticated 1930s style, an exaggerated smile across her face, a fur wrapped round her shoulders. When you unfold the original cover, you discover her lying peacefully on a sofa, marked by her trials but serenely beautiful.

Would *Baltimore* have been a slightly less ugly album, slightly less pompous, had Nina had some sort of control over it? It's hard to say. We're led to believe that neither Nina nor CTI's team meant to do anything more than get another album out. Although there are few redeeming moments on the album, it is vulgarly called 'a hit'. As the *All Music Guide* columnist Joseph McCombs remarked, 'Simone simply covers too much ground and there's too little attention paid to how songs flow together'. Matthews's arrangements are literally stunning. Where did he get the idea of overloading the two traditional songs on the album with violins, reverb, choirs? That's either totally ignoring the subject or displaying a certain amount of incompetence. When you have a singer and a pianist of Nina's quality, the idea is to give them the space to express themselves as much as possible, and not these garish, suffocating colours. Even the choice of songs for *Baltimore* leaves us sceptical. Who had the strange idea of recording the slight 'Rich Girl' by the Californian duo Hall & Oates? Nina? Really?

It's not important. All indications were that *Baltimore* was Nina's last-chance album, and it is here that she achieved her coup. The single 'Baltimore', a Randy Newman cover, managed to enter the American and British charts, if only discreetly. *Baltimore* put Nina back in the saddle, earning respectable sales, bringing her back into contact with the record industry without having to kowtow. She even met with the people from RCA to discuss the possibility of a new contract. But it seems that her tantrums in the Belgian studio found their way to the ears of the industry bigwigs. Soon RCA let her know that her financial demands and her determination to control her own artistic work were not in keeping with their policy. So Nina was caught up, once again, in the old pattern. Just like what happened with her album for Bethlehem, armed with the hit 'Porgy', her record company ignored her.

It took a shock to persuade Nina to take the risk of starting all over again.

After an appearance on stage at Fisher Hall in New York on 11 December 1978, Nina Simone set off for a tour of Israel. Two dates in the Holy Land: the first on Christmas Day in Bethlehem church, the second in Tel Aviv on New Year's Eve. From the moment she stepped off the plane, Nina was welcomed with open arms. At the airport, where the mayor came to greet her on the tarmac, she was met by a throng of fans who invaded the arrivals hall: 'It took us four hours to get away from the airport, straight to a civic reception.'[15]

During those two concerts, Nina felt her soul purified, her faith rekindled. Not her Christian faith – she felt too abandoned by Him to still be able to worship Him without fear – but by pure faith, her faith in life, in the power of prayer and singing. On 31 December 1978, during her concert in the church in Tel Aviv, Nina Simone entered a trance, and invited the audience to invade the stage in what she claims was one of the most powerful spiritual moments of her life.

In the early days of 1979, Nina Simone left Israel refreshed, alive again: 'I'd realized something very important while I was in the Holy Land; I had nobody to rely on but myself and my father's spirit, and I was going to have to get used to the fact.'[16]

9

'ONE MORNING I TOOK
A LOOK AT CIVILIZATION'

NINA RETURNED to Switzerland feeling invigorated by her Israeli experience. She knew she had to find a way to leave the country, it was just too depressing, and her personal effects were still strewn around between Barbados, Liberia and the United States. Lisa was still at boarding school and Nina was already thinking about moving to Paris.

Before taking the plunge, she accepted a gig in New York, where the Village Gate was offering her several weeks' residency during the month of February 1979. A short column by John S. Wilson with the headline 'Nina Simone makes her first appearance on the New York jazz club scene in ten years' was published in the *New York Times* on 24 February 1979. The article emphasized that those concerts bore 'Nina Simone's particular touch'.

The artist who'd gone underground for several years was trying to get back on her feet both financially and artistically. Nina Simone was famous, yet unknown to the younger audience she'd set her mind on winning over. To do that, she'd play her trademarks, 'Mississippi Goddam' and 'Porgy', every night, then throwing in some classics by the Beatles, Joan Baez and Dylan, and some traditional gospel songs. As for the rest, her provocative behaviour on stage made the show.

Then she went back to Switzerland. Indeed, although Nina always declared she'd left Switzerland for good after the revelation she experienced in Israel, she kept a pied-à-terre in Geneva until at least

1982, having left Prangins to move into a tower in Geneva close to the airport.

The period Nina Simone spent in Switzerland is one of her most troubled, and it's hard to follow her tracks without losing them altogether. There she is, re-emerging where no one expected her to. The treasure hunt takes us all the way to Montreal, Canada, in the summer of 1980.

On 18 July, Nina played at Place des Arts, in the Salle Wilfrid-Pelletier. The concert was recorded and would years later be released as a semi-official live record called *The Rising Sun Collection*. Its seven songs include the usual 'Mississippi Goddam' and 'Ain't Got No/I Got Life', a short a cappella version of 'Be My Husband', and 'Let It Be Me', Nina Simone's adaptation of a standard by Gilbert Bécaud and Pierre Delanoë.

At the end of the concert, Nina had a brush with the management of the hotel she was staying in. Her friend (and future president of her international fan club) Roger Nupie tells that: 'Nina was meant to be staying with someone in Montreal, but it didn't work out so she had to check into a chic hotel in town. Weeks went by before the hotel management reminded her that she had to pay her bill. Nina replied: "I can't, darling, I have no money, I am a poor woman. I can play a concert in your hotel as compensation, but no more than fifteen minutes." Not only did the management of the hotel agree, but Nina played the game right through to the end. And what did she play? This is what she told me: "I played this divine thing by Camille Saint-Saëns [meaning a theme from *Samson and Delilah*, which was created in Weimar in 1877] that I'd already played at Carnegie Hall, and one or two love songs. And that's it. There were fourteen people in the room and everyone clapped. I took a bow and went back to my hotel room. I've never made that much money in my entire life.'

Then Nina returned to Switzerland again. Why didn't she just leave this country she claimed to despise? The question remains unanswered. Roger Nupie provided a clue: 'Nina had mixed feelings about Switzerland, but she loved the country because it was quiet. She often said she was bored there and she felt like she was living in a cemetery, but she felt comfortable there too! I remember hearing her saying the same thing about Africa sometimes. Nina was never happy anywhere. It was as though some outside force was set on destroying everything whenever things were going well for her. It was beyond her. Whenever she found peace, she missed the excitement, and whenever the excitement got too much, she couldn't deal with it.'

There was another and more pragmatic reason for her prolonged stay in Geneva. Nina was trying to get her career back on track and had surrounded herself with people who were organizing a tour in Switzerland and Germany. Those who were close to her at the time bear testament to this: she was going through a hollow patch and was trying to get back on track. She performed in Switzerland, Belgium and Germany, at venues that held five hundred on average. Many people evoke a woman who was emotionally unstable, manic-depressive, subject to phases of utter despondency or repressed aggression that alternated with manic phases where she could prove pretty voluble. All agree that this unpredictability was also obvious on stage.

The papers reporting on the concerts Nina played over that period all emphasize their shock value. In those days she'd show up on stage in a long leather coat reminiscent of those worn by the Gestapo, throwing the crowd a despising glare as she sat down at her piano, letting her coat slip open while she played a few arpeggios. This now fuller-figured, forty-something-year-old woman would then get up and take it off to reveal tight-fitting shorts, then stand there, proudly and defiantly staring at the audience. Only once she was sure she'd made an impression, to the point where you could have heard a fly buzzing around the room, she'd get to work without a second glance at her astounded audience.

Those who accompanied her during those concerts recalled that over time it gets harrowing to work with someone who acts like that, but you had to make do because the outcome of the concert depended on it. Nina knew this and would add a touch of cruelty as though saying, 'Without me, there is nothing.'

This was also the time where pirate copies of Nina's records came raining down. This flurry is understandable on account of the artist's several-year-long break from recording, which led to her concerts being pirated. For the most part, those were radio recordings and tapings of the poorest sound quality. One day, Nina saw some of those records in the window of a shop she happened to be passing by in Switzerland. She walked in and began to dig out all the pirate records bearing her name from the boxes, fully intending to take them with her without paying. The shop assistant protested, Nina fulminated. Only the intervention of Jean-Claude Arnodon, a leading figure of Radio Suisse Romande who was her road manager on that tour, helped avert a tragedy. 'But I understand where Nina was coming from,' he said. 'Those were days where she was in such dire need of money that those pirate records were purely and simply money that she didn't earn!'

Al Schackman was part of Nina's entourage over that period. I was surprised to hear how little interaction there was between him and her at that time. 'Her relations with her musicians, most of whom we didn't know, were strictly confined to work,' Jean-Claude Arnodon told me. 'I don't recall there being any special bond or comradeship there. I sometimes felt that her musicians were just flunkeys to her. She didn't spend any time with them off stage.' Here's the picture: a band of musicians frustrated to be stuck working for a manic-depressive diva whose heyday was over ten years past.

Then came the big jump and the move to Paris, in 1981. Nina wrote that she came alone, set on leaving Switzerland for good. She rented a small flat near the Porte d'Orléans, then went in search of gigs on her own, without a manager. All the promoters she met showed interest, but they demanded exclusive rights and wanted to take care of all financial aspects. Nina claimed that she refused all those propositions outright for fear of being tricked once more, eventually getting a gig in a small club in the Latin Quarter called Les Trois Maillets.

But research revealed that the reality of it might have been somewhat different. First of all, for much of 1981, Nina kept her place in Geneva. She actually travelled to France at the invitation of a jazz club in Tours, Le Petit Faucheux, which can't have held more than eighty people. The promoters put her up in a beautiful hotel in town, but soon Nina's concert antics wore out the patience of the organizers, who decided to cancel her gigs. Then, finding herself penniless, she was asked to settle her hotel bill. Unable to do so, she contacted Yves Chamberland, a Parisian producer who until 1975 had made records with most French pop artists, from Sheila to Henri Salvador. Mr Chamberland was also the owner of the Davout studio, the ultimate shrine of jazz in the capital. Nina'd been put in contact with him through Alain Farhi, the co-founder of the New Morning concert hall, first in Geneva, then Paris. When Yves Chamberland got Nina Simone's call, she talked about making a record with him; Chamberland asked her to come and meet him to discuss the possibility.

It's said that Nina Simone arrived at Gare Montparnasse with just $50 in her pocket. As she got off the train, she was greeted by Luc Rubinstein, Arthur Rubinstein's nephew and a close friend of Claude Nougaro's. Following a first meeting with Yves Chamberland in which he and Nina agreed on the terms of a one-record deal, Luc Rubinstein provisionally arranged for her to stay with Claude Nougaro.

Jean-Michel Boris, who was Bruno Coquatrix's nephew and would spend forty years as the artistic director of the Olympia concert hall, tells us this anecdote: Marcia, Claude's Brazilian wife, installed Nina in the guest room and warned Nougaro that they had a guest for the night. Claude reacted to the news with glee: 'Nina Simone in my home, how wonderful!' When he came home in the middle of the night, he ran into the room she was sleeping in. Panic-stricken, she leapt out of bed and chased him all over the house, brandishing a knife while Claude screamed: 'But Nina my love, it's me, it's Claude!' In the end, Nina spent but a few days with Nougaro before he showed her the door.

After that, she stayed at various Parisian hotels, including the plush Regina, on the place des Pyramides. The recording sessions for what would become the album *Fodder on My Wings* began in Davout's studio A, in January 1982. Yves Chamberland (who himself confessed to having refrained from any artistic input on the record) hired three musicians to back up the diva: Paco Sery, Sylvain Marc and Sydney Thiam. The sessions spanned three weeks, punctuated by the pianist's usual fits, like the time she fired a blank shot at a young man acting as her chauffeur and 'escort'. After that incident and a strict warning from Yves Chamberland, Nina swore to finish recording the album in two days. She kept her word.

Fodder on My Wings turned out to be Nina Simone's last major studio record. It was released on CY Records and distributed by Carrere.

During an interview she gave on Radio Suisse Romande, she said this about the title track:

> I wrote 'Fodder in her Wings' on the balcony of my apartment in Switzerland. One morning I took a look at civilization from the height of the tower I lived in. I listened to the silence and watched those people doing the same thing, the same way, at the same time. I saw children all dressed in the same uniforms, carrying their books, their satchels, going to school, all those people walking the line to go to the grocery store, businessmen setting off in their cars, phone operators rushing off to work..., and I thought: 'What am I doing here?' Then I thought of the title of the movie *The Asphalt Jungle*. I've never seen the film but I know it's about some Western civilization that lives surrounded by concrete. That's how the word 'fodder' came up: 'manure'. The lyrics of the song tell the story of a bird that falls into a pile of manure, breaking a wing in its fall, no longer able to fly. It has a third eye though and it can see that those creatures we call 'human beings' don't know how to live, let alone give. Just like me, that bird is the reincarnation of another being. Despite its broken wing, it tries to break free from the fodder and manages to fly short distances from one country to the next. The ending to the song lets the listener decide whether the bird finds peace... or not, if its wing heals and if it manages to find release from this awful place, or whether it fails and falls back on the ground, into the manure. This is the story behind 'Fodder in her Wings'.

And the thinly veiled story of Nina Simone's own odyssey.

Jacques Bonni, the owner of the jazz club Les Trois Maillets, is a well-known character in Paris's Latin Quarter. In the business since 1966, he's the founder of Polymagoo which was the epicentre of student protests in May 1968, and he bought the Trois Maillets in 1977. Located on rue Galande, this maze of cellars dates back to the construction of Notre Dame cathedral. The basement is home to a concert hall with a vaulted ceiling and the capacity to hold about one hundred people. During its first few years in business, the Trois Maillets didn't do too well. Not until it hosted Nina Simone in 1982 and sold out night after night. Jacques Bonni was one of the pianist's Good Samaritans during her stay in Paris, and although the months she spent at the Trois Maillets didn't quite help to revive her career, that little place with its medieval feel provided her with some kind of anchorage, a relative stability that she seemed to be denied elsewhere.

Their meeting was quite fantastic. Nina was playing in Troyes, and after the concert ended she sat down on the steps of a church, counting the notes of her fee, when she was attacked by some gang who took off with her meagre wages. No one knows quite how the pianist managed to make it back to Paris, but she found shelter at the Novotel at Porte de Bagnolet, and from there called Maurice Cullaz, who back then was the president of the Jazz Club de France, asking for his help. Cullaz, for some reason unknown to Jacques Bonni, called him up on the spot. 'How would you feel about hosting Nina Simone at the Trois Maillets?'

A meeting was set up at the Novotel the following day at 9 p.m.

'I showed up at that first meeting about ten or fifteen minutes late,' Jacques Bonni tells. 'She moaned, then calmed down and said: "Let's go and eat in the hotel restaurant, you're buying!" As soon as she sat down, Nina demanded that I give her four thousand francs. It was quite a large amount and I didn't even know this woman, so I suggested we talk about it first and try to come to some arrangement. She looked at me, furious, took hold of the table and pushed it over. The restaurant fell completely silent. When she calmed down, I proposed to start over. We talked business and came to an agreement. Nina was desperate but she never let it show.'

Nina Simone spent almost a year at the Trois Maillets, a fairly lacklustre time for her. The months performing in that cellar felt like she'd returned to square one. One wanders around the place looking for some trace of Nina, but in vain; there are no photos of the diva, nothing bearing witness to her passing through those walls. The only marks on the vaults are the arms and initials of the families that built the place or, further in, the iron gate of a cell said to have held the poet François Villon when the Trois Maillets was turned into a prison in the fifteenth century. Squeezing up against those bars, all one makes out in the dark are cases filled with empty bottles.

Still, this is the place where Nina tried to get her career and finances back on track and to regain her mental balance. She made a pretty good living with Jacques Bonni, not least because tickets to her concerts cost 100 francs, the pianist making between ten and fifteen thousand a night depending on attendance, which was excellent considering the capacity of the venue. Word spread across Paris like wildfire. 'Nina Simone is playing at some tiny club in the Latin Quarter.' The news was barely believable. The audience would come and stand in the stifling heat to watch her inconsistent concerts that featured the same repertoire night after night, seeing her randomly alternate between magic and mediocrity, scandals and genius, anger and moments of pure grace: 'At her most amazing, Nina could literally transport you somewhere else,' Jacques Bonni recalls. 'When someone can make you feel that way even just once, it makes you hope to experience it again one day. And so the public kept coming back just to relive that moment of pure magic, even though just a few minutes later she might break the charm and start to yell.'

Just what did Nina Simone's Parisian life consist of in those days? A succession of hotel rooms, no friends to speak of except for Jacques Bonni, no steady lovers, just one-night stands where Nina turned into a sexual predator, sometimes offering those men money in exchange for a night of passion, occasionally getting ripped off in the process.

Money became an obsession. No alcohol, or only in private. Tranquillizers. Relapses? There were several of those, at regular intervals, some of them alarming. When Nina heard of Samuel Doe's coup in Monrovia, or when Lisa, now of legal age, left Switzerland to go back to live in the United States with her father. That was a terrible blow. Of her difficult relationship with her daughter, Nina wrote: 'Too much had happened between us and I had never spent the time I should have done with her when she was younger. There was no way I could make her understand how I just never had the time and how much I wished that I had.'[1] Soon thereafter, Lisa enrolled in the US Army. They wouldn't meet again until the late 80s.

Nina's mere physical presence left a strong mark through her years in Paris: a presence that was magnetic, intense, intimidating, constantly surfing the fine line between allure and annoyance.

Above all, Nina needed the energy and attention of others in order to survive; that was her poison, the essence of her art and her manipulation. Her appetite turned her into a vampire who thrived on the constant renewal of an entourage she was quick to suck dry. There is no shortage of absurd, incoherent, funny, even violent stories from this time. Nina once returned to Switzerland for the weekend, only to call up Bonni from Geneva airport screaming that the plane was full and she wouldn't be able to make it back to Paris that night as she'd promised, passing him on to the airport manager to back up what she said. Nina then had a fit of hysterics and tried to force her way onto the plane to Paris before security stopped her at the last minute. She showed up at the Trois Maillets three days later with some guy in tow to whom she'd promised 5,000 francs if he drove her to Paris.

Jacques Bonni laughs about it now. He laughs with that special tenderness he feels for this woman he took into his den and who despite all his efforts to steady her couldn't stop herself from disappearing or diving into trouble head first.

Over those years, Nina gave several performances at Paris's Palais des Glaces. During one of the gigs she actually deigned to honour, the manager Raymond Gonzalez happened to be there. Raymond was a product of the New York culture. Born in Hell's Kitchen and of Catalan, Galician and Puerto Rican descent, he had moved to Europe in the early 70s, living in Spain, then Germany before ending up in Paris. Gonzalez was no newcomer to the business when he met Nina Simone.

His track record included collaborations with tough characters, including Chuck Berry and Kid Creole and the Coconuts. When asked about that night at the Palais des Glaces, Raymond recalls Nina with her hair in long braids, clad in a black slip dress that clung to her bulging curves, a knife at her waist ('plain for all to see', he adds).

They were introduced at the end of the concert. In those days, Raymond Gonzalez was the artistic director of the Pamplona festival in the Spanish Basque Country. Nina insisted on playing there and once she got hold of Gonzalez's number, she harassed him until he pencilled her in for the 1982 festival. After that, she disappeared off the radar. A few days before the show, still without any news from her, Gonzalez started to worry. He heard that she was due to perform in Switzerland and was probably staying at the Geneva flat she'd kept. So he caught a plane to Geneva, hoping to get her to Pamplona in time for her concert two days later.

In those days, there were only two weekly flights to Pamplona from Madrid. Gonzalez made his way to Nina's flat but found no one there. He left her a message explaining that he'd come and fetch her in morning at 7 o'clock to catch the 9 a.m. flight, and that if they missed that plane, it would be impossible for them to make it to the festival in time.

The next day, Gonzalez went to Nina Simone's flat as planned. The door was open. He came in to find her blind drunk, a large glass of cognac in hand. She didn't seem surprised to see Gonzalez sit down, hardly noticing his worried expression. She said she had enough money to do without that concert. Upset, Raymond Gonzalez told her that he was going back to Spain, he would tell the organizers her concert was cancelled, and that he felt disappointed, as the audience would be too... As he got up to move towards the door, he heard her scream: 'You haven't got any balls!' He asked her why. She replied: 'Because you don't know how to handle me. You should've called a cab right away.' She then ordered a taxi herself, airport-bound. Halfway there, she pulled out a knife and threatened the driver, who was a tough nut and feigned indifference. Once they got to Geneva airport, Gonzalez called up the festival to say that Nina Simone was with him but she wasn't in a fit state to play. Pamplona refused to cancel her set.

Raymond Gonzalez warned them: considering the state Nina was in and as she didn't have a manager, he would escort her to the festival as her agent.

When she made it to Pamplona at last after a stopover in Madrid, Gonzalez heard that the diva's luggage had been lost in transit. Nina had nothing suitable to wear on stage and the concert was now but a few hours away. It was the weekend and all the shops were shut. He had to call the sister of one of the organizers to the rescue, get her to reopen her boutique and ask Nina to pick out an outfit. Nothing was to her liking, nothing fitted her: she would go on stage wearing the same brightly coloured African boubou she'd been wearing since Geneva. Back at the hotel, she demanded to go down to the pool, only to show up there naked and brandishing three bottles of champagne. Raymond Gonzalez protested, but Nina wouldn't listen. She threw a tantrum, declaring that she no longer wanted to play. Gonzalez lost it: 'Fuck you!' She regained her composure just as he moved to leave: 'Wait! Give me the list of songs you want to hear tonight.' He was at his wits' end, but making a last effort, he handed her a list and begged her to go and get dressed. They drove to the festival. Nina demanded to be paid up front, in full and in cash, otherwise she wouldn't play. The audience was waiting and a clamour of dissatisfaction was rising up: it was too late for the organizers to back out. They paid cash, ignoring the advice of Raymond Gonzalez who suggested they get the star to sign a receipt.

At long last, Nina got up on the stage that had been set up in a park downtown. She sat down at her piano, tried out a few arpeggios, but she was too drunk to play a single harmony. The audience, its patience sorely tried by the delay, began to boo her. Gonzalez felt disaster loom when Nina began to insult the crowd until she had to be escorted off stage. Frustration showing on his face, Raymond Gonzalez turned to face her – only to hear her say, 'I really need to pee.' There were no facilities nearby and Raymond asked her to wait until they were back at the hotel, but right then, unable to hold it any longer, Nina lifted up her boubou, crouched down and urinated right there on the ground. Horrified, Gonzalez tried to mop up the puddle with the first piece of paper he could find... a poster of Nina Simone. She watched him, aghast: 'But that's as if I'd peed on myself!'

The next morning, Raymond Gonzalez was told that Nina Simone was going to be sued by the festival for outrageous behaviour. Raymond attempted a parry: 'You can't put Nina in jail, for the simple reason that she played the concert for free.' The man in front of him laughed out loud until the New Yorker asked him to prove that the pianist had been paid. Without a receipt or official record of the transaction, they couldn't. Gonzalez reminded them that he wasn't speaking in his capacity as festival organizer now but as Nina Simone's agent during her stay in Spain.

Gonzalez was fired on the spot, and his client was asked to leave Spain within forty-eight hours under threat of legal action. But the first flight out of Pamplona wasn't for three days. Waiting was not an option; they had to flee as fast as they could.

Raymond Gonzalez found Nina back at the hotel. The diva had transformed into a little girl filled with anguish at the thought that she'd done something terribly wrong. He explained the situation to her, addressing her as though she were a child: 'Nina, we're going to play cops and robbers. We're the robbers. You've never been here, and you'll never come back. We're going to leave town now because the sheriff is after us. Now, you're going to do exactly as I say and I don't want to hear you say a single word. OK?' They eventually made it down to Biarritz in a mad rush. When Raymond Gonzalez was done telling me about his crazy ride with Nina, I asked him why he'd taken all those chances to get an artist who'd got him into serious trouble out of this critical situation. 'Because I knew that she was a remarkable artist and because it hurt me to see such a fine lady being humiliated like that.'

Two months after that lucky escape, Nina left Switzerland for good and moved to Paris. Jacques Bonni found her a three-bedroom flat in a house a stone's throw from Parc Montsouris, in the south of Paris, acting as her guarantor. Nina moved her piano and a few pieces of furniture into the flat, but the hundred-plus square yards remained largely unfurnished. And dirty too, if those who came to visit are to be believed.

By the end of winter 1982, Nina had regained a semblance of stability, giving concerts at the Trois Maillets with musicians who'd taken part in the *Fodder on My Wings* sessions. During this period, she was contacted by Assas University, which offered her a concert at the annual party organized by the student council. Jacques Bonni negotiated the diva's fee; tickets were set at 100 francs and it was agreed that Nina would get a cut of the profits. Last but not least, he advised her to sign a contract for a concert of two forty-minute halves, knowing full well that Nina often cut her shows short.

Having made peace with Nina, Raymond Gonzalez was designated to go and fetch her from the Grand Hôtel, where she had been put up for the night. Gonzalez found her quietly sitting in her room. She was calm, with no signs of nerves. A reassuring picture, except perhaps for the wine stain on her purple dress.

They dived into a cab and rushed towards the rue d'Assas, reaching the university just a few minutes late. Rumour had gone round that the artist wouldn't show up. The audience, feeling cranky, began to boo her as she appeared. She asked: 'Why are you upset? Everything's fine. I'm here.' Nina gave a stellar concert in front of an audience of two thousand and got a standing ovation. People from the Olympia happened to be in the hall after her performance and offered her a gig on boulevard des Capucines.

The Olympia show took place on 16 February 1983. It was a disaster. Nina was still too fragile to cope with the pressures of such a major event. According to Raymond Gonzalez, 'In those days she was just like a lost child; the merest obstacle seemed insurmountable to her.' And for good reason. In the space of ten months, moving from the cellar of Trois Maillets to treading the boards of the Olympia was a challenge that Nina wasn't psychologically fit to be facing. But despite it all, offers started pouring in once again, most of them tempting, exclusive. Alas, from the New Morning where she just left her audience standing there to the Théâtre des Champs-Elysées where she showed up on stage wrapped in a leopard-print coat nearly forty-five minutes late to give a concert that lasted no more than... fifteen minutes, her antics soon discouraged French promoters from hiring her.

In the spring of 1983, she travelled to London to honour a commitment and temporarily left her flat in the care of Jacques Bonni. What she really did was dump it on him, leaving him with her car and four months' rent to pay. The day that Bonni got to the Parc Montsouris flat, he was surprised to come face to face with the bailiffs, who seemed just as confused as him, as all the furniture had disappeared.

Even though the whole Paris episode didn't fully succeed in reviving her career, those years gave her a breather that allowed her to overcome her depression, to forge a few new friendships and to record *Fodder on My Wings*, a beautifully crafted album. She also enjoyed the services of a competent manager in the person of Raymond Gonzalez (this was exactly what she'd been missing since her split from Andy Stroud) and found herself a new Good Samaritan in Jacques Bonni, who had a lot to do with her regaining her equilibrium. So it's disturbing that in her autobiography Nina cast such a harsh eye on those years, swearing that at Les Trois Maillets 'The fans... never materialized,'[2] and going as far as asserting that 'I wasn't earning enough to live on at the club, and my savings – what little I had – gradually trickled away... I had to sell my car, my furniture and my jewels.'[3] A picture of disgrace in complete disproportion to reality. But how could she help feeling bitter when in just a few years she'd shifted from the luxury of Carnegie Hall to the boards of some tiny club in Saint-Michel?

She knew that just playing gig after gig wasn't going to lead her anywhere, and that on top of that, her inconsistency had made promoters wary of her. Though the records *Baltimore* and *Fodder on My Wings* had done reasonably well, Nina understood that there was little to be expected from record labels. She had to find another way. She'd obtained the rights to the video that was shot of one of her concerts in the south of France. She now wanted to get it released, but for that she needed to find a distributor. She went to the United States in search of one. Why in a country she despised and where she'd fallen into oblivion rather than in Europe? It remains a mystery, or, according to her friend Roger Nupie, 'an example of a logic that was Nina Simone's very own'.

She resurfaces in June 1983 in New York, at a concert at the Swing Plaza, after which she travelled to California. She arrived in Los Angeles with her videotape, but the doors of the distributors remained tightly shut. She did, however, meet the manager of Videopix: Anthony Sannucci.

Strictly speaking, Sannucci wasn't a producer but a businessman whose sole interest was money. At Videopix, he worked in partnership with Eddie Singleton, a former Motown musician who was also head of VPI, a small independent label that specialized in R&B.

Sannucci was interested in Nina's proposition, but only on one condition: he wanted to be her manager. She declined, intent on never again letting someone stick their nose in her business, but once she got back to Paris and was faced with the same dead end of clubs and pointless gigs, she called Sannucci back and took him up on his offer. Raymond Gonzalez was fired without a word of warning.

Back in LA, she moved into a studio apartment that belonged to her new patron and soon the team got busy recording a new album. A tour of the USA, then Europe was set up and they tried to disentangle Nina Simone from her problem with the IRS.

During those months, Nina and Sannucci became 'friends', so far as their respective interests required, even visiting Las Vegas together, this place Nina used to so despise. Nina was transformed, filled with hope: 'I was enjoying being part of an organization again, and having the responsibility for many of my concert and recording arrangements taken off my hands. But the reason I most liked Sannucci was that he was lucky; he nearly always won whatever he gambled on, and he certainly struck lucky with me.'[4] That would remain to be seen. The album *Nina's Back*, born from their partnership and released in 1985 by the label VPI, didn't turn into the hit they'd banked on, due to serious distribution problems and also its mediocre quality. By the time of its release, the team had already split up and *Nina's Back* failed to benefit anyone.

But in the summer of 1984 this failure was yet to come, and Nina went on the road again. Temporarily at peace with America, her public and the club circuit, she even looked pleased when she came and played at New York's Blue Note in July. A review in the *New York Times* said: 'Isn't her music wonderful? It's the salt of the earth!'[5] She returned to the Blue Note in March 1985, and even honoured the Newport Jazz Festival (meanwhile renamed the Kool Jazz Festival) with her presence in July, eight years after standing up George Wein.

Yet the place to look for traces of Nina's rebirth as an artist in the 80s isn't here in America but in a club in London. In the autumn of 1984, the diva took up an offer from one of Europe's shrines of black music (and jazz): Ronnie Scott's.

This club in Soho, which had been set up in October 1959 by Ronnie Scott and Pete King, two English musicians, turned the British jazz scene upside down at a time when the restrictions imposed by the Musicians' Union made it almost impossible for London to host American artists. After a trip to New York to explore all its jazz clubs, Ronnie Scott founded his den in a basement in Gerrard Street, which would end up hosting the cream of American jazz in the 60s, including Charlie Parker, Miles Davis and Dizzy Gillespie. Ronnie Scott's moved into its definitive premises at 47 Frith Street in the summer of 1965. With a capacity of 250 and a narrow stage in the heart of the club, this reddish-hued venue became one of the world's jazz beacons and a necessary stopover for any blues artist passing through London.

In 1984, Nina Simone played at Ronnie Scott's from 8 to 21 January, then 6 to 11 February. In *Break Down & Let It All Out* Sylvia Hampton says that for her third visit in autumn, Nina was convinced that her fans would be waiting for her at Heathrow as she arrived, just like in the 60s. Sylvia had to explain to her that times had changed, and that all those fans now had families to look after and other priorities than going to the airport at 6 a.m. This angered the singer.

Did she even realize? She hadn't had a hit in Europe since the 60s and was no longer the flavour of the month or even featured in the music press or on radio playlists, she'd given a dizzying number of concerts in recent years that had the whiff of wreckage, yet she refused to acknowledge that her glory days were in the past. It would take a miracle to revive that flame. And yet this miracle would happen;

maybe she already sensed it. Maybe the 'high priestess of soul' knew her destiny had a surprise for her that was beyond her wildest dreams.

The third series of concerts at Ronnie Scott's was scheduled from 15 to 20 October 1984. Before then, Nina spent a few days in a rest-home in Oxford, then she returned to London, where she stayed at the Grosvenor House Hotel in the West End with Singleton, Sannucci, and her brother Sam Waymon. But a few days before the concerts were due to take place, the gang was hit with some rotten luck: due to his papers not being in order, Nina's drummer was stuck at US customs. Martin Drew, the club's resident drummer, had just left to go on tour with Oscar Peterson. A replacement was urgently needed. Sam remembered that in the winter of 1983 he'd noticed a young British drummer – handsome face, long hair, rock'n'roll jacket – and who, more importantly, played well. At the time, the boy had been touring with a London-based big band called Superjazz, which played at Ronnie Scott's. So they rang up the pretty boy: Paul Robinson.

Twenty years have passed but Nina Simone's last drummer (and one of her best) displays an attractive vitality. Paul picks me up at Andover station, an hour from London, and takes me to his remote home in the countryside. He introduces me to his little girl and tells her I'm here to chat about Nina. In the kitchen hangs a framed photo of a smiling Nina with the child in her lap.

Paul Robinson doesn't beat around the bush. I've barely accepted the customary cup of tea and already he launches into it. 'I played with Nina Simone for close to twenty years. Mainly because I knew this woman was a genius.'

He tells me how he came to listen to Nina Simone after Pete King's telephone call. She was playing with three English musicians 'but it wasn't working,' he says, 'these guys were doing their thing without even listening to her'. Paul jumped on board the next day. There were no rehearsals ('she never rehearsed') and their first contact was frosty, as Nina, as usual, crossed the room to solemnly get up on the stage of the club. Paul Robinson is an 'old-fashioned kind of guy', not the type to be easily impressed; maybe that's why it worked between them.

Backed up by this creative and strong-minded drummer, the pianist began her artistic rebirth with a series of triumphant shows.

During the first week, Sam Waymon accompanied them, giving vague instructions, timidly playing a little Hammond organ and percussion and singing backing vocals. 'Nina never told you what to play,' Paul Robinson adds. 'She didn't know how to tell the other musicians what she wanted them to do. She did her thing, hoping the others would follow her.' On the first few nights, Paul didn't know much of the pianist's repertoire. He wasn't actually aware quite how much of a cult artist he was backing. Sam Waymon soon faded into the background, and every night for three weeks, the drummer was the only one supporting her on stage. He observed her, improvised, following her closely without ever losing track. Later, he was often told that his work with Nina was the best artistic combination the pianist had ever found; first because when the drummer was the only back-up she had, lazy Nina couldn't rely on her band to play on without her whenever she felt like it. With just Paul there, there was no choice: she had to play, and sometimes they'd touch the sky.

There is a record of those nights: *Live at Ronnie Scott's*, an album that was also released as a video. This recording is one of the last live testaments to Nina's genius and opens with a classic, 'God God God', inspired by a poem she once read on a gravestone, followed by the grace of 'Fodder in Her Wings', the perennial 'I Loves You Porgy', and a swing track that was going to turn her destiny around again: 'My Baby Just Cares for Me'.

After the concerts, getting to sleep before 6 a.m. was difficult, and Nina fell prey once more to fits of anxiety and loneliness. Singleton and Sannucci understood nothing of her fears. Sam was used to them but didn't want to get involved, so they all left her as she lost herself in darkness.

In the daytime, her crises dissipated. She drank litres of lemon tea to lubricate her voice, acted like a star under all circumstances, took ages getting ready to go out, even to go out to dinner, showing up dressed like an African queen at a restaurant on the King's Road. At night she liked to keep people waiting, delaying her entrance at the club by half an hour and meeting the crowd without acknowledging her waiting public. She'd get up on stage without a word, sit down behind the keyboard without even glancing at her drummer who was poised and ready, and launch into the first chords.

The last series of performances at Ronnie Scott's began on 15 October 1984. It was only due to last a week originally, but turned out so successful that it was extended until 17 November. Every week and without consulting Nina, Sannucci would add new dates. The artist let it go the first few times, but soon she and her manager began to disagree. She'd accuse him of keeping her out of business decisions, and he'd stand his ground. Suspicions, lies, the tone got sharper. Then came anger and eventually a major fall-out.

Raymond Gonzalez happened to be in London for the final week of those gigs. He hadn't heard a word from Nina for months, yet he decided to go and see her at Ronnie Scott's. He got a table close to the stage, watched her as she walked across the room, straight past, without seeing him, and sat down at her piano. The first part of the concert went well, but as she finished a song she seemed upset and addressed her audience: 'I want to dedicate this song to my former manager. I wish he was here with me right now.' Somewhere in the room, Sannucci and Singleton cringed in silence. Earlier there'd been a violent argument and Nina had thrown them the accusation, 'Neither of you knows how to look after me!' She hadn't said a word since, and now she was missing her old manager and publicly at that! Then Nina suddenly spotted Gonzalez, smiled at him and in her baritone said into the microphone, 'Hello daaaaarling...'

At the end of that show and again without consulting her, Sannucci scheduled another week of gigs. She fired him when she found out: 'I was a different person from the woman who he had met in his office in LA a few years before', she wrote.[6] But above all, she'd spoken with Gonzalez, and Gerrit de Bruin, her Dutch friend, had come to join them in London. She held hopes for a fresh start and perhaps saw the promise then of the family being brought back together.

Nina Simone didn't show up for that third week. She must have thought this would teach Sannucci a lesson, but Pete King was the one who was put in the impossible situation of having to refund a week's worth of sold-out tickets.

He gets upset now when the matter is brought up; an older gentleman of imposing build, Pete King's voice is slow, deep and measured as he speaks. I know people who would have used the opportunity to vent their anger at an artist who let them down so badly, yet all he chose to say was that 'Nina Simone was a person who was difficult to work with,' mentioning that 'her attitude was pretty tough'. In fact Pete King never forgave Nina for disappearing on him like that. His was a club famous worldwide; Ronnie Scott's picked the artists who played there, and the place carries on a certain tradition and a constant regard for quality. According to Mr King: 'Nina Simone saw things differently. She gave off the impression that she was the one who'd picked you. She didn't want to work with people who employed her.' To the point that she never called to apologize.

Nina never played at Ronnie Scott's again. Clearly, she wouldn't have been welcome there. Jacques Bonni says that shortly after her outburst, she rang him up to ask him to join her in the Caribbean. He agreed, and then forgot that he had. Nina was deeply offended and severed all ties with him.

She left England in December 1984, took a few weeks' holiday in Trinidad then went to Holland where the promise of a new life awaited.

10

SOMEWHERE BETWEEN THE BLACK KEYS AND THE WHITE I FOUND MY BALANCE

BACK FROM Trinidad, Nina joined Gerrit de Bruin in Nijmegen, an old town in Holland less than an hour away from Amsterdam. Gerrit and Nina had met in the 60s, at a concert the pianist had given in Central Park. Back then, this man who would become Nina's closest friend was a photographer. As the crowd pressed dangerously against the stage and it threatened to collapse, Gerrit had helped Andy get Nina to safety. Later on, Gerrit became a kind of beacon in Nina's life and even an 'Uncle Gerrit' to Lisa. Nina and Gerrit were reunited at the Hotel Belvoir, where she had set up camp. She'd left Paris for good and now lived out of a suitcase. Gerrit assured her that she'd never achieve any kind of stability living like that, and that the time had come for her to settle down and invest in a flat; and why not here, where he'd be able to look after her and her interests?

She told him that she didn't have that kind of money, so Gerrit and Raymond Gonzalez struck a deal with her: if she committed to honouring all her concerts and complying with her medical treatment, they would do everything in their power to get her career back on track. She agreed. The first objective they set themselves was to get Nina back into shape, physically and mentally. First and foremost, she needed to rest in order to gradually get her appetite for life back. The next thing was to build a solid team around her with whom she'd gradually start working again, but for this project to be viable, Nina had to agree to move to Nijmegen for a while. Letting her carry on living at the hotel was out of the question; the time had come for her to get back something like an normal life.

Gerrit worked out what she earned, lent her money and helped her get a mortgage so she could buy a flat a few minutes away from his own house and a few steps from the Belvoir hotel. This was the ideal choice – it would allow Nina to enjoy the facilities of the four-star establishment (swimming pool, restaurants, gardens, and so on), and it was only minutes from the town centre.

With eight concerts in Holland under her belt, organized by Gonzalez and produced by Freddie Martinez, a maths teacher turned promoter, Nina finally moved into her new flat. As soon as she was settled, she covered it with pictures and posters of herself. 'She was obsessed by her lost youth,' Gerrit confided. 'She was also keen on listening to her own records.'

I met Gerrit de Bruin at his home in Cap d'Agde. We spent the day listening to several dozens of unreleased tracks of Nina's, digging into folders of private pictures (most of them unpublished), with me asking him all about the years he'd got to spend by Nina's side. Gerrit told me about their unique friendship, the kind that marks one's life for ever. 'What a friend she was!' he loved to say over and over, as he uncorked a bottle of wine, set it down in front of us and drank from his glass in tiny sips. Patiently, as though playing back the reel of this long-lost love, Gerrit told me his story with Nina; a story entwining moments of anger and tenderness. He outlined the clashing feelings that inhabited this woman. I encouraged him to let those memories surface and tell me what Nina Simone's life was like. Gerrit, after a few digressions, summarized it as 'A life filled with shame, fear, suffering and regrets'.

Later, I asked him why he was so devoted to her. 'Because she put a spell on me!'). He started into this anecdote with delight. One afternoon, as he was busy with his wine business, he got a call from Nina, who'd just moved into her Nijmegen flat:

'Gerrit, you gotta come down right now, it's important!'

'I'm working, I can't just take off like that...'

'You have to come. I'm waiting for you!' and she hung up, just like that. Gerrit hesitated; after all, it could be a real emergency. He put on his jacket, got in the car and rushed over. Once he'd parked, he ran up the stairs and burst in to find her looking radiant in an evening gown: 'Gerrit, I'm ready to give you the best concert of my entire life!' Nina planted herself behind her keyboard and started to play for her flabbergasted friend. Once the shock wore off, Gerrit sat himself down and burst out laughing. Defeated, he decided to just enjoy this once-in-a-lifetime show – which ended up lasting no less than five hours! 'She'd give you moments like those to thank you,' Gerrit said, 'but she'd never give you any money. Because money was what she needed to save herself. I've never known another friend like her in my whole life. She was true in her own special way. True and disconcerting.'

Over their forty years of friendship, Gerrit's love for Nina stayed boundless and unwavering. His affection reached past the usual limits of friendship. So involved was he in the diva's life that he called his first daughter... Nina.

The Nijmegen era lasted about three years. Happy days. Nina hadn't enjoyed that kind of balance since her split from Andy Stroud. The devastating attacks were still there, dangerous to Nina and those who surrounded her and mostly the result of her refusal to comply with her medical treatment. A Damocles' sword that gave Gerrit no choice but to hire a doctor to check up on her daily.

This might sound like an amusing anecdote, but 'Whenever Nina stopped taking her medication for two weeks, all hell broke loose!' Gerrit explained. 'Her episodes could last up to three days, during which she was out of control. When Nina came to her senses, she remembered everything she'd done and felt crippled with shame.' Like the day in 1989 when in Paris, in the lobby of the Grand Hôtel, she assaulted a stranger who was looking at her a little too intensely. To prevent a bloodbath, Gerrit had to get her out of the hotel and bundle her into a taxi ('Towards the Eiffel Tower, quick!'). Months later, in Nijmegen, Nina once said to him out of the blue: 'Thank you for getting me out of trouble at the Grand Hôtel!'

But what about when Nina was alone when she was hit by one of her episodes? I was told of one in particular which occurred in

Canada in the 80s: one day, at the end of a concert that had been fairly uneventful, she just disappeared. She was found on a railway platform two days later, several miles from where she had last been seen, with no idea who she was or what she'd been doing during that time.

Nina's illness was first made public by Sylvia Hampton and David Nathan in their book *Break Down & Let It All Out*: 'In fact, her infamous bouts of rage were caused by a chemical imbalance that left her prone to sudden and intense depression, underpinned by bleak, wild fury. Put bluntly, she suffered from a mental illness that often blighted her happiness. Tragically, the illness was a closely guarded secret only a few shared.'[1]

Since then, tongues have loosened and there's been open talk of disease, of a mineral imbalance in her brain that caused what is called bipolar disorder and made her sway between periods of melancholic depression and manic excitement. Although the disease only became apparent in adulthood, the imbalance had always been there, latent. Nina was born sick and no one ever suspected it. The first signs emerged in the mid-60s and reached a devastating climax during her tour with Bill Cosby. Later on, the disease gradually worsened as she moved through her various escapades to Liberia, Switzerland and France.

As I talked to people in researching this book, I often heard that 'Had she not been this amazing artist, she would have been sectioned and locked up in a psychiatric hospital!' But as Sylvia Hampton emphasizes in her book,[2] Nina's art and her madness were closely linked. Nina would never have expressed such intense feeling and drama without her bipolar disorder; she could never have reached the excess and depth that captivated even someone as uncompromising as Miles Davis, who confessed to feeling dazzled by her music. If one listens to 'Sinnerman' in this light, it is clear that what she managed to express in this song passes the ordinary confines of music to explore the abyss of a torn soul.

Her everyday life, and that of those around her, was dominated by fear. As Gerrit de Bruin recalled, 'When Nina fell prey to her episodes, we were helpless. All we could do was to give her drugs.' In the mid-80s she was on the highest therapeutic dose allowed: 16 milligrams daily of Trilifan®, a powerful neuroleptic prescribed for manic phases.

Nina's bipolar disorder explains a lot about her behaviour, her violence, the absurd choices she made, her despair and her chronic inability to achieve happiness. Her moments of lethargy too, as depression is characterized by an intellectual slowdown that sinks the sufferer into a state of stupor. On the other hand, the patient can also be overcome by a feeling or urgency during manic phases, which drags him or her into a cycle of hyperactivity and elation.

Gerrit and Raymond Gonzalez decided to employ someone to take care of Nina Simone full-time. This was where Jackie Hammond stepped in, a young woman of Ghanaian origin whom they'd met in London and hired to assist her in her day-to-day life. A lady in waiting, so to speak, who was gentle, attentive and bubbly. On her first visit to Nijmegen, Jackie Hammond was struck by panic and wanted to leave immediately. 'When Jackie arrived,' Gerrit recalls, 'Nina suddenly threw a major fit. She began to scream, to threaten everyone, and got violent. Jackie was scared and wanted to leave. I calmed her down and explained to her that there were no more flights that day so she'd have to stay until morning anyway; after that she was free to leave if she wanted to. I could tell she was frightened, so I slept on the sofa. During the night, I spent a long time explaining to her how Nina functioned, how to react to her crises and how to go about calming her down. When she woke up, Nina was all smiles; she came out of her bedroom, saw Jackie and greeted her with a big smile and a "Hello daaaaarling."'

Sweet Jackie would end up spending several years with this makeshift family, following the pianist to Brazil, the States and on each of her trips in Europe.

This Dutch period undeniably saw Nina's artistic and psychological reawakening. There were a few hitches here and there, like at the Boston Symphony Hall in 1986, where Nina was two hours late getting on stage, forcing Freddie Hubbard, the trumpet player who opened the show, to play the equivalent of two concerts just to keep the audience entertained. She then gave a half-hearted performance of which the columnist Ernie Santosuosso wrote that 'she should have stayed at the hotel'.[3] Despite this episode, she toured England and Holland with renewed energy and regularly returned to rest up at her place in Nijmegen. Rumour had spread in the showbiz world that Nina's concerts were on the way back up, that she'd become manageable and had a solid team looking after her interests. Nijmegen became the team's headquarters, the springboard for Nina Simone's career revival in Europe. This was where Gerrit de Bruin, Alvin Schackman, Jackie Hammond, Raymond Gonzalez, the percussionist Leopoldo Fleming and Bobby Hamilton, all of whom loved Nina and knew about her problems, would gather around the artist to get her back on track. 'We had to seize the market,' Gerrit likes to say. All the more so as at the dawn of 1987, Nina's recomposed family, aka the 'A-Team', was in for a big surprise: global success, no less!

A few months before that, the team was joined by a character who would play an important part in Nina Simone's life. A Belgian admirer whom Gerrit had been spotting at her concerts over the past few months, a guy with glasses who'd wait at the artists' exit, a bunch of flowers in hand. His name was Roger Nupie.

I met Roger in Antwerp, in a small Chinese restaurant on Lange Dijkstraat. Roger Nupie is the president of her international fan club, but that doesn't begin to describe this man's devotion to the pianist's memory. Roger has spent over thirty years compiling unpublished documents and rare recordings. He would often introduce Nina at the start of her performances. But above all, Roger was Nina's friend, and one as loyal as they come, for the last fifteen years of her life.

For Roger, the story began when he was fourteen years old. He'd just bought a compilation called *Heart and Soul* and experienced what I later would with 'Sinnerman': the certainty that this music had always been there, just waiting to be acknowledged. Roger became a die-hard fan, endearingly mad in his own way, braving the rain and cold just to shyly offer the diva his bunch of flowers. Gerrit noticed him a few times and one day went up to him, asking for his number. One day the stranger got a call at Nina's request: 'Come and join us in Holland, we'd like to get to know you.'

'The first time I met Nina was at her place in Nijmegen,' Roger tells me. 'I wasn't meant to stay longer than an hour, but I ended up staying the whole weekend. We'd found each other. It felt a little like I'd come home. Later on, once we'd become friends, I shared that impression with her. Nina wasn't in the least bit surprised and replied in a very "Simone"-like manner: "But of course, daaaarling, you were Heaven-sent."' In no time at all, Roger became part of the gang.

But Nina was already getting bored of the little Dutch town's quietness and asked to move to Amsterdam. Gerrit found her a large furnished flat on the top floor of a beautiful building right on the canals. The Nijmegen place was sold immediately. 'We'd bought it in dollars for the equivalent of three hundred thousand guilders,' Gerrit says. 'When the Nijmegen place was sold, the dollar was very weak, so Nina almost doubled her investment!' After a house-warming party whose guests included Miriam Makeba (there is a picture of Nina and Miriam sitting side by side, beautiful and proud in their gold-threaded boubous like African nobility), her drummer Bobby Hamilton and his niece moved into the Amsterdam flat with Nina and Jackie. There, as she happily tells in her autobiography, her social life blossomed once again, replete with receptions, parties and opera premières.

Miriam lived near Brussels back then; little information is available about their relationship since the Monrovian years, but we know that Miriam, together with Stokely Carmichael, came and saw Nina in Switzerland several times, and that she and Nina met again in Paris, where the American tried to convince Miriam to perform with her at the Trois Maillets, but to no avail. Since then, even though the two friends rarely saw each other and made do with swapping news on the phone, they kept in touch, especially when Miriam came to live in Belgium. In 1991 she invited Nina and Dizzy Gillespie to take part in a studio album. Nina chipped in with a verse of 'I Shall Be Released' which she recorded in one take, and the evening ended in a Brussels restaurant where Miriam had invited her tribe. A little drunk, she began to talk about her ex-husbands. Nina suddenly panicked and took Roger and Gerrit, who'd come with her, aside:

'She keeps talking about all her men and I don't have any, what am I going to say?'

'That you've got two: you've got us!'

But the men, lovers and husbands, who'd made their mark on Nina's life were either far way or gone for ever, like Errol Barrow, who'd died of a heart attack on 1 June 1987.

1987. The year that Nina Simone made her comeback and took revenge on the music industry.

Nina's state of mind at that time is illustrated by these extracts from an interview she gave *L'Humanité* in 1992:

'You say you were robbed by record companies...'

'There was one company in particular that stole my albums and my royalties. When its boss came to Switzerland, I went and found him: "Where's my money?" And he said: "We're not going to give you any money," so I told him: "We'll see about that!" I had a gun on me and I chased him into a restaurant and tried to kill him. I missed.'

'What advice would you give young artists?'

'Don't ever get into the music business! It's awful! You have to fight to get paid and to get your rights respected. They exploit your name. Some of them pirate your records and release them and never pay you a cent. Sometimes they put your names on concert bills when you're not even meant to be part of the show! Anything to attract the audience and then you get the blame for not being there... You have to be lucky and get a hit, or else...'[4]

Or else you disappear. Nina knew this all too well, having had to wait until 1987 to get back to the forefront of the international scene, after an absence that lasted almost fifteen years, only intermittently making it to the top.

This comeback took the form of a twist of fate when thirty years after it was originally recorded for Bethlehem Records, 'My Baby Just Cares for Me' ('one of the slightest [songs] I'd ever recorded'[5]) was chosen by Chanel as the soundtrack to the international campaign for its most famous fragrance, Chanel No. 5.

In 1959, Nina had given up her rights to 'My Baby Just Cares for Me' to Syd Nathan, by virtue of the American 'work made for hire' rule: when a work is commissioned, if the contract so stipulates, it becomes the property of the employer in exchange for a flat payment. Since then, the Bethlehem catalogue had changed hands until it was bought by Charly Records, a London-based label that specialized in reissuing black American music from the 50s, 60s and 70s. Charly had become the owner of the song's copyright and so Nina would miss out on a million dollars, which was enough to get her worked up to the point where she confused theft, piracy and legal business.

Nina's lawyers, one of whom was Steven Ames Brown, joined the fight to find some kind of compromise, some loophole in the contract that might profit the performer of 'My Baby Just Cares for Me'. Gerrit de Bruin tells the story: 'In 1959, Nina had given up her broadcasting rights – radio, records, and so on – but not rights for use in advertising. That's what allowed her to get money out of "My Baby Just Cares for Me". On the other hand, the song remained the property of Charly Records and it wasn't until its third release that it eventually became a hit again' – entering the British charts at number five and topping the French Top 50.

So why did Chanel choose this song in particular? What is pretty likely is that earlier in 1987, Chanel's publicity people noticed 'My Baby''s cult following in British clubs, saw it featured on the playlists of trendy DJs and an object of genuine devotion at the Mud Club, a place to be seen in 80s London.[6]

When Chanel bought the rights to 'My Baby Just Cares for Me' for its international campaign, the company was unaware that the rights owned by Charly Records didn't extend to advertising. In the end, Steven Ames Brown, the lawyer responsible for Nina Simone's international interests, managed to obtain $150,000 from Charly Records, but this failed to placate Nina; she called the label owners thieves in front of British TV cameras. Charly Records immediately sued her for defamation. They reached an agreement and the story died down. A rather more worrying rumour was going around, saying that Nina had assaulted the head of Charly Records in a restaurant when he offered her a cut of 'My Baby Just Cares for Me''s sales, but no one at Charly seemed to want to talk about it.

Despite those unpleasant events, Nina did well out of the whole story and cashed in a handsome sum, owing mainly to a new law passed in the States that allowed artists who had been cheated in the 50s and 60s to renegotiate their rights. Work-for-hire contracts could be submitted for review after twenty-five years. In the end, it took until March 1995 for a San Francisco court to grant Nina Simone ownership of fifty-two of her original recordings.[7]

Summer 1987. Nina Simone's career was soaring once again. Gerrit and the gang did everything in their power to make the most of the incredible opportunity created by the success of 'My Baby Just Cares for Me'. Especially with popular radio stations playing the single on loop (and TV screens showing an animated video clip about the nocturnal love of a couple of cats, including the now cult sequence where a piano plays the song's solo on its own). Concerts all over Europe, interviews, TV shows, press shoots. A brand new audience provided further proof of the resurrection of Nina Simone's career. 'I had done it without pandering to the music industry. I still said the same things I always did, that the music industry is full of thieves, that America is a racist country and those black citizens who involved themselves in the movement were still being punished twenty years later.'[8]

That same year, Verve released *Let It Be Me*, the first album of Nina's to be published by a major label since *It Is Finished*, in 1974. A live album recorded at the Vine Street Bar & Grill in Hollywood, all *Let It Be Me* did was to opportunely rehash the pianist's trademark tracks ('My Baby Just Cares for Me', 'I Want a Little Sugar in My Bowl', 'Fodder in Her Wings', 'Baltimore'...) with a few traditional tunes thrown in for good measure like 'If You Pray Right (Heaven Belongs to You)'.

Later came the album *Live at Ronnie Scott's*, in memory of the night of 17 November 1984 in London. Then *Live & Kicking*, a concert recorded in the States in 1985 by the Singleton/Sannucci duo, a live album whose main merit was that it offered a raw version of 'Pirate Jenny' Nina hardly ever played in concert any more as it needed too much of a dramatic build-up.

Swept up by this flood of releases, Nina embarked on a summer festival tour, whose climax was her performance at the Montreux Jazz Festival on 10 July 1987 for the Jazz Aid evening held by Sally Burton, widow of Richard Burton, and which also featured Memphis Slim, Dee Dee Bridgewater and Randy Crawford. Everyone agreed that the concert was a success, even though Roger Nupie says that just a few hours before her appearance the diva locked herself into her hotel bathroom, screaming through the door that 'The only thing they're interested in is to watch me play!' Maybe she felt like a circus freak again, after all those years spent suffering the public's indifference. It took Roger pretending to pack his bags and get ready to leave the hotel for a fuming Nina to finally deign to emerge from the bathroom.

Though the pianist's moods continued to be highly volatile, her financial situation on the other hand had stabilized. Her troubles with the American tax authorities had come to an end and offers for handsomely remunerated concerts came pouring in: Japan, Australia and the whole of Europe, everyone wanted a piece of her. Nina even briefly performed at a reception hosted at one of the Loire castles in honour of the French president François Mitterrand. Last, and something that would remain one of Nina's and Raymond Gonzalez's most treasured memories, came this performance in the Valencia bullring. 'We were concert's producers,' Raymond recalls. 'Only a few tickets had sold, and the rain had stopped barely an hour before the start of the concert. I was convinced we were heading for a disaster, but Nina was serene and kept saying to me, "Don't worry Raymond, they'll come." As soon as the rain stopped, seven thousand people filled the stands. Nina took her spot at the centre of the arena and started to sing in the light of the sunset, as the audience lit candles. Nina played three hours that night; it was magical, one of her most beautiful concerts' – given in what she called 'the middle of a flickering universe'.[9]

There were other triumphs and other standing ovations. Right in the middle of her return to grace, in 1988 she was offered a concert in Nigeria with Miriam Makeba. Nina returned to Yorubaland for the second time. This time around, the festival had been organized by a Nigerian tribal chief to support the campaign to end apartheid in South Africa. The event was financed by a New York banker and due to be held at the National Stadium in Lagos, featuring 750 musicians from all over Europe, South Africa and the United States. Only Nina and Miriam managed to be paid in advance. The team landed at Lagos's Murtala Muhammed Airport and showed up at customs for passport control.

Raymond Gonzalez recalls: 'The soldiers at the border insisted on keeping our passports; they'd confiscate them from all arrivals without a word of explanation. I gave instructions for no one to move until they were returned to us, and after several minutes' negotiations they eventually gave them back. We got into the cars and drove to a hotel in the centre of Lagos. As soon as we got there, we were told how disorganized the whole thing was. Nina and Miriam's concerts, which were originally scheduled for 9 p.m., were pushed back to 2 a.m., then 3 a.m., supposedly because protocol had us pencilled in for several official protests the Nigerian government had organized. In the end, one of the organizers came and told us that we wouldn't be playing until 8 a.m.! Miriam, Nina and I went and found the tribal chief to explain to him that we demanded to play at the time originally agreed, otherwise we were going straight back to the airport. The chief told us: 'You don't understand; you're going to be here at 8 a.m. and you will give your concerts.' We went back to the airport without telling the organizers and miraculously we managed to board a plane to Europe. Later on we were told that another musician who'd also complained had apparently been burned alive in the hotel lobby!'

1988 saw Nina back in Paris. The setting of her former 'disgrace' was about to welcome her for two exceptional concerts: one at the Palais des Congrès on 6 June and another at the Olympia on 30 September. 'My Baby Just Cares for Me' had just made it to gold status in France and platinum in England.

In Paris, while she was staying at the Grand Hôtel on place de l'Opéra, Nina received a large parcel filled with perfumes from the Chanel house. Her return to France was a major event that mobilized most of the French press, with everyone from *Libération* to the *Quotidien de Paris* coming to meet the diva and writing about her sold-out concert at the Olympia in their columns.

The journalist Yves Bigot bravely interviewed Nina and presented her like this in an article published on the day of the Palais des Congrès concert: 'What a matron. For ten years now we've seen her bounding up on stage at the Montreux Festival, wrapped in black leather with her steel wristbands, insulting any man in sight, whipping the hell out of her harem and threatening to cut loose her Dobermans! It will have taken all of Claude Nobs's patience to refrain from calling the Vaud police every time she stormed the stage to sing a few a cappella African songs, only to immediately demand her fee... But it all turned around last year. Nina now tops all the European Top 50 charts.'[10]

Slightly less in the know, the *Quotidien de Paris* published an article in September under the headline 'Nina Sold-Out'. 'Not a single ticket left for Nina Simone at the Olympia tonight. Jazz and retro are back in fashion,'[11] the article said, explaining that 'You have to go and see Nina Simone because vocal jazz is music with brains and any nostalgic approach is essentially anti-artistic. What we're about to see on stage is a form of art, not some memento from the fifties.'

The two concerts were a resounding success and earned Nina another Olympia gig on 16 February 1989. And an article in *Le Figaro* under the headline 'Nina Simone, African Queen! After crossing the desert, the ebony diva's smooth and powerful comeback',[12] preceded by a portrait in *L'Express* entitled 'Nina Simone is back from the wilderness. She was never really gone.'[13] Those lines ring a little strange when you think how often Nina had sunk into the abyss over the previous ten years, which recalls an old African adage that 'Death may swallow the man, but neither his name nor his reputation.'[14]

A prisoner of her own hypersensitivity, Nina Simone was experiencing her revival with Damocles' sword threatening to annihilate her at any moment. Even though those close to her took it in turns to ensure that she took her medication and to soothe her in times of anguish, Nina remained alone with her demons, life's demands and those of her career.

There was something about this woman that exuded dread. A lack of self-confidence channelled into aggression which she hid behind her diva mask. Roger Nupie recalls once seeing Nina storm into a room, instantly transforming the energy of the space: 'She scared people. Everyone told her, "You're difficult, you're a diva," and I think that at some point she began to feel she had to act like one.'

Nina Simone had become her own worst enemy. She who when she realized she was feared would take it to extremes and make your life a misery, could also take on the demeanour of some adorable old auntie who worried about you and kept giving you the whole 'daaarling' treatment. In those days of sycophancy, the gang would bend over backwards with kindness and bear the unbearable, in situations where others would have walked away. But as I've often been told, those people were motivated by their love of Nina and guided by the feeling that it was their mission to look after this woman, 'to give her back some of what she gave us through her music and her personality', in Roger Nupie's words. 'Love. That's the only reason we put up with anything from her,' he continues. 'There were times when I was tempted to flee to save my own life, but I'd always return to her in the end, because something compelled me to, and Nina was perfectly aware of our devotion. She played on it without ever pushing us to the end of our tethers because she also wanted to keep us by her side. Even during her episodes, when she was no longer able to control herself, she bore this in mind. It was very unnerving.'

When we met, Paul Robinson, her drummer at the time, emphasized the special relationship that existed between Nina and those who worked close to her. The select few who'd stuck around had managed to decipher the 'Simone logic' and understood her bipolar personality. 'When I joined the band,' Paul recalls, 'a lot of people asked me the same question: "Is Nina really that hard to handle?" And I'd say "No, she isn't, she just can't stand not to get what she wants." I was able to work with Nina because of my attitude towards it all. As a musician, it wasn't a question of what kind of drummer I was, it was about my understanding of her personality. Nina needed to have strong people around her, and if anyone showed any sign of weakness, she immediately used it to attack them.'

In the end, the point of tension between Nina and her band wasn't the violence of her attacks; everyone had learned to deal with those. The main problem for those who worked with Nina was money, which was a central obsession of hers. By the end of the 80s the diva was being paid handsomely, on average about $20,000 a show in France and in Canada; yet those who worked with her during that period concur that Nina always made sure to hold on to as much as possible of the fees the promoters paid her, sometimes at the expense of her musicians. Her relationship with money was compulsive and she squandered it away, insisting on dining in the most expensive restaurants, staying in the most exclusive palaces at her managers' expense, but without ever giving her band members a pay rise or a bonus.

That was the logic of a woman who despite being quite aware of her friends' good intentions could at any moment set her sights on a new face, let herself be influenced by complete strangers and thereby ruin her protectors' efforts to guard her from the vultures who had circled since her return to grace. 'To Nina, the right person was the one who happened to be around when she was at her loneliest,' Gerrit explains. This weakness would be Nina's downfall, but not for a few years yet: the coming months of the early 90s would be filled with happiness.

Happiness, that is, in her work and friendships, since in private, as she sings in 'Another Spring':

Sometimes the night comes down on me
And I know what's ahead
An evening in this cold old house
With no one to say goodnight to me when I go to bed
An evening in this cold old house
With no one to say goodnight to me when I go to bed

Nina Simone's sex life was a desert and this void turned her into a predator whenever she was attracted to a man. She'd get aggressive, pounce on him, intimidate him and this obviously only made him flee. There's no shortage of witness accounts regarding her sexual appetite and the times of drought she went through. A void so deep and so violent that she'd sometimes pay a heavy price or do something crazy to soothe her craving for affection. Paul Robinson didn't beat about the bush when I brought up the issue, and quietly assured me: 'No one wanted to fuck her. She scared men off.' He then evoked that trip to Los Angeles when Nina stayed at the Four Seasons, a five-star palace in Beverly Hills, while her musicians made do with more modest lodgings a few blocks away. On a whim, she bought herself a $3,000 return trip to the south of France, where some lover awaited. After a pause, Paul continued: 'But none of us had to live with the kind of pressures she was under. You have to understand that Nina was a black woman, not so young any more; single, without a healthy sex life... and who sometimes had to pay for men to fuck her.'

Obviously, this emotional void reflected something much deeper, the chronic feelings of insecurity that had plagued her existence ever since her split from Andrew Stroud. 'For me, when my father was around she had a certain schedule, which kept things balanced. When they separated and I went to live with her, she was not the same person I remembered living in Mount Vernon. I remember thinking that she had turned into a monster. Mommy was selfish in a lot of ways and I often felt if she had taken two seconds to consider people around her, especially me, who depended on her 100 per cent, she would have made a different decision with her behaviour.'[15] Those are the words of Nina's daughter Lisa. They provide a brutal account of Nina's downfall after her separation from Andy and her inability to deal with the events in her professional, family and personal life.

This was a woman (and a terribly romantic one) who couldn't imagine living without a man by her side. A husband. Through her obsession with marriage, Nina desperately searched for someone to rule her life, for a man to take care of her, to guarantee her money, stability and affection. Her attitude towards sex was just the expression of the turmoil caused by this craving for love. This desperate quest for closeness sometimes led her to offer up her bed and her trust to strangers in passing, giving it all away in the hope, each time, that he'd be the one, asking them to marry her on the first night, or sometimes, when there was no eligible suitor in sight, offering herself to the men in her close entourage. Most of those who have a part in her history had their turn and each of them rejected the diva's advances, sometimes gently, sometimes less so.

In 1990, as she worked on her autobiography *I Put a Spell on You*, Nina Simone's public image was that of a sacred monster. A blend of pasionaria and temperamental diva as capable of giving phenomenal concerts as of walking off the stage for a fleabite. Nina Simone, who'd captivated them all since her return to centre stage, was now the subject of the wildest fantasies and speculations. Was there anything that the press hadn't reported or made up about her? Though it had never given Nina's music the respect and consideration such demanding work deserved, it often provided exaggerated accounts of her outbursts, telling of her holding record label owners at gun- or knifepoint, her late arrivals on stage those evenings she sank into depression in her hotel room. Her scenes at the Lido and elsewhere, her incitements at New York's Avery Fisher Hall when as she appeared, already two hours late, she said to the audience: 'I know you spent twelve hours standing in line to get your tickets but I'm worth every cent!' That night, she'd unexpectedly played a version of Bob Marley's 'No Woman, No Cry', a song she also covered during her last ever performance at Montreux on 13 July 1990.

By now something of a legend, Nina had reached the pantheon of cursed artists, somewhere between Maria Callas and Billie Holiday. 'Yes, I think I'm a little volatile!' she admitted with a smile when interviewed for Frank Lords's film *The Legend*. 'I don't blow my top easily, that's not true. I am very emotional. Very self-disciplined, but very emotional. If I don't like something I say so right away... But I've got a pretty bad temper!'

As a random example, take a 1990 concert at the Royal Theatre Carré in Amsterdam. Nina's staff had gone to great lengths to make sure she didn't find out that the jazz singer Dee Dee Bridgewater was opening the show. Why? Because Nina had slapped her at Tel Aviv airport a few months earlier, when she learned they were due to play on the same night (the story doesn't say how Dee Dee reacted to this).

Nina was due on at midnight and Dee Dee Bridgewater was opening at eleven. A half-hour interval was agreed to allow the latter to disappear via one wing of the building while Nina came on stage through a door at the other end. She fell for it, never to find out how hard her team had worked to spare her.

Then came a collaboration with Pete Townshend, The Who's guitarist, on his solo album *The Iron Man*, appearances on albums by Maria Bethânia and Miriam Makeba, and an invitation to the march held to commemorate Martin Luther King's birth, on 21 January 1991, by his widow Coretta Scott King's side. This, aside from touring, was how Nina Simone spent her time up to the publication of *I Put a Spell on You*, the autobiography she penned together with Stephen Cleary, a young British film-maker.

Cleary met Nina at Ronnie Scott's in 1984. He went up to her and offered to film one of her concerts. Nina agreed on the condition that she got paid several days in advance. He gave her the money, then, as he didn't hear back from the artist, called her, worried, a few days before the agreed date. Nina reassured him: 'But of course I'll be there, daaarling!' She was true to her word and the concert was filmed. Six years later, Nina got in touch with Cleary to write her memoirs.

There had been plenty of applicants for the job. Some proved unable to cope with working with Nina Simone for more than a few days and quit the project, including the black American poet Nikki Giovanni and the writer Amiri Baraka (formerly LeRoi Jones), a friend from her years fighting for the movement and the author of *Blues People*. A woman, also (whose name is nowhere to be found), who worked with Nina for a few months before getting fired on a whim. According to Roger Nupie, the woman suggested calling the book *Memoirs of a Black Princess*. Pantheon Books, the autobiography's US publisher, demanded that Nina change the title as they didn't deem it suitable for the American market. In the end, the project was put in the hands of Stephen Cleary.

Those who followed the project's progress all tell of how badly the young Englishman suffered in the process. Nina kept going back on things she'd asserted just the day before, disregarding dates and factual accuracy, often revising the story or glossing it over when she didn't just leave out the murkier bits. Talking about *I Put a Spell on You* actually led Roger Nupie to warn me regarding my own book: 'The Simone logic is highly unusual. Don't try and find any coherence or chronology to it, you'd just be wasting your time and you'll never get to the end of it. Even with my archives, some parts of her life are so garbled and contradictory that I haven't managed to make any sense of them. During the writing of her book, Nina couldn't remember what year certain events had taken place. Stephen Cleary was tearing his hair out; whenever he'd try and retrace the facts without managing to put an accurate date on it, Nina would say: "Just use any old date, I don't care!"'

Which may explain some of the inaccuracies, mistakes and omissions in her autobiography, which, although it's often self-indulgent, at least allowed readers to understand the role the artist had played in the movement. That that stage of American political and social life hardly made any waves in Europe in the 60s. In France, only a few left-wing intellectuals took an active interest in the matter and it took the work of Jean-Luc Godard (who included Black Power poetry in his film *Sympathy for the Devil*) and the involvement of Jean Genet (who wrote the preface to *Soledad Brother* by the black activist George Jackson) for the civil rights movement to draw the left-wing intellectual community's attention.

The publication of her memoirs helped to soften Nina Simone's image, showing her endearing side whilst giving her a dramatic dimension which endeared her to a wider audience that mainly knew her for her hits like 'My Baby Just Cares for Me', 'Porgy' and 'Ne me quitte pas'.

Those 'Memoirs of a Black Princess' were warmly greeted by the French press, which gave Nina a lot of column space, once again allowing her to broach her favourite topics: the sacrifice of her family life for her work, the struggle of blacks against white power, her relentless search for love, money of course, and her views on the music industry...

'Your autobiography reveals a less unpredictable, gentler, more moving side of Nina Simone...'

'Thank you. People only know the singer, not the woman, and I'm glad to be revealed at last. I used to be an innocent, loyal, beautiful young woman. I was too pure and I paid for that. Showbiz is a fierce jungle and I've met a lot of bastards, but all things considered, I've been pretty lucky, even though I sacrificed everything for my career.'

'Is this an admission of regret?'

'Absolutely. The woman was sacrificed for the artist's benefit. This is why I lost so many men; my love life's been sporadic and disappointing: too much instability, too much travel, no time to stop. I met a man in Algeria a month ago but that doesn't mean I'll see him again. Nowadays it hurts me not to have a social life, a family life, a man. I'd like to get married, but the man I'm looking for now will have to be rich. A pauper would just rob me. I'd never marry a man who was poor. I like money too much.'

'Exactly what do you do with your money?'

'I save it up; I'm planning on moving to Africa and to stop working in about two or three years. I'm going to live in Africa and my ambition is to become a UN ambassador. I'll make some records from time to time still, but no more concerts, they're too tedious... The only reason I still do them now is for the money, although I used to love being on stage, the crowd... I even have this gift of being able to hypnotize my audience... I could make them laugh and I could make them cry, but now I'm just no longer inspired by music at all.'[16]

No longer inspired by music, but still filled with dreams for the future, writing in the final pages of her autobiography: 'Right now I'm as close to happy as I can be without a husband to love. I started to work on this book, looking back over a life which, after thinking about for months and months, I have no regrets about. Plenty of mistakes, some bad days, and, most resonant of all, years of joy – hard, but joyous all the same – fighting for the rights of my brothers and sisters everywhere; America, Africa, all over the world, years where pleasure and pain were mixed together.'[17]

She is fifty-nine years old, she thinks the game is over and that she's won it as she proudly signs autographs 'Dr. Nina', as she tells anyone who'll listen that what she enjoys most these days 'is having enough money to turn down things I don't want to do'. She wants to retire from the business and stop bowing down to the never-ending circus of her tours.

On the occasion of the publication of her memoirs, one final accolade awaited Nina at the Olympia, where she played a week of sold-out concerts from 23 to 27 October 1991. The French press, who had been singing her praises for several months by then, met the event with great acclaim. The *Journal du Dimanche*, in an article entitled 'Nina Simone, cursed child of blues', allowed her to expand on her failed ambition: 'My goal was to become a concert pianist, and I had what it took! Bach for instance held no secrets for me, Bach is beautiful! I could have been the first black musician to become a concert artist, the first...'[18] Forty years on, she still hadn't digested her failure to get into the Curtis Institute! *Le Monde* chose to focus its portrait on her activism, opening its piece with this strapline: 'Nina Simone, her heart and politics. From fighting for civil rights to love songs, the African-American pianist returns to Europe.'[19] For *L'Humanité*, Nina was 'A rebel diva'.[20] The *Quotidien de Paris*, on the other hand, expanded on her love of classical music, her aborted career as a concert pianist, this 'centre of gravity of the civil rights struggle' who had 'travelled to South Africa', her contempt for slavery and her recent visit to the slave market of Elmina, in Ghana.[21] Then there was *La Croix*, which was more interested in Nina Simone's more tragic aspects, setting aside sensationalism to look at the pianist's contradictions: 'I live between a black world and a white world,' she said to Anne Pichon, 'between the black keys and the white keys of my piano, but I've found my balance.'[22] To the journalist who wanted to know whether she considered herself strong, Nina replied: 'Yes. Now that I've experienced the death of friends, a child, I know that nothing can get to me any more. First of all because I've always worked hard; no one should ever have to work as hard as I did, except to make money. And I am guided by a strong spirituality which is present in all my songs and every action in my life.'[23]

Those few press snippets are an attempt to recreate Nina's state of mind a few days before her concerts at the Olympia. We find her on fine form and playing the part of exasperated diva to perfection.

Her five shows at the Olympia were the last traces of Nina's dazzling art to be seen in Paris. Between panic attacks, a war of nerves with the Olympia's managers, and the constant pressure on Raymond Gonzalez, who was still the commander of the Nina enterprise, those five concerts would against all odds turn out a major success. And yet mistrust was rife on the boulevard des Capucines, and with reason:

the venue staging the show, the Olympia, had already experienced difficulties with the pianist, not least with her catastrophic concert in 1983.

Her bad reputation preceding her, Jean-Michel Boris, the Olympia's artistic director, awaited Nina with some apprehension: 'I'd left Christian Chassaing in charge of looking after her because I couldn't stand her. She got on my nerves. Contact with her was always really weird, very frosty, especially when it was about money. She'd been taken advantage off quite badly by American agents and hadn't always been paid, so her attitude towards her employers was very harsh. Christian Chassaing had managed to build a good rapport with her – which wasn't easy – so he was the one who took care of Nina Simone that week.'

In those days Christian Chassaing was Jean-Michel Boris's assistant, and he'd got personally involved when she came to boulevard des Capucines, to the point of drafting the concert programme himself. Working with Raymond Gonzalez, he took care of the whole event. Ticket prices were set at 240 and 190 francs (£30 and £24), Nina was put up at the Grand Hôtel, and a car was put at her disposal to take her to the concert hall (two hundred yards away). They agreed on a $16,000 fee, which earned Christian Chassaing a booming 'You're a slave-driver! See what you're paying me? Anywhere else I'd get forty-five thousand dollars!'

Viviane Priou, an independent press officer, was hired by the Olympia to ensure extensive media coverage. 'As far as the public was concerned, Nina Simone hadn't been around for years,' she explains. 'We had to create the event, but in the end the interviews all went pretty well, and even Yves Saint Laurent came to one of the concerts with his people.'

Viviane Priou's role that week was of key importance – key to Nina Simone's well-being and to making sure the interviews ran smoothly. As Gerrit and Jackie informed her of the pianist's attacks, Viviane also made sure she got some time in between interviews: 'I'd been warned about her character and her hatred of interviews,' she says. 'I'd also been informed that Nina was on lithium. I soon realized that when she wasn't well, her jaw would move from side to side. When I sensed she was getting cranky or saw her jaw begin to wiggle, I'd stop the interviews. I'd take her for a wander, a break or to lunch. Journalists had been warned that I might break off the interviews at any time.'

One afternoon, Viviane decided that Nina needed an hour's rest and the press officer invited Nina and Jackie to join her for a drink at the Closerie des Lilas, a legendary spot in literary Montparnasse. Nina showed up at the Closerie looking impressive in her leopard-print coat. Noticing that a wedding reception was being held in the restaurant, they went and sat down on the terrace. The newlyweds recognized Nina Simone and offered her a glass of champagne. She took the glass, knocked it back, stuck her hand in a plate of canapés and stuffed them into her mouth. Then she said: 'Another one.' The petrified young couple got their picture taken with Nina, then ordered her another drink, which she also drained in one gulp. Then a third. No one dared refuse her anything any more.

Although Nina's mental health was fairly stable that week in Paris, she wasn't safe from relapses. Those attacks were usually dealt with by Gerrit or Jackie in private, but when they struck in the midst of press interviews, they could lead to absolute disasters.

Still, except for an unfortunate lunch at Lucas Carton, Nina was a good sport with giving interviews during her stay in Paris. With Raymond and Gerrit keeping watch behind the scenes and accompanied by Al Schackman, Leopold Fleming and Paul Robinson on stage, Nina felt comfortable, playing one good show after another, though keeping everyone guessing about her much-feared late arrivals at the Olympia. 'She showed up at one concert over forty-five minutes late,' Christian Chassaing recalls. 'The audience was screaming "Refund!" When she finally came on stage, she exclaimed, just like she had at Assas: "What's wrong with you? I'm here!" Then gave a fabulous show, facing the audience and winning them over. Regardless of how she treated the audience, she always managed to charm them. She always got a standing ovation at the end.'

Her return to the Olympia three years later would prove an utter disappointment, giving a taste of what would turn out to be Nina Simone's last descent into hell.

11

'SO WHILE YOU'RE IMITATING AL CAPONE I'LL BE NINA SIMONE'

BOUC-BEL-AIR is ugly, there's nothing interesting here. In the middle of the countryside ten minutes from Aix-en-Provence, only a stone's throw from the motorway, the Platanes estate is a charmless group of houses with faded orange walls. There are no shops anywhere near, just a service station five minutes away on foot, and only a bus, if you can find it, to get into the centre of Aix. Yet this is where Nina Simone bought a house in 1992, on a whim and without even taking advice from her entourage. The building is still there, hidden behind a badly tended hedge.

Getting out of the car, I scanned the untidy garden. Seen from the roadside, the house is sadly ordinary, one large upstairs room and four rooms on the roughly ninety-square-yard ground floor. A few crooked trees in the garden and a garage built as an extension. I was trying to find signs of life behind those walls when the owner made a sudden appearance, calling from the doorway and asking me: 'What are you looking for?'

I introduced myself and explained that I was looking for Nina Simone's house. 'This is it.' She didn't invite me inside and seemed to be in a rush when I tried to ask her a few questions. 'I only met her once when I came to view the house before buying it. That's all I can tell you.'

As I turned to leave, she added: 'The neighbours were happy to see her go. She didn't leave good memories behind in the area. Speak to the neighbours over there,' she said, pointing to a house hidden behind a hedge, 'she used to go skinny-dipping in their pool without asking!' No one answered when I called at their house. There was no reason to stay around here.

Gerrit de Bruin told me of Nina's whim when she bought this house, probably the first one she had visited in the region: 'She was influenced by a guy she met in Amsterdam. She told him that she planned to buy a house in the south of France and he offered to help her. No one knows how it happened, but she came across this house and decided to buy it straight away. She had already made a ten per cent down payment (84,000 francs) at the notary's office when she called me to tell me the news. Overcome with excitement, she explained that Amsterdam's climate wasn't to her liking and that she wanted to live close to Aix-en-Provence. I warned her straight away that once she was settled in Bouc-Bel-Air it would be hard for us to come and visit her very often. She answered: "You've only come to see me twice a month since I've been in Amsterdam. Come to Bouc-Bel-Air once a month and that'll be perfect." I protested. I explained that life in France would be difficult for her, that if it was only a question of money we could still go back on the deal, give up the ten per cent deposit, she could make that amount back in a single concert. But she didn't want to hear any of it.'

Soon after that, Nina described her new property to Sylvia Hampton in glowing terms: 'I just bought a home in France in Aix-en-Provence, just near the mountains. So now I've nearly got three homes. I bought some land in Ghana and I'm building a beach home there and of course I still have a condo in Hollywood. It's strange how life turns out. From having nowhere to call home, I've now got a choice and that's good because I hate feeling tied down. I need to be able to move around so I don't get bored.'[1]

Nina was on holiday in Ghana when her furniture was moved from Amsterdam to Bouc-Bel-Air, the task left to Gerrit de Bruin and Roger Nupie. Neither of them had been to the house before when they parked their van in the Platanes estate. They found a gloomy interior in dire need of freshening up, faulty electrics, a narrow kitchen, a small living room, a garden that hadn't been maintained for years, two bedrooms on the ground floor and a first-floor room that could be used as a guest room. Nothing special. Everyone who came to visit her in Bouc-Bel-Air would make the same comment: 'It was terrible. We couldn't understand what she was doing there.' The move caused new problems, the most significant in her life over the last few years. Too isolated, far from Aix town centre, too far from Amsterdam, Antwerp and Paris for Gerrit, Raymond and Roger to visit regularly, the Bouc-Bel-Air house would become the scene of new dramas.

The first was a mysterious fire in the summer of 1993. On 26 June 1993 Reuters news agency published this dispatch:

> The American signer Nina Simone was hospitalized Saturday morning in Aix-en-Provence after sustaining injuries in the fire that completely destroyed her villa in Bouc-Bel-Air (Bouches-du-Rhône), we have learned through the police. The fire began at night. According to initial inquiry findings, the singer, who was severely inebriated at the time of the incident, may have caused the accident herself. Nina Simone, 60, was only saved from the flames thanks to the intervention of her bodyguard. She has been admitted to the Aix-en-Province hospital in a state that causes 'no alarm'.

Accounts differ as to exactly what happened. According to some sources, Nina set her mattress alight and the room was consumed by flames. Gerrit, who was there that night, injured her against the broken glass of a window as he tried to get her out of the villa. The accident and subsequent hospitalization forced Nina to cancel her appearance at the Nice Jazz Festival on 24 July 1993. Raymond Gonzalez offers a less dramatic version of events, explaining that fax-machine paper had piled up on the floor and a poorly extinguished cigarette or perhaps a short-circuit had set it alight.

There are other versions. In one, Nina deliberately set her furniture alight, and then a few days later called her insurer to reimburse her 'on the spot!' Whatever the truth about the source of the fire, the incident pushed Gerrit to set up a rotating guard for Nina Simone.

One of the first to join her in her Bouc-Bel-Air house was Roland Grivelle, her road manager for European and American tours. He came to see about the house, freshen up the walls, and install the gas and new electrics. He stayed with her for a while, just as Jackie Hammond did, and then had to leave to deal with other matters.

When no one could be with her in Bouc-Bel-Air and she was left to her own devices, Nina would see the ghosts of the past return and would baulk at following her medical treatment. Alone in Bouc-Bel-Air and without a car to travel to Aix-en-Provence as she pleased, deprived of company, bit by bit losing her places to hide, the diva sank into solitude. 'I remember a telephone conversation in which she told me she didn't need to take her medication any more,' Gerrit confided in me. 'She said that a new world was opening up to her. I protested, warning her that that world was going to change if she didn't take her treatment properly. I told her to give up the whim of living in the south of France and to come back to Holland where we could look after her. But she wouldn't hear of it. She was convinced she'd made the right decision.'

Nina got into her neighbours' bad books quickly. One of them later complained to a *France-Soir* journalist: 'She drinks a lot, and when she doesn't know what to do, she fires a gun into the air. The police have already been several times to disarm her.'[2]

I managed to catch up with one of the kids from the neighbourhood who has since become one of the top house DJs in France. Master H (Hassen Gouaned) grew up in Bouc-Bel-Air and remembers when the American lived in the area: 'We often saw her walking her little dog in the street and talking to herself. She became the local attraction. To many people, she was "the crazy American". Personally, I was intrigued because my parents had her records. Her house was surrounded by tall hedges and we didn't know what was going on inside. There were few comings and goings, but sometimes we'd hear shouting, and on the odd occasion music.'

1992. Nina Simone left for Los Angeles, where she was due to record the album *A Single Woman* under the guidance of Michael Alago, the A&R director of Elektra Records whom she had met at a Carnegie Hall concert in 1987. The record's production was entrusted to

André Fischer, notably responsible for Natalie Cole's multi-platinum *Unforgettable*. Among the songs Nina was planning to record were 'Sign o' the Times' by Prince (which wouldn't make the final cut), 'Papa, Can You Hear Me?', a Barbra Streisand cover from the film *Yentl*, the traditional song 'I Know It Was the Blood', and 'Wake Up Everybody' from Harold Melvin & the Blue Notes. Alas, the production team had a very specific idea of the material to be recorded for this album. Even its title harked back to Elton John's classic *A Single Man*.

Alvin Schackman and Paul Robinson were called during the session going on at the Village Studio in Hollywood. Nina thought the recording was great: 'I feel good, I'm not killing myself to get it done and the people I'm working with seem to appreciate what I do and show me respect.'[3] Paul Robinson has a different view: 'I only played on two of the songs on the album. The producers preferred to replace me with one of their house drummers. Lots of them were arseholes, but there were also a lot of well-meaning people. The repertoire that André Fischer chose for Nina wasn't suited to her, but he didn't care. He had his own vision of Nina and wouldn't budge from it.'

In the end, *A Single Woman* included songs such as 'If I Should Lose You', a standard that Nina had already recorded in the 60s, 'The Folks Who Live on the Hill', which she dedicated to the memory of Errol Barrow, and 'Il n'y A Pas d'Amour Heureux', a poem by Louis Aragon to a Georges Brassens melody that Jacques Bonni had suggested she should adapt during the pianist's years in Paris.

A Single Woman was released in 1993. The critics welcomed a subdued Nina Simone, offering her more romantic, seductive and voluptuous side. Her voice was draped in a deluge of strings and a thousand tricks aimed at giving the record a luxurious gleam. In spite of that, sales didn't live up to the record company's expectations. And, following several scandals during Nina's promotion of the album in the United States, particularly in the wings of NBC's *Tonight Show*, Elektra decided to abandon its investment and the album's promotion ceased suddenly. *A Single Woman* was Nina Simone's last studio album.

That wasn't the first time Nina would scupper such opportunities because of her inability to control her emotions. Raymond Gonzalez says that shortly after 'My Baby Just Cares for Me's triumph he received a telephone call from Ahmet Ertegün, the legendary co-founder of Atlantic Records, the man who discovered Ray Charles and Aretha Franklin. 'One of Ahmet Ertegün's big projects was to get Nina Simone to do an album for him,' he explains. 'We were in negotiations, but he had been very clear about his conditions. He refused to speak to Nina directly about the project, stating quite clearly that if Nina ever called him, that would be it, he'd drop the project. I spoke to Nina about it, I explained what was at stake, what an album with Ahmet Ertegün could represent, but she couldn't help contacting him and saying: "You're going to negotiate with me, I want a million dollars!" I didn't know anything about that call. Several weeks went past without any word from Ahmet Ertegün, and when I finally managed to get in touch with him, he told me about Nina's call and that as a result the project wouldn't be going ahead.'

In May 1994 Nina Simone spent some time in Tunisia, where she got involved with a young man of twenty-five, Mohamed. She had been engaged for a series of three concerts at the Olympia and was forced to leave her lover to go to Paris the same day that Nelson Mandela, who had become President of South Africa, came to Tunis.

She arrived in Paris with her nerves in tatters and Raymond had to deal with her on his own (Gerrit had opted to go on holiday). Roger Nupie had been contacted to provide a firm hand but he initially refused out of tiredness. It would take a desperate call from Raymond for him to change his mind: 'I could hear Nina screaming behind him. He didn't have a clue what to do to calm her down. I really hesitated, but in the end I set off for Paris. I was there for three very difficult days spent watching her twenty-four hours a day, to make sure she took her medication, but nothing could make her. Nina was in a terrible state of psychological distress.'

Serious disagreements erupted with the Olympia team. To begin with, Nina refused to promote her concerts and tickets sales were slow. Christian Chassaing, who had originally planned a week of performances, was forced to cut the pianist's residence to three days, from 16 to 18 June 1994. On average, audiences were no more than

1,200 paying concert-goers each night, plus a few hundred invited guests, for a capacity of 2,000. In the end, the Olympia lost money.

Each evening, Christian Chassaing's patience was sorely tested. The diva demanded to receive her complete fee in cash before even heading to the stage. 'Traditionally,' Christian explained, 'we pay artists half before the concert and the other half afterwards. Nina's case was an extreme. I even had to threaten her with prison one night to make her get on the stage!'

Each passing night saw the same round of tantrums, fighting, stage hysterics, wardrobe aberrations, contempt, indifference. She put everyone to the test: the audience, technicians, organizers. As if she was demanding they prove they were worthy of hearing her sing. Yet the thoughtful Nina – in her own sometimes clumsy way – was not far away and could sometimes be seen, as on the evening of the second concert. Roger Nupie accompanied her back to her hotel. He was due back in Antwerp early the next morning and slept on a sofa in his suite. When he awoke, Nina was sitting beside him, holding out a breakfast tray with a rose in a little jar. She said, 'Look outside, Roger.' He moved over to the window and saw, in the middle of the deserted place de L'Opéra, in the early morning mist, a black man waiting. At the man's feet was a dalmatian that resembled the one he had had years before. She declared: 'It's for you!'

Two months later, on 20 August 1994, during a German tour, Nina Simone would have to cancel a concert in Lörrach because of a nervous breakdown.

She was but a shadow of her former self, a vulgar reflection of the beauty who had trod the boards of the Old World in the late 60s. Obese, ill and being watched over by a shrink ('So many years spent sitting on a piano stool can screw you up'). Crises, resignations, cancelled concerts, contempt for audiences, organizers and even her musicians. Her heart just wasn't in it any more, not in her work, a lover, pleasure or desire. Only pain and isolation remained.

Of course, 'they' appeared from time to time to take care of her, but their presence never lasted more than a few nights, a week sometimes. Adamo, a Cameroonian she met at the Trois Maillets, lived with her for a time, then he left again. Jackie would visit from time to time, as would Gerrit, Raymond and Roger, of course.

It's at this point that Isabelle Terrin entered Nina Simone's life. Her appearance in this book is, in a way, a bit of a happy accident. I had contacted her about an issue that pitted Nina Simone against the French courts in the summer of 1995; Isabelle was her lawyer. It is strange that Gerrit, Roger, Raymond and co. don't know her name, because as well as Nina's lawyer she was her close friend during the Bouc-Bel-Air era.

They met by chance in 1994 at the Aix-en-Provence court building, had a coffee and had dinner together that very night at Isabelle's house. 'She was looking for simple times with simple people,' she said. That was the start of a close friendship that would last through the 90s. 'I discovered a hypersensitive woman with a difficult, imposing presence,' Isabelle Terrin says. 'She was incapable of looking after her house or eating properly – to the point that a neighbour was bringing her food at that time. Nina just wasn't adapted. She set her kitchen on fire one day trying to cook eggs. Another time, her electricity was cut off because she hadn't paid her bills and I found her on the floor in tears, moaning: "After all I've given France, they could at least give me electricity!" I had only known her for a few months, and all of a sudden she asked me to leave everything for her, leave my work and family. Then she started sobbing: "If you knew the people who gave up everything for me and who lost everything!"'

When they met, Nina Simone was going through a difficult time, marked by an incident that had left her lastingly traumatized: 'Some people had broken into her house while she was away and had defecated in her living room,' Isabelle Terrin explains. 'That threw her into a state of terrible distress.' Paul Robinson had already told me about this incident. It happened a few days after a concert in Marseille in 1994. Some members of the audience in the first few rows stood up, blocking the view of the people behind them, who then started to protest. Nina thought she was being booed and started insulting the audience: 'You fucking French!' Then she left the stage and refused to return.

Over the following days, her house was vandalized, floors and walls smeared with excrement. In order for a police investigation to be held, Nina had to file a complaint for damages, a procedure that required the plaintiff to pay a deposit of 10,000 francs (£1250). Nina refused and no investigation was ever opened, but according to Isabelle Terrin, the police suspected a small far-right group of being responsible.

After the incident, Nina took refuge with Isabelle Terrin in Aix-en-Provence, in her beautiful home only a few minutes from the city centre. There was a large terrace and a swimming pool in which Nina enjoyed bathing. A photo still sits on a coffee table showing her in a white bathing suit, paddling in the pool with a huge smile on her face.

Isabelle's husband and son were there too, who called Nina the 'Black Mummy', and were astonished at first to see this big black lady devour her food rather than tasting it, confused when she poured some of her champagne on the ground before downing the glass in one ('Libation!') and when she covered her plate with a napkin when she was finished eating. But it was an angel who had come into their home, an angel with the occasional scent of poison, a sort of old exhausting aunt, but a rare person who was also generous and attentive in her own way. When we met, the words Isabelle used to describe Nina particularly touched me: 'Nina changed my life.' That's what resonates. Because, despite her pain, Nina still had the power to shine some of her sorcerous grace on you, and so refine you, release you. At the same time, her charms could also destroy you.

On 25 July 1995, Nina made the headlines after shooting at a fifteen-year-old boy with a nine-millimetre air-pistol because he was 'making too much noise' while swimming in a neighbouring villa's pool. The teenager suffered injuries from fragments on different parts of his body.

Nina was immediately 'investigated for assault with a weapon and possessing a category-four weapon without authorization'.[4] She was taken before a judge the next day and had the case postponed until 23 August 1995. She was required to surrender her passport to the police as part of her probation. Her public defender, Jean-Paul Mouélé, declared that 'health reasons could explain an act that she immediately regretted and so stated to the police'.[5] In court she was described as a depressive, fragile, harassed woman. The psychologist the court ordered to examine her confirmed that she was 'incapable of assessing the consequences of her actions', 'she sometimes lacks the ability to control herself', and finally was suffering, at sixty-two years of age, 'a terrible solitude. No one supports her any more, either from within her family or among her friends',[6] according to the expert.

Nina Simone, who was not present at the trial, was given an 'eight-month suspended prison sentence, eighteen months' probation and forbidden from purchasing or possessing a weapon'.[7] She was sentenced by the Aix-en-Provence criminal court to pay a fine 'of 3,000 francs, to pay 20,000 francs in civil damages and to undergo medical treatment. Her lawyer, Mr Jean-Paul Mouélé, was not authorized to plead in his client's absence'.[8]

Isabelle Terrin made sure that Nina was defended before the court of appeals. She argued the particular context, a mutual lack of understanding between the American and her neighbours, the children's repeated provocations of her, racist insults, the tension between Nina and her neighbours fed by the fact they couldn't understand one another yet were compelled to live side by side. Finally, Isabelle pointed out that Nina's presence in Bouc-Bel-Air was not welcome and that her illness played a central role in her behaviour. After confirming that Nina had paid the civil damages, the court quashed the conviction of 23 August 1995 and declared her free.

After this episode, and even though Nina hadn't performed on stage for almost two years, the members of her close guard decided to take turns in taking care of her in Bouc-Bel-Air.

Paul Robinson, who hadn't worked with Nina in nearly two years, received a call not long after. She wanted him to come and see her. 'I didn't really want to go, but I owed it to her,' he said. 'I packed my drum kit in the car boot, thinking that we'd practise. I drove all night from London to the south of France and arrived in Bouc-Bel-Air mid-afternoon. It was hot as hell and I was exhausted. I rang the doorbell and her dog Shadow started barking. After a few minutes, Nina finally appeared. She was wearing an old, dirty Columbo-style raincoat, a blue African dress, sunglasses and had a pencil in her hair. She came towards me and said "Hi, Paul" as if it was perfectly normal for me to be there, and then let me in. I set the parts of my drum kit in a corner, then she sat down in front of me and took off her sunglasses: she had a huge black eye. I didn't ask any questions and gave her the bottle of champagne I'd brought. We drank it while we talked. I remarked that the house was full of surveillance cameras. I mentioned the incident when she shot at the kid, but she just swept it aside, saying, "He was making too much noise!"'

Paul Robinson's patience was really put to the test when a few normal, everyday incidents Nina-style occurred: she screamed at some kids playing in front of the chemist's where she was picking up a prescription; at the supermarket the target of her anger was a security guard. 'At that moment,' Paul Robinson remembers, 'I said to myself: "I've had enough, I want to go home." While she was waiting for me in town to have lunch, I got my drums out of the house by propping a ladder up against a window, and headed back towards London. A few months later, Nina decided to tour again and Raymond called me. He said: "You should call Nina and explain to her why you disappeared." I did, I told her an unlikely story that she bought without asking any questions.'

Not long after, it was Roger Nupie's turn to visit Nina. He stayed in Bouc-Bel-Air for a week, making sure she was following her medical treatment to the letter, taking care of her, trying to entertain her and trying to get her past the anxiety that had been torturing her since her brush with the courts. During his stay, Roger witnessed strange goings-on: 'At that time, Nina was only sleeping a few hours a night. We were sitting at the kitchen table very early one morning. I'd made breakfast and we were eating omelettes, and I got up to put *Caught Up* on the record player, a Millie Jackson record that Nina really liked because the lyrics were very sexual. She would play Millie Jackson for days sometimes. She'd sit at the piano and play along with the songs or ask me to dance. When I came back into the kitchen, a small, narrow room, I found Nina in the company of an enormous black dog.

'"Where did that dog come from?"

'"He's been here the whole time, Roger."

'That worried me. I had never seen that dog in the time I'd been in the house, and the doors had been closed all morning. Still, there it was, sitting at her feet. Nina began to laugh: "You can stroke it if you want." But I didn't want to, I was scared. I declined her offer and we went back to eating as if nothing had happened, the dog still lying at her feet. We started talking again, I'd forgotten the dog was there when she interrupted me to say: "If you look out the window, you'll see the dog is outside now."

'"Where is it, Nina?"

'"He's sitting in the car. He's waiting on us to go shopping."'

As Roger Nupie was telling me this story, I saw the hair on his arms and his neck stand up when he got to this part. He was reliving the scene and, only a few inches in front of him, having a private conversation that sometimes made me feel a strange presence at our table, I could see terror in his eyes.

'David, don't believe me if you don't want to, but I can tell you that I got up from the table, I went to the window overlooking the street, looked towards the car and the dog was sitting inside!'

'What was that dog? A vision? Her father?'

'What else?! We finished our breakfast in silence, got up, locked the house and took the car to Aix. I drove on the way there and watched the dog in the rear-view mirror. It was sitting there in the back, not moving at all. When we arrived in town, we parked and went to do our shopping, leaving the dog in the car. When we got back it was gone. I was relieved, but worried too. Nina drove on the way back. She was dangerous at the wheel as ever, then, suddenly, she began honking the horn and laughing. "Look Roger, look at the dog!" It was sitting on the hard shoulder watching us drive past. I never saw it again after that.'

'Did you ask her about the dog?'

'Yes, later I asked her to explain the dog to me, but she just answered: "Come on Roger, I don't need to explain it to you. You know perfectly well who that dog was." I decided never to bring the subject back up.'

'Because you were worried?'

'No. Because, really, in her case, it wasn't really that strange after all. That sort of thing was part of Nina Simone. Remember, she was the high priestess of soul.'

When I spoke to Gerrit de Bruin about Roger Nupie's stay in Bouc-Bel-Air, he told me that Nina received a visit from her elder brother, Carrol Waymon, at the time. Carrol was a psychologist in San Diego, a member of the Association of Black Psychologists whose aim was to 'have a positive impact upon the mental health of the [American] Black community'. Carrol Waymon hadn't seen his sister for years. He arrived one day to see how her health was. At the time, Roger was having difficulties with Nina, to such an extent, Gerrit told me, that he wasn't sleeping any more as he was worried she would burst into his room in his sleep and attack him in the middle of one of her rages. Carrol looked after his sister during his stay. He may have been the one who suggested to Nina that she return to the United States for a while, as she flew off to Hollywood shortly afterwards. Another crisis was waiting for her there, followed by a spell in a Los Angeles psychiatric hospital and a meeting that would shake and eventually destroy the fragile balance holding together Nina Simone's close guard.

Before flying off to California, Nina first spent some time in Tunis with Mohamed. Other than this lover, did Nina have any other affairs during the Bouc-Bel-Air years? Isabelle Terrin told me she remembered at least one man, a forty-something white man living in Aix, with whom Nina had had a romantic relationship for a few months. Probably weary of his girlfriend's attacks, the man left her. His excuse was that it had become 'impossible to make love to a legend'. That man confided in Isabelle that his relationship with Nina wasn't working between the sheets, that although Nina liked to talk about sex constantly, in reality she was totally passive and unable to achieve any pleasure.

And Mohamed. We know nothing about Mohamed other than that he was Nina's last exploit. She was convinced that he was the one she would marry and grow old with. In a disjointed letter to Isabelle written from her Hollywood hotel on 17 October 1995, Nina talked about her Tunisian lover. She also mentioned – and it's an indicator in trying to link the flow of events to Nina's psychological state at that time – a forthcoming visit to an LA clinic.

Hollywood, 17 October 1995

Dear Isabelle,

I was very touched by your very sensitive letter. I hesitated in responding to you because of the extraordinary suffering I went through in Bouc-Bel-Air. In any event, it was you who said that my problem (in your opinion) was that I love too intensely. And you explained it to me in such well-chosen words.

Being 'beautiful' and black, being a woman, being as famous in familiar countries as in countries that are unknown is both extraordinarily joyous and painful. Being ME. We share the pain (obviously), but not at the same level.

I'm not planning on coming back to Bouc-Bel-Air for the moment. The only judgement I trust in [referring to her recent trial] is my own and that of a few (very few) friends... I had to rely on white people because at the time and even today (and unfortunately, over the last 500 years, my people, ignorant, poor, rich or famous alike, have been hunted, raped, massacred, babies ripped from their mothers' wombs, from the wombs of the women of Gorée). Yes, I've seen all that, Isabelle. So the only thing that's new about what's going on in Bosnia is that it involves whites. It is possible (but highly unlikely) that (as a race) WHITE PEOPLE have changed. Racism is a problem that I will always face. My 'father', you see, ordered me to spend six months a year until I die in Africa, where I am free.

I've been married twice, I've lost four children because I worked too hard – and my only surviving daughter (I've seen her) is beautiful and LOST. She doesn't have the slightest idea what to do.

I'm a beautiful and intelligent woman, I attract all hot-blooded men (smiles). It's true. Dogs, cats and children too.

And I've never given up the freedom to walk peacefully in the streets. All the 'black stars' are here with me, the living and the dead, I'm friends with Nat King Cole's family – Princess Fernandez isn't here, but some mutual friends are... I'm waiting in this hotel.

I have to know what my situation in Bouc-Bel-Air is – according to what I've been told, those newspaper whores wrote I'd taken 18 months' probation. The bad publicity surrounding my arrival here has set off unrest that I can't deal with on my own. Customs have already seized my red car since I arrived on the 29th of August. I'm refusing to give even the briefest of interviews to anyone. In particular, '33' have sent me four faxes from Paris about a documentary on Billie Holiday. For $1,000. Listen, Isabelle – that's an insult, even a double insult: the bastards have the cheek to ask me to betray a woman whose spirit made Porgy a success! My God! They'll rot in hell before I'll do anything of the sort. Billie Holiday is dead (basically because she always refused the feeding pipe that MEN offered her on the condition that she slept with them first)...

As for my love (Mohamed), he has not only asked me to marry him, but he has also got his hands on appropriate clothing for a huge party in Tunisia. Isabelle, he's had to deal with it all alone, even though he's only twenty-five, because my wedding gown is already prepared and tailored. I don't know if it's going to work. He can't come here to be with me for the moment. He's slow to appreciate the cruelty of life, especially here in the United States. His 'honesty' is quite simply frightening. He gets in touch every three days and I cry every night. He's so young and pure. He has really touched my heart and soul. It's both frightening and so rare.

I'm sure I've spoken to you about Mohamed before. The French refuse to allow him into France, and the Americans refuse to allow him into America. That's why I'm stuck. I have to rest here in the hotel (only a few minutes away from my apartment) until I've calmed down and to give Nina Simone some time for herself. That will be a first.

You can get in touch with me here. I'm looking forward to your thoughts on everything I've written.

With love,

Nina.

A few weeks after this letter was sent, and after Nina had a violent attack, one of the Waymon sisters, in agreement with Carrol, had her admitted to a Californian psychiatric hospital.

That's where Nina met Clifton Henderson. Who was he really? A nurse she met in that Californian hospital, as Nina and he both stated? A fellow patient she met during her weeks in care, as others have suggested to me? An intern that Nina, drugged with tranquillizers, mistook for a doctor? It is said that during this stay, Clifton had Nina sign some papers granting him a salary for life. That was impossible to verify.

However, if there is something we can say for sure, it's that after she met Clifton, the semblance of peace kept alive, for better or worse, by Gerrit and Raymond since the mid-80s would crumble away before disappearing altogether.

Little by little Clifton Henderson strengthened his influence over Nina until he became the new leader in her entourage.

Marc Penniman, Nina Simone's accountant and also Little Richard's brother, was looking for a safe pair of hands to look after her in the south of France. That's when Nina spoke to him about this black nurse she had met in hospital and told him that she got on well with him. Penniman met Henderson and offered him the job of Nina's private nurse in Bouc-Bel-Air. He accepted and moved in during 1996. Isabelle Terrin remembers his arrival: 'It was fantastic, because someone had to look after her full-time.' He lived with Nina all year round, looked after her, made sure she took her medication. He got her out of the house too, kept her busy. For the first few years, Clifton was accepted by everyone 'as long as he did his job properly'. But soon a new recruit was taken on: Javier Collado.

Javier was living in Paris when he met Nina Simone. At twenty-three, he was trying to break into the Parisian music scene. He had worked with Tyrone Dennis, ex-keyboard player with the Wailers, and for several weeks with Marla Glenn, an androgynous blues singer who was Nina's personal assistant during her time in Holland. Clifton was looking for someone to help him, as his role as a nurse had gradually grown to personal secretary too. A little put off by the lady's character, Javier initially refused the offer, but in the end moved into Bouc-Bel-Air a few months later. Javier Collado was officially taken on as Nina Simone's bodyguard: 'She was quite paranoid,' he said, 'she wanted someone there to protect her.' But above all, Javier became Clifton Henderson's assistant, as well as a full-time member of Nina's band.

Nina set off again on an international tour in 1996 (to Brazil, Beirut, the United States and Australia), after two years without touring. Because of her delicate state of health, Raymond Gonzalez ensured that the performances were spaced at least three days apart. Everyone felt that 'Nina hadn't played interesting music for ten years'; Paul Robinson thought she was using up her last musical reserves. 'From 1996, Nina was exhausted and had lost all taste for touring. Her only motivation was money and the perks of the profession: luxury hotels, great restaurants, first-class travel...' Over the last six years of her career, Nina Simone gave no more than fifty performances.

'Nina always said: "I work like a dog! I go from concert to concert!"' Gerrit told me, annoyed. 'It's not true! How many concerts did she give between 1974 and 1988? No more than a hundred and thirty, including the shows at the Trois Maillets. Over the last few years of her life, she didn't play more than fifteen to twenty times a year.'

Paradoxically, Nina Simone was reaping honours and distinctions. On 19 July 1998 she was invited to the gala given in Johannesburg for Nelson Mandela's eightieth birthday. It was his first official appearance with his new wife, whom he had met soon after leaving prison in 1990.

Accompanied by Isabelle Terrin, Clifton Henderson and Javier Collado, who was in charge of everything and anything Nina needed, she joined the party for which Desmond Tutu, Stevie Wonder, Danny

Glover and Michael Jackson had made the trip. In front of the South African TV cameras, they all got up on stage to sing 'Happy Birthday' to Nelson Mandela. That was the only time Nina shared a stage with Michael Jackson, for whom she didn't hide her affection. She even defended him in an interview with the journalist Alison Powell, accusing Quincy Jones of having used him for his own ends:

'I distinctly remember meeting Michael on a plane many years ago when he was little, and I said to him, "Don't let them change you. You're black and you're beautiful." But of course, he was influenced by his family and everybody else... I think that the person who's responsible for Michael's tragedy is Quincy Jones [who co-produced his albums *Thriller* and *Bad*]. You can quote me.'

'How is he responsible?'

'It was Quincy who married a girl from Sweden [Oolah]. And with Quincy with all them white women, poor little Michael didn't know what to do. Michael needed somebody to emulate, and I think he did everything that Quincy Jones told him to do. That is what I believe.'[9]

Letting out a huge laugh, Isabelle Terrin told me how the diva was 'stuck' on the 'King of Pop''s music for months and wouldn't go anywhere without his cassettes. She would listen to him religiously by the poolside and answer his complaints: 'Oh, poor little thing! What have they done to you?' or 'Oh yeah, my boy, I understand you!' So during Nelson Mandela's birthday celebrations in Johannesburg, Isabelle was expecting Nina and Michael to fall into one another's arms, but the two were happy to greet each other politely, as vague acquaintances would do.

The invitation to Nelson Mandela's birthday was the start of a series of honours celebrating Nina Simone as a 'figure in the black struggle worldwide'. In December 1998 in Abidjan, Nina was named an honorary ambassador of Côte d'Ivoire, then the next year she was presented in Philadelphia with the title Honorary Doctor in Music and Humanities, before receiving a Diamond Award for Excellence in Music from the Association of African American Music in June 2000, again in Philadelphia. During the ceremony, she couldn't hold back her emotion or her satisfaction at avenging the humiliation she suffered forty years earlier at the hands of the Curtis Institute. The

Institute recognized its error in quite a strange way and awarded Nina an honorary degree shortly before her death.[10] She got her revenge.

During the ceremony in Philadelphia, the poet Sonia Sanchez, the musician Kenny Gamble and the singer Jill Scott came to pay homage to her, Scott even daring to sing 'My Baby Just Cares for Me' in front of Nina, who was amused by her cheek. That Jill Scott, a soul artist close to the hip hop band The Roots, would come and pay her dues to Nina was neither surprising nor an isolated case. During the 90s, the new generation of American soul and hip hop (a single musical family regardless of the labels created by the record industry) had openly recognized the debt they owed Nina Simone's work. In 1996, radios across the world were playing the Fugees' hit 'Ready or Not', in which the singer Lauryn Hill raps 'So while you're imitating Al Capone / I'll be Nina Simone / And defecating on your microphone.' This was an explicit indication of Nina's influence, not just as a musician, but as an artist involved in the struggle, a strong woman, enlightened and determined. The most important figures in this new generation of female American artists (Erykah Badu, Missy Elliott, Mary J. Blige) claimed to be followers of Nina Simone.

Their big sister from a bygone age, but whose influence was dominant on hip hop and so-called 'neo soul', Nina Simone became a key inspiration.

But Nina was far from realizing what influence she had over all of this new generation, as she was more concerned with her physical and psychological health.

12

'AFTER THAT IT'S ALL JUST PAIN'

CLIFTON HENDERSON took power progressively. From 1997, Nina's personal nurse was the only person living with her from day to day. Gradually, he extended his influence.

There were several early signs of his intentions, but no one seems to have taken them seriously. When he asked Raymond Gonzalez if he would make 'a good manager' during a tour in Brazil in July 1997, Raymond burst out laughing: 'Are you taking the piss?'

Although her entourage didn't see it coming, Nina seemed to sense Clifton's designs. In fact, on that same Brazilian tour, she wanted to fire him one day on a whim. It was Gonzalez who saved him his job, yet soon Gonzalez would be the first victim of his manipulations: 'I thought, he's a nurse, he does his job well, he's part of the family now, he's no danger. Furthermore, letting him go meant no longer having anyone to look after Nina in Bouc-Bel-Air, and no one wanted to run that risk.'

The first crisis openly pitting the close guard against Clifton Henderson wasn't long coming. At a concert in the Royal Albert Hall in London, Al Schackman found him with a baksheesh worth $5,000 belonging to the show organizer. 'What shocked us about the story,' Roger Nupie says, 'wasn't so much the amount of money Clifton had got, but that Nina didn't do anything about it. In times gone by she would have cut the hand off anyone who touched her money. But that evening she didn't say anything, because she knew that if Clifton left no one would be living with her in Bouc-Bel-Air.' Everyone reckoned that if Clifton was allowed to take the upper hand like that it was mainly because Nina no longer had the strength to resist. 'Before, she could stand up to people with bad intentions,' Gerrit de Bruin explains, 'but at sixty-six years of age, and more than forty spent on her career, she couldn't any more. And her medical treatment had taken too much of her strength.'

From 1999, Clifton influenced Nina's choices and, one by one, pushed away the members of the close guard. In turn, Javier Collado came to live in Bouc-Bel-Air and kept Nina company, leaving the new leader free to tend to her 'private' affairs.

Two clans were formed: the old guard against Henderson and Collado. Why did those two start going against Gerrit and Raymond? People have told me that Javier's wish was to accompany Nina on stage and that when Clifton offered him that chance in exchange for his loyalty, he seized it.

We need this duo's explanations to fathom what was going to happen. Clifton has failed to respond to my many interview requests; Javier agreed to a telephone interview between Paris and Valence, where he now lives. I wanted to understand the reasons why they had taken charge of Nina's life in that way. Here's his response: 'From the first few months after my arrival, I was shocked by the disorder that ruled,' Javier Collado says. 'Why was Nina, for example, earning so little money from concerts through Raymond? Why were the musicians allowed to eat in restaurants and leave Raymond the bill? Clifton and I had the feeling that many people had taken advantage of a system for a long time and we wanted to put things back in order. That's where the decision to remove Raymond Gonzalez from Nina's business dealings came from, from the fact that we had observed bad management of her interests.'

I protested, arguing that at the time, Clifton Henderson was employed as a nurse and secretary, certainly not as a manager. Nina's business dealings didn't concern him, so I asked how he had the nerve to intervene. 'When you see things you believe are not normal,' Javier responded, 'you have to choose either to refuse to accept them or allow them to continue. Clifton's job was to manage Nina's personal life. But seeing as professional and personal issues were closely linked in her case, how could he look after one side and ignore the other? A time came when he was forced to choose: either stay where he was, only managing Nina's medical and personal life, witnessing abuses and buttoning his lip, or get involved in her professional life, which was having an impact on her psychological health.'

Raymond Gonzalez was dismissed in 2000. 'I was the first on the list,' he said. 'Clifton was in complete control. My influence over Nina dwindled and disappeared. She was no longer listening to me, Clifton interfered with all my decisions, I was of no use any more. It was over.'

Everything collapsed like a row of dominos. With Gonzalez out of the way, Isabelle Terrin would be next, even though a few years earlier she had welcomed the nurse to Bouc-Bel-Air with open arms. For Isabelle, things changed 'when Nina decided to return to the stage in 1999. New faces were beginning to circle round her, some of them attracted by her "fortune" and her celebrity.' At the time, Isabelle Terrin had proposed to Clifton that she look after Nina's legal affairs, as she was worried that she'd never seen a signed contract and knew Nina's official matters were in trouble: 'I was made to see that my presence was no longer welcome, and soon I began thinking that it was dangerous to be too interested, too close.'

Why all this manoeuvring? What was Clifton Henderson really up to? Was he after Nina's fortune? Her earnings consisted of income from ASCAP, royalties from record sales and radio play, concert fees... There was really no fortune. Perhaps we should look elsewhere for the source of the disagreements that split her previous and new management. We need to consider another angle: the possession of original, unreleased masters entrusted by Nina to Gerrit years before so that he could transfer them to digital format.

I've had the opportunity to listen to a few of the unreleased recordings. It's quite simply fantastic music, worthy of appearing among the pianist's best recorded work. Maybe they were the spoils that the two camps were fighting over. 'We fought for three years to try to recover those tapes. Unsuccessfully,' Javier Collado confirmed. But neither he nor Clifton could demand the return of the recordings, only Nina, their legal owner. I risked another question: 'What did Nina think about all these quarrels?' 'She trusted us,' Javier assured me.

How can we separate the truth from the lies? But above all, how can we explain why Nina allowed her old friends to be cut off from her like that? They all knew her very particular concept of friendship and loyalty. 'Friendship was a short-term commitment for her,' Gerrit explains. 'As long as you were giving her what she wanted, you were her best friend. You could be her best friend for thirty years and then be completely forgotten about the next day.'

Even so, how could they not feel cheated, betrayed, when some of them had listened to that woman's problems constantly, when they'd loved her, advised her, encouraged her...

In 2000, with Raymond Gonzalez dismissed, Gerrit rejected ('They wouldn't let her come to the phone,' he says, 'and when I visited the door was kept firmly shut'), Isabelle forgotten, Clifton officially became Nina Simone's manager. The old guard fell out of favour and became *personae non gratae*. Regardless of whether they visited Bouc-Bel-Air, or the Carry-le-Rouet house where Nina moved in 2000, or whether they called and insisted on speaking to their friend, the answer was always the same: 'Nina isn't here,' 'Nina can't come to the phone right now.' Then, finally: 'Nina doesn't want to hear from you any more.'

Gerrit, exasperated by the use of false pretexts to refuse to put his old friend on the phone, travelled down to the south of France, went to the house, rang the bell and, greeted by a stranger, was told that the diva wasn't home yet. He could see her lounging in the garden over the shoulder of this stranger blocking his path. He shouted: 'Nina! It's Gerrit!' She turned and, smiling, invited him to join her.

'Gerrit! I'm pleased to see you. Why didn't you come sooner?'

'Because they wouldn't let me.'

Silence.

'It was painful for all of us to see her so dependent on her new entourage,' Roger Nupie said. 'And her physical state was getting worse as the months went by. Clifton had convinced her that her old friends had abandoned her and that he was the only person left to look after her. She must have thought Clifton was the only person she could count on.'

Roger told me he went to a concert Nina was due to play at. Having got backstage, he managed to get close to her. Surprised to see him,

Nina exclaimed: 'Where did you disappear to, man? How long have you been here?' Roger told her that he'd been staying at a hotel in town for two days.

'Why didn't you come see me sooner?'

'I couldn't. Your entourage wouldn't let me near you.'

She wouldn't accept that. 'She knew,' Roger stated, explaining that sometimes Nina would make such terrible decisions or behave so badly that later she would be ashamed to admit to it. 'That day, the only thing she could think of to break the ice was: "Do you still love me, daaarling?" And as usual, I melted: "Of course I love you!"' Trying to make it up to him, she proposed that he go out on stage first and introduce her to the audience. 'Just like the good old times.' Of course, he agreed.

From 2000, none of Nina's old friends could testify to her state of health, as she secluded herself in her Bouc-Bel-Air home. I found an article published in the French monthly magazine *Jeune Afrique* in May 2003, by the Benin journalist Francis Kpatindé. He met Nina for the first time in 1992 at the Grand Hôtel in Paris in the company of Jean Adamo, a friend of the pianist's from Cameroon. Her autobiography had just come out, and for a week she had willingly taken questions from the press.

'We exchanged details after the interview,' Francis remembered. 'She would call me every two weeks from Amsterdam, sometimes for nothing at all, just to chat...' One day, in 2000, after months of silence she got in touch again. True to her brutal form, she ordered him to get on a plane and come and see her in Bouc-Bel-Air. He accepted. Upon arriving at Marseille airport, he jumped in the first taxi he could find. 'I gave the driver the address in Bouc-Bel-Air and he immediately turned round and said: "You're going to that nut's place! She's always causing problems. She's got such a bad reputation among my colleagues that no one will drive her any more!"'

As he arrived, Francis Kpatindé could see Nina waiting for him on the house's front step, looking majestic in a yellow and green boubou. She threw her arms around him, screaming, and immediately dissolved into tears. He tried to handle the situation as best he could, still unaware of why she had called him. She led him by the arm into the living room, where he discovered a modest interior, piles of records from Nina's collection strewn across the floor. The artist, who was constantly searching for her lost youth, showed them to him with pride. Marc, a young black American who the lady of the house would routinely scold through the day, interrupted them in the living room. Francis and Nina went and sat on the terrace facing the little garden. She asked Marc for a pastis and then he brought lunch out. 'Disgusting food, a tasteless salad and instant soup.' They had hardly finished when Nina began to get restless, ordering Francis to call a local dog trainer to get her dog Shadow under control. Francis did as asked and contacted several agencies specialized in training big dogs, 'but they were all too expensive,' he explains. 'Nina was bawling so loud behind me that one of the people I called even said: "That woman is nuts! She's the one that needs training!"'

Then Nina moved on to her favourite topic: con men, vultures in the business. 'She struck the table violently and screamed: "I want my money back!"' Francis Kpatindé remembers. Later, once she had calmed down, a neighbour came to visit. 'The woman was obviously the only person Nina got on with in the neighbourhood,' he explained. She came for tea, they talked a little, she tidied up the living room, then left again.

Mid-afternoon he ordered a taxi to take him back to the airport. On the doorstep, he said goodbye to Nina, sank into the car and, as it started up, turned to see the diva one last time. 'She seemed frozen behind the garden gate. She seemed terribly alone.'

In 2000, Nina Simone left her villa in Bouc-Bel-Air permanently to move to a house by the sea, in Carry-le-Rouet, near Marseille. Javier had shown her the resort during their drives. They would come down on weekends, sit on the old cafés' terraces and eat grilled sardines. Nina was taken by the place and spoke to Clifton about it. He suggested she sell her house in Bouc-Bel-Air to invest in another, more suited to her status. The Platanes house was sold for 1,200,000 francs, which was immediately reinvested in a villa in Carry-le-Rouet costing 3,500,000 francs.

During the same period, on 11 August 2000, Nina performed at the Marciac jazz festival, in Gers. She first demanded a five-star hotel, then a helicopter, but she changed her mind and asked for a Cadillac, before changing her mind one last time and demanding a limousine. Finally, having already got on the organizers' nerves, she made a scene about wanting the room of Wynton Marsalis, a regular at the festival. In the end, Nina and her troupe were housed in a residence in Auch, in the heights of Marciac, with a Mercedes at their disposal.

On the Monday, at midday, she held a press conference in the Château de Pallanne before being made a Mousquetaire d'Armagnac, as the likes of Dee Dee Bridgewater and Gérard Houiller had been before her. She arrived at the ceremony in a horse-drawn carriage and was honoured by Aymeri de Montesquiou, senator for Gers and the last surviving descendant of the Marquis de Montalet, one of Louis XIII's officers. Nina addressed the assembly, promising to be 'an honourable and worthy Mousquetaire all [her] life',[1] speaking about France as the homeland of human rights and digressing about her meeting with Nelson Mandela in Johannesburg, which she called the 'most beautiful day of my life' in somewhat hesitant French.

The day after her performance in Marciac, the journalist Serge Loupien summed it up vividly in the daily paper *Libération*: 'A few minutes before the show, the crammed marquee's atmosphere was electric. The volunteer controllers, who are normally so relaxed, almost apologized for the tension that had overcome them. The photographers were mad because of the first three minutes which they are normally given. The lighting engineers were tearing their hair out about the star's latest demand: pink light only. This was the situation in which Nina Simone finally made her appearance.'[2]

Escorted to her piano on the arms of two black men in dark suits, Nina wore a green dress with sequins, a blue sash and the cross of the Mousquetaires d'Armagnac. Visibly flattered by that honour, she showed the audience her award several times. She had a Ghanaian fly swatter in her hand, a symbol of power among black people and of spiritual survival despite slavery.

That night, she performed a string of her classics without pulling any surprises ('Black Is the Color of My True Love's Hair', 'Here Comes the

Sun', 'Just Like a Woman', 'I Loves You Porgy', 'Mississippi Goddam'...), regularly interrupting her show with statements in support of the civil rights movement, as if time had stood still for her.[3] In spite of her frailty and the inconsistency of her performance, the audience in Marciac behaved superbly, supporting her through to the very last note, paying homage despite the feeling of former glories preserved. Because, as Serge Loupien noted in *Libération*, Nina Simone 'has become a modern-day Billie Holiday'.[4] Further on in the article, he opined that the pianist, in her rambling, had 'joined the list of damned, exhausted artists: the Vince Taylor of recent years, Chet Baker, Charlie Parker...'[5]

Nina: a Callas who would never stop singing. As Pierre-Jean Rémy wrote in his biography of the opera singer: 'So... she suddenly appeared as the heroine of an opera invented by and for herself. As a solitary woman lost in a man's world where men ask women to sing and be beautiful for them, to touch the sublime and make them cry.'[6] So she was applauded, and the hurrahs weren't for the fat black woman crumpled on the stage, playing 'Porgy' and 'Four Women' for the umpteenth time, but for an invention – her immortal double, her shadow – a status that supplants the real woman with a legend.

Like Callas, 'our' Nina wasn't a tigress, a mad or fickle woman; she was fragile. Nina, 'like Violetta in *La Traviata* – who trembles... who dies of consumption... and who makes us tremble'.[7]

Because it's in the wings, in private, that the final scene is sealed, the death of the tragic actress who has become a queen without a kingdom through the perceptions of the men around her, the audiences, the vultures, alcohol, regrets. Once she returned to the routine of her house in Carry-le-Rouet, how could she forget that there was no husband, no lover, no children, no tenderness waiting for her there? One day followed another in the fog of fears that was only held in check by medication. Then a new day would dawn, like the last one, wreathed in fear, shame, boredom and resentment. As she wrote at the beginning of the 90s and published in her memoirs: 'All these years, I've received very little love, I've had very little time for love. It haunts me, especially at night, when I'm alone.'[8]

Obviously, she thought of her daughter. Lisa, who had since married and become a mother herself, but with whom she couldn't overcome the successive abandonments. Lisa, who would probably never forgive that selfish mother, but who, strangely, had started a career in music under the name Simone. She performed in *Jesus Christ Superstar*, then in *Rent*. In 1998 she joined Liquid Soul, an acid jazz group from Chicago, and then gained success on Broadway in 2001 through her role in the musical *Aida*, with music by Elton John. She also tried to launch a solo career and would sometimes join Nina on stage, the only place mother and daughter were able to communicate.

On 8 June 2001, Nina Simone gave her final concert in Paris, on stage at the Palais des Congrès. Posters showing the diva from head to toe were stuck up around the capital. Despite the disappointments of her most recent appearances in France, the press unanimously welcomed this tour: 'At once a survivor, an amazon and a highly sensitive woman, her performance at the Palais des Congrès – which is (nearly) sold out – is without doubt a great event.'[9] Why an event? Because her odyssey was nearing its end. And everyone could sense it.

A well-informed article by Alain Sarraute published in *Le Figaro* stated: 'An expressive singer and a master pianist, Nina Simone is above all an incorrigible rebel who disregards principles and tramples on established classifications.' Further on: 'Was it her impecunious childhood that fed her desire for revenge? While her whims have exasperated producers more often than they won their favour, her adventurous and stormy love life didn't help, and her quarrels with the American courts... made the situation even worse. That earned her a career of ups and downs, saved at each reprieve by an audience under the spell of her warm and husky voice, and her uncommon personality.'[10]

Le Parisien carried the title 'Nina Simone, queen for a night', announcing: 'At a one-off concert tonight at the Palais des Congrès, Nina Simone, 68, the blues and soul diva, will regale us with her unforgettable interpretations of "My Way" and "Ne me quitte pas". A rendezvous with a legend.'[11] The article featured an interview with the pianist in which she stated: 'I really don't care if people love me or hate me. I know my attitude is misunderstood sometimes, but believe me, it's not easy to be a living legend. But I've changed quite a lot over the years and I'm not necessarily what people believe I am: the conscience of the black people.'

What the press didn't know was that Nina Simone was suffering from breast cancer. For the second time, I have been told. Clifton Henderson and Javier Collado decided that she should undergo surgery in a Parisian hospital, followed by breast reconstruction. A few days after the operation, Nina suffered an allergic reaction that forced her back into the operating room. She was placed under observation in the hospital and didn't check out until the day before her Palais des Congrès concert.

Why did she agree to perform in these conditions and why was she allowed? Roger Nupie (the only member of the A-Team not to be ousted by Henderson and Collado), who introduced her in the Parisian auditorium before she came on stage, says: 'I think she only gave those last few concerts, and in particular the one in Paris, because of her love for the audience, as it was physically painful for her to play. Nina, who in the past had always demanded a get-out clause in her contracts, insisted on playing in Paris. That was the last time I saw her on stage, and I had the feeling things had gone too far. She was suffering too much, it had become inhumane.'

When I spoke to Javier Collado by telephone, I asked him about that last appearance in Paris: 'Knowing she was weak, why did you allow her to play?'

'Because she decided to!' he said. 'Nina had realized over the previous few years that her biggest mistake, for almost thirty years, had been balking at playing concerts, cancelling them for all sorts of bad reasons. Even though she was comfortable in Carry-le-Rouet, she hadn't had a great private life, she didn't have a family or a husband. What did she have left? Her audience.'

Gerrit goes further: 'Over her last few years, Nina wanted to honour all her engagements because she knew that when she was on stage people applauded her, she felt good, and for a few moments she'd be safe from her worries and all the shit going on around her.'

So the concert in Paris went ahead. It was a disaster – some of the saddest, most lifeless music she had ever performed. A whiff of death haunted the flavourless performance, which began after a delay that everyone forgave her for. At 400 francs a ticket, they all accepted that waiting was part of the ritual. She played the same set as in Marciac, then, shortly after 'Porgy', only a half-hour into the show, she left the stage. This left her musicians to play their solos on a stage too big for them to last long without her. The audience wriggled impatiently in their seats. After what seemed like hours, doubts began to grow as to whether Nina would come back. They didn't really care what songs she played, as long as she came back. One last time.

Nina Simone's elephantine shape finally reappeared, escorted by two men dressed in black and moving slowly, exhausted and defeated. She was sat down behind her piano again. She seemed doubtful and turned to the audience: 'What would you like to hear?' A smart-ass thought it was a good idea to suggest 'Ne me quitte pas', and a twilit melody began to fill the room. After that, two or three more songs completed her performance and the organizers agreed that she had fulfilled her contract. Helped again by the two men, Nina stood up from her stool with great difficulty, moved to the front of the stage, seeming to accept her martyrdom with each step, and grimaced a smile as she was handed some flowers, as if the death ceremony required her to be sent back to her solitude with her arms filled with bouquets.

Just then a young man at the back of the room tore down the Palais des Congrès's stairs four at a time towards the stage. In a matter of seconds he was so close he could touch the diva. He did nothing. He had no roses in his arms. He was happy to stand before her, acknowledging the end of an era in his red T-shirt. And there, standing before her, he cried '*Je t'aime*' and, smiling, blew her a few kisses. For a few brief seconds, his eyes met those of the old lady crippled by pain. She smiled at him, turned again, and, absorbed in the immensity in front of her, seemed to think: 'This is the last time we'll see each other, isn't it?' And while the flashes crackled, the stage was suddenly filled with bodyguards, a pointless act, as Nina had disappeared.

After that last date in Paris, Nina Simone, at sixty-eight years of age, gave ten American concerts during July 2001, cutting across

New York, Portland, Saratoga, Los Angeles, Chicago and Detroit, and finishing her journey with a final performance on British soil, at the Bishopstock Festival near Exeter, in Devon, on 26 August 2001.

She had told Gerrit several times: 'I'll die when I'm seventy, because after that, it's all just pain.' Nina had confided in Roger Nupie: 'I've not had the life I wanted, as I wanted it. But I'll die when I want.'

Secluded away in her Carry-le-Rouet house, kept in bed by a cancer that had now spread, a growing tumour in her brain making speech difficult, Nina gradually let herself fade away. Far from all this craziness, from those guys that, I have been told, forgot about her in her room (Raymond Gonzalez even confirmed: 'In the end, no one helped her go to the toilet. She was left to do it in her bed!'). Far from the guys that didn't answer when she begged for a bit of company, who were happy to simply feed her and forget about her the rest of the time. 'She wanted to leave,' Roger told me. 'She wanted to get out of that shit.' Just to die.

What a tragic sequence of circumstances. A few years before, before Nina's interests, and her friendship, got away from them, Raymond and Gerrit had thought they would be able to release those hundreds of hours of unheard recordings and thus guarantee Nina peace in her final days. Those royalties would have paid for her house in the south of France, financed the construction of her home in Ghana. She could have spent the spring and the summer in France, and the rest of the year in Africa, they thought. She would have been visited frequently and people would have made sure she was well looked after. She would have had a happy life. More or less. But that's not how things panned out. Nina faded away in a beautiful house a few yards from the sea. During the last few months of her life she was unable to walk or get down the stairs on her own. She was wracked with fear – of dying alone, upstairs in her room while she could hear them laughing and scheming in the living room. Nina no longer had the strength to fight or to throw them out as she would have in times gone by. Nina, the trapped tigress, had become dependent, cut off from her old friends, and in her agony no longer even dared to get annoyed 'for fear that they wouldn't feed or wash her any more', according to Gerrit. Clifton Henderson and Javier Collado deny this.

Nina Simone died on 21 April 2003 in her house in Carry-le-Rouet at the age of seventy. According to Clifton Henderson, who was at her bedside, 'Nina hadn't been feeling well for a while, she died of natural causes.' In truth, cancer had spread throughout her body and overcame her.

On the day of the funeral, Gerrit made the journey to Carry-le-Rouet to say goodbye to his friend. He was not allowed in. There was simply too much accumulated tension, family mess, jealousy, bad feeling and hostility. Javier Collado confirmed that he refused to allow Gerrit into the house as Nina had passed away and thus he no longer had any business there... But the reasons are of little importance. In his emotional slump, Roger remains the only one who attempts to temper his words: 'You have to realize that it was complicated for everyone around her at the end. Certain people may not have had bad intentions but their choices, on the other hand, have been shown to be bad. But something strange happened, something unforgivable.'

The funeral took place on 25 April 2003. A mass was held in the Notre Dame de l'Assomption church in Carry-le-Rouet in the presence of three hundred people including Clifton Henderson, Javier Collado, Paul Robinson, Lisa and her husband, Miriam Makeba and Isabelle Terrin. A message from Elton John rested on a bed of yellow roses, saying 'We were the greatest and I love you'. Shortly after Nina's death, he declared to the journalist Ingrid Sischy: 'I think she was the greatest female artist of the twentieth century'.

The French culture minister Jean-Jacques Aillagon declared: 'The family of jazz has lost one of its most beautiful souls and one of its most beautiful voices, a splendid voice singing of love and the roots and struggles of her life.' What family was he talking about? For what it was worth, he offered a wreath in the name of the French Republic.

Nina Simone's funeral began with a pre-recorded 'Ne me quitte pas'. Lisa sang a tribute to her mother, and Father Guy de Fatto, artists' chaplain and former jazz bassist, declared during his sermon that 'Of course Nina wasn't perfect, but she fought for the rights of blacks in the United States, and for that reason alone, I'm sure she's up above now. Thank you, Nina.'[12] Then four bearers dressed in black took the coffin away. Two other ceremonies were held in her memory that day: one in New York and one in Tryon.

In accordance with her wishes, the body of Nina Simone was cremated in Saint-Pierre cemetery in Marseille and her ashes were scattered in several different African countries. That was scant consolation for a woman who wished to die on the continent of her ancestors.

Nina's death was covered unenthusiastically in the media of the country where she ended her days, such as *Elle* magazine, which on 28 April 2003 accorded her just three lines, with no photo: 'Sometimes violent, often capricious, always unpredictable, the passionate militant embodied swing-style bohemia with humour and panache. Her deep voice will continue to resonate in the air.'[13] Visibly more concerned, the daily *Libération* made two attempts to salute Nina's memory. On 22 April 2003 it ran the title: 'Aged 70, the American jazz singer was an activist for the black cause her entire life'. The next day, *Le Monde*'s Véronique Mortaigne paid her vivid tribute, not flinching from the dark truths beneath the smooth image routinely accorded to the dead: 'Nina, carried away by alcohol and false paradises, was abandoned by everyone and abandoned everyone in turn, bearing a solitary cross, bound by moods and jealousy, by petty swindling lovers that left with the good times. Moods and jealousy... She sometimes had sudden flashes of inspiration that would lead her to leave concert halls, to everyone's disappointment. Other times, her concerts were beautiful and profound, carrying halls and stadiums into swing and warmth.'[14]

On the day of Nina Simone's funeral, the inhabitants of Carry-le-Rouet were amazed to see the rows of limousines parked in front of the church. The most curious asked around and found out that Nina Simone had been living in their village for three years. That she had died there. Yet no one remembers seeing her stroll down their streets or along the beach. And though I asked, no one remembers even the slightest incident happening at the house she was living in. The closest neighbours say the villa was quiet, with few comings and goings.

The villa is still inhabited – the shutters are wide open – but the swimming pool seems to have been covered over for months. Leaves have gathered on top and the garden seems abandoned.

I rang the doorbell but no one answered. I walked around, on the beach then along the charming streets, looking for a terrace café to wait in, maybe ask a few questions. But no one remembers Nina here. No, no one ever got a whiff that she was living in one of the villas. However, I was very quickly told of an American, a black guy, who spoke hesitant French. He had a black Mercedes. It had to be black. Some say they saw him several times, aimlessly wandering the town's streets, talking to himself. He comes to eat here sometimes, I was told. All alone. We've never seen him with anyone else. He has lunch or dinner, doesn't seem interested in talking to anyone. Then he gets back in his Mercedes and leaves. No one knows his name.

AUTHOR'S NOTE

THIS PROJECT was born as Laurent Garnier and I were putting the finishing touches to *Électrochoc*. During the months we spent writing that work, Nina Simone's music was our soundtrack. On 21 April 2003, we learned of the artist's death and I immediately began researching her life. I had no clear aim at first; perhaps I was only planning a radio programme in her memory. At the time, I only had a few scraps of information about Nina's life, gathered from interesting anecdotes, legends surrounding her, and her most popular recordings. Soon, as my research advanced, I became impassioned by my project and accumulated a great deal of information from several interviews with the people who crossed her path, who assisted her in her odyssey, or quite simply, who loved that extraordinary woman.

Anyone who begins to seriously research Nina Simone is first of all struck by the very limited number of works about her. *I Put a Spell on You*, her autobiography, published by Presses de la Renaissance in 1991 under the title *Ne me quittez pas*, has been out of print in France for ten years or so. The original version, published by Ebury Press and Pantheon Books in 1991, can still be found in English-language bookshops. It's a contrived, sterilized autobiography. Whole passages of Nina Simone's life are largely 'put right', while the drifting in her existence is quite simply omitted. Nevertheless, *I Put a Spell on You* is a good starting point in trying to understand the chronology of her life.

More recently, Sylvia Hampton and David Nathan, the founder of Nina Simone's first English fan club in the 1960s, published *Break Down & Let It All Out*, a remarkable biography mainly focused on the diva's periods in the UK. That book brings us a little closer to seeing the artist's multiple personalities and throws a gripping light on her private life and chaotic career.

Of course, Nina Simone's plentiful discography is a never-ending source of information and indicators for a biographical project. Listening to each of her albums allows us to understand Nina's artistic development, to locate her influences and the mood of the periods she embodied, because, as the American musician and poet Camille Yarbrough[1] stated, 'Her music was a response to the social situation we were living through.'

Although Nina Simone's art largely drew from traditional music, spirituals, the blues, folk and classical music, it was a unique artistic mix. Look as you might, you won't find anything like her work anywhere in American music. This freshness assures the listener they are before art that still has a currency in the present. Is that why today a wide range of artists, from the most polished singers (Diana Krall, Norah Jones...) to the most elegiac rockers (Placebo, Muse, Marilyn Manson...), from the most cutting-edge hip hop (Missy Elliott, Mos Def, Talib Kweli, Saul Williams...) to black gospel-folk (Lauryn Hill...), from certain traditional soul and jazz (Meshell Ndegeocello, Erykah Badu...) to the most experimental rock (A Silver Mount Zion...), claim Nina Simone as an influence – when not imitating her outright?

I searched for references to Nina Simone in a wide range of press and radio archives (*New York Times*, *Le Temps*, *Libération*, *Le Monde*, Radio Suisse Romande, *Paris Match*, AFP dispatches, *Jazz Hot*, etc.) until I was able to build a satisfactory chronology of the events that she lived through, from her childhood in Tryon to her last move to Carry-le-Rouet in 2000.

During my research, I learned at my cost that reconstructing a timeline of the events that punctuated her life is impossible. There are simply too many unverifiable myths, shadowy areas, unknowns, and that's without even mentioning the whole years of her life that are unaccounted for, in particular her periods in Liberia and Switzerland. In spite of that, this book has been structured around a chronology that is as close as possible to the course of her life.

To build this timeline I spent two years, from London to New York, from Montreux to Antwerp, from Johannesburg to Aix-en-Provence, from Amsterdam to Paris, attempting to speak with the people who met, surrounded or loved Nina during her life's long trek.

My first discovery was realizing just how strong a code of silence shrouds her memory. An omertà has become the rule for the most shadowy parts of her life. It was hard to loosen people's tongues and I was often confronted with people who simply refused to speak, such as the famous jazz pianist I met at the Montreux Jazz Festival who dismissed me, saying: 'I've seen things about her that are too difficult and that I don't want to speak about. Go away!' The conversation had been friendly up to that point... Other people declined saying they also planned to write a book about Nina – there are apparently at least four in the works.

Some of my interview requests remain unanswered: the director of one of the world's largest music festivals; that wonderful South African singer; Nina's own daughter, who clearly didn't want to speak about the subject and bring up its memories. I came to understand why as I entered the mysteries of Nina's life, thanks to a number of new records I was shown here and there, but above all, thanks to those who agreed to answer my questions without holding their tongues.

I wanted to use this biography to explore the antagonistic relationships Nina had with her blackness, her music, her fans, her need for love, and with sex. I discovered Nina the sacrificed child, Nina the African witch, Nina the mother, unable to offer her daughter the affection she herself hadn't known, Nina the visionary and Nina the crazy woman. I also found shipwrecked Nina, taken in by Good Samaritans in Europe, many of whom offered me their help, advice and support. I thank them for that.

This book aims to pay tribute to Nina Simone's memory and her art, and show just why this peerless *tragédienne* deserves to be recognized as a true American genius.

Rest in peace, Nina.

ACKNOWLEDGEMENTS

I WISH to thank the following people for their assistance and hospitality: Isabelle Terrin, Roger Nupie, Gerrit de Bruin and Raymond Gonzalez.

Thank you to those who, during my research, offered their assistance and memories: Jean-Claude Arnodon, Charles Aznavour, Ilene Barnes, François Bensignor, Johanne Blein and Le Temps, Jacques Bonni and Les Trois Maillets, Jean-Michel Boris, Pierre-Marie Bougri, Robert Boutin, Solomon Burke, Yves Chamberland, Christian Chassaing and the Olympia, Nik Cohn, Javier Collado, Jeremy Collingwood, Paulette Coquatrix, Jeni Dahmus and the Juilliard School, Nabih Daouh, Lorraine Gordon and the Village Vanguard, Céline Gorier-Bernard, Pierre Grandjean, Roland Grivelle, Olivier Horner, Pete King and Ronnie Scott's, Francis Kpatindé, The Last Poets, Jacqueline Ledent-Vilain, Willy Lieser, Frank Lords, Greil Marcus, the Montreux Jazz Festival, Mimi Perrin, Elsa Prat-Carrabin, Viviane Priou, Radio Suisse Romande, Vincent Ravalec, Diana Reeves, Hervé Riesen and Couleur 3, Paul Robinson, the Reverend Barbara Ruth and Detroit's Second Baptist Church.

I wish to acknowledge the following people for their inspiration: David Beaugier, Marc Benaïche and Mondomix (www.mondomix.com), Sophie Berbar-Sollier, Didier Bonvin, Laurent and Delia Garnier, Gérard Suter and Radio Paradiso, and Marushka Vidovic. Very special thanks to Benoit de Vilmorin.

I also wish to acknowledge Béatrice Lecomte, Charles Arsène-Henry, Camille Kuntz and Alexandre Boldrini for the beautiful feeling they have given this book.

Finally, without the patience, support and passion of Olivia de Dieuleveult, this book's original editor, this project would have never come to fruition.

NOTES

1. THE FIRST NOTES OF THE MELODY

1   Nina Simone with Stephen Cleary, *I Put a Spell on You* (Da Capo Press, 2003), p. 2

2   Simone, *I Put a Spell on You*, p. 4

3   J.M. Coetzee, *Disgrace* (Penguin Books, 2000), p. 6

4   Simone, *I Put a Spell on You*, p. 13

5   Simone, *I Put a Spell on You*, p. 13

6   Simone, *I Put a Spell on You*, p. 16

7   Simone, *I Put a Spell on You*

8   Frank Lords (director), *Nina Simone: The Legend*

9   Mildred Clary, *Mozart, la lumière de Dieu* (Pygmalion, 2004)

10 LeRoi Jones, *Blues People* (William Morrow, 1999)

11 Simone, *I Put a Spell on You*

12 Simone, *I Put a Spell on You*, p. 19

13 Simone, *I Put a Spell on You*, p. 22

14 Simone, *I Put a Spell on You*, p. 23

15 Simone, *I Put a Spell on You*, p. 24

16 Clary, *Mozart, la lumière de Dieu*

17 Clary, *Mozart, la lumière de Dieu*

18 C. Vann Woodward, quoted in W.T. Lhamon Jr., *Raising Cain* (Harvard University Press, 1998), p. 151

19 Simone, *I Put a Spell on You*

20 Simone, *I Put a Spell on You*, p. 32

21 Simone, *I Put a Spell on You*, p. 31

22 Simone, *I Put a Spell on You*, p. 30

23 Simone, *I Put a Spell on You*, p. 29

24 Simone, *I Put a Spell on You*, p. 32

25 Juilliard Summer School Catalog, 1950

26 Ronald L. Morris, *Le Jazz et les gangsters* (Le Passage, 2002)

27 Frank Lords (director), *Nina Simone: The Legend*

2. FROM RENUNCIATION TO REVELATION

1   Simone, *I Put a Spell on You*

2   Simone, *I Put a Spell on You*, p. 44

3   Frank Lords (director), *Nina Simone: The Legend*

4   James Brown, *I Feel Good: A Memoir of a Life of Soul* (New American Library, 2005)

5   Simone, *I Put a Spell on You*, p. 170

3. SOMETHING INSIDE HER COMES ALIGHT

1   Simone, *I Put a Spell on You*, p. 63
2   Simone, *I Put a Spell on You*, p. 65
3   Simone, *I Put a Spell on You*, p. 65
4   Simone, *I Put a Spell on You*, p. 66
5   *New York Times*, 13 September 1959
6   Simone, *I Put a Spell on You*, p. 69
7   Simone, *I Put a Spell on You*, p. 74
8   Simone, *I Put a Spell on You*, p. 71
9   Charles Aznavour, *Le Temps des avants* (Flammarion, 2003)
10 Simone, *I Put a Spell on You*, p. 77

4. 'I KNOW WHAT THE WORLD HAS DONE TO MY BROTHER'

1   *Jazz Hot* no. 212 (1965)
2   Simone, *I Put a Spell on You*, pp. 80–1
3   Simone, *I Put a Spell on You*, p. 86
4   Speech given by Martin Luther King in Birmingham, 23 January 1955
5   Marie-Agnès Combesque, *Martin Luther King, un homme et son rêve* (Le Félin, 2004)
6   Combesque, *Martin Luther King*
7   Combesque, *Martin Luther King*
8   Martin Luther King, Jr./Clayborne Carson (ed.), *The Autobiography of Martin Luther King, Jr.* (Warner Books, 2001)
9   Combesque, *Martin Luther King*
10 Clayborne Carson et al. (ed.), *The Papers of Martin Luther King, Jr.*, Volume IV: *Symbol of the Movement* (University of California Press, 2000), p. 490
11 Carson et al. (ed.), *The Papers of Martin Luther King, Jr.*, Volume IV
12 This protest song and slogan was inspired by a spiritual and popularized by Pete Seeger, one of Bob Dylan's main influences.
13 Pierre-Jean Rémy, *Callas, une vie* (Albin Michel, 1997)
14 Rémy, *Callas, une vie*
15 Simone, *I Put a Spell on You*, p. 85
16 *New York Times*, 13 April 1963
17 Simone, *I Put a Spell on You*
18 Simone, *I Put a Spell on You*
19 Simone, *I Put a Spell on You*, p. 87
20 Bruce Chatwin, *The Viceroy of Ouidah* (Penguin Books, 1988)
21 Ryszard Kapuściński, *The Shadow of the Sun*, p. 82
22 Charles Johnson and Patricia Smith, *Africans in America: America's Journey Through Slavery* (Harcourt Brace, 1998)
23 LeRoi Jones, *Blues People*, p. 57
24 Johnson and Smith, *Africans in America*
25 LeRoi Jones, *Blues People*, p. 53
26 LeRoi Jones, *Blues People*, p. 95

27 Richard Wright, *Black Boy* (HarperCollins, 2005)

28 Ronald L. Morris, *Le Jazz et les gangsters*

29 David Margolick, *Strange Fruit* (HarperCollins, 2001)

30 Margolick, *Strange Fruit*

31 Richard Wright, *Black Boy*

32 James Baldwin, *The Fire Next Time* (Modern Library, 1995)

33 Baldwin, *The Fire Next Time*, p. 75

34 Combesque, *Martin Luther King*

35 Combesque, *Martin Luther King*

36 John F. Kennedy, televised press conference, 11 June 1963

37 Combesque, *Martin Luther King*

38 Combesque, *Martin Luther King*

39 Combesque, *Martin Luther King*

40 David J. Garrow, *The FBI and Martin Luther King, Jr.: From "Solo" to Memphis* (WW Norton & Co., 1981)

41 Combesque, *Martin Luther King*

42 Simone, *I Put a Spell on You*, p. 89

43 Simone, *I Put a Spell on You*, p. 90

44 Simone, *I Put a Spell on You*, p. 90

45 Alison Powell, 'The American Soul of Nina Simone', *Interview*, January 1997

46 Simone, *I Put a Spell on You*, p. 104

47 Simone, *I Put a Spell on You*, p. 94

48 Simone, *I Put a Spell on You*, p. 91

49 Simone, *I Put a Spell on You*

50 Bob Dylan, *Chronicles: Volume One* (Simon & Schuster, 2004)

51 Miriam Makeba with James Hall, *Makeba: My Story* (New American Library, 1987)

52 Makeba, *Makeba: My Story*

53 Simone, *I Put a Spell on You*, p. 98

54 Makeba, *Makeba: My Story*

55 Simone, *I Put a Spell on You*

56 Brown, *I Feel Good*

57 www.nobel-paix.ch/bio/mandela.htm

58 Combesque, *Martin Luther King*

59 Combesque, *Martin Luther King*

60 Combesque, *Martin Luther King*

61 Frank Lords (director), *Nina Simone: The Legend*

62 Baldwin, *The Fire Next Time*, p. 65

63 Baldwin, *The Fire Next Time*

64 Baldwin, *The Fire Next Time*, p. 73

65 Baldwin, *The Fire Next Time*

66 Baldwin, *The Fire Next Time*, p. 50

67 Sylvia Hampton with David Nathan, *Nina Simone: Break Down & Let It All Out* (Sanctuary, 2003), p. 41

68 Ahmadou Kourouma, *Waiting for the Wild Beasts to Vote* (Vintage, 2004)

69   Simone, *I Put a Spell on You*, p. 107

70   Bob Dylan, *Chronicles: Volume One*, p. 275

71   Bob Dylan, *Chronicles: Volume One*

72   'Décibels', *France Culture*, 24 May 2004

73   Simone, *I Put a Spell on You*, p. 92

74   Hampton, *Break Down & Let It All Out*, p. 58

75   Hampton, *Break Down & Let It All Out*, pp. XX–64

76   Simone, *I Put a Spell on You*, p. 87

77   *New York Times*, 16 January 1965

78   Nik Cohn, *Awopbopaloobop Alopbamboom* (Grove Press, 2001), p. 38

79   *Jazz Hot* no. 212

80   Margolick, *Strange Fruit*, p. 42

81   Baldwin, *The Fire Next Time*

82   Margolick, *Strange Fruit*, p. 19

83   Margolick, *Strange Fruit*, p. 1

84   Margolick, *Strange Fruit*, p. 57

85   Angela Y. Davis, *Blues Legacies and Black Feminism* (Pantheon, 1998)

5. 'HELL IS RIGHT BESIDE ME'

1   Combesque, *Martin Luther King*

2   Martin Luther King, *Where Do We Go from Here: Chaos or Community?* (1967)

3   Bobby Seale, *Seize the Time: The Story of the Black Panther Party and Huey P. Newton* (Black Classic Press, 1996), pp. 69–72

4   Combesque, *Martin Luther King*

5   Combesque, *Martin Luther King*

6   King, *Where Do We Go from Here*

7   King, *Where Do We Go from Here*

8   Simone, *I Put a Spell on You*, p. 118

9   Hampton, *Break Down & Let It All Out*, p. 31

10   Frank Lords (director), *Nina Simone: The Legend*

11   © Acontresens 2002–2005

12   King, *The Autobiography*, p. 338

13   Combesque, *Martin Luther King*

14   Greil Marcus, *Mystery Train* (Penguin Books, 1997), p. 68

15   J. Edgar Hoover, FBI COINTELPRO memo 'Counterintelligence Program, Black Nationalist Hate Groups, Racial Intelligence' (100-448006), 4 March 1968

16   Barney Hoskyns, *Waiting for the Sun* (St Martin's Press, 1996)

17   Hoskyns, *Waiting for the Sun*,

18   Combesque, *Martin Luther King*

19   Combesque, *Martin Luther King*

20   Combesque, *Martin Luther King*

21   Simone, *I Put a Spell on You*, pp. 112–13

22   Simone, *I Put a Spell on You*, p. 112

23   Interview by Francis Dordor, *Les Inrockuptibles* no. 442, 19 April 2004

24   Hampton, *Break Down & Let It All Out*, p. 39

25   Lloyd Bradley, *Bass Culture* (Viking, 2000)

26   Simone, *I Put a Spell on You*, p. 113

27   Frank Lords (director), *Nina Simone: The Legend*

28   Frank Lords (director), *Nina Simone: The Legend*

29   Simone, *I Put a Spell on You*

30   Hampton, *Break Down & Let It All Out*, p. 166

31   James Brown, *I Feel Good*

32   Hampton, *Break Down & Let It All Out*, p. 45

33   See the documentary *The Weather Underground*, by Sam Green and Bill Siegel, 2002

34   Makeba, *Makeba: My Story*

35   Simone, *I Put a Spell on You*

36   Frank Lords (director), *Nina Simone: The Legend*

37   Simone, *I Put a Spell on You*, p. 116

38   Hampton, *Break Down & Let It All Out*, p. 52

39   Simone, *I Put a Spell on You*

40   Hampton, *Break Down & Let It All Out*, p. 68

41   Hampton, *Break Down & Let It All Out*, p. 66

42   Hampton, *Break Down & Let It All Out*, p. 67

43   *St. Louis Post-Dispatch*, 4 October 1967

44   Interview with Katherine Dunham, *St. Louis Post*, 4 October 1967

45   Hampton, *Break Down & Let It All Out*, p. 62

46   *New York Times*, 27 October 1965

47   'An Evening with Nina Simone', promotional interview for *Black Gold*, RCA, 1970

48   'An Evening with Nina Simone'

49   'An Evening with Nina Simone'

6. THERE'S NO WAY OUT OF OUR TROUBLES

1   Simone, *I Put a Spell on You*, p. 119

2   *New York Times*, 12 October 1971

3   Simone, *I Put a Spell on You*, p. 135

4   Simone, *I Put a Spell on You*, p. 121

5   Simone, *I Put a Spell on You*, p. 128

6   Hampton, *Break Down & Let It All Out*, p. 82

7   Hampton, *Break Down & Let It All Out*, p. 86

8   Simone, *I Put a Spell on You*, p. 136

9   Maya Deren, *Divine Horsemen: The Voodoo Gods of Haiti*, quoted in John Edgar Wideman, *Damballah* (Mariner Books, 1998)

10   Simone, *I Put a Spell on You*

11   Frank Lords (director), *Nina Simone: The Legend*

7. THE COMAPNY OF GHOSTS

1   Ryszard Kapuściński, *The Shadow of the Sun*, p. 238

2   Lloyd Bradley, *Bass Culture*

3   Ryszard Kapuściński, *The Shadow of the Sun*, p. 240

4   'Histoire du Liberia', www.africa-onweb.com/pays/liberia/histoire.htm

5   Ryszard Kapuściński, *The Shadow of the Sun*, p. 243

6   Ryszard Kapuściński, *The Shadow of the Sun* p. 244

7   Simone, *I Put a Spell on You*, p. 138

8   Simone, *I Put a Spell on You*, p. 140

9   Simone, *I Put a Spell on You*

10 Simone, *I Put a Spell on You*, p. 141

11 Simone, *I Put a Spell on You*, p. 142

12 Jim Harrison, *True North* (Grove Press, 2004), pp. 278–9

13 Simone, *I Put a Spell on You*, p. 142

14 Simone, *I Put a Spell on You*, p. 142

15 Morrison, *Beloved*, p. 49

16 Simone, *I Put a Spell on You*, p. 145

17 Simone, *I Put a Spell on You*, p. 148

18 Simone, *I Put a Spell on You*, p. 153

19 Ryszard Kapuściński, *The Shadow of the Sun*, p. 244

8. ADRIFT

1   Simone, *I Put a Spell on You*, p. 154

2   Simone, *I Put a Spell on You*, p. 155

3   Rémy, *Callas, une vie*

4   Rémy, *Callas, une vie*

5   Rémy, *Callas, une vie*

6   Simone, *I Put a Spell on You*, p. 157

7   Simone, *I Put a Spell on You*, p. 157

8   Hampton, *Break Down & Let It All Out*, p. 93

9   Simone, *I Put a Spell on You*

10 Simone, *I Put a Spell on You*, p. 159

11 Simone, *I Put a Spell on You*, p. 159

12 *New York Times*, 24 June 1972

13 Simone, *I Put a Spell on You*, p. 161

14 Hampton, *Break Down & Let It All Out*, p. 95

15 Simone, *I Put a Spell on You*, p. 164

16 Simone, *I Put a Spell on You*, p. 164

9. 'ONE MORNING I TOOK A LOOK AT CIVILIZATION'

1   Simone, *I Put a Spell on You*, p. 168

2   Simone, *I Put a Spell on You*, p. 166

3   Simone, *I Put a Spell on You*, p. 167

4   Simone, *I Put a Spell on You*, p. 170

5   *New York Times*, 13 July 1984

6   Simone, *I Put a Spell on You*, p. 172

10. SOMEWHERE BETWEEN THE BLACK KEYS AND THE WHITE...

1   Hampton, *Break Down & Let It All Out*, p. 11

2   Hampton, *Break Down & Let It All Out*

3   Ernie Santosuosso, 'History of the Jazz & Blues Festival', www.boston.com/jazzfest/history.shtml

4   Interview by Fara C., *L'Humanité*, 22 February 1992

5   Simone, *I Put a Spell on You*, p. 170

6   Laurent Garnier and David Brun-Lambert, *Électrochoc* (Flammarion, 2003)

7   Hampton, *Break Down & Let It All Out*, p. 12

8   Simone, *I Put a Spell on You*, p. 171

9   Simone, *I Put a Spell on You*, p. 173

10   Yves Bigot, *Libération*, 6 June 1988

11   *Le Quotidien de Paris*, 30 September 1988

12   Jean-Luc Wachthausen, *Le Figaro*, 16 February 1989

13   Nicole Le Caisne, *L'Express*, 3 February 1989

14   Kourouma, *Waiting for the Wild Beasts to Vote*

15   Hampton, *Break Down & Let It All Out*, p. 166

16   Richard Gianorio, 'Nina Simone cherche millionnaire', *France Soir*, 10 February 1992

17   Simone, *I Put a Spell on You*, p. 176

18   Carlos Gomez, *Journal du Dimanche*, 20 October 1991

19   Véronique Mortaigne, *Le Monde*, 25 October 1991

20   Fara C., *L'Humanité*, 17 October 1991

21   *Quotidien de Paris*

22   Anne Pichon, *La Croix*, 21 October 1991

23   Anne Pichon, *La Croix*, 21 October 1991

11. 'SO WHILE YOU'RE IMITATING AL CAPONE...'

1   Hampton, *Break Down & Let It All Out*, p. 144

2   Christian Rodat, *France-Soir*, 24 August 1995

3   Christian Rodat, *France-Soir*, 24 August 1995

4   Guy Benhamou, *Libération*, 24 August 1995

5   Guy Benhamou, *Libération*, 24 August 1995

6   Guy Benhamou, *Libération*, 24 August 1995

7   Christian Rodat, *France-Soir*, 24 August 1995

8   Christian Rodat, *France-Soir*, 24 August 1995

9   Powell, 'The American Soul of Nina Simone'

10   Hampton, *Break Down & Let It All Out*

12. 'AFTER THAT IT'S ALL JUST PAIN'

1   Cécile Soule, *France-Soir*, 9 August 2000

2   Serge Loupien, 'Les divagations de Nina Simone', *Libération*, 11 August 2000

3   Loupien, 'Les divagations de Nina Simone'

4   Loupien, 'Les divagations de Nina Simone'

5   Loupien, 'Les divagations de Nina Simone'

6   Rémy, *Callas, une vie*

7   Rémy, *Callas, une vie*

8   Simone, *I Put a Spell on You*

9   *Journal du Dimanche*, 3 June 2001

10 Alain Sarraute, *Le Figaro*, 6 June 2001

11 Alain Morel, *Le Parisien*, 8 June 2001

12 AFP dispatch, 25 April 2003

13 *Elle*, 28 April 2003

14 Véronique Mortaigne, *Le Monde*, 23 April 2003

AUTHOR'S NOTE

1   Especially known for the soul classic 'Take Yo' Praise' from 1975.